YORK MEDIEVAL TEXTS

General Editors

ELIZABETH SALTER & DEREK PEARSALL

The King's Manor, University of York

Middle English Religious Prose

N. F. BLAKE

Senior Lecturer in English Language,
University of Liverpool

EDWARD ARNOLD

© N. F. BLAKE 1972

First published 1972 by
Edward Arnold (Publishers) Ltd
25 Hill Street, London W1X 8LL

Cloth edition ISBN 0 7131 5610 4
Paper edition ISBN 0 7131 5611 2

Printed in Great Britain by
Billing & Sons Limited, Guildford and London

Preface

The present series of *York Medieval Texts* is designed for undergraduates and, where the text is appropriate, for upper forms of schools. Its aim is to provide editions of major pieces of Middle English writing in a form which will make them accessible without loss of historical authenticity. Texts are chosen because of their importance and artistic merit, and individual volumes may contain a single work, coherent extracts from a longer work, or representative examples of a genre. The principle governing the presentation of the text is to preserve the character of the English while eliminating unnecessary encumbrances such as obsolete letters. Glossary and explanatory notes operate together to clarify the text; special attention is paid to the interpretation of passages which are syntactically rather than lexically difficult. The introduction to each volume, like the rest of the apparatus, is designed to set the work in its proper literary context, and to provide the critical guidance most helpful to present-day readers.

The present volume, which contains a selection of the religious prose from the Middle English period, is designed to introduce the reader to the richness and diversity of Middle English prose. Since separate volumes in this series may be devoted to them at a later date, selections from the most famous prose works have not been included. The pieces date from the twelfth to the fifteenth centuries, and they illustrate the wide range of interests of medieval churchmen. Each piece is presented in its entirety so that it can be appreciated as a literary work in its own right. But both in the introduction and in the notes the editor has drawn attention to the many parallels among the selections themselves and to the many points of contact between them and Middle English poems. It is hoped that not only will the prose be studied for its own intrinsic merit, but also that the pieces will provide students of Middle English poetry with first-hand information of the religious concerns and ideas of the time as a background to their reading. All the selections have been newly edited from the manuscripts.

Acknowledgements

I am indebted to the librarians of the following institutions for the provision of photographic material and permission to reprint works in their charge: the Bodleian Library (II, V, VI); the British Museum (III, X); Cambridge University Library (VII); Corpus Christi College, Cambridge (IX); Henry E. Huntington Library (VIII); Lambeth Palace Library (I); and Lincoln Cathedral Chapter Library (IV).

I acknowledge with gratitude the provision of some research grants by the University of Liverpool to carry out the necessary research. Professor Cross and Dr. David Mills of Liverpool University have offered me much constructive advice. I am grateful to the two general editors, Derek Pearsall and Elizabeth Salter, for including this volume in their series and for their help at many stages of its preparation.

N. F. B.

Contents

Introduction

Development and Extent of Middle English Prose

THE title of this book does not imply that Middle English religious prose is a definite and readily discernible entity; it is used as a matter of convenience to convey the broad limits of the selection. Indeed, in Middle English not only is it sometimes difficult to decide exactly what is prose and what poetry, but also the period witnessed such a marked change in both style and subject-matter that early Middle English prose has more in common with Old English, and later Middle English prose more in common with Tudor prose, than either has with the other. A brief review of the early development of prose in England will provide the justification for this statement.

Since literary prose was not written by the Anglo-Saxons before their conversion to Christianity, there was no indigenous prose style similar to the poetic or alliterative one. When literary prose started to be composed it was based on Latin models and was often no more than straightforward translation; and as English had few of the words and constructions found in Latin, the resulting prose was clumsy. It was natural that later writers should seek to improve the quality of the prose style. They used two methods: firstly, they imitated their Latin originals in general rather than in particular by following the techniques of Latin rhetoric without necessarily trying to adapt all Latin constructions to English; and secondly, they employed some of the stylistic features characteristic of Old English poetry. Since that poetry is composed in alliterating half-lines, later Old English prose writers borrowed alliteration, balance and variation which are their principal hallmarks. Different writers deployed these features in various ways, but two trends in this adaptation of poetic techniques to prose are discernible: one associated with Ælfric, the other with Wulfstan. In the former alliteration is used to bind together balanced phrases, which are often lengthy, by letting it extend beyond the compass of a single phrase. In the latter the alliterating words are confined to one phrase, frequently only a doublet, whereby each phrase becomes an independent rhythmical unit.

Both Ælfric and Wulfstan were clerics, as were most of their imitators, and a tradition became established that those who wrote on religious topics followed one of the stylistic patterns associated with these two writers. The differences between them are not great and later authors often made use of both. These two patterns formed a style, which may be called the alliterative prose style. It survived the Norman Conquest, though it ceased to be the only style, for one result of the Conquest was that many of the senior positions in English sees and religious houses were filled by French clerics and monks, and when these ecclesiastics encouraged writing in English, they preferred the adoption of the French style and ideas familiar to them. In this way a new English style developed, though in the early

A*

Middle English period its influence was limited for it had not the uniformity, tradition or authority of the alliterative style. It gained ground most speedily in the east of the country, as the Trinity and Kentish collections of sermons show. In the west, however, Bishop Wulfstan,[1] an Englishman, remained in possession of his see at Worcester till his death in 1095. Here at least continuity was preserved between the Old and Middle English periods; scribes and writers were trained as a matter of course in the existing tradition, so that not only were the writings of such Old English authors as Ælfric copied, but also many new works, strongly influenced by the Old English homiletic style and matter, were composed there and in the neighbourhood. Of these *The Life of St. Chad* appears to be the earliest extant.

Although it can be shown that the Old English homiletic tradition continued unbroken at Worcester, it is possible that in other centres the style associated with this tradition survived to some extent, for early Middle English prose works usually show some influence of the alliterative tradition. Thus in this sentence from the *Lambeth Sermon on Sunday*

Gif hwa wule witen hwa erest biwon reste tham wrecche saule, to sothe ic eow segge thet wes Sancte Paul the apostel and Mihhal the archangel. (6–8)

one can trace the alliteration of *w* in *wule, witen, biwon* and *wrecche*, and of *s* in *saule, sothe, segge* and *Sancte*. The alliteration is there, though it is uncertain whether it is fortuitous or not. But as this writer does use other rhetorical devices, such as rhyme, probably his alliteration is intentional and does represent an echo of the traditional style. It has ceased, however, to be the dominant feature of his style. Writers in the west of the country, on the other hand, continued to use alliteration as a major stylistic feature, though they also employed other techniques to make their prose studied, ornate and rhythmical. Thus in *The Wooing of Our Lord* the alliterative rhythm is insistent:

Jesu, swete Jesu, mi druth, mi derling, mi drihtin, mi healend, mi huniter, mi haliwei, swetter is munegunge of the then mildeu o muthe. Hwa ne mei luve thi luveli leor? Hwat herte is swa hard that ne mei tomelte i the munegunge of the? (1–4)

Each phrase forms an independent unit because the alliteration is rarely carried on from one phrase to the next, with the result that these units are linked together more because they are of the same length and weight than by any rhythmical or syntactical unity; the model is Wulfstan rather than Ælfric. Yet the author's use of synonyms shows that he was moving away from a complete reliance on the alliterative style: he was creating a style that in its intensity and excess would convey the devotional feelings of the author. The older style is still used, but it has been adapted to meet the requirements of the new spirituality of the twelfth century; and although this new style may strike a modern reader as florid and

---

[1] Not to be confused with Archbishop Wulfstan of York, the writer.

breathless, it was developed for a specialized end. A parallel development is found in *Holy Virginity*: the traditional alliteration is an important, but not the only, stylistic technique used, though it is employed more frequently in passages of deep emotion and intensity: other features such as balance, rhyme, rhythm and word-repetition are found. Thus the traditional late Old English prose was transformed into the highly wrought and studied prose of the early Middle English period; and this was prose of a high technical standard put to the service of special religious needs.

This style, primarily associated with Worcester and the west in the early Middle English period, spread northwards. Although it had originally been used for various types of religious writings, it became confined more and more to mystical works and treatises of fervent spirituality associated with them. This development took place partly because of the suitability of such a style to convey the range and intensity of rare religious experience and partly because a similar style was used for comparable writings in Latin. Indeed the existence of this Latin style raises doubts as to the indigenous nature of the alliterative style of fourteenth-century writers, though the continuity of the vocabulary and the availability of the earlier texts in the fourteenth century go a long way to dispel them. This style, still modified by the admixture of rhetorical devices, was used by Rolle and to a much lesser extent by Hilton and the author of *The Cloud of Unknowing*. Through its use these authors managed to achieve a personal, homogeneous style even though the majority of their works were based on continental originals and models; there is nothing 'foreign' about their writings.

A change in English prose, which consisted in the displacing of the native alliterative style by a French-based style, can be traced during the fourteenth century. We have already seen that some early Middle English texts were influenced by French language and style; and in England many works were written in Anglo-Norman, that dialect of French used in England. But the major works of early Middle English prose had been composed in the traditional style, though they had not remained untouched by continental influences. France, however, had undergone a cultural renaissance in the twelfth and early thirteenth centuries, and French literary works came increasingly to be regarded elsewhere as the correct models to follow. It is probable that the English nobility became acquainted with such works through the campaigns and conquests of the Hundred Years' War; and as members of the nobility grew richer and more enlightened they imitated their French counterparts by patronizing literature, so that the style and intention of religious literature underwent considerable modification at this time. The Church, for its part, was troubled with heresy within its own body and with the attacks on its wealth and secularization, of which the satire in *The Perversion of the Works of Mercy* is not untypical. The Church was no longer in a position to remain the sole haven for or patron of writers, though it continued to support and encourage them. Contemplative and polemical writers still used the alliterative style, which became even more closely identified with the Church. But such writings, though important in themselves and popular with certain sections of society, no longer formed the mainstream of English prose; they were regarded increasingly as provincial. Naturally this development was one that happened only gradually; there was no sudden change.

The rise of the nobility as patrons changed the approach as well as the style of religious prose. Much early Middle English prose is written by clerics for other clerics or for their disciples: it either explains the rules for living within a community or describes the higher states of religious experience. It usually presupposes a knowledge of the basic tenets of a Christian education. Late Middle English prose, on the other hand, is more explanatory and consolatory: being addressed to laymen it explains the fundamentals of the Christian religion. It is more romantic and colourful in its approach to religion in order to make the instruction more palatable. Exotic topics like the quest of Seth are commoner in late Middle English prose. The reader's interest could also be aroused by clothing a subject in an elaborate literary allegory. Such allegories were superimposed upon the texts like a kind of intellectual puzzle, as in *The Abbey of the Holy Ghost*, and have little in common with the traditional religious allegory which sought to expound biblical passages and images; but allegory is a subject to which we shall return. Characteristic of this change between the two periods is the piece *Remedies against the Seven Deadly Sins*, which is an adaptation of part of the *Ancren Riwle*. The earlier work had been written as a guide for certain ladies as to how they should conduct their lives within the small community which they comprised. The author of the later work took over only certain aspects of the former one in order to develop them at greater length. From these he produced a treatise on the seven deadly sins suitable for private reading, which was not in any real sense designed as a guide to the conduct of one's life. It describes, it does not direct, the predominant impression being that this is religion at second hand. Neither the author nor the reader is as involved in the later work as he had been in the earlier one.

It is significant that *Remedies against the Seven Deadly Sins* is translated from French, for the majority of the selections in the second half of this book resemble it in this. Some, such as the *Golden Legend*, may indeed go back beyond the French versions to Latin originals, but Latin was no longer so important an influence on English prose. Latin had lost its predominance to French in works designed for a wider audience, for French had become the fashionable language. Consequently there are innumerable translations from French in the late Middle English, and the prose found in them may be called 'courtly prose'; it is characteristic in particular of those works translated from or modelled upon a continental French source and intended for a member of the nobility. The kings, as the foremost members of that nobility, often set the lead in patronizing literary works, and as their courts gradually came to be based permanently on London, so courtly prose became increasingly associated with London and the south-east.

The two terms 'alliterative prose' and 'courtly prose' are not parallel, since the first defines a style and the second the audience. Such a distinction is necessary, however, because there is little stylistic uniformity in the works of courtly prose. As writers of this prose were reacting against the traditional English style and its vocabulary, they had nothing other than their French source to imitate or to serve as a model; and as they were translating from French because of that language's fashionable elegance, they no doubt wanted to keep as close to their original as possible. Hence courtly prose is characterized by literal translation of its sources with the result that there is a great diversity in style, although it is in general clumsier and far less technically accomplished than the prose of the alliterative tradition. The problems its writers faced were not unlike those which had faced the early Anglo-Saxon translators of Latin texts: they had to force English into the patterns of a supposedly superior language. Naturally they made the same sort of mistakes: they assumed the original must be elegant and make sense although they could not always understand it, so they were satisfied with a literal English version. Elegance in French was thought to produce elegance in English; but unfortunately the result was all too often rough and sometimes simply unintelligible. The balanced rhythm of the earlier prose gives way to a string of simple paratactic sentences, as in the later pieces in the selection. French idioms and constructions are freely imported into English, where they are assumed to make as good sense as in the original. Such features as a tautologous subject or the omission of the pronoun as subject or object are usually the result of literal translation. Nevertheless, the courtly writers did also want to elevate their style and to bring it up to the level of French. To do this they adopted the simple expedient of introducing French loanwords into their prose, since these gave it a cultured and fashionable look. The later selections contain many unusual words which have been borrowed from French: the homeliness of the earlier vocabulary has been lost. This emphasis upon elevation also results in the use of two or three words where one would have done.

Some of these features may be seen in the following passage from *The Life of St. Edmund*:

> And so by one assent theye chose Seynt Edmond to proclayme the popys wylle. And soo he dyd that charge full welle and dyligently thurgh this londe, and moche people he causyd to take the crosse and for to go into the Holy Londe. (175–8)

The rhythm and force of the early style are gone. The paratactic construction of the passage gives it a simple appearance, but that simplicity is deceptive because the translator has sometimes failed to use English expressions and constructions: the inversion of verb and object in *moche people he causyd* and the absence of a parallel construction in '*to take* the crosse and *for to go* into the Holy Londe' upset the fluency of the sentence. There are several words of French origin, *assent*, *proclayme*, *charge*, *dyligently* and *causyd* though none is as strange as some which occur. The initial result of the subservience of English prose to French was the loss of its strength and forcefulness.

It should not be inferred from the above that all late Middle English prose is clumsy, for the period is characterized by a great range in the quality of its prose. Whereas in the early Middle English period the alliterative tradition tended to make prose pieces less diverse in quality, in the later period the quality of a text was determined by the prose of the French original and the outlook of the translator. Since French prose was anyway less uniform than English and since the translations varied from the free to the utterly slavish, the range is enormous. In general, however, the style of the later selections is less proficient than that of the earlier ones. But it must be remembered that these pieces represent a new start for English prose in a direction which affected its whole future development; and we should not expect the founders of a tradition to be as proficient as its later beneficiaries.

This brief sketch of the development of Middle English prose provides the background for a consideration of the problem raised at the beginning of this section: how can one decide whether a piece is in prose or verse? We saw, for instance, that late Old English writers like Ælfric and Wulfstan adopted many of the techniques of Old English poetry to embellish their prose. Alliterative poetry is a poetry of stress which allows the poet considerable freedom as to the number of syllables per line. Stressed syllables are linked by alliteration within the line, but the absence of rhyme means that there is often little obvious connection between one line and the next, though naturally the sense as well as balance, parallelism and variation provide some. When alliteration was extended to prose, which then adopted a rhythm based on stressed alliterative syllables, the difference between the two forms became small. Indeed some Old English alliterative prose, such as the sermons of Ælfric, is sometimes printed in modern editions as though it consisted of lines of poetry. For the Old English period, however, poetry and prose may be distinguished because the former uses a specialized vocabulary and a stricter alliterative rhythm. But changes which affected the language in the transition period from Old to Middle English also affected alliterative poetry—the vocabulary was simplified, the rhythm became looser and the line longer. These changes made alliterative poetry even closer to alliterative prose, so that a prose writer who uses a fairly strict rhythmical pattern of alliteration may find himself writing something which is to all intents and purposes alliterative poetry. Thus the lines quoted earlier from *The Wooing of Our Lord* could be arranged as poetry:

> Jesu, swete Jesu, mi druth, mi derling, mi drihtin,
> Mi healend, mi huniter, mi haliwei,
> Swetter is munegunge of the then mildeu o muthe.
> Hwa ne mei luve thi luveli leor? (1-3)

This free arrangement of alliterative stresses, which would be unusual in Old

English, could be paralleled from Middle English poetry. Generally, however, even in Middle English the rhythm in prose is not maintained at such a level throughout; there are passages on a lower emotional and rhythmical plane. While this applies also to some extent to poetry, there is an attempt in that medium to maintain the alliterative pattern with some consistency.

This difficulty in determining the boundary between prose and poetry is not confined to alliterative prose. In the later Middle English period transposition from one form to the other was frequent. The prose *Life of St. Edmund* is an adaptation of the poetic version found in the *South English Legendary* and frequently it has taken over the vocabulary and rhythms of the poem, some parts hardly differing from the poetic text. Even in cases where such an adaptation is not in question, the medium of a given piece is sometimes a matter of dispute. *John Gaytryge's Sermon* is printed as poetry in one modern edition, and it has been suggested that *The Life of Adam and Eve* was written in long lines which have been corrupted in transmission.[1] For just as alliteration was used as a decoration in prose, so was rhyme; and as early rhyming poems did not necessarily adhere to a regular syllabic line (no doubt because this was not part of the English poetic tradition) the two forms could easily converge.

Although I am confident that the pieces reproduced here are best printed as prose in a modern edition, perhaps one should not press the point too far since the modern distinction between prose and poetry as separate entities had not been established in Middle English times. Indeed the very words *poetry* and *prose* were anglicized only in the fourteenth century. In the Middle Ages the distinction made was among varying levels of style (high, middle and low) and not between two different forms. Prose and poetry could both be written in a high or a low style, and neither form was considered more appropriate for a particular style. On the contrary, there was more similarity between poetry and prose in the high style than between prose in the high and in the low style. Often indeed, for the more elementary forms of religious instruction, poetry rather than prose was used because it was simpler and more readily remembered. Prose was in many ways the more sophisticated medium. It is significant that such conscious stylists as Hilton and the author of *The Cloud of Unknowing* used only prose for their compositions, and this may have been because they were writing for a limited and educated audience. It should also be remembered that Middle English writers did not think that certain subjects were more suitable for prose and others for poetry; as we have seen, texts were transposed from one to the other quite easily. The modern idea that certain themes are more poetic was unknown. Prose could be used to express the whole range of human ideas and emotions; it was in no way the mere utilitarian thing that it has increasingly become.

It must therefore be emphasized that in Middle English prose is a specialized

[1] T. F. Simmons and H. E. Nolloth, *The Lay Folks' Catechism* (London 1901), and M. Day, *The Wheatley Manuscript* (London 1921), pp. xxvi–xxvii.

and sophisticated means of literary composition. And while it may be true that it does not rise to the highest flights of expression achieved by individual Middle English poets, the general level of Middle English prose is overall far higher than that of Middle English poetry. It is rare to come across bad Middle English prose. At the same time, because prose was used regularly by clerical writers for a limited range of subjects, it is easier to trace the development of medieval ideas, sensibilities and literary characteristics through it than through poetry. So although it has many points of similarity with poetry, it has important characteristics of its own. Some of these will be described in the following sections.

Religious and Social Background

As so many medieval works are anonymous it is hardly surprising that the authors of most of the pieces in this collection are unknown; but it is not without significance that such authors or translators as have been identified are generally clerics of one sort of another. John Gaytryge was a Benedictine monk at York, and the author of the *Epistle of Discretion of Stirrings* was the priest who wrote *The Cloud of Unknowing*. The author of the original Latin version of the *Golden Legend* was an archbishop of Genoa, and the compiler of the French collection of the *Somme le Roi* (in which *The Art of Dieing* was included) was the Dominican Lorens d'Orléans, confessor to King Philip the Bold of France. The knowledge of Latin, the scriptures and the fathers found in the other texts suggests that they also were written by clerical authors. The Lambeth sermons were certainly by a priest, and *Holy Virginity* was doubtless written by the same priest who wrote the other religious pieces associated with it. The author of *The Wooing of Our Lord* was familiar both with the English mystical tradition and with the tradition of ecstatic prayers to Christ; he was quite possibly a monk. The authorship of the Wycliffite *The Perversion of the Works of Mercy* is uncertain. Although Wyclif was not the author, it may well have been written by someone who like himself was in orders; it must have been written by one of the intellectual leaders of the Wycliffite movement. The latter pieces are mostly translations, usually from French. The translators were probably not in orders, but since they translated literally their contribution was in any event small; their originals were, as far as we can tell, written by clerics more often than not.

Since these pieces were written by clerics or religious, it is understandable that they exhibit the same moral outlook and religious bases, for they were all produced for instruction and exhortation. They differ however in detail and approach because they were composed for different audiences and purposes. Here we are on less certain ground, though this section will try to examine these aspects in order to provide the necessary background for an understanding of the selections.

One of the foremost duties of the Church was the teaching of God's word, and one of the commonest ways of performing this duty was through sermons.

Two types of sermon are found in the Middle English period: the ancient and the modern. The latter was associated with the universities and the friars, for 'modern' sermons were often written in Latin and were usually based on the instructions for composition found in the *Artes Praedicandi*—manuals for preachers which outlined how sermons might be constructed and subdivided. The audience's enjoyment came from appreciating the form of the sermon with its arrangement into parts to support the logic of the argument; hence such sermons were normally addressed to sophisticated audiences. Space did not permit the inclusion of a sermon of this type here. The other or 'ancient' type of sermon was the descendant of the older homily and is characterized by the absence of any formal approach to structural composition. Such sermons are freer in their overall structure and rely principally upon narration and exempla for their effects. The modern sermon, which was introduced into England in the thirteenth century, never managed to oust the ancient type, which was in any case more suitable for use with less well-educated audiences. The *Lambeth Sermon on Sunday* belongs to the ancient type. It makes a direct appeal to the audience's emotions by portraying the pains of hell, the efficacy of Paul's intercession and the mercy of Christ; its intellectual content is small. It has, however, obvious points of contact with apocryphal literature as exemplified in this book by *The Life of Adam and Eve*.

The task of providing instruction for the layman fell upon the clergy. Such an arrangement presupposes that the clergy were themselves sufficiently educated for this purpose, which was not always the case for the Church in England was composed of two types of minister: the intellectual elite who had attended university and the parish priests who were often as uneducated as their parishioners. The ignorance of these priests was a permanent scandal in the Church and numerous attempts were made to improve their educational level. A major reform movement was inaugurated at the Fourth Lateran Council in 1215 and its lead was followed in England by Archbishop Pecham of Canterbury, who issued his Constitutions for the reform of the clergy in 1281. These were in Latin and gave a simple outline of the essential tenets of the Christian faith. His work was taken as a model by a fourteenth-century reformer, Archbishop Thoresby of York, whose catechism of 1357 is an expansion of Pecham's Constitutions. Thoresby's Latin catechism was translated into English by a monk of St. Mary's Abbey, York, and hence is known as *John Gaytryge's Sermon*, though it hardly merits the name of sermon. It is a systematic arrangement of the elements of the Christian faith which every Christian, priest and parishioner, must know. Although it contains a few literary flourishes, it is designed as a straightforward text containing plain statements of belief. No attempt is made to cajole, to threaten or to persuade; fact is here all-important. Gaytryge's English version was made at Thoresby's request and included in his Register. While the English translation may be a comment on the ignorance of Latin among the clergy, it also testifies to the archbishop's wish to make the catechism known as widely as possible so that the task of educational reform could go forward. In this he was evidently successful, for not only was the work known to John Foxe in the sixteenth century, but an adapted version was produced in the late fourteenth century by the Lollards so that it could be used for their propaganda purposes.

Wyclif and the other Lollard leaders had received their training within the Church, since that was the only place where intellectual instruction could be had, and they therefore used the Church's own weapons in their attack upon it. Usually in the English works this meant that they drew a vivid contrast between the Church as it existed in the fourteenth century and the ideal as expressed in religious writings of what it should be and was indeed considered to have been in earlier ages. Hence *The Perversion of the Works of Mercy* adopts the simple procedure of comparing the Church's own teaching on the seven works of mercy with the life of the average ecclesiastic, particularly that of the friars, in contemporary England. It should, however, be emphasized that *The Perversion of the Works of Mercy* contains little that could not be found in more orthodox criticisms of the Church, for as we have seen there were many who were only too conscious of the shortcomings of the clergy and tried to do something about them. Satire and complaint were genres which were commonly used to express such views. *The Perversion of the Works of Mercy* contains nothing which is not orthodox, and its criticisms could be readily paralleled from *Piers Plowman* and other fourteenth-century works. Wyclif and his followers diverged from the traditional critics both by their attack on some dogmas of the Church and through arousing the suspicions of the state by their direct appeal to the people. While the former was usually argued in Latin treatises, the latter necessitated the use of English—and an English that was not too sophisticated. Although *The Perversion of the Works of Mercy* is not without subtlety, it is easy enough to see how pieces like this with their attack on the established order and their appeal to a more primitive form of Christianity would have attracted the sympathy of the lower classes. *The Perversion of the Works of Mercy* has much in common with sermons and satires: it takes a piece of Christian teaching and shows how it might be observed and how it is usually neglected. It does this with examples drawn from contemporary society readily understandable to all and expressed in a trenchant language. The passage would lend itself to forceful delivery as easily as the *Lambeth Sermon on Sunday* would.

Not all religious works were intended to explain general points of faith to a wide audience since the Church also had to cater for the instruction of those who had undertaken a more specialized form of religious life. Those who joined a community or who were inspired to follow in the footsteps of the contemplatives needed spiritual guidance. A text which may have originated in this way is *Holy Virginity*, for while it was certainly intended as a piece of propaganda for the nunneries, it may have been written more specifically at the request of or for the edification of a particular community of devout women. Of its companion pieces the *Ancren*

Riwle was composed for the guidance of certain noble women living in a small community, and both *St. Katherine* and *St. Marharete* were written for the edification of women. Indeed, the necessity of providing women with suitable literature was responsible for the composition of many works in English, since few of them knew Latin. Because of its ambivalent attitude towards women, the Church may at times have been embarrassed by such communities, though it could not ignore them. At first women were attached to existing orders whose rules were modified where necessary to accommodate them, but from the thirteenth century special orders for women were established. In all cases, since women could not be ordained as priests, their spiritual life had to be regulated and supervised by men, who would write works for their instruction and encouragement. *Holy Virginity* should be understood against this background.

In it we can trace the two medieval attitudes to women, for a woman had caused man to fall in the Garden of Eden and a woman had provided man with the means of salvation by the birth of Christ. Woman therefore symbolized the temptress and the mother of the Saviour, and the contrast between complete bliss and utter degradation (the two alternatives open to man) seemed to find its most pungent expression in the mortal life of womankind. The method the author has adopted is not unlike that found in many sermons. In some ways it combines the ancient and modern types of sermon, for it commences as an allegorical exposition of a text from the *Psalms* and then proceeds to a direct appeal to the audience's emotions by portraying the bliss of virginity and the torments of marriage. The latter, though doubtless exaggerated, provide an excellent corrective to the view of woman found in the majority of the Middle English romances.

The *Epistle of Discretion of Stirrings* was likewise written for a limited audience. Ostensibly a letter written to a young contemplative who had enquired how far he should follow certain promptings to special ascetic practices, it may have been intended by its priestly author for all who were inclined to the contemplative life, since in manuscripts it is generally found in company with other treatises on mysticism. Mysticism, or contemplation as it should more correctly be called, was an important element in medieval Christianity: those who cut themselves off from the world, in order to concentrate their whole being on the Godhead, hoped that the soul might eventually achieve a union, however brief, with it. Although mystical elements are found in the writings of St. Augustine and Gregory the Great, it was only when the works of the pseudo-Dionysius became more widely known in the West as a result of their translation into Latin and when St. Bernard popularized what has been called his 'philosophy of love' that mysticism became a pervasive influence on Western Christianity. In England many early Middle English texts like *Holy Virginity* and *The Wooing of Our Lord* show some knowledge of the meditative processes which were often preparatory to mystical states: it is the fourteenth century, however, which is the great age of

English mysticism. That century saw the emergence of Richard Rolle, Walter Hilton, Dame Juliana of Norwich and the author of *The Cloud of Unknowing*, identified as the author of this piece as well. These four differ among themselves in both approach and influence. Whereas the writings of Rolle, for example, are largely descriptive of his periods of ecstatic union with Christ, those of the author of *The Cloud of Unknowing* are advisory. They direct intending contemplatives how to conduct themselves and how to approach the contemplative life. Caution is his watchword, and he evidently deplored the influence exerted by Rolle. He differs also from the other English mystics in the influence of the pseudo-Dionysius found in his writings. Pseudo-Dionysius, who was a Christian Neoplatonist, was probably a sixth-century Syrian ecclesiastic. His writings in Greek were translated into Latin in the ninth century and many commentaries on them were written by Western teachers. Because he accepted that God was absolutely incomprehensible to man on account of his different nature, he advocated the negative approach to contemplation, by which a contemplative was urged to aspire to a state of nothingness; in this respect the title, *The Cloud of Unknowing*, is itself significant. In the *Epistle of Discretion of Stirrings*, however, the author is more a counsellor and guide, warning of the dangers of false promptings within, who nevertheless encourages his pupil to persevere in the attempt to know himself better in order to achieve the final union. He shows himself to be a wise and patient adviser.

Other works of instruction in this volume are *Remedies against the Seven Deadly Sins* and *The Art of Dieing*, though both were addressed to lay noblemen rather than to clerics. The former was probably composed in its French form for Margaret, the sister of Edward IV who married Charles the Bold of Burgundy, a pious lady responsible for the composition of many moral and didactic works. The piece provides an account of each sin and its opposite virtue, supported by patristic quotations and illustrative examples. The descriptions of the sins and the virtues are very general: there is never any guidance to the reader as to how he could face his own particular problems. The application of the virtues to individual circumstances was evidently the job of the reader himself. Hence while the work is lively with many narrative felicities, its use as a practical help was limited. It could be read by almost any audience at any time with equal profit. *The Art of Dieing* is different in that it forms part of a compendium known as *The Book of Vices and Virtues*, which contained lengthy discussions of those tenets of the Christian faith so briefly listed in *John Gaytryge's Sermon* and which could thus be considered a comprehensive guide to a Christian life. *The Art of Dieing*, or *Ars Moriendi*, had however been a separate text before its inclusion in *The Book of Vices and Virtues*. The title *Ars Moriendi* is applied to works of several different types: the earlier examples, like this one, are designed to encourage people to lead better lives; the later ones are more in the nature of battles between an angel and a devil for the soul of a dying man; and others, generally from the fifteenth century, are collections of prayers for the dying. All emphasize the ever-present nature of death with the consequent necessity to prepare for it, though the earlier examples are not so morbidly conscious of death as the later ones. Yet the result is that there is little instruction of the accepted kind: the work is a mixture of threats and blandishments to get Christians to improve themselves, with little practical guidance as to how this might best be done. *The Art of Dieing* is, however, more sophisticated than the *Lambeth Sermon on Sunday* since it tempts as much as it frightens.

Not all texts were intended for instruction; some were meant for use privately or as part of the divine service. *The Wooing of Our Lord* is a prayer which falls into this category. It has close connections with the mystical Christianity associated with St. Bernard. The founder of the Cistercian order of monks, St. Bernard sought to temper the austere asceticism of that order by encouraging his monks to achieve a heightened communion with Christ through prayer. The language of his own writings is emotive and personal, and it owes much to the imagery and tone of the *Song of Songs*, on which he wrote an influential commentary. His work inspired many others to write prayers and hymns in both Latin and the vernacular. *The Wooing of Our Lord* exhibits the same intensity of language and emotion—it is hardly fortuitous that it contains an echo of the hymn *Jesu dulcis memoria* which has been attributed to St. Bernard—and it may conceivably have been written by an English Cistercian.

The connection of *The Abbey of the Holy Ghost* with the cloistered life is of a different nature. Designed ostensibly for people who wished to enter a community but were unable to do so, it may originally have been written for a female audience since the monastic life portrayed is that of a convent. It sets out to show how people who are obliged to spend their days physically under secular conditions might nevertheless live spiritually as though members of a community. But the framework of the allegorical convent, which may have been suggested by secular allegories such as the *Roman de la Rose*, is largely superficial. Characters like the Abbess Charity and the Prioress Wisdom merely represent certain virtues; they do not come to life or take any action until they merge with the personified virtues and vices of the psychomachia of a different tradition. Only then does some drama enter the work. For the most part the piece is constructed on the well-tried method of assembling certain passages from the Bible, the meaning of which is then expounded with the help of patristic commentaries and traditional learning. The allegorical framework obscures this basic pattern and was doubtless incorporated to make the work more palatable to an audience accustomed to allegorical fantasies.

The remaining works in the volume, *The Life of Adam and Eve* and the two extracts from the *Golden Legend*, may be considered historical, even though two of them are mainly apocryphal and the other one has many legendary elements. But the medieval attitude to the past was very different from our own. To us it seems simply that medieval historians could not or would not distinguish between history and legend. To them a belief in the divine creation and ordering of the universe presupposed that God was revealed through historical events. So what was significant was not the event itself, but what that event revealed of God and his purpose: the spirit and not its particular physical manifestation was the true reality. Thus it was really immaterial whether Constantine had his vision on the banks of the Tiber or of the Danube; only the vision itself was important. Not unnaturally such an attitude could lead to an adjustment of certain happenings or even to their invention to make God's ways to man more explicit. But this was usually done in an effort to get to the true reality and not in any attempt to deceive. At the same time there was a natural curiosity about those persons in the Bible of whom the canonical books provide only brief glimpses. Stories which catered for this taste were popular from an early date and typical of them is *The Life of Adam and Eve*. Not only did this work fill in the details of the life of Adam and Eve, but it also sought to underline the appropriateness of Christ's role as the second Adam. For Seth was given the seed of the tree whose fruit Adam and Eve had eaten, and from that seed sprang the tree whose wood was used ultimately to make Christ's cross. The cross therefore represented both the fall and the salvation of man, and embodied within itself the pattern of man's history. After the crucifixion the cross was buried only to be found later by St. Helena, and parts of it, whether genuine or not, were to be found throughout Christendom. The story of the finding of the cross was important as a testimony to the genuineness of the fragments of the true cross and as an example of how one should strive for what is right. Helena had struggled against all the odds to find the cross and in this she had been helped by God. The value of such writings as *The Finding of the True Cross* to the Church was that they offered instruction through history about how God assists those who believe in him: no man need be alone in his struggle in this world.

The message of *The Life of St. Edmund* is similar. The saints were venerated either because their lives were a model of holiness and piety or because the way in which they died could offer encouragement and strength to those who remained behind. Saints' lives of the latter type concentrate principally upon the great climax of the martyrdom, whereas those of the former kind consider the whole life of the saint. For, as in the case of St. Edmund, the saint must appear to have been marked out from earliest childhood: he has overcome the enemy not in one glorious fight, but in the steady struggle of everyday existence. The witness for such a life is cumulative and all details of the saint's life are important. As the possibilities for martyrdom diminished, so the model lives of these saints increased in importance for, though ordinary humans like the rest of us, they show how the devil and the flesh can be overcome.

The Material and its Arrangement

Although the Bible is the basic text of Christianity, it rarely provides the principal material or theme of Middle English religious literature. It appears most frequently as an authority for a moral judgement or as a yardstick by which to judge human behaviour. Thus it may provide the characters who appear, such as St. Paul in the *Lambeth Sermon on Sunday* and Adam and Eve in *The Life of Adam and Eve*, but it does not supply the actions they undertake; these are usually of a more recent date. Similarly, biblical texts may be used to support the argument of a passage, as in the various references to *1 Corinthians* and to the parable of the wise and foolish virgins in *Holy Virginity*, even though the biblical texts have only a general relationship with the theme under discussion. In *The Abbey of the Holy Ghost* the author has linked two passages from the *Psalms* (1: 2 and 77: 12) simply because they both happen to contain the word *meditabor*, even though there is otherwise little connection between them. Biblical characters and stories were used as examples and models: Mary Magdalen was a standard symbol of penitence. And all the time there are echoes of biblical imagery and language. So although the Bible has rarely provided the immediate material of these texts, it is always present in the background.

More important for the genesis of religious prose was the Church's daily round of worship. While the services were in Latin, parts of it such as the sermon could be delivered in the vernacular. The congregation would need to be informed of what was being celebrated. The lives of the saints and accounts of other events which were commemorated in the Church's calendar, such as the finding of the cross, arose from the need to provide material which could be used in this way. So the lives of past Christians and accounts of important events in the history of Christianity naturally form a large part of Christian religious prose. As we saw in the last section, medieval Christians accepted that as God had created the world, everything in it showed some attribute of the divinity, provided only that its essential meaning was extracted. Historical events were part of God's grand plan for the human race, while all organic and inorganic life contained some attribute of its creator. There was a message and meaning in everything, and the writer of a religious tract had literally the whole world as his possible material.

The way in which the author presented his material could be decided by the material itself or the occasion for which it was written. A saint's life will be based round the life of the saint and the miracles performed in his name. A sermon, if it is the modern type, will be developed in accordance with the recommendations of the *Artes Praedicandi*. The *Epistle of Discretion of Stirrings* is cast in the epistolary form which had its own rules of composition based ultimately upon classical example. A satire is normally based on a straightforward contrast as in *The Perversion of the Works of Mercy*. A debate was a contest of wits between two real, assumed or allegorical personages to discuss the rights and wrongs of a particular action or theme. Some texts, however, were simple disquisitions which fall into no particular category.

Even when the author was writing within a well-defined genre, he had considerable latitude in working out his theme. There were several accepted methods he could use and these tend to recur in the texts: often one of them may be used to provide the framework while the others appear incidentally. One such method was allegory, which may for our purposes be divided into two types: biblical allegory and personification. The former arose through exegesis. Some form of interpretation of the Bible was necessary because there were many apparent inconsistencies within it; much in the Old Testament, at a literal level, was disturbing or even distasteful; and as the Old Testament was regarded as foreshadowing the New Testament it had to be read in a way which would bring out the parallelism between the two. The early fathers had developed allegory as a means of solving these difficulties. Their interpretations were handed down in several ways. Later commentators incorporated much of what had been suggested by earlier ones, and as at the universities such commentaries formed part of the curriculum the allegorical method was perpetuated. When Vulgate manuscripts were copied the scribes frequently included one or other of the important commentaries with the text so that the reader almost inevitably read the Bible in the light of what the commentators had said. Otherwise the average author probably picked up the traditional teaching from various compendia and florilegia, collections of material suitable for particular occasions and purposes, or from earlier writings on that topic which they were about to treat. Contemplatives would be familiar with established mystical works and would naturally tend to use the same passages from the Bible with their relevant explanations in their own writings; and the same applied to writers on other subjects. Reliance on previous authority took precedence over any desire for originality: writers wanted to pass on the established truth, not to propound new ideas. Hence it is not surprising that two quite separate and disparate works should interpret a particular passage of the Bible in the same way. The Wycliffite *The Perversion of the Works of Mercy* and the mystical *Epistle of Discretion of Stirrings* both interpret the 'windows' of *Jeremiah* 9: 1 as the five wits, for they were both inheritors of the same tradition of biblical scholarship and interpretation. Authors of vernacular works rarely used a thoroughgoing form of biblical allegory, and the nearest approach to it in these texts is the opening of *Holy Virginity* where a passage from the *Psalms* is allegorized. More usually biblical allegory appears incidentally, which may make it more difficult to appreciate since we today are not always aware of the background. It was common, for example, to allegorize the occurrences of Sion in the Bible as the heavenly home, the goal of our strivings and the pattern of our behaviour so that Sion came to stand for heaven with all that that entails. Similarly Babylon became associated with hell, evil and sin. The author of *Holy Virginity* was thereby enabled to use Sion and Babylon knowing that they carried with them their biblical connotations and allegorical force. The allegorical method produced highly charged symbols, which may seem lifeless or wooden to a modern reader but which were pregnant with meaning to the writer and his audience.

Personification allegory, by which abstract qualities are endowed with human characteristics, also has a long history and, though not specifically Christian, it was used by Christian writers from an early period. It was at first particularly associated with battles between personified vices and virtues. As a mode of writing it lends itself especially to those pieces which describe a difference of opinion: the debate between the soul and the body, the battle between the four daughters of God and those of Satan, or the strife between the seven virtues and the seven vices. Personification here adds drama, humour and human interest in what could otherwise be arid intellectual debates. The result of its use was that some abstract qualities were usually thought of in partly human terms. Wit (reason) and Will (physical pleasure) so frequently appeared in a personified guise that medieval authors found it difficult to think of them simply as abstracts; they seem to retain part of their personification even in contexts where a simple abstract would be sufficient. So the editorial capitalization in this volume should be considered as tentative; it is not always possible to be certain how much personification was intended. In later medieval times personification allegory was adopted by secular writers in the vernacular, particularly in France, where it found its most influential expression in the *Roman de la Rose*. This work set a fashion for allegory among courtly writers and this fashion was taken up by English writers, as the Middle English translation, the *Romaunt of the Rose*, testifies. This use by secular authors gave personification allegory new life and no doubt inspired its use by those religious authors, such as the writer of *The Abbey of the Holy Ghost*, who wanted to pander to the new fashion.

Another method which was employed to develop the material was the use of numbers. In *Matthew* 25: 31–46 the dead at the Day of Judgement are divided into sheep and goats depending on whether in this life they had performed six things. But six was not a number which appealed to the medieval mind and it was soon changed to seven, for those numbers which were most popular were three and four, and their sum, seven, and their multiple, twelve. The ten commandments were frequently divided into two groups of three and seven each, as in Gaytryge's sermon, to make them fit these numbers, and the other groups in that sermon consist of the fourteen points of faith (two groups of seven each), the seven sacraments, the seven virtues, the seven works of mercy and the seven deadly sins. Even in a work like the *Lambeth Sermon on Sunday* the popular numbers keep recurring: there are seven flames from the oven, twelve principal devils, seven bitter waves, seven prison-locks, the old bishop led by four devils, and Sunday honoured for three reasons. In no instance is the number of material importance in so far as it would make little difference whether there were ten or twelve principal devils, except that the number twelve implies that these principal devils were hell's equivalent to the twelve apostles. The use of similar numbers allows such correspondences to be suggested, if not actually stated. Of the numbers mentioned three and seven occur most frequently. The former allows for a triangular arrangement of parallelism and contrast which is easy to follow, as in: good, better, best; virgin, wife, widow; heaven, earth, hell; charity, wisdom, meekness—to choose some which occur in these selections. The latter, on the other hand, allows the author to indulge in one of the favourite medieval pastimes, that of categorization, within a framework which is not too big and which can be subdivided in its turn into three and four. Apart from categorization, medieval authors liked to compose lists of things, a taste which an arrangement into seven gratified. Lists were not invariably arranged numerically, for on occasion they are simply introduced by *some* as at the beginning of *The Wooing of Our Lord*.

The numerical arrangement could appear either incidentally, as in the *Lambeth Sermon on Sunday*, or as the framework of a text which was then expanded. The elaboration of this framework could take several different forms, some of which may be illustrated from the seven deadly sins. One was to personify the sins so that the characteristics of each could be exemplified through one person: this was the method adopted by Langland in *Piers Plowman*. Alternatively the sins could be equated with different animals, for animal symbolism was well developed in the medieval period. A full-scale development of this method is found in Hilton's *Scale of Perfection*, but instances of individual animals representing a certain sin occur not infrequently in many works. A third possibility was that the sins could be subdivided into various lesser sins which sprang from the greater ones; Gower used this method in his *Confessio Amantis*. The first subdivision could be further subdivided if necessary. A quite different method, the one adopted in *Remedies against the Seven Deadly Sins*, was to show how the sins might be countered; often indeed the sins were paired off with the corresponding virtues. The remedies for the sins could be subdivided in their turn: for example, in *Remedies against the Seven Deadly Sins* patience, the antidote of wrath, is divided into three levels. Other approaches are possible,[1] but these examples are sufficient to reveal how works which started with the same basic pattern could become quite varied in their development.

In most methods, however, the different subdivisions would normally be illustrated by *exempla*. An exemplum was a short narrative story used to illustrate a particular point or moral: the parables of Christ are the prototypes for Christian writers. They could be drawn from the Bible, lives of saints, history, contemporary events or classical literature, and they varied in length from a few lines to several pages. The extended type is found more frequently in secular literature: the stories in Gower's *Confessio Amantis*, for example, are so long that they almost destroy the confessional framework into which they are inserted. Typical of religious prose are the examples in the *Lambeth Sermon on Sunday* of the bishop and the maiden tormented by the devils in hell because of their faults in this life

[1] For artistic representations of the vices and virtues see A. E. M. Katzenellenbogen *Allegories of the Virtues and Vices in Medieval Art* (London 1939), particularly plates xl and xli.

and those in *Remedies against the Seven Deadly Sins* taken for the most part from episodes in the life of Christ. They are short, often picturesque, and contain a moral—and this was sufficient for the purposes of the writer of religious prose. Exempla of this kind would keep alive the reader's or listener's attention and make the moral stick in his mind. In cases where the use of exempla was carried to an extreme they could become more important than the teaching they were supposed to illustrate. In the *Lambeth Sermon on Sunday* it would have been easy to extend the examples of the punishments of sinners almost indefinitely. Consequently exempla were criticized by some writers; but these selections do not exhibit their abuse.

Where a numerical framework is not used, pieces of religious prose will often be constructed around some form of contrast or parallelism based on all or some of the following real or ideal ways of life: the customary existence of man following material pleasures, the life of the true Christian, and the future life whether in heaven or in hell. In *Holy Virginity*, for example, the author makes his main contrast between the states of virginity and marriage, but there are minor contrasts between the former and the angelic life and between the latter and the state of widowhood. A hierarchy is established among these various ways of life, and their benefits and shortcomings are pointed out so that the whole adds up to a comprehensive picture of woman's existence, though the ostensible subject is virginity. For a thing is known as much by what it is not as by what it is. *The Wooing of Our Lord* is based on the proposition that those human attitudes which arouse love in men are found in a higher and purer state in Jesus, who ought therefore to be the object of our loving. The piece is worked out by contrasting each attribute as it appears in men and as it appears in Christ. In the *Epistle of Discretion of Stirrings* the contrast is between living in solitude and in public with the attendant behaviour suitable for one's own life and circumstances. *The Abbey of the Holy Ghost* is constructed round parallelism rather than contrast, for it exhibits that common medieval idea that the internal life is mirrored in the external one. *The Perversion of the Works of Mercy*, on the other hand, has not only the rigid structure of the numerical pattern of the seven works of mercy but also a thoroughgoing contrast between the life of the friars and of other religious as it actually is and the ideal to which it ought to conform. Here the two structural methods are united.

These comparisons and parallelisms embody the Christian view of the world based on the interpretations of the Bible. Through Adam man had fallen into original sin and could be raised from that state only through Christ's sacrifice. So in this life, though we are sinful by inheritance, we must try to emulate Christ's sacrifice; those who are content to remain in Adam's state will go to hell, while those who follow Christ can expect salvation. The contrast between the life of the spirit and that of the flesh (Wit and Will) was exemplified in the lives of Christ and Adam, and naturally Christian writers devoted considerable space to the two prototypes of these lives. An emphasis upon Christ is natural enough, though as Christ is the second Adam it is his humanity which is most frequently commented upon, for in our aspiration for heaven we emulate Christ's life on earth. On the other hand, it was not simply an interest in the exotic or a desire to fill lacunae in the biblical narrative which led to the creation of such works as *The Life of Adam and Eve*. Such accounts revealed how man had come to be in his present condition, they underlined why suffering was necessary, and they continually stressed that this state was not permanent. Seth had fetched a branch of the tree of life from paradise and he was promised that it would bloom at the appointed time: the way to salvation was being prepared for man. To achieve it man had to overcome the flesh through suffering and win through to a state of blessedness. In the writings of an emotional and passionate Christian, in for example *The Wooing of Our Lord*, the physical sufferings of Christ on the cross could be equated in a moving manner with those of the recluse in her cell. For other authors, such as the less extreme writer of the *Epistle of Discretion of Stirrings*, it meant adjusting the pattern of one's life in a manner suited to one's individual disposition, for not everyone was equipped to live a spiritual life at such an elevated level. It was sufficient to follow Christ in one's own way. But those whose lives most closely approximated to that of the divine prototype were regarded as models for the rest of us; indeed, they were generally canonized. Their lives were useful examples in that they showed what man—any man—could achieve with determination and the grace of God. *The Life of St. Edmund* is best appreciated in this way. In it, while his sufferings and physical repressions are pointed out, they are not emphasized. The life concentrates upon the temptations to which he was exposed and how he overcame them. The whole is little more than a compendium of vignettes or exempla illustrating the workings of various virtues—virtues which we ought to have and to practise. His life shows that we too can follow the divine example.

Although they had the example of Christ and his saints to speed them on the pilgrimage of this life, most men were content to remain in the life of Adam, of the flesh. Hence writers depicted the contrast between the life led by the average person and the life they could, indeed should, have led. This resulted in those pictures of contemporary life which are such a feature of some Middle English prose. In this volume the liveliest and most memorable of these is the picture in *Holy Virginity* of the lot of married women who have so many duties and cares that they never have a moment's peace; the demands of marriage and parenthood rob them of all tranquillity. Descriptions like this help to bring these works alive for us, but they are realistic only in a limited way. The author, who was in any event a priest unacquainted with a domestic routine, has picked out the worst domestic misfortunes that could afflict a wife and has presented them as though they happened continually, to create a sense of unwavering misery and disaster. Nor are all descriptions of contemporary life necessarily accurate pictures of their times. In *The Perversion of the Works of Mercy* there is much that is traditional in the attack on the friars' way of life; the author based his descriptions as much on other men's words as on his own observations.

The portrayal of mankind in medieval works was strongly influenced by *Matthew* 25: 31–46 in which men are divided into sheep and goats. As everyone earned heaven or hell by his deeds in this life, there seemed to be place for only two types of men: the good and the bad. There is rarely any question of a man being compounded of a mixture of both. This absence of any middle ground led to that portrayal of people who are impossibly wicked or righteous. And because conversion or repentance was considered immediately effective, it was possible for a man to change from one state to the other all at once, as Judas does in *The Finding of the True Cross*. This simple opposition of good and bad was reinforced by the medieval understanding of the cosmos in which this world is placed between heaven above and hell below. It is typical that the dreamer in *Piers Plowman* should see the deep dungeon and the tower of truth on either side of the field full of folk. The presence of these two absolutes on either side of human life, the two poles between which it flows, made it difficult in religious literature to portray men as other than black or white. At the same time it accounts for that preoccupation with the other worlds, for this life is a preparation for the next. This life is a staging post which is important only in so far as it determines where we go on the next stage of our voyage. But the next life, being eternal, is ultimately far more important. Our true home, from which we were expelled by the wiles of the serpent, is in paradise and the purpose of religious prose is to help us to find our way back there.

Since it is so difficult to give a convincing picture of heaven which is not at the same time flat and uninteresting, the majority of writers preferred to employ their eloquence on descriptions of hell. Typical of such descriptions is the account of hell in the *Lambeth Sermon for Sunday*. It is traditional in that it concentrates on the flames, the stench, the torments and the devils' terrifying figures. Hell is physical and concrete; it is also personalized since the punishments meted out are to some extent tailored to the various crimes committed on earth. Descriptions of paradise, on the other hand, are far less vividly realized. Partly this is because such descriptions concentrate on what is not rather than what is in paradise, and partly because they simply provide a list of some of the qualities found there. In *The Art of Dieing* paradise is portrayed in this way:

There is the joyeful companye of God, of aungeles and of halewen. There is plente of al goodnesse, fairenesse, richesse, worschipe, joye, vertues, love, wit, and joye and likynge everemore lastynge. There is non ypocrisie, ne gile, ne losengerie, ne non evel-acord, ne non envye, ne hunger, ne thrist, ne to moche hete, ne cold, ne non yvele, ne non akynge of heved, ne drede of enemys, but everemore festes grete and realle weddynges with songes and joye withouten ende (130–37)

Here is none of the immediacy, particularity or force which is found in descriptions of hell; the author does not seem to be so engaged. Not unnaturally this criticism does not apply to descriptions of paradise found in contemplative writings which are among the most moving; but unfortunately the examples of contemplative writing in this volume contain no such descriptions.

Descriptions of hell were as traditional as descriptions of the shortcomings of the friars. Because the instruction offered by the clergy covered the same sort of subject so frequently, set methods of developing certain themes were evolved. Often this culminated in the expression of an idea within a set rhetorical or imaginative framework. Thus it became customary to express the decay of temporal things in contrast to the permanence of spiritual ones through the lips of men who had been rich or powerful on earth, but who at death retained nothing. In *The Art of Dieing* the theme is expressed like this:

> And that witnesseth wel the kynges, the erles, the prynces, and the emperoures, that hadde sum tyme the joye of the world, and now thei lyen in helle and crien and wailen and waryen and seyn: 'Alas, what helpeth now us our londes, oure grete power in erthe, honoures, nobeleye, joye and bost? Al is passed—ye, sonner than a schadewe or foul fleynge or a quarel of an arblawst; and thus passeth oure lif: now be we bore and thus sone dede. . .'.   (13–19)

Many similar examples could be found in both Old and Middle English literature, and together they form what are commonly known as *topoi* (sing. *topos*). Such topoi (or 'motifs') were obviously useful to the writers of religious prose, as indeed to all other writers, because when writing about a given subject they could illustrate it by using one of these ready-made topoi suitably adapted to their own purpose.

Another device used to drive home the instruction was the use of proverbial phrases, for like topoi and exempla such proverbs brought the teaching within the comprehension of an audience and made it seem part of their everyday experience. We find Middle English equivalents of such proverbs as 'All that glitters is not gold' (II, 97), 'Ease makes thief' (II, 233), 'When need is highest, help is nighest' (III, 143–4), and 'Who loves to dwell at home knows little good' (VIII, 64–5). The use of such proverbial expressions may also have been encouraged by the Bible since both *Proverbs* and *Ecclesiasticus* are full of pithy sayings. The latter book, though later regarded as apocryphal by the Anglican Church, was very popular in the Middle English period and many quotations from it are found in these selections. Yet although writers relied on such helps to composition as are described in this section and although their work frequently covers much the same ground, the texts themselves exhibit a notable variety of range and approach.

Achievement

The need to provide religious instruction was a continuing one and prose to satisfy this need was written throughout the Middle English period. As Christian ideas and attitudes were themselves continually changing, a selection of Middle English religious prose is a microcosm of medieval Christianity. Religious prose was written at many centres in the country, and perhaps for this reason it was less susceptible to sudden changes in literary taste though it could not ultimately escape their influence. Religious prose is therefore a good medium through which to trace the continuity and change of literary style and expression. Yet, as mentioned in the opening section, prose was a sophisticated medium particularly reserved for intellectual and cultured audiences and it naturally exhibits the structural organization and subtle use of language that such audiences would expect. A study of Middle English poetry may leave an impression that where it exists Middle English literature is pedestrian, with one or two notable exceptions. A knowledge of Middle English religious prose can correct that distorted view by revealing how competent a level of literary expression was maintained throughout the Middle English period. However, the range of prose covered in this volume is large enough to make it impossible to formulate any generalizations about the achievement of Middle English religious prose. It may be best to base some general observations around a single text, the *Epistle of Discretion of Stirrings*.

In the last section possible methods for a text's composition were discussed; many of these texts have a rigid, but by no means an inflexible, structure. The *Epistle of Discretion of Stirrings* consists of three sections: a brief introduction and the author's answers to his correspondent's two questions. The introduction states in a general way the whole problem of living publicly or in seclusion and emphasizes that the latter is good only when it is informed by grace. The two specific questions are then put down and an answer to each is provided in turn. The development of each answer is parallel. Each commences with the author's insistence on his lack of competence to answer the question, and both answers are worked out in terms of a central image. In the first it is the crown of life, in the second the two eyes. These images provide a pivot around which the author can develop his teaching and make it colourful. Yet although the two answers are parallel, they are also complementary in that they represent two stages in his pupil's education. The first consists in the necessity of knowing oneself and of being able to understand one's own inward impulses, the second is learning to love God, who will then guide one's actions so that one knows instinctively what to do. This instinctive behaviour is the operation of grace, and the conclusion thus completes the cycle of the teaching by linking up with the message of the introduction. The framework is quite perfect in its way: it controls without mastering the material; the teaching is put across clearly and tactfully. This work is by no means an isolated example. While the brevity of pieces such as these has naturally prevented the authors from diverging too far from their subjects, their structure is not a negative virtue. The result is planned; it did not simply come about. Even in extended works of Middle English religious prose, which are too long for this volume, there are many examples of careful structure.

Similar attention to detail is evident in the construction of the paragraphs, as the following example shows:

> Thou askist me counseil of silence and of speking, of comon dieting and of singuler fasting, of duelling in cumpany and of onely-wonyng bi thiself. And thou seist that thou art in gret were what thou schalt do: for, as thou seist, on the to partie thou art gretly taried with speking, with comyn eting as other folk don and, thou seist, with comyn wongyng in cumpany; and on the tother partie thou dreddist to be streitly stille, singuler in fasting and onely in wonyng, for demyng of more holyness then thou art worthi and for many other perils. For oftetymes now thees daies thei be demyd for moost holy and fallen into many perils that moost are in silence, in singuler fasting and in onely-duelling.
> (3-13)

In the first sentence the three contrasted pairs, speaking—silence, eating in public —eating in private, and living in a community—living as a recluse, symbolizing two different ways of life, are put forward. These are rearranged in a different pattern in the next sentence, for the three activities which make up each way of life are put together, and each group of three is contrasted as a whole against the other. First the three 'public' activities and then the three 'private' activities are put forward. But the second sentence is continued by the inclusion of the pupil's fears of the 'private' activities: being considered too holy and other dangers. The threefold pattern is varied by this change to two. And these two fears then introduce the last sentence, though in a slightly different form, for those who are thought to be holy often fall into these other dangers. And they are thought holy because they practise the three 'private' activities which are then listed. The final sentence is thus a reverse structure of the second part of the second sentence, though its conclusion returns to the dominant three pattern, which unites it with the opening sentence. Each sentence is thus contrasted and linked with the others and the whole is tightly knit. Yet the sense flows readily enough, and there is no sense of tedium even though the same ideas are constantly repeated.

The care which went into the arrangement of the sentences within the paragraph is paralleled by the attention to the choice and disposition of the vocabulary. The three word-groups of the first sentence are linked by sound and rhythmical pattern although they are constrasted in meaning. The single words of the first pair are bisyllabic and alliterate with each other. The second pair consists of two adjective-noun groups, which are united by the echo of the -ing at the end of each verbal noun. This rhyme is repeated in the third pair, except that here it comes internally in each phrase which consists of a noun-preposition-(pro)noun group. A sense of progression is attained by the increasing length of the constituent parts of the three pairs; and the pairs themselves are linked partly by the occurrence of the -ing ending in all the groups and partly by repeating the alliterating letter of the first pair in one of the words of the second group. These features recur throughout the paragraph and help to provide that close interaction of sound and sense which is so characteristic of the author.

The control exhibited by the writer and his ability to compose long sentences (such as the one at ll. 56–68) with perfect clarity is attributable to the accumulated expertise of the alliterative tradition within which he was writing and to the precepts of the rhetoricians which were used as guides. Both alliteration and the repetition of an ending like -ing (technically known as *homoeoteleuton*) were techniques recommended in the rhetorical manuals. Such manuals encouraged not only the use of figures of sound, but also the arrangement of sentences into regular and methodical patterns. Even in a work with such a practical purpose as *John Gaytryge's Sermon* a straightforward statement falls into two natural balanced groups:

> This manere of knawynge had oure formefadyrs in the state of innocence that thay ware mad in; and so sulde we hafe hade if thay had noghte synnede— noghte so mekill als hally saules hase now in heven, bot mekill mare than man hase now in erthe. (15–18)

Authors learned from the rhetoricians to manipulate sentences with the maximum effectiveness. More recently, however, the growth of the view that it is impossible to separate meaning and form has often led to a deprecation of rhetoric as a mode of composition, since it seems to put expression above everything else. But the classical concept of rhetoric was that it provided the means to give the material its most suitable and convincing expression; and this is generally how it is used by writers of Middle English religious prose. It is true that, particularly in later medieval poetry, rhetorical precepts are sometimes followed for their own sake in a spirit of exhibitionism; but this fault is much less common in religious prose, where the more practical subject-matter may well have inhibited such fanciful exhibitions. In religious prose rhetoric was a beneficent influence which resulted in the composition of a powerful, rhythmical prose.

The sober tone which the author of *Epistle of Discretion of Stirrings* cultivated discouraged the highest flights of lyricism or figurative language. Yet the piece does contain some images used to good effect. The traditional image of the soul's journey in the form of a ship passing through storms and calm weather reminds one of English poetry, and the equally common image of a crown to symbolize perfection has been enlivened and made contemporary by the inclusion of the fleur-de-lys. More striking images, however, are found in such works as *The Wooing of Our Lord* and *Holy Virginity*, which are more emotional in tone and language. In the former the wound which Longinus inflicted on Christ's side is interpreted as Christ opening his heart so that we can read the 'love-letter' written in it. Other arresting images include Christ's spittle at the crucifixion washing away the sins of the world and his conquest of the devil because of and in spite of his hands being nailed to the cross. Less striking perhaps, but equally effective, is

B

the succession of metaphors (ll. 129ff.) to symbolize virginity in *Holy Virginity*.
They make of that passage a small prose poem of moving lyricism. Indeed, both
these texts are notable for their lyricism, which is achieved not so much through
a more exotic vocabulary as through a more extended use of alliteration as we
saw in an earlier section. Prose was thus in the hands of the religious writers a
medium which could express a wide range of human experience and emotion.
It deserves close study and attentive reading.

THE TEXT

In common with other editions in this series letters are given a modern form:
þ, ð, ðð and dð all appear as *th*; ʒ is represented by *gh*, *w* or *y* as appropriate; initial
ff appears as *f*; the use of *i/j* and *u/v* follows modern practice; and in the early
texts the variation between ð and *d* is corrected silently except in the group *dl*,
e.g. *wurdliche* (I, 98), which may represent a sound change.

Abbreviations are expanded silently. Some may be expanded differently in
different texts (þ may be either *thet* or *that*), but they are expanded consistently
within any one text. There are many cases in which it is difficult to determine
whether an abbreviation is intended or what it might represent. I have ignored
the rounded stroke over *p(e)*, which might be represented as *ppe*. The superior
curled flourish at the end of a word has been interpreted as *re* only when necessary;
otherwise it has been ignored. The strokes through *h* and *l* are disregarded. The
macron is interpreted as *n*, *m* or *i* as necessary. The contraction *Jhu(s)* has been
expanded to *Jesu(s)*; so where *Jhesus* and *Jherom* are written in full, these have
been altered to *Jesus* and *Jerom* for consistency's sake.

The punctuation is modernized except that in the genitive singular an apostrophe
is added only between a consonant and the genitival *s*. The paragraph division is
editorial, and chapter headings and numberings in the original are omitted. The
word division is also editorial; but like the expansion of the abbreviations it is not
consistent throughout all the texts. Thus in the early texts the pronouns with *self*
are represented as two words, in the later texts as one.

Otherwise the texts represent the manuscripts and early printed book faithfully,
except that where a correction has been made in a manuscript by the scribe this is
taken to be the true manuscript reading. Departures from the manuscript or
printed book are recorded in the footnotes: the form before the colon being the
editorial form, the one after it the manuscript form. Where a corrected form has
been based on another manuscript, this is indicated immediately after the editorial
correction by the word *sic* with the relevant manuscript abbreviation in brackets.
The correction may not represent the word(s) in the other manuscript literally,
since I have occasionally modified the spelling to bring it into line with the con-
ventions in the base manuscript. The key for the abbreviations used in the apparatus
criticus and notes will be found in the appropriate introductory section of each

passage; but usually a single letter, e.g. A, indicates a variant MS from the base one, and two or more letters, e.g. RB, indicate a different version of the text.

The editor's notes are at the bottom of each page. Previous editions are referred to by the names of their editors. Other abbreviations used include OED and MED for the *Oxford English Dictionary* and the *Middle English Dictionary* respectively, and P.L. for *Patrologia Latina*.

Select Bibliography

N. L. Beaty, *The Craft of Dying: a Study in the Literary Tradition of the Ars Moriendi in England* (New Haven and London 1970).

J. W. Blench, *Preaching in England in the Late Fifteenth and Sixteenth Centuries* (Oxford 1964).

M. W. Bloomfield, *The Seven Deadly Sins* (Michigan 1952).

W. W. Capes, *The English Church in the Fourteenth and Fifteenth Centuries* (London 1900).

R. W. Chambers, 'On the Continuity of English Prose from Alfred to More and his School', *Harpsfield's Life of More*, ed. E. V. Hitchcock. EETS o.s. 186 (London 1932). Also reprinted separately 1933.

T. M. Charland, *Artes Praedicandi: contribution à l'histoire de la rhétorique au moyen âge* (Paris 1936).

R. D. Cornelius, *The Figurative Castle: A Study in the Mediæval Allegory of the Edifice with Especial Reference to Religious Writings* (Bryn Mawr 1930).

C. Dawson, *Mediaeval Religion and other Essays* (London 1934).

M. Deanesly, *A History of the Medieval Church 590–1500*, 3rd edn. (London 1934).

M. Deanesly, *The Lollard Bible and other Medieval Biblical Versions* (Cambridge 1920).

C. D'Evelyn and A. J. Mill, *The South English Legendary*, 3 vols. EETS o.s. 235, 236, 244 (London 1951–7).

J. H. Fisher, 'Continental Associations for the *Ancrene Riwle*', *PMLA* 64 (1949), 1180–9.

E. Gilson, *The Mystical Theology of St. Bernard* (London 1940).

H. Grundmann, *Religiöse Bewegungen im Mittelalter*, 2nd edn. (Hildesheim 1961).

A. E. M. Katzenellenbogen, *Allegories of the Virtues and Vices in Medieval Art from early Christian Times to the Thirteenth Century* (London 1939, reprinted 1964).

J. Leclercq, *The Love of Learning and the Desire for God* (New York 1961).

B. L. Manning, *The People's Faith in the Time of Wyclif* (Cambridge 1919).

J. R. H. Moorman, *Church Life in England in the Thirteenth Century* (Cambridge 1945).

M. Morgan, '*A Talking of the Love of God* and the Continuity of Stylistic Tradition in the Middle English Prose Meditations', *Review of English Studies* n.s. 3 (1952), 97–116.

M. Morgan, 'A Treatise in Cadence', *Modern Language Review* 47 (1952), 156–64.

J. A. Mosher, *The Exemplum in the Early Religious and Didactic Literature of England* (New York 1911).

J. J. Murphy, 'Rhetoric in Fourteenth-Century Oxford', *Medium Ævum* 34 (1965), 1–20.

G. R. Owst, *Preaching in Medieval England* (Cambridge 1926).

G. R. Owst, *Literature and Pulpit in Medieval England* (Cambridge 1933).

W. A. Pantin, *The English Church in the Fourteenth Century* (Cambridge 1955).

J. D. Peter, *Complaint and Satire in Early English Literature* (Oxford 1956).

H. G. Pfander, *The Popular Sermon of the Medieval Friar in England* (New York 1937).

P. Pourrat, *La spiritualité chrétienne*, vol. 2 (Paris 1946).

F. M. Powicke, *The Christian Life in the Middle Ages and other Essays* (Oxford 1935).

E. M. C. Quinn, *The Quest of Seth for the Oil of Life* (Chicago 1962).

D. W. Robertson, 'The Doctrine of Charity in Medieval Literary Gardens: A Topical Approach through Symbolism and Allegory', *Speculum* 26 (1951), 24–49.

G. Shepherd, *Ancrene Wisse: parts six and seven* (London and Edinburgh 1959).

B. Smalley, *The Study of the Bible in the Middle Ages* (Oxford 1941).

R. W. Southern, *Western Society and the Church in the Middle Ages* (London 1970).

J. Walsh, *Pre-Reformation English Spirituality* (London 1965).

J.-Th. Welter, *L'exemplum dans la littérature religieuse et didactique du moyen âge* (Paris 1927).

M. S. Westra, *A Talkyng of þe Loue of God* (The Hague 1950).

A. Wilmart, *Auteurs spirituels et textes dévots du moyen âge latin* (Paris 1932).

T. Wolpers, *Die englische Heiligenlegende des Mittelalters* (Tübingen 1964).

E. Zeeman, 'Continuity in Middle English Devotional Prose', *JEGP* 55 (1956), 417–22.

I Lambeth Sermon on Sunday

MS. Lambeth Palace Library 487, which contains the 17 Lambeth sermons and some other religious literature, was written at the end of the twelfth century. Its provenance is disputed. The sermons are fairly broad in scope, and the one for Sunday is a good example of the type. In *2 Corinthians* 12 St. Paul claimed he had been taken up to the third heaven where he heard unspeakable words. This statement led to apocryphal accounts of what he might have seen there, in much the same way as stories about other biblical characters developed to fill lacunae in the Bible (*cf.* VI). The apocryphal account of St. Paul's voyage, which was very popular, was written in Greek, but survives only in the Latin version known as the *Visio Pauli.* Several French and English versions are extant, there being at least one prose and four poetic English versions other than the Lambeth sermon. The prose version, in British Museum MS. Add. 10056 from the fourteenth century, has most in common with the Lambeth sermon, though the Lambeth sermon has many individual touches of its own such as Paul's pleading with Christ. The arrangement of the story as a sermon has also necessitated a number of changes.

Editions: R. Morris, *Old English Homilies,* First Series. EETS o.s. 29 & 34 (London 1867–8).
J. Hall, *Selections from Early Middle English 1130–1250* (Oxford 1920).

[L]eofemen, yef ye lusten wuleth and ye willeliche hit understonden, we eow wulleth suteliche seggen of tha fredome the limpeth to than deie, the is icleped Sunedei. Sunedei is ihaten thes Lauerdes dei, and ec the dei of blisse and of lisse and of alle irest. On thon deie tha engles of heofene ham iblissieth, forthi the tha erming-saulen habbeth rest of heore pine. Gif hwa wule witen hwa erest biwon reste tham wrecche saule, to sothe ic eow segge thet wes Sancte Paul the apostel and Mihhal the archangel.

Heo tweien eoden et sume time into helle, alswa heom Drihten

---

3. icleped Sunedei: iclepeth su sunedei

---

2. Brit. Mus. Harl. 2851 of the *Visio Pauli* has the title *Privilegia Diei Dominicae;* and *fredom* here has the sense of a 'special right, privilege'.

het, for to lokien hu hit ther ferde. Mihhal eode biforen and Paul com   10
efter, and tha scawede Mihhal to Sancte Paul tha wrecche sunfulle the
ther were wuniende. Therefter he him sceawede heghe treon eisliche
beorninde etforen helle-yete, and uppon than treon he him sceawede
the wrecche saulen ahonge: summe bi tha fet, summe bi tha honden,
summe bi the tunge, summe bi the eren, summe bi the hefede, summe
bi ther heorte. Seothan he him sceaude an oven on berninde fure;
he warp ut of him seofe leies, uwil[ch]an of seolcuthre heowe, the alle
weren eateliche to bihaldene and muchele strengre then eani thing to
tholien; and therwithinnen weren swithe feole saule ahonge. Yette
he him sceawede ane welle of fure and alle hire stremes urnen fur   20
berninde. And tha welle biwisten xii meister-deoflen, swilc ha weren
kinges, to pinen therwithinnen tha earming-saulen the forgult weren;
and heore awene pine nevre nere the lesse thah heo meistres weren.
Efter thon he him sceawede the sea of helle and innan than sea
weren vii bittere uthe. The forme wes snaw; that other is; thet thridde
fur; thet feorthe blod; the fifte neddren; the siste smorther; the
seofethe ful stunch—heo wes wurse to tholien thenne efr eni of alle
tha othre pine. Innan than ilke sea weren unaneomned deor: summe
fether-fotetd, summe al bute fet; and heore eghen weren al swilc swa
fur and heore ethem scean swa deth the leit amonge thunre. Thas ilke   30
nefre ne swiken, ne dei ne niht, to brekene tha erming-licome of tha
ilca men the on thisse live her hare scrift enden nalden. Summe of

15. eren: eghen   18. thing: thurg
25. snaw: swnan

10. In the original legend Paul had gone from earth while still a man, so naturally
he is taken by Michael who is the guide.

15. eren: the Latin texts have auribus. By hefede is probably meant 'hair', for the
Latin texts have capillis.

16. heorte: possibly a corruption of (h)earme, cf. Lat. brachiis.

17. he: that is, the oven.

24. the sea of helle: this may be an echo of the 'lake of fire and brimstone' of Revelations 20: 10.

26. smorther: 'smoke'; in most versions we find 'lightning' (Lat. fulgur).

28. unaneomned: that is, without name. Being unknown in this world these animals
had no name.

30. Thas ilke: may refer to the animals alone, or to the animals and the seven waves
as well.

32. scrift: this probably implies both the confession of sins and the resulting penance
imposed. Those who do not atone for their sins in this world will do so in the next;
cf. II, 297–8.

than monne sare wepeth; summe swa deor lude remeth; summe ther
graninde siketh; summe ther reowliche gnegheth his awene tunge;
summe ther wepeth; and alle heore teres beoth berninde gleden
glidende over heore awene nebbe; and swithe reowliche ilome
yeigheth and yeorne bisecheth that me ham ibureghe from tham uvele
pinan. Of thas pinan speketh David, the halie witeghe, and thus seith:
'*Miserere nostri, Domine, quia penas inferni sustinere non possumus,*
40 Lauerd, have merci of us forthon tha pinen of helle we ham ne mawen
itholien.'

Seothan he him sceawede ane stude inne middewarde helle (and
biforen tham ilke stude weren seofen clusterlokan) thar neh ne mihte
nan liviende mon gan for than ufele brethe. And therwithinna he him
sceawede gan on ald mon thet iiii deoflen ledden abuten. Tha escade
Paul to Mihhal hwet the alde mon were. Tha cweth Mihhal, heh
angel: 'He wes an biscop on othre live, the nefre nalde Cristes lawen
lokien ne halden; ofter he walde anuppon his underlinges mid wohe
motien and longe dringan thenne he walde salmes singen other eani
50 other god don.' Herefter iseh Paul hwer iii deoflen ledden an meiden
swithe unbisorweliche; and yeorne escade to Mihhal hwi me heo swa
ledde. Tha cweth Mihhal: 'Heo wes an meiden on other live thet wel
wiste hire licome in alle clenesse, ah heo nalde nefre nan other god don;
elmesyeorn nes heo nefre, ah prud heo wes swithe and modi, and
lighere and swikel, and wrethful and ontful—and forthi heo bith
wuniende inne thisse pine.'

Nu bigon Paul to wepen wunderliche, and Mihhal, heh engel, ther

---

42. ane: and   47. othre: eothre

39–41. Not a biblical quotation, though it is modelled on prayers found in the
psalms. It may come from a version of the *Gospel of Nicodemus*, on which see Xa, 2.

40. *ham:* a tautologous object pronoun referring to *pinen.*

43. *clusterlokan:* 'a lock, prison-lock'; *cf.* OE *cluster-loc.* In the Latin versions there
is a *puteum signatum vii sigillis,* which in the fourteenth-century English prose version
is a *put ylokke with seven lockes.*

47. The bad bishop figures frequently in medieval exempla. Here his *underlinges*
are his tenants. He pays more attention to extorting rents from his tenants than to
attending to episcopal duties. *Cf.* the quotation about Benno II of Osnabrück given in
R. W. Southern, *Western Society and the Church in the Middle Ages* (London 1970),
p. 182.

50ff. For the medieval attitude to 'chastity without charity' *cf.* II, 613*ff.*

weop forth mid him. Tha com ure Drihten of heveneriche to heom
on fures liche and thus cweth: 'A, hwi wepest thu, Paul?'

Paul him onswerde: 'Lauerd, ic biwepe thas monifolde pine the   60
ic her in helle iseo.'

Tha cweth ure Lauerd: 'A, hwi nalden heo witen mine lawe the
hwile heo weren on eorthe?'

Tha seide Paul him mildeliche toyeines: 'Louerd, nu ic bidde the,
yef thin wille is, thet thu heom yefe reste la hwure then Sunnedei a
thet cume Domesdei.'

Tha cweth Drihten to him: 'Paul, wel ic wat hwer ic sceal milcien:
ic heom wulle milcien the weren efterward mine milce tha hwile heo
on live weren.'

Tha wes Sancte Paul swithe wa, and abeh him redliche to his   70
Lauerdes fet and onhalsien hine gon mid thas ilke weord the ye mawen
iheren. 'Lauerd,' he cweth tha, 'nu ic the bidde for thine kinedome
and for thine engles and for thine muchele milce and for alle thine
weorkes and for alle thine haleghen and ec thine icorene that thu heom
milcie, thes the rether thet ic to heom com, and reste yefe then Sunnedei a thet cume thin heh Domesdei.'

Tha onswerede him Drihten mildere stevene: 'Aris nu, Paul, aris.
Ic ham yeve reste alswa thu ibeden havest from non on Saterdei a
tha cume Monedei's lihting, thet efre forth to Domesdei.'

Nu, leofe brethre, ye habbeth iherd hwa erest biwon reste tham for-   80
gulte saule. Nu bicumeth hit therfore to uwilche Cristene monne
mucheles the mare to halighen and to wurthien thenne dei the is
icleped Sunnedei, for of tham deie ure Lauerd seolf seith: 'Dies Domini-

---

59. fures: wunres   **63.** on: en

---

59. *fures:* Morris emended the MS *wunres* to *thunres* 'of thunder', though the
resulting sense is not entirely happy. The suggestion *fures* is Hall's and is based on a
passage from another sermon on Sunday from the Lambeth MS: *ure Drihten wile
cumen dredliche in fures liche.*

68. *weren efterward:* 'sought for'.

75. *thes the rether thet:* 'all the sooner because, particularly because'.

78. *non:* that is, 3 o'clock on Saturday afternoon when the Sunday festival com-
menced.

83ff. These quotations are from the so-called *Sunday Letter,* which was a letter
written by Christ in Latin threatening those who failed to observe Sunday with
judgement. It was said to have fallen from heaven. It probably originated in southern
France in the sixth century.

B*

cus est dies leticie et requiei, Sunnedei is dei of blisse and of alle ireste;
*Non facietur in ea aliquid nisi Deum orare, manducare, et bibere cum pace
et leticia,* Ne beo in hire nathing iwrat bute chirche-bisocnie, and
beode to Criste, and eoten, and drinken mid grithe and mid gledscipe;
Sicut dicitur, pax in terra, pax in celo, pax inter homines, For swa is ise[i]t,
grith on eorthe, and grith on hefene, and grith bitwenen uwilc Cristene
90 monne.' Eft ure Lauerd seolf seit: '*Maledictus homo qui non custodit
Sabatum,* Amansed beo the mon the Sunnedei nulle iloken.'

And forthi, leofemen, uwilc Sunnedei is to locan alswa Esterdei,
for heo is muneghing of his halie ariste from dethe to live and munegheing of tham Halie Gast, the he sende in his apostles on thon dei
the is icleped Witsunnedei; ec we understondeth thet on Sunnedei
Drihten cumeth to demene al moncun. We awen thene Sunnedei
switheliche wel to wurthien and on alle clenesse to locan, for heo hafth
mid hire threo wurdliche mihte the ye iheren mawen. Thet forme
mihte is thet heo on eorthe yeveth reste to alle eorthe-threlles, wepmen
100 and wifmen, of heore threl-weorkes. Thet other mihte is on heovene,
forthi tha engles heom resteth mare thenn on sum other dei. Thet
thridde mihte is thet tha erming-saule habbeth ireste inne helle of
heore muchele pine.

Hwa efre thenne ilokie wel thene Sunnedei other tha other halie
dawes, the mon beot in chirche to lokien swa the Sunnedei, beo heo
dalneominde of heofeneriches blisse mid than Fedre, and mid than
Sunne, and mid than Halie Gast a buten ende. Amen. *Quod ipse
prestare dignetur qui vivit et regnat Deus per omnia secula seculorum. Amen.*

---

101. heom: hem heom   **106.** Fedre: Ferde

---

86. *hire:* that is, Sunday. The feminine is taken over from the Latin; it is also used
to refer to Sunday later, *cf.* ll. 93, 97–9.

92ff. Certain important events were thought to have taken place or to be going to
take place on Sundays. Here Easter, Whitsun and Doomsday are mentioned; but other
sermons on the Sunday theme also claim that Christ's birth and baptism, not to mention
many important Old Testament events, took place on a Sunday.

98ff. These three details underline the universality of Sunday since they link heaven,
earth and hell together. *Cf.* VI, 402–4.

104–5. *other halie dawes:* that is, feast days of obligation, when people were obliged
to stay away from work and go to church.

105–6. *beo heo dalneominde:* 'let them be partakers'.

107–8. 'If it so be that he who lives and reigns as God world without end deem it
worthy to grant.'

II Holy Virginity

Holy Virginity survives in two manuscripts: Bodley 34 [B] (c. 1210), which also includes *St. Katherine, St. Juliana, St. Marharete* and *Sawles Warde*, and British Museum Cotton Titus D 18 [T] (c. 1220), which also contains *St. Katherine, Sawles Warde, The Wooing of Our Lord* (*cf.* III) and the *Ancren Riwle*. Both are collateral copies of a common original. B is unusual in that not only is its language consistent within itself (a rare enough feature in Middle English) but also linguistically it is identical in all but the smallest details with Corpus Christi College Cambridge MS. 402 of the *Ancrene Wisse* (c. 1230), even though that manuscript was written by a different scribe. The originals of both manuscripts must have been written in the same dialect area, and the copies were no doubt made soon afterwards. This means that somewhere in the West Midlands, probably Herefordshire, there was an area in which texts were written in a standardized language; this language is only imperfectly preserved in T. Yet the existence of texts of a similar nature in a standardized language coming from one locality indicates that there was a strong religious and literary tradition which was centred on one or several religious houses.

Holy Virginity, the prose homily *Sawles Warde*, and the lives of the saints Katherine, Juliana and Margaret form what is known as the Katherine Group of texts. It is significant that the three saints are women and that *Holy Virginity* is in praise of female chastity, since *Ancren Riwle*, a closely allied text, was itself composed for three noble ladies in a community. Within the Katherine Group *Holy Virginity* is exceptional in that no Latin source for it is known. It has been compared, somewhat unconvincingly, with later poems on virginity like *A loue ron* and *Of clene maydenhod*.

While modern readers may find themselves out of sympathy with its strident tone, the skill with which it is constructed and the powerful quality of the language are striking. It is edited here from B.

Editions: O. Cockayne, *Hali Meidenhad;* re-ed. by F. J. Furnivall. EETS o.s. 18 (London 1922). [B and T]
A. F. Colborn, *Hali Meiðhad* (Copenhagen 1940). [B and T]

'*Audi, filia, et vide et inclina aurem tuam, et obliviscere populum tuum et domum patris tui.*' David, the psalm-wruhte, speketh i the Sawter

1. *Ps.* 45: 10; translated at ll. 4–5. The allegorical development of this quotation follows traditional lines; *cf.* for example Jerome's *Breviarium in Psalmos* (P.L. 26: 1016–17) and Bede's *In Psalmorum Librum Exegesis* (P.L. 93: 722).

towart Godes spuse, thet is euch meiden thet haveth meith-theawes,
ant seith: 'Iher me, dohter, bihald ant bei thin eare, ant foryet ti folc
ant tines feader hus.' Nim yeme hwet euch word beo sunderliche
to seggen. Iher me, dohter, he seith; dohter he cleopeth hire forthi
thet ha understonde thet he hire luveliche lives luve leareth as feader
ah his dohter ant heo him as hire feader the blitheluker lustin. Iher
me, deore dohter, thet is yeorne lustne me with earen of thin heavet;
10 ant bihald, thet is opene to understonde me the ehnen of thin heorte;
ant bei thin eare, thet is beo buhsum to mi lare.

Ant hwet is nu this lare thet tu nimest se deopliche ant learst me se
yeo[r]ne? Low this: foryet ti folc ant tines feader hus. Thi folc he
cleopeth, David, the yederunge inwith the of fleschliche thonkes the
leathieth the ant dreaieth with har procunges to fles[ch]liche fulthen,
to licomliche lustes, ant eggith the to brudlac ant to weres cluppunge,
ant makieth the to thenchen hwuch delit were thrin, hwuch eise i the
richedom thet theos leafdis habbeth, hu muche mahte of inker streon
awakenin. A, fals folc of swikel read, as thi muth vleth as thu schawest
20 forth al thet god thuncheth ant helest al thet bittri bale thet is therunder
ant al thet muchele lure thet terof ariseth. Foryet al this folc, mi
deorew[u]rthe dohter, seith David the witege, thet is thes thonkes
warp ut of thin heorte; this is Babilones folc, the deofles here of helle,
thet is umbe forte leaden into the worldes theowdom Syones dohter.

Syon wes sumhwile icleopet the hehe tur of Jerusalem, ant Syon
ase muchel on Englische ledene ase heh sihthe; ant bitacneth this tur
the hehnesse of meith-had the bihald as of heh alle widewen under

---

3. meith-: mei|ith   9. yeorne: yeornne

13-14. *he cleopeth, David:* a tautologous subject is common in ME: 'he, David, interprets as'.

18. There is a constant contrast in this text between the highest spiritual rewards of virginity and the highest secular benefits of an elevated social status.

19. *as thi muth vleth as:* 'how your mouth speaks flatteringly when you . . .'; *cf.* MED *flen* v. (3).

24. The contrast between Sion, the heavenly home, and Babylon, the seat of evil, goes back to *Revelations* 14. In this text Sion is portrayed as a tower enclosing the virtues which is attacked by the devil and his troops. The comparison with a besieged castle is common; *cf.* Grosseteste's *Château d'Amour*.

25. Omission of a part of the verb 'to be' occurs sporadically: 'And Syon (is) . . .' *Cf.* l. 100. T has *and seith Syon ase muchel.*

hire ant weddede bathe, for theos ase flesches threalles beoth i worldes
theowdom ant wunieth lah on eorthe. Ant meiden stont thurh heh lif
i the tur of Jerusalem, nawt of lah on eorthe, ah of the hehe in heovene 30
the is bitacnet thurh this. Of thet Syon ha bihalt al the worlt under
hire, ant thurh englene liflade ant heovenlich thet ha lead, thah ha
licomliche wunie upon eorthe, ant is as i Syon the hehe tur of heovene
freo overalle from worldliche weanen. Ah Babilones folc, thet ich ear
nempnede the deofles here of helle, thet beoth flesches lustes ant
feondes eggunge, weorrith ant warpeth eaver towart tis tur forte
keasten hit adun ant drahen into theowdom thet stont se hehe therin,
ant is icleoped forthi Syones dohter.

Ant nis ha witerliche akeast ant into theowdom idrahen the of se
swithe heh stal, of se muche dignete, ant swuch wurthschipe as hit is to 40
beo Godes spuse, Jesu Cristes brude, the Lauerdes leofmon thet alle
thinges buheth, of al worlt leafdi as he is of [al] lauerd, ilich him in
halschipe, unwemmet as he is ant thet eadi meiden his deorrewurthe
moder, ilich his hali engles ant his heste halhen, se freo of hire seolven—
ha nawhit ne thearf of other thing thenchen bute ane of hire leofmon
with treowe luve cwemen, for he wule carie for hire, thet ha haveth
itake to, of al thet hire bihoveth hwil ha riht luveth him with sothe
bileave—nis ha thenne sariliche, as ich seide ear, akeast ant into theowdom idrahen the of se muchel hehschipe ant se seli freodom schal
lihte se lahe into a monnes theowdom swa thet ha naveth nawt freo of 50
hire seolven, ant trukien for a mon of lam the heovenliche Lauerd,
ant lutlin hire leafdischipe ase muchel as hire leatere were is leasse
wurth ant leasse haveth then hefde ear hire earre; ant of Godes brude
ant his freo dohter, for ba toyederes ha is, bikimeth theow under mon
ant his threl to don al ant drehen thet him liketh, ne sitte hit hire se
uvele; ant of se seli sikernesse, as ha wes ant mahte beon under Godes
warde, deth hire into drechunge, to dihten hus ant hinen, ant to se
monie earmthen, to carien for se feole thing, teonen tholien ant gromen

---

28. worldes: world|des   **40.** wurthschipe: wurthsjchipe

39ff. This long sentence is cast as a question. Is she not truly humiliated who gives
up all the advantages of a heavenly life on earth in order to become a man's servant
through marriage? The *of se swithe heh stal* (39–40) is parallel to *of se muchel hehschipe*
(49); but the second part of the balanced question is given only with the latter parallel.

46–7. *thet ha haveth itake to:* 'to whom she has committed herself'.

51–2. *trukien* and *lutlin* are infinitives dependent upon *schal* (49).

55–6. *ne sitte hit hire se uvele:* 'however wretched it makes her'.

ant scheomen umbestunde, drehen se moni wa for se wac hure, as the
60 worlt foryelt eaver ed ten ende? Nis theos witerliche akeast? Nis this
theowdom inoh ayein thet ilke freolec thet ha hefde hwil ha wes
Syones dohter? Ant thah nis inempnet her nawt of heovenliche luren
the passith alle withuten evenunge.

Sikerliche swa hit feareth. Serve Godd ane ant alle thing schule the
turne to gode; ant tac the to him treowliche ant tu schalt beo freo
from alle worldliche weanen ne mei nan uvel hearmi the, for as Seinte
Pawel seith: 'Alle thing turneth then gode to gode, ne mei na thing
wonti the, the berest him thet al wealt inwith thi breoste.' Ant swuch
swettnesse thu schalt ifinden in his luve ant in his servise, ant habbe
70 se muche murhthe throf ant licunge i thin heorte, thet tu naldest
changin thet stat thet tu livest in forte [beo] cwen icrunet. Se hende
is ure Lauerd thet nule he nawt thet his icorene beon her withute
mede, for se muchel confort is in his grace thet al ham sit thet ha seoth.
Ant thah hit thunche othre men thet ha drehen hearde, hit ne derveth
ham nawt, ah thuncheth ham softe ant habbeth mare delit thrin then
ei other habbe i licunge of the worlt. This ure Lauerd yeveth ham her
as on earnnesse of eche mede thet schal cume threfter. Thus habbeth
Godes freond al the frut of this worlt, thet ha forsaken habbeth, o
wunderliche wise ant heovene ed ten ende.

80 Nu thenne, on other half, nim the to the worlde, ant eaver se thu
mare havest se the schal mare trukien ant servin, hwen thu naldest
Godd, thes fikele worlt ant frakele, ant schalt beo sare idervet under
hire as hire threal on a thusent wisen; ayeines an licunge habben twa
ofthunchunge[s], ant se ofte beon imaket earm of an ethlich mon thet
tu list under for nawt other for nohtunge thet te schal lathi thi lif ant
bireowe thi sith thet tu eaver dudest te into swuch theowdom for
worldliche wunne, thet tu wendest to biyeotene, ant havest ifunden

60ff. In addition to the loss of those mortal benefits which are associated with
virginity in this life, marriage can involve the loss of heavenly ones. The thought is
developed in the following paragraph.

67. *Romans* 8: 28. The sense is: all things turn out well for the good.

72. *her*: that is, in this life.

73. 'Everything they see they find agreeable (suits them).'

81–2. The 'world' is the subject of *schal* (81), but 'you' understood is the subject
of *schalt* (82).

86. *bireowe*: that is, cause you to repent of the time.

87. It is common to suggest that the pleasures of the world are only superficially
enjoyable; they cannot last long.

weane thrin ant wontrethe rive. Al is thet tu wendest golt iwurthe to
meastling; al is nawt thet ti folc, of hwam I spec thruppe, biheten the
to ifinden. Nu thu wast thet ha habbeth bichearret te as treitres, for 90
under weole i wunnes stude thu havest her ofte helle; ant bute yef thu
withbreide the, thu bredest te thet other, as doth thes cwenes, thes
riche cuntasses, theos modie leafdis of hare liflade. Sothliche yef ha
bithencheth ham riht ant icnawlecheth soth, ich habbe ham to witnesse,
ha lickith honi of thornes, ha buggeth al thet swete with twa dale of
bittre—ant thet schal forthre i this writ beon openliche ischawet.
Nis hit nower neh gold al thet ter schineth; nat thah na mon bute
ham seolfen hwet ham sticheth ofte. Hwen thus is of riche, hwet
wenest tu of the poure the beoth wacliche iyeven ant biset on uvele,
as gentile wummon meast alle nu on worlde the nabbeth hwerwith 100
buggen ham brudgume onont ham ant yeoveth ham to theowdom of
an etheluker mon with al thet ha habbeth? Weilawei, Jesu Godd,
hwuch unwurthe chaffere! Wel were ham weren ha on hare brudlakes
dei iboren to biburien. Forthi, seli meiden, foryet ti folc as David
bit; thet is, do awei the thonckes the prokieth thin heorte thurh licomliche lustes ant leathieth ant eggith towart thullich theowdom for
fleschliche fulthen. Foryet ec thi feader hus, as David read threfter:
thi feader he cleopeth thet untheaw thet streonede the of thi moder,
thet ilke unhende flesches brune, thet bearninde yeohthe of thet licomliche lust bivore thet wleatewile werc, thet bestelich yederunge, thet 110
scheomelese sompnunge, thet ful of fulthe stinkinde ant untohe dede.
Hit is thah i wedlac summes weies to tholien, as me schal efter iheren.

Yef thu easkest hwi Godd scheop swuch thing to beonne, ich the
ondswerie Godd ne scheop hit neaver swuch, ah Adam ant Eve turnden
hit to beo swuch thurh hare sunne ant merden ure cunde thet is untheawes hus, ant haveth, mare hearm is, al to muche lauerdom ant meistrie
thrinne. This cunde merreth us thet David cleopeth thi feadres hus,
thet is the lust of lecherie thet rixleth therwithinnen. Foryet ant ga ut
throf with wil of thin heorte, ant Godd wule efter the wil yeove
strengthe sikerliche of his deore grace. Ne thearf thu bute wilnin, ant 120

---

107. fleschliche: flecsliche   109. bearninde: bearnninde
116. hearm: hear|rm

---

95. That is with misery in this world and eternal damnation.
100. Cf. l. 25.
116–17. Take *sunne* as the subject of *haveth; thrinne* = 'in our nature'.

leote Godd wurchen; have trust on his help. Ne schalt tu na thing godes bisechen ne luvien thet he hit nule endin. Eaver bidde his grace ant overkim with hire help the ilke wake cunde the draheth into theowdom ant into fulthe fenniliche akeasteth se monie. '*Et concupiscet rex decorem tuum*, Ant thenne wule', seith David, 'the king wilni thi wlite;' the king of alle kinges desiri the to leofmon. Ant tu thenne, eadi meiden, thet art iloten to him with meith-hades merke, ne brec thu nawt thet seil thet seileth inc togederes. Halt thi nome, thurh hwam thu art to him iweddet, ne leos thu neaver for a lust ant for
130 ethelich delit of an hondhwile thet ilke thing the ne mei neaver beon acoveret.

Meith-had is thet tresor thet beo hit eanes forloren ne bith hit neaver ifunden. Meith-had is the blostme thet beo ha fulliche eanes forcorven ne spruteth ha eft neaver: ah thah ha falewi sum chere mid misliche thonkes, ha mei eft grenin neaver the leatere. Meith-had is the steorre thet beo ha eanes of the est igan adun i the west neaver eft ne ariseth ha. Meith-had is thet an iyettet te of heovene; do thu hit eanes awei ne schalt tu neaver nan other swuch acovrin. For meith-had is heovene cwen ant worldes alesendnesse thurh hwam we beoth iborhen,
140 mihte over alle mihtes ant cwemest Crist of alle. Forthi thu ahest, meiden, se deorliche witen hit for hit is se heh thing ant se swithe leof Godd ant se licwurthe, ant thet an lure thet is wit[h]uten coverunge. Yef hit is Godd [leof] thet is him seolf swa ilich, [nis] hit na wunder, for he is leoflukest thing ant buten eaver euch bruche, ant wes eaver ant is cleane over alle thing, ant over alle thinge luveth cleannesse. Ant hwet is lufsumre thing ant mare to herien bimong eordlich thing then the mihte of meith-had bute bruche ant cleane ibrowden on him seolven, the maketh of eordlich mon ant wummon heovene engel, of heame hine, of fa freont, help of thet te hearmith? Ure flesch is ure fa
150 ant heaneth us ant hearmith se ofte as ha us fuleth. Ah yef ha wit hire

---

128. Halt: Hwalt B, Hald T   145. cleannesse: cleainnesse

124–5. *Ps.* 45: 11. This verse follows the one which opens the text.
129. In the author's conceit a virgin is the wife of Christ.
147. *ibrowden*: Colborn translates as 'resembled', but perhaps the more usual sense of 'clasped, pulled tight' gives an adequate meaning; the *him seolven* is dative singular.
149. *help of thet te hearmith*: 'a help out of that which harms you'.
150. *yef ha*: that is, if virginity.

withute bruche cleane, ha is us swithe god freond ant help of treowe
hine, for in hire ant thurh hire thu ofearnest, me[i]den, to beon englene
evening i the eche blisse of heovene—ant with god rihte hwen thu hare
liflade i thi bruchele flesch bute bruche leadest.

Engel ant meiden beoth evening i vertu i meith-hades mihte, thah
eadinesse ham twinni yetten ant totweame. Ant thah hare meith-had beo
ed[i]ure nuthe, thin is the mare strengthe to halden ant schal with mare
mede beo the foryolden. This mihte is thet an thet i this deadliche lif
schaweth in hire an estat of the blisse undeadlich i thet eadi lond as
brude ne nimeth gume ne brudgume brude, ant teacheth her on eorthe   160
in hire liflade the liflade of heovene, ant i this worlt thet is icleopet
lond of unlicnesse edhalt hire burde in cleannesse of heovenlich cunde
thah ha beo utlahe therof, ant i licome of lam ant i bestes bodi neh
liveth heovene engel. Nis this mihte of alle swithe to herien? This is yet
the vertu the halt ure bruchele veat, thet is ure feble flesch as Seinte
Pawel leareth, in hal halinesse; ant as thet swote smirles ant deorest
of othre, thet is icleopet basme, wit thet deade licome thet is therwith
ismiret from rotunge, alswa deth meidenhad meidenes cwike flesch
withute wemmunge, halt alse hire limen ant hire fif wittes, sihthe ant
herunge, smechunge ant smellunge, ant euch limes felunge, thet ha ne   170
merren ne ne mealten thurh licom[lich]e lustes i fleschliche fulthen the
Godd haveth thurh his grace se muche luve iunnen, thet ha ne beoth of
the ilich bi hwam hit is iwriten thus thurh the prophete thet ha in hare
wurthinge as eaveres forroteden, thet is eaver euch wif thet is hire
were threal ant liveth i wurthinge, he ant heo bathe. Ah nis nawt bi

---

151. god: godd

163. therof: threof

158. i this (sic T): is the

171. lustes (sic T): lustest

---

162. *lond of unlicnesse:* the world is unlike our real home, which is Paradise or
the heavenly Jerusalem, from which we were exiled by the sin of Adam and Eve
(*cf.* l. 114). Through the merits of virginity maidens can experience a small foretaste
of what our heavenly home is like. The theme of exile is a common one in medieval
religious literature.

164-6. The reference is probably to *1 Corinthians,* a text which our author draws
from extensively.

169. The five senses are the means through which man sins, hence the necessity
for keeping them in check; *cf.* 215*ff.* and VII, 175–7.

172-3. *of the ilich bi hwam:* 'like those of whom'.

173. This sentence represents the spirit, if not the actual words, of many prophetic
utterances.

theos iseid thet ha forrotieth thrin, yef ha hare wedlac laheliche haldeth. Ah the ilke sari wrecches the i the fule wurthinge unwedde waleweth beoth the deofles eaveres, thet rit ham ant spureth ham to don al thet he wule. Theos walewith i wurthinge ant forrotieth thrin a thet ha
180 arisen thurh bireowsunge ant healen ham with soth schrift ant with deadbote.

Eadi meiden, understont te in hu heh dignete the mihte of meith-had halt te. Ah se thu herre stondest beo sarre offearet to fallen, for se herre degre se the fal is wurse. The ontfule deovel bihalt te se hehe istihe towart heovene thurh meith-hades mihte, thet him is mihte lathest, for thurh hire Leafdi meith-had the hit bigon earst, the meiden Marie, he forleas the lauerdom on moncun on eorthe, ant wes helle irobbet ant heovene bith ifullet; sith the folhin hire troden, meiden, gan as heo dude, the offrede hire meith-had earst to ure Lauerd for-hwon thet
190 he cheas hire bimong alle wummen forte beon his moder ant thurh hire meith-had moncun alesen. Nu bihalt te alde feond ant sith [the] i this mihte stonde se hehe ilich hire ant hire sune, as engel in heovene, i meith-hades menske, ant toswelleth of grome ant scheoteth niht ant dei his earewen, idrencte of an attri healewi, towart tin heorte to wundi the with wac wil ant makien to fallen as Crist te forbeode; ant eaver se thu strengeluker stondest ayein him, se he o teone ant o grome wodeluker weorreth, for swa muche the hokerluker him thuncheth to beon overcumen thet thing se feble as flesch is, ant nomeliche of wummon, schal him overstihen. Euch fleschlich wil ant lust of leccherie the

---

183. offearet: offea|aret   190. wummen: wummem

---

186. 'Through the virginity of her Lady'. T reads *ure* for *hire*.

187. The reference is to the harrowing of hell, which Christ, born of the Virgin, accomplished after the crucifixion.

188. Understand the devil to be the subject of *sith*, though Furnivall takes it to be Mary. Translate: 'The devil sees you, maiden, follow her footsteps and go the same way which she who first offered her virginity to our Lord did.'

193. Like that of the castle, the image of the devil's arrows appears frequently in descriptions of the struggle between the vices and virtues. The virgin's defence against them is the shield of reason.

199ff. The opposition between wit (reason) and will (carnal pleasure) is frequent in medieval literature, as for example in *Sawles Warde*. Often these two, like the seven sins, are personified, though in this text the personification is not carried through consistently.

ariseth i the heorte is thes feondes fla. Ah hit ne wundeth the nawt 200
bute hit festni in the ant leave se longe thet tu waldest thet ti wil were
ibroht to werke. Hwil thi wit edstont ant chastieth thi wil, thah thi
lust beore to thet te leof were, ne hearmeth hit te nawiht ne suleth thi
sawle, for wit is hire scheld under Godes grace. Hwil the scheld is ihal,
thet is the wisdom of thi wit thet hit ne breoke ne beie, thah thi
fleschliche wil fals beo therunder ant walde as hire luste, thes feondes
flan fleoth ayein alle on him seolven. Ant loke wel hwervore: ure
licomes lust is thes feondes foster, ure wit is Godes dohter; ant ba
beoth us inwith. Forthi her is aa feht ant mot beon aa nede, for ne
truketh neaver mare hwil we her wunieth weorre ham bitweonen. Ah 210
wel is him thet folheth Wit, Godes dohter, for ha halt with Meith-
had thet is ure suster.

Ah thi wil, on other half, of thet licomliche lust halt with Leccherie
thet is the deofles streon, as heo is, ant sunne hire moder. Leccherie o
Meith-had with help of fleschlich wil weorreth o this wise. Hire forme
fulst is sihthe. Yef thu bihaldest ofte ant stikelunge on ei mon, Leccherie anan riht greitheth hire with thet to weorrin o thi meith-had, ant
secheth erst upon hire nebbe to nebbe. Speche is hire other help. Yef
ye threfter thenne speoketh togedere folliche ant talkith of unnet,
Leccherie seith 'Scheome the menske of thi meith-had,' ant tuketh hire 220
al to wundre, ant threat to don hire scheome ant hearmin threfter.
Ant halt hire forewart, for sone se cos kimeth forth, thet is hire thridde
fulst, thenne spit Leccherie to scheome ant to schendlac Meith-had
o the nebbe. The feorthe fulst to bismere ant to merren meith-had, thet
is unhende felunge. Wite hire thenne, for yef ye thenne hondlith ow
in ei stude untuliche, thenne smit Leccherie o the mihte of Meith-had
ant wundeth hire sare. Thet dreori dede on ende yeveth thet deathes
dunt; weila thet reowthe! Ne acwiketh neaver Meith-had efter thet
wunde. Wei the sehe thenne hu the engles beoth isweamet the seoth
hare suster se seorhfuliche aveallet ant te deoflen hoppin ant kenchinde 230

---

207. fleoth (*sic* T): beoth   **223.** fulst (*sic* T): fulht

---

213f. 'On the other hand, desire of physical pleasure joins forces with Lechery who is born of the devil, just as desire is; and her mother is sin.' Good and evil are portrayed as two warring families.
222. 'And Lechery keeps her word', i.e. she inflicts injury upon virginity.
229. *Wei the sehe:* 'Woe to him who might see . . .'.

beaten honden toyederes; stani were his heorte yef ha ne mealte i teares.

Wite the, seli meiden; me seith thet eise maketh theof. Flih alle the thing ant forbuh yeorne thet tus unbotelich lure mahe of arisen; thet is on alre earst, the stude ant te time the mahten bringe the on mis forte donne. With othre untheawes me mei stondinde fehten. Ah ayein Lecherie thu most turne the rug yef thu wult overcumen ant with fluht fehten. Ant sothes yef thu thenchest ant bihaldest on heh towart te muchele mede thet meith-had abideth, thu wult leote lihtliche ant
240 abeoren blitheliche the derf thet tu drehest onont ti fleschliche wil ant ti licomes lust, thet tu forberest her ant ane hwile leavest for blisse thet kimeth therof withuten eani ende.

Ant hwuch is the blisse? Low, Godd him seolf seith thurh the prophete: 'Theo the habbeth from ham forcorven flesches lustes ant haldeth mine sabaz, thet is haldeth ham i reste from thet fleschliche werc ant haldeth me forewart, ich bihate ham,' he seith, 'i mi kineriche to yeoven ham stude ant betere nome then sunen ant dehtren. Hwa mahte wilni mare? *Eunuchus qui seminaverunt sabata mea, et cetera.*' Hwa mei thenche the weole, the wunne, ant te blisse, the hehschipe of
250 this mede thet tes ilke lut word bicluppeth abuten? Ich chulle, he seith, yeoven ham stude ant nome betere then sunen ant dehtren. Sulli biheste; ah hit is ilich thet thet ham is bihaten: to singen with engles hwas feolahes ha beoth thurh liflade of heovene the yet ther ha wunieth fleschliche on eorthe; to singe thet swete song ant thet englene dre[a]m utnume murie, thet nan habbe ne mei bute meiden ane singen in heovene; ant folhin Godd Almihti euch godes ful hwiderse he eaver wendeth, as the othre ne mahe nawt thah ha alle beon his sunen ant alle hise dehtren. Ne nan of thes othres crunen, ne hare wlite, ne hare weden ne mahen evenin to hare, se unimete brihte ha beoth ant schene
260 to biseon on.

Ant hwet bith hare anes song, ant efter Godd hare anes yong hwiderse he eaver turneth, ant hare fare se feier bivoren alle the othre? Understond ant nim yeme, al hare song in heovene is forte herien Godd of his grace ant of his goddede. The iweddede thonkith him thet ha, lanhure hwen ha alles walden fallen dunewart, ne feollen nawt

242. therof: threof

231–2. Note the confusion of genders here.
244 ff. Isaiah 56: 4–5.   246. me: 'to, with me'.

with alle adun for wedlac ham ikepte—the ilke lahe the Godd haveth
istald for the unstronge. For wel wiste ure Lauerd thet alle ne mahten
nawt halden ham i the hehe of meith-hades mihte, ah seide tha he spec
throf: '*Non omnes capiunt verbum istud*, Ne undervoth nawt,' quoth he,
'this ilke word alle. *Quis potest capere capiat*, Hwase hit mei underneo-   270
men underneome, ich reade,' quoth he. Other is thet Godd hat, ant
other is thet he reat. The ilke thinges Godd hat thet mon mot nede
halden the wule beon iborhen, ant theo beoth to alle men o live iliche
imeane. His reades beoth of heh thing ant to his leoveste freond, the
lut i thisse worlde, ant derve beoth to fullen, ant lihte thah hwase
haveth riht luve to him ant treowe bileave. Ah hwase halt ham earneth
him overfullet ful ant overeorninde met of heovenliche mede. Swuch
is meith-hades read thet Godd ne hat nawt, ah reat hwuchse wule
beon of the lut of his leoveste freond ant al his deorling deore don his
read ant earnin him crune up o crune. Alswa Seinte Pawel yeveth   280
read to meidnes, the meidnes beoth as he wes, ant seith thet wel is ham
thet swa ham mahen halden; ne hat he hit nan other weis (for eaver se
deorre thing se is derure to biwitene): ant yef hit were ihaten ant
nawt tenne ihalden, the bruche were deadlich sunne.

Forthi wes wedlac ilahet in hali chirche, as bed te seke, to ihente the
unstronge the ne mahen stonden i the hehe hul ant se neh heovene as
meith-hades mihte. This is thenne hare song the beoth i lahe of wedac:
thonki Godd ant herien thet he greithede ham, lanhure tha ha walden
of meidnes hehschipe a swuch stude into lihten, thet ha neren nawt
ihurt thah ha weren ilahet, ant hwetse ha thrin hurten ham with ealmes-   290
deden healden. This singeth thenne iweddede thet ha thurh Godes
milce ant merci of his grace tha ha driven dunewart i wedlac etstutten
ant i the bed of his lahe softeliche lihten. For hwase swa falleth of
meith-hades menske thet wedlakes hevel-bedd nawt ham ne ihente, se
ferliche ha driveth dun to ther eorthe thet al ham is tolimet, lith ba ant

---

269ff. *Matthew* 19: 11–12.

275-6. 'And easy, however, for those who have a fitting love and firm faith towards him.'

280. The author probably had *1 Corinthians* 7: 8 in mind here. The author refers to *1 Corinthians* frequently, as it is a text in which the problems of chastity and marriage are discussed.

281-2. 'It is well for them who may keep them in this way (i.e. they are favoured who live in this manner).'

290. 'And that they might through charitable deeds atone for whatever [sins] they inflicted on themselves therein (i.e. in marriage).'

lire. Theos ne schulen neaver song singen in heovene ah schulen
weimeres leo[th] a mare in helle, bute yef bireowsunge areare ham to
live ant heale ham with soth schrift ant with deadbote. For yef ha thus
beoth acwiket ant imaket hale, ha beoth i widewene reng ant schulen i
300 widewene ring bivore the iweddede singen in heovene. Thet is thenne
hare song: to herien hare Drihtin ant thonkin him yeorne thet his
mihte heolt ham i cleanschipe chaste efter thet ha hefden ifondet
flesches fulthe ant yettede ham i this worlt to beten hare sunnen.
Swote beoth theos songes, ah al meidenes song unilich theose, with
engles imeane, dream over alle the dreames in heovene. In heore ring,
ther Godd seolf ant his deore moder, the deorewurthe meiden, the
heovenliche cwen, leat i thet eadi trume of schimminde meidnes, ne
moten nane buten heo hoppin ne singen for thet is aa hare song:
thonki Godd ant herien thet he on ham se muche grace yef of him
310 seolven thet ha forsoken for him euch eorthlich mon, ant heolden
ham cleane aa from fleschliche fulthen i bodi ant i breoste, ant i stude
of mon of lam token lives Lauerd, the king of hehe blisse. For-hwi he
mensketh ham se muchel bivoren alle the othre as the brudgume deth
his weddede spuse. This song ne muhen nane buten heo singen.

Al, as ich seide ear, folhith ure Lauerd ant tah nawt overal; for i
the menske of meith-had ant in hire mihte ne muhen nane folhin
him ne thet eadi meiden, englene leafdi ant meidenes menske, bute
meidnes ane. Ant forthi is hare aturn se briht ant se schene bivoren alle
othre thet ha gath eaver nest Godd hwiderse he turneth. Ant alle ha
320 beoth icrunet the blissith in heovene with kempene crune, ah the
meidnes habbeth up o theo the is to alle iliche imeane a gerlondesche
schenre then the sunne, *auriole* ihaten o Latines ledene; the flurs the
beoth idrahe thron ne the yimmes thrin te tellen of hare evene nis na
monnes speche. Thus feole privileges schawith ful sutelliche hwucche
beoth ther meidnes ant sundrith ham from the othre with thus feole
mensken world buten ende.

302. cleanschipe: clen|nschipe
316. muhen: muhten B, muhe T   322. *auriole* (*sic* T): an urle
323. yimmes thrin te: yimmies thrin ne B, yimstanes thrin te T

---

304. Understand a part of the verb 'to be': 'but the song of a virgin is totally different from these'.

307. *schimminde*: T has *schimerinde*, which is more usual; but other forms in texts
of the Katherine Group suggest that there was a verb *schimmen*.

321. In addition to that (i.e. crown) which is common to all.

Yef of thes threo hat, meith-had ant widewehad ant wedlac is the
thridde, thu maht bi the degrez of hare blisse icnawen hwuch ant bi hu
muchel the an passeth the othre, for wedlac haveth frut thrittifald in
heovene, widewehad sixtifald, meith-had with hundretfald overgeath   330
bathe, loke thenne herbi hwase of hire meith-had lihteth into wedlac
bi hu monie degrez ha falleth dunewardes. Ha is an hundret degrez
ihehet towart heovene hwil ha meith-had halt, as the frut preoveth; ant
leapeth into wedlac, thet is dun neother to the thrittuthe, over thrie
twenti ant yet ma bi tene. Nis this ed en cherre a muche lupe dunewart? Ant tah hit is to tholien, ant Godd haveth ilahet hit, as ich ear
seide, leste hwase leope ant ther ne edstode (lanhure nawt nere thet
kepte him) ant drive adun swirevorth withuten ikepunge deope into
helle. Of theos nis nawt to speokene for ha beoth iscrippet ut of lives
writ in heovene.   340

Ah schawi we yet witerluker, as we ear biheten, hwet drehen the
iweddede thet tu icnawe therbi hu murie thu maht libben, meiden,
i thi meith-had over thet heo libbeth, to eche the murhthe ant te
menske in heovene thet muth ne mei munnen. Nu thu art iweddet ant
of se heh se lahe iliht, of englene ilicnesse, of Jesu Cristes leofmon, of
leafdi in heovene into flesches fulthe, into beastes liflade, into monnes
theowdom, ant into worldes weane. Sei nu hwet frut ant for hwuch
thing meast. Is hit al forthi other ane dale thervore? Beo nu soth-
cnawes forte keli thi lust with fulthe of thi licome. For Gode hit is
speatewile forte thenche thron, ant forte speoken throf yet speatewilre. 350
Loke thenne hwuch beo thet seolve thing ant thet dede to donne.
Al thet fule delit is with fulthe aleid as thu turnest thin hond; ah thet

349. cnawes (*sic* T): cwawes

---

327. T omits *Yef*, which makes the sense more fluent. The general sense of B is:
If you can understand how much one of these states passes the others, realize from that
how much she falls who relinquishes her virginity.

334-5. Three times twenty plus ten, i.e. seventy (from a hundredfold to thirtyfold).

337-9. Lest anyone should leap and not remain there—indeed there being nothing
to restrain him—and fall down headlong into hell.

347-8. Relate what benefit you have and what was your principal reason for doing
it. Is it entirely for that reason (i.e. fleshly lust) or only partly therefore?

348-9. *Beo nu soth-cnawes*: 'confess'. *Soth-cnawes* is peculiar to the language of the
texts in the Katherine Group. Understand a part of the verb 'to be' here. 'Confess
(it was) to cool your lust through physical sin'.

352-3. *As thu turnest thin hond*: 'in a short while'; cf. VIII, 19-20, and l. 663. The

ladliche beast leafeth ant lest forth, ant te ofthunchunge throf longe threfter. Ant te unseli horlinges, the unlaheliche hit hantith, [dreheth] in inwarde helle for thet hwilinde lust endelese pine bute yef heo hit leaven ant hit on eorthe under schrift bitterliche beten. Forhohe forte don hit thet te thuncheth uvel of ant eil forte heren, for-hwen hit is thullich ant muchele ladluker then ei wel-itohe muth for scheome mahe seggen. Hwet maketh hit iluvet bituhhe beasteliche men bute
360 hare muchele untheaw, thet bereth ham ase beastes to al thet ham lusteth, as thah ha nefden wit in ham ne tweire schad as mon haveth ba of god ant of uvel, of kumelich ant unkumelich, na mare then beastes ant dumbe neb habbeth—ah leasse then beastes yet, for theos deth hare cunde, bute wit thah ha beon, in a time of the yer? Moni halt him to a make ne nule efter thet lure neaver neomen other; ant mon thet schulde habbe wit ant don al thet he dude efter hire wilnunge fo[l]heth thet fulthe in eaver euch time ant nimeth an efter an, ant moni—thet is wurse—monie toyederes.

　　Lo nu hu this untheaw ne eveneth the nawt ane to wittlese beastes,
370 dumbe ant broke-rugget ibuhe towart eorthe, thu thet art i wit wraht to Godes ilicnesse ant i riht bodi up ant heaved towart heovene forthi thet tu schuldest thin heorte heoven thiderwart as thin eritage is ant eorthe forhohien; nim yeme hu this untheaw ne maketh the nawt ane evening ne ilich ham, ah deth muchel eateluker ant mare to witen the forschuptest te seolf, willes ant waldes, into hare cunde: the leoseth thenne se heh thing, the mihte ant te biheve of meith-hades menske, for se ful fulthe, as is ischawet thruppe. Hwase of engel lihteth to iwurthen lahre then a beast for se ladli cheaffere, loki hu ha spede.

pleasures of the flesh soon turn sour; the delight is brief, but the consequences last much longer.

354. *hit*: here, sexual intercourse. In the next clause neither MS has a verb, but one such as *dreheth* seems to be required; *cf.* l. 467.

369. 'Behold, now, how this immorality not only makes you resemble beasts without reason . . .'. Take the *ne* with *nawt*; *cf.* l. 373. This clause is parallel with that starting *nim yeme* at 373; the balancing 'but also' clause is given only with the second 'not only'. Man consists of two parts: a mortal one which is bestial in nature and a spiritual one which resembles the angels.

370. *ibuhe towart eorthe*: that is, bent to the ground and unable to look beyond the physical act of keeping alive by eating grass, etc.

374f. 'But also it does something more terrible and blameworthy to you who transformed yourself into their nature of your own accord: you lose then such a noble thing . . .'. In 375–6 *se heh thing* is the subject of *leoseth*, and *the* is dative.

Nai, thu wult seggen, for thet fulthe nis hit nawt. Ah monnes elne is muche wurth, ant me bihoveth his help to fluttunge ant te fode. Of wif ant weres gederunge worldes weole awakeneth ant streon of feire children the gleadieth muchel the ealdren. Nu thu havest iseid tus, ant thuncheth thet tu havest iseid soth. Ah ich chulle schawin hit al with falsschipe ismethet. Ah on alre earst, hwet weole other wunne se ther eaver of cume, to deore hit bith aboht thet tu the seolf sulest fore ant yevest thin beare bodi to tukin swa to wundre ant feare with se scheomeliche, with swuch uncoverlich lure as meith-hades menske is ant te mede, for worldlich biyete. Wa wurthe thet cheaffeare for ei hwilinde weole sullen meith-had awei, the cwen is of heovene, for alswa as of this lure nis nan acoverunge alswa is euch wurth unwurth her towart. Thu seist thet muche confort haveth wif of hire were the beoth wel iyederet, ant either is alles weis ipaiet of other. Ye, ah hit is seltscene on eorthe! Beo nu thah swuch hare confort ant hare delit, hwerin is hit al meast buten i flesches fulthe other in worldes vanite, the wurtheth al to sorhe ant to sar on ende? Ant nawt ane on ende, ah eaver umbehwile for moni thing schal ham wreathen ant gremien ant make to carien, ant for hare othres uvel sorhin ant siken; moni thing ham schal twinnin ant tweamen, thet lath is luvie men, ant deathes dunt on ende either from other, swa thet ne bith hit nanes weis thet tet elne ne schal endin in earmthe; ant eaver se hare murhthe wes mare toyederes se the sorhe is sarre ed te twinnunge. Wa is him, forthi as Seint Austin seith, thet is with to muche luve to ei eorthlich thing iteiet, for eaver bith thet swote aboht with twa dale of bittre, ant a fals wunne with moni soth teone. Ah wel is hire thet luveth Godd, for him ne mei ha nanes weis, bute yef ha lihe him ant his luve leave, neaver mare leosen, ah schal ifinden him aa swetture ant savurure from worlde into worlde aa on ecnesse.

Thu speke thruppe of monnes help to flutunge ant to fode. Wala, lutel therf thu carien for thin anes liveneth, a meoke meiden as thu art ant his deore leofmon the is alre thinge lauerd, thet ye ne mahe lihtliche,

---

392. ah (*sic* T): ahi   **401.** twinnunge: twimmunge

393-4. 'Even if a man is a wife's comfort, of what does that comfort consist if not of physical sin or worldly vanity?'

398-9. The transience of earthly love with the sorrow which its inevitable loss entails is a common homiletic theme; it occurs frequently in Old English poetry. *Cf.* l. 95.

400. There is no escaping that that vigour will end in misery.

thet he nule gleadliche ifinde the largeliche al thet te bihoveth. Ant
tah thu wone hefdest other drehdest eani derf for his deorewurthe
luve, as the othre doth for monnes, to goderheale him the hit tholeth:
to fondi the hwether thu beo treowe; ant greitheth thi mede monifald
in heovene. Under monnes help thu schalt sare beon idervet, for his
ant for the worldes luve the beoth ba swikele, ant wakien i moni care,
nawt ane for the seolf ase therf Godes spuse, ah schalt for monie othre
ase wel for the lathe ofte as for the leove; ant mare beon idrechet then
ei drivel i the hus other ei ihuret hine; ant tin anes dale bruken ofte
420 with bale ant bitterliche abuggen. Lutel witen herof the selie Godes
spuses the i the swote eise withute swuch trubuil i gastelich este ant i
breoste reste luvieth the sothe luve ant in his anes servise hare lif leadeth.
Inoh wel ham is her, ah unlich elleshwer. Alle worldes weole ham is
inoh rive; al ha habbeth therof thet ha wel wilnith. Al thet eaver Godd
isith, thet ham wule freamien. Ne mei na worldlich unhap bireavin
ham hare weole for ha beoth riche ant weolefule inwith i the heorte as
the este ant al the eise is, ther as the othre beoth godlese ant ignahene—
nabben ha neaver se muchel withuten i the worlde—for thet ha beoth
offearet eaver forte leosen ant yiscith thah efter muchel muche deale
430 mare.

With earmthe biwinneth hit, with fearlac biwiteth hit; forleoseth hit
with sorhe. Swinketh to biyeotene, biyeoteth forte leosen, leoseth
forte sorhin. Thus this worldes hweol warpeth ham abuten. Theoves
hit steoleth ham, reavers hit robbith, hare overherren witith ham ant
wreatheth, mohthe fret te clathes, ant cwalm sleath thet ahte. Ant tah
nane of theos ne makie to forwurthen weole ther ase muchel is, eaver
se ther mare is se ma beoth thet hit wastith. Ant nat ich neaver hwi me
seith thet heo hit al weldeth thet wullen ha nullen ha biwinneth ant
biwiteth hit to se monie othre, nawt ane to hare freond ah to hare fan

434. hit (2): hit | hit

---

411. God will provide for his own; cf. Luke 12: 22–30.
413. Understand a part of the verb 'to be' here: 'it is for his benefit who endures it'.
423. Although they are happy with what they have here, it is nothing to the happiness they will have in the next world.
424 f. 'All that which God ever provides, that will be of advantage to them.'
427. godlese ant ignahene: destitute (of spiritual welfare and happiness).
433. The reference is to the wheel of fortune; see H. R. Patch, The Goddess Fortuna
in Medieval Literature (Cambridge, Mass. 1927), pp. 147–77.

fulle; ne habben ne mahen throf thah ha hit hefden isworen bute hare 440
anes dale.

This is nu forthi iseid thet tu seidest thruppe thet ter walde wakenin
of wif ant weres somnunge richesce ant worldes weole thet tu understonde hu lutel hit freameth ham yet her i this worlt, teke thet hit
reaveth ham the hehe riche of heovene bute ha poure beon therin
with halinesse of heorte. Thus, wummon, yef thu havest were efter
thi wil ant wunne ba of worldes weole, the ne[de] schal itiden. Ant
hwet yef ha beoth the wone, thet tu nabbe thi wil with him ne weole
nowther ant schalt grenin godles inwith westi wahes ant te breades
wone brede thi bearnteam, ant teke this liggen under lathest mon thet 450
thah thu hefdest alle weole he went hit te to weane? For beo hit nu
thet te beo richedom rive ant tine wide wahes wlonke ant weolefule
ant habbe monie under the hirdmen in halle ant ti were beo the wrath
other iwurthe the lath swa thet inker either heasci with other, hwet
worltlich weole mei beo the wunne? Hwen he bith ute, havest ayein
his cume sar care ant eie. Hwil he bith et hame alle thine wide wanes
thuncheth the to nearewe, his lokunge on ageasteth the, his ladliche
nurth ant his untohe bere maketh the to agrisen. Chit te ant cheoweth
the ant scheomeliche schent te, tuketh the to bismere, as huler his hore
beateth the, ant busteth the as his ibohte threl ant his ethele-theowe. 460
Thine banes aketh the ant ti flesch smeorteth the; thin heorte withinne
the swelleth of sar grome, ant ti neb utewith tendreth ut of teone.
Hwuch schal beo the sompnunge bituhen ow i bedde? Me theo the
best luvieth ham tobeoreth ofte thrin thah ha na semblant ne makien
ine marhen; ant ofte of moni nohtunge, ne luvien ha ham neaver swa,
bitterliche bi ham seolf teonith either. Heo schal his wil muchel hire
unwil [drehen] with muche weane ofte. Alle his fulitoh[s]chipes ant
his unhende gomenes, ne beon ha neaver swa with fulthe bifunden,
nomeliche i bedde, ha schal wulle ha nulle ha tholien ham alle. Crist
schilde euch meiden to freinin other to wilnin forte witen hwucche 470

---

453. were (*sic* T): weres   **456.** Hwil (*sic* T): Hwel
462. tendreth (*sic* T): tendreith

---

447. 'Necessity shall befall you'; the reading *nede* is from T.

449. *grenin*: the sense is probably 'to lament, gnash the teeth' from OE *grennian*, though 'to become green' (i.e. to become ill) would also be possible, *cf.* l. 522.

462. *tendreith*, if kept, would be a plural.

463-4. 'But those who love each other best often quarrel in bed.'

467. The omission is supplied from T.

ha beon, for theo the fondith ham meast ifindeth ham forcuthest ant
cleopieth ham selie iwiss the nuten neaver hwet hit is ant heatieth thet
ha hantith. Ah hwase lith i leifen deope bisuncken, thah him thunche
uvel throf he ne schal nawt up acoverin hwen he walde.

Bisih the, seli wummon, beo the cnotte icnut eanes of wedlac,
beo he cangun other crupel, beo he hwuch-se-eaver beo, thu most
to him halden. Yef thu art feier ant with gleade chere bicleopest alle
feire, ne schalt o nane wise wite the with unword ne with uvel blame.
Yef thu art unwurthliche ilatet, thu maht ba to othre ant to thi were
480 iwurthen the unwurthre. Yef thu iwurthest him unwurth ant he as
unwurth the, other yef thu him muche luvest ant he let lutel to the,
hit greveth the se swithe thet tu wult inoh-reathe, ase monie doth,
makien him poisun ant yeoven bale i bote stude; other hwase swa nule
don, medi with [mede] wicchen ant forsaken, forte drahen his luve
towart hire, Crist ant hire cristendom ant rihte bileave. Nu hwet
blisse mei theos bruken the luveth hire were wel ant ha habbe his
lathe other cunqueari his luve o thulliche wise?

Hwenne schulde ich al habben irikenet thet springeth bituhe theo
the thus beoth iyederet? Yef ha ne mei nawt temen, ha is icleopet
490 gealde; hire lauerd luveth hire ant wurthgeth the leasse; ant heo as
theo thet wurst is throf biwepeth hire wurthes ant cleopeth ham wunne
ant weolefule the temeth hare teames. Ah nu iwurthe hit al thet ha
habbe hire wil of streon thet ha wilneth, ant loki we hwuch wunne
throf hire iwurthe. I the streonunge throf is anan hire flesch with thet
fulthe ituket, as hit is ear ishawet; i the burtherne throf is hevinesse
heard sar eaver umbestunde; in his iborenesse alre stiche strengest ant
death otherhwiles; in his fostrunge forth moni earmhwile. Sone se
hit lihteth i this lif mare hit bringeth with him care then blisse, nomeliche to the moder. For yef hit is misboren, as hit ilome ilimpeth,
500 ant wonti ei of his limen other sum misfeare, hit is sorhe to hire ant to al
his cun scheome, upbrud in uvel muth, tale bi mon alle. Yef hit wel
iboren is ant thuncheth wel forlich, fearlac of his lure is anan with him
iboren for nis ha neaver bute care leste hit misfeare a thet owther of

497. fostrunge: fost|trunge

---

476. *cangun*: Colborn derives from Northern French *cangoun* with the semantic
development from 'changeling' via 'ugly person' to 'fool'.

484. *medi with* [*mede*] *wicchen*: 'bribe witches with money', i.e. purchase the services
of witches. Neither MS has *mede*.

ham twa ear leose other. Ant ofte hit itimeth thet tet leoveste bearn ant iboht bitterlukest sorheth ant sweameth meast his ealdren on ende. Nu hwet wunne haveth the moder the haveth of thet forschuppet bearn sar ant scheome bathe ant fearlac of thet forthlich a thet ha hit leose for gode, thah hit nere neaver for Godes luve, ne for hope of heovene, ne for dred of helle?

Thu ahtest, wummon, this werc for thi flesches halschipe, for thi 510 licomes luve ant ti bodies heale over alle thing to schunien, for ase Seinte Pawel seith: 'Euch sunne thet me deth is withute the bodi bute this ane.' Alle the othre su[n]nen ne beoth bute sunnen, ah this is sunne ant ec uncumelecheth the ant unwurthgeth thi bodi, suleth thi sawle ant maketh schuldi towart Godd, ant fuleth thi flesch ec. Gulteth o twa half: wreathest then Alwealdent with thet suti sunne, ant dest woh to the seolf ant tu al willes se scheomeliche tukest.

Ga we nu forthre ant loki we hwuch wunne ariseth threfter i bur-therne of bearne hwen thet streon in the awakeneth ant waxeth ant hu monie earmthen anan awakeneth therwith, the wurcheth the wa 520 inoh, fehteth o thi seolve flesch ant weorrith with feole weanen o thin ahne cunde. Thi rudie neb schal leanin ant ase gres grenin, thine ehnen schule doskin ant underneothe wonnin, ant of thi breines turnunge thin heaved aken sare; inwith i thi wombe swelle thi butte the bereth the forth as a weater-bulge; thine thearmes thralunge, ant stiches i thi lonke, ant i thi lendene sar eche rive, hevinesse in euch lim; thine breostes burtherne o thine twa pappes ant te milc-strunden the the of striketh. Al is with a weolewunge thi wlite overwarpen. Thi muth is bitter ant walh al thet tu cheowest, ant hwetse thi mahe hokerliche underveth, thet is with unlust, warpeth hit eft ut. Inwith al thi weole ant ti weres wunne 530

524. swelle: swelin (T and B)

---

512. *1 Corinthians* 6: 18.

516. *suti*: the sense here is 'foul' and at l. 558 where it is used as a quasi-noun as 'foulness', though the word seems otherwise to be unrecorded; it is doubtless related to OE *sot* 'soot' and *besutian* 'to soil'.

524 ff. The emotional heightening has led to an elliptical style with the omission of the finite verbs (*cf.* ll. 494–7). The sense is: Your womb (shall) swell in your belly which projects out from you like a water-butt; (there will be) pain in your guts, stitches in your side; frequent pain in your loins and heaviness in every limb; the weight of your breasts (will cause pain) in your two nipples and in the streams of milk which flow from you. *Swelle* is an infinitive dependent on *schal* (l. 499); the form *swelin* is hardly likely in this dialect. The word *lonke* is rare, but its meaning is clear.

530f. 'You are withering in the midst of your joy and your husband's pleasure.

forwurthest. A wrecche! The cares ayein thi pinunge thra[h]en
bineometh the nahtes slepes. Hwen hit thenne therto kimeth, thet sore
sorhfule angoise, thet stronge ant stikinde stiche, thet unroles uvel, thet
pine over pine, thet wondrinde yeomerunge, hwil thu swenchest
terwith i thine deathes dute scheome teke thet sar with the alde wifes
scheome creft, the cunnen of thet wa-sith, hwas help the bihoveth ne
beo hit neaver se uncumelich; ant nede most hit tholien thet te therin
itimeth. Ne thunche the nan uvel of, for we ne edwiteth nawt wifes
hare weanen thet ure alre modres drehden on us seolven, ah we scha-
540 with ham forth forte warni meidnes thet ha beon the leasse efterwart
swuch thing ant witen herthurh the betere hwet ham beo to donne.

Efter al this kimeth of thet bearn ibore thus wanunge ant wepunge,
the schal abute midniht makie the to wakien other theo the hire stude
halt the thu most forcarien. Ant hwet the cader-fulthen ant bearmes:
umbestunde to feskin ant to fostrin hit se moni earmhwile? Ant his
waxunge se let ant se slaw his thriftre, ant eaver habbe sar care ant
lokin efter al this hwenne hit forwurthe ant bringe on his moder sorhe.
Thah thu riche beo ant nurrice habbe, thu most as moder carien for al
thet hire limpeth to donne. Theose ant othre earmthen the of wedlac
550 awakenith Seinte Pawel biluketh in ane lut wordes, *Tribulaciones
carnis, et cetera.* Thet is on Englisch 'Theo thet thulliche beoth schulen
derf drehen.' Hwase thencheth on al this ant o mare thet ter is ant
nule withbuhe thet thing thet hit al of awakeneth, ha is heardre iheortet then adamantines stan ant mare amead, yef ha mei, then is meadschipe seolf, hire ahne fa ant hire feont, heateth hire seolfen.

Lutel wat meiden of al this ilke weane, of wifes wa with hire were,
ne of hare werc se wleateful the ha wurcheth imeane, ne of thet sar ne

---

531. cares: carest B, care T	**533.** stikinde (*sic* T): stinkinde
535. i (*sic* T): ant	**557.** werc (*sic* T): were

Wretch, your anxieties in respect of the spasms of agony (i.e. of the future birth of her
child) rob you of sleep at night.'

532ff. The phrases introduced by *thet* (532–4) are in apposition to *hit* (532).

533. *unroles*: Colborn derives from OE *un-*, ON *ró* and OE *-leas*.

534–5. The sense is: while you in the fear of death are in labour therewith (i.e.
with the birth), there is shame in addition to the grief of . . .

544f. 'And what of the soiled bedding and your breasts: from time to time to swaddle
it, and to feed it so many tedious times.'

550. *1 Corinthians* 7: 28, 'Nevertheless such (i.e. who marry) shall have trouble in
the flesh.'

of thet suti i the burtherne of bearn ant his iborenesse, of nurrices
wecches ne of hire wa-sithes, of thet fode fostrunge hu muchel hit is ed
eanes in his muth famplin, nowther to bigan hit ne his cader-clutes. 560
Thah this beon of to speokene unwurthliche thinges, thes the mare ha
schawith i hwuch theo[w]dom wifes beoth the thullich mote drehen
ant meidnes i hwuch freodom the freo beoth from ham alle. Ant
hwet yef ich easki yet, thah hit thunche egede, hu thet wif stonde the
ihereth hwen ha kimeth in hire bearn schreamen, sith the cat et te
fliche ant ed te hude the hund, hire cake bearnen o the stan ant hire
kelf suken, the crohe eornen i the fur; ant te cheorl chideth? Thah hit
beo egede isahe hit ah, meiden, to eggi the swithe ther frommart
for nawt ne thuncheth hit hire egede thet hit fondeth. Ne therf thet seli
meiden, thet haveth al idon hire ut of thullich theowdom as Godes 570
freo dohter ant his sunes spuse, drehe nawiht swucches. Forthi, seli
meiden, forsac al thulli sorhe for utnume mede thet tu ahtest to don
withuten euch hure. For nu ich habbe ihalden min biheaste thruppe
thet ich walde schawin with falschipe ismethet thet te moni an seith ant
thuncheth thet hit soth beo of the selhthe ant te sy thet te iweddede
habbeth, thet hit ne feareth nawt swa as weneth thet sith utewith, ah
feareth al other weis of poure ba ant riche, of lathe ba ant leove, thet
te weane ihwer passeth the wunne ant te lure overal al the biyete.

Nu thenne, seli meiden thet David cleopeth dohter, iher thi feader
ant hercne his read thet he the i the frumthe of this writ readde. Foryet 580
ti folc thet liheth the of weres ant worldes wunne, thet beoth thine
thohtes the swikelliche leathieth the towart alle weane; ant forsac thi
feader hus, as hit is thruppe iopenet, ant tac the to him treowliche.
With him thu schalt wealden as with thi were iweddet worlt buten
ende heovenliche wunnen. Eadi is his spuse hwas meith-had is unwemmet; hwen he on hire streoneth ant hwen ha temeth of him, ne swinketh ne ne pineth. Eadi is the were hwen nan ne mei beo meiden bute
yef heo him luvie, ne freo bute yef heo him servi hwas streon is un-
deathlich ant hwas marheyeve is the kinedom of heovene.

Nu thenne, seli meiden, yef the is weole leof, nim the him to lauerd 590
thet wealdeth al thet is ant wes ant eaver schal iwurthen for, thah he
beo richest him ane overalle, the alre measte poure the him to were
cheoseth is him wel icweme. Yef thet tu wilnest were the muche wlite

---

561. *thes the mare*: 'so much the more', cf. I, 75.
590ff. For the general development of this passage, cf. III.

habbe, nim him of hwas wlite beoth awundret of the sunne ant te mone, up o hwas nebscheft the engles ne beoth neaver fulle to bihalden. For hwen he yeveth feierlec to al thet is feier in heovene ant in eorthe, muchele mare he haveth withuten ei etlunge ethalden to him seolven. Ant thah hwen he thus is alre thinge feherest, he underveth blitheliche ant bicluppeth swoteliche the alre ladlukeste ant maketh ham seove sithe schenre then the sunne. Yef the were leof streon, nim the to him under hwam thu schalt i thi meith-had temen dehtren ant sunen of gasteliche teames, the neaver deie ne mahen ah schulen aa bivore the pleien in heovene. Thet beoth the vertuz thet he streoneth in the thurh his swete grace, as rihtwissnesse ant warschipe ayeines untheawes, mesure ant mete ant gastelich strengthe to withstonde the feond ant ayein sunne, simplete of semblant, buhsumnesse ant stilthe, tholomod-nesse ant reowfulnesse of euch monnes sorhe, gleadschipe i the Hali Gast ant pes i thi breoste of onde ant of wreathe, of yisceunge ant of euch untheawes weorre, metelec ant miltschipe ant swotnesse of heorte, the limpeth alre thinge best to mei[th]-hades mihte. This is meidenes team, Godes sune[s] spuse, thet schal aa libben ant pleien buten ende bivoren hire in heovene.

Ah thah thu, meiden, beo with unbruche of thi bodi ant tu habbe prude, onde other wreathe, yisceunge other wac wil inwith heorte, thu forhorest te with the unwiht of helle ant he streoneth on the the team thet tu temest. Hwen thi were, Alwealdent, thet tu the toweddest sith ant understont tis thet his fa forlith the ant thet tu temest of him thet him is teame lathest, he forheccheth the anan, as hit nis na wunder, ant cwetheth the al cwite him thet tu of temest; ne kepeth he with na mon ant hure with his famon nan half dale. The luvieth eawiht buten him ant hwetse ha for him luvieth ha wreatheth him swithe. Over alle thing wite the thet tu ne temi Prude bi thes deofles streonunge, for heo of alle untheawes is his ealdeste dohter. Earst ha wakenede of him the yet he wes in heovene, forneh with him evenald, ant swa hire keaste ure Feader sone se ha ibore wes from the heste heovene into

---

623. his: hiss

---

603. Through her spiritual marriage with Christ a virgin produces her children, the virtues. But if she exhibits pride or other sins, her spiritual marriage is with the devil rather than with Christ. Neither the virtues nor the sins are arranged into a group of seven, as became usual in the medieval period.

613ff. Cf. the maiden in I, 52ff.

helle-grunde bute coverunge ant makede of heh engel eatelukest deofel. The thus adun duste hire heovenliche feader, hwet wule he don bi hire eorthliche modres the temeth hire in horedom of then lathe unwiht, the hellene schucke? Hwen Godd se wracfulliche fordemde his heh engel the streonede hire in heovene, hwet wule he don bi thet 630 lam ant wurmene mete the of the deofel temeth hire in eawbruche on eorthe?

Yef thu havest with meith-had meokelec ant mildschipe, Godd is i thin heorte; ah yef ther is overhohe other ei prude in, he is utlahe throf: for ne muhen ha nanes weis beddin in a breoste, ne ne mahten nawt somet eardin in heovene. Theonne Godd weorp hire, sone se ha iboren wes. Ant as thah ha nuste hwuch wei ha come theonewart, ne con ha neaver mare ifinden nan wei ayeinwart. Ah earmthe her on eorthe bihat eche wununge alle hire modres, al beon ha meidnes, with hare aweariede feader in inwarde helle. Wite the, meiden, with hire. 640 Ha cwikede of cleane cunde as is in engles evene, ant cleaneste breosten bredeth hire yetten. The beste ha asaileth ant wel ha der hopien to beo kempe over mon, the overcom engel. Nis ha nawt i clathes ne i fea-hunge utewith thah hit beo merke throf ant makunge otherhwiles; ah under hwit other blac ant ase wel under grei ase under grene, ant aa ha luteth i the heorte. Son se thu telest te betere then an other, beo hit hwervore se hit eaver beo, ant havest of ei overhohe ant thuncheth hofles ant hoker of eawt thet me seith the other deth yetten, thu merrest thin meith-had ant brekest ti wedlac towart Godd ant of his fa temest.

Ne tele thu nawt ethelich, al beo thu meiden, to widewen ne to 650

635. mahten: maken B, muhen T   639. bihat (*sic* T): bihalt
640. aweariede: awenriede B, awariede T

627-8. 'What will he, who thus cast down her heavenly father, do to her mortal mothers?' Pride, who is portrayed as a woman, is the antithesis of the Virgin Mary, and thus the latter's humility is stressed; *cf.* ll. 666ff. In the author's conceit she is both the daughter of Satan in heaven and the progeny resulting from sinful man's intercourse with the devil on earth.

635. *ha*: that is, humility and pride, which symbolize God and the devil.

638-39. The sense of the passage is difficult in B, but can be understood as: Their wretchedness on earth promises (i.e. is a foretaste of) to all her mothers that eternal life with their cursed father in hell. An emendation of *hare* to *hire*, i.e. Pride's, is possible.

641ff. Pride, the chief of the seven deadly sins, seduces even the best humans.

650. 'Although you are a maid, do not hold widows and married women cheap.'

C

iweddede. For alswa as a charbucle is betere then a jacinct i the evene
of hare cunde ant thah is betere a briht jacinct then a charbucle won,
alswa passeth meiden onon[t] te mihte of meith-had widewen ant
iweddede ant tah is betere a milde wif other a meoke widewe then a
prud meiden. For theos for hare sunnen thet ha i flesches fulthe folhith
other fulieth leoteth ham lahe ant ethliche ant beoth sare ofdret of
Godes luthere eie, ant as the eadi sunegilt, Marie Magdaleine, with
bittre wopes bireowseth hare gultes ant inwardluker luvieth Godd
alswa as heo dude for hare foryevenesse; ant te othre, the haldeth ham
660   unforgult ant cleane, beoth ase sikere, unlusti ant wlecche unneathe i
Godes luve withuten euch heate of the Hali Gast the bearneth se lihte
withute wastinde brune in alle his icorene; ant te othre in an heate of an
honthwile beoth imelt mare ant iyotten i Godd then the othre in a
wlecheunge al hare lif-sithen. Forthi, eadi meiden, Godes sunes spuse,
ne beo thu nawt trust ane to thi meith-had withuten other god ant
theawfule mihtes, ant overal miltschipe ant meokeschipe of heorte
efter the forbisne of thet eadi meiden over alle othre, Marie Godes
moder. For tha the heh engel Gabriel grette hire ant brohte hire to
tidinge of Godes akennesse, loke hu lah ha lette hire tha ha ontswerede
670   thus bi hire seolven: 'Efter thi word,' quoth ha, 'mote me iwurthen;
low her, mi Lauerdes threl.' Ant tah ha ful were of alle gode theawes,
ane of hire meokelec ha seide ant song to Elizabeth: 'For mi Lauerd
biseh this thuftenes meokelec, me schulen cleopien,' quoth ha, 'eadi
alle leoden.' Nim yeme, meiden, ant understont herbi thet mare for
hire meokelec then for hire meith-had ha lette thet ha ifont swuch
grace ed ure Lauerd. For al meith-had meokelec is muche wurth, ant
meith-had withuten hit is ethelich ant unwurth. For alswa is meiden i
meith-had bute meokeschipe as is withute liht eolie in a lampe. Eadi

---

651. charbucle (*sic* T): charbuche   **657.** as (*sic* T): al   **669.** lah (*sic* T): thah

---

651. Comparison of the virtues with gems is common; *cf.* the poem *The Pearl.*

655ff. *theos* (655): those who sin and repent; *te othre* (659): those who are virgins
but also proud; *te othre* (662): those who are virgins and also meek.

657. In the West Mary Magdalen was identified with the woman 'which was a
sinner' (*Luke* 7: 37) and so developed into a foremost example of a penitent. Her
tears of repentance are frequently portrayed in medieval art. *Cf.* V, 28.

664f. *Cf. Piers Plowman* C. ii. 176–86.

670–1. *Luke* 1: 38.   **672–4.** *Luke* 1: 48.

678. The author probably had the story of the five wise and the five foolish virgins
in mind here (*Matthew* 25: 1–13).

Godes spuse, have theos ilke mihte thet tu ne thunche theostri, ah schine ase sunne i thi weres sihthe; feahi thi meith-had with alle gode theawes the thuncheth him feire. 680

Have eaver i thin heorte the eadieste of meidnes ant meith-hades moder ant bisech hire aa thet ha the lihte ant yeove luve ant strengthe forte folhin i meith-had hire theawes. Thench o Seinte Katerrine, o Seinte Margarete, Seinte Enneis, Seinte Juliene, ant Seinte Cecille, ant o the othre hali meidnes in heovene hu ha nawt ane forsoken kinges sunes ant eorles with alle worldliche weolen ant eorthliche wunnen, ah tholoden stronge pinen ear ha walden neomen ham ant derf death on ende. Thench hu wel ham is nu ant hu ha blissith thervore bituhe Godes earmes, cwenes of heovene. Ant yef hit eaver timeth thet ti 690 licomes lust thurh the false feont leathie towart fles[ch]liche fulthen, ontswere i thi thoht thus: 'Ne geineth the nawt, sweoke. Thullich ich chulle beon in meidenes liflade ilich heovene engel. Ich chulle halde me hal thurh the grace of Godd, as cunde me makede, thet paraise selhthe undervo me al swuch as weren ear ha agulten, his eareste hinen. Allunge swuch ich chulle beon as is mi deore leofmon, mi deorewurthe lauerd, ant as thet eadi meiden the he him cheas to moder. Al swuch ich chulle wite [me] treowliche unwemmet as ich am him iweddet, ne nulle ich nawt for a lust of ane lutle hwile, thah hit thunche delit, awei warpe thet thing hwas lure ich schal biremen withuten coverunge ant 700 with eche brune abuggen in helle. Thu wrenchfule ful wiht, al for nawt thu prokest me to forgulten ant forgan the blisse up o blisse, the crune up o crune of meidenes mede, ant willes ant waldes warpe me as wrecche i thi leirwite, ant for thet englene song of meith-hades menske with the ant with thine greden aa ant granin i the eche grure of helle.' Yef thu thus ontswerest to thi licomes lust ant to the feondes fondunge, he schal fleo the with scheome. Ant yef he alles efter this inoh-reathe etstonde ant halt on to eili thi flesch ant prokie thin heorte,

680. i thi (*sic* T): ant ti   **686.** ane (*sic* T): ane ne
690. ti (*sic* T): tu   **693.** heovene engel: heovene e[*tear*]englel

---

684f. The lives of Katherine, Margaret and Juliana are found in B. All these saints, who lived in the first centuries of Christianity, are invoked here as virgin saints and thus they are proper models for the recipients of this text. *Enneis* is St. Agnes.

690. *ti*: for the emendation *cf.* l. 706.

695. *ha*: Adam and Eve; *his*, that is the devil's, though Furnivall understands it as 'its' referring to paradise.

ant ti Lauerd Godd hit theaveth him to muchli thi mede, for as Seinte
710 Pawel seith: 'Ne bith nan icrunet bute hwase treoweliche i thulli feht
fehte ant with strong cokkunge overcume hire seolf,' for thenne is the
deofel with his ahne turn scheomeliche awarpen, hwen thu, as the apostle
seith, ne schalt tu beon icrunet bute thu beo asailet. Yef Godd wule
cruni the, he wule leote ful wel the unwiht asaili the thet tu earni
therthurh kempene crune. Forthi hit is the meast god thet, hwen he
greveth the meast ant towart te with fondunge wodeluker weorreth,
yef thu wel wrist te under Godes wengen, for thurh his weorre he
yarketh the—unthonc in his teth—the blisse ant te crune of Cristes
icorene.
720 Ant Jesu Crist leve hire, thurh thi blescede nome, alle theo the
leaveth luve of lami mon forte beon his leofmon; ant leve ham swa
hare heorte halden to him thet hare flesches eggunge ne the feondes
fondunge ne nan of his eorthliche limen ne wori hare heorte wit ne
wrenche ham ut of the wei thet ha beoth in iyongen; ant helpe ham
swa in him to hehin towart heovene a thet ha beon istihe thider as
hare brudlac schal in al thet eaver sel is with thene seli brudgume thet
siheth alle selhthe of sitten buten ende. Amen.

717. Godes: Goder

710–11. *1 Corinthians* 9: 25.

718. *unthonc in his teth:* 'unwillingly in his own despite'. Found elsewhere in the
Katherine Group, this phrase may be a conflation of *his unthonkes* 'unwillingly' and
in his teth 'in defiance of him'.

720. The sense is difficult but may be understood as: And Jesus Christ, may you
through your blessed name grant it (i.e. the joy of heaven) to all those who . . . T reads
leve the thurh his.

725. *hehin:* 'to ascend'; but T has *hihin* 'to hasten', which may be the original reading.

III   The Wooing of Our Lord

This text is found in British Museum Cotton Titus D 18 (*cf.* II). Its authorship is unknown, but its close relationship with the Katherine Group shows that it was composed in the West Midlands in the first half of the thirteenth century. The *Wooing* exhibits similarities with the seventh part of the Ancren Riwle, in which the nature of love is discussed, though that work probably exercised a general rather than a particular influence over the author of the *Wooing*. Together with several other short pieces like the *Hymn to our Lady* and the *Orison of Our Lord*, it forms a group of texts known as the Wooing Group. They are all lyrical prayers addressed to either the Virgin or God. The emotional phraseology of the pieces in the group was influenced by the language of the *Song of Solomon* and by secular love lyrics. In this respect they may be compared with Middle English lyrics addressed to the Virgin.

The Wooing was used as one of his two sources by the fourteenth-century author of *A Talking of the Love of God* (TLG), found in the Vernon manuscript (*cf.* VI). It is possible that the author of TLG used a later copy of the *Wooing* rather than that in Titus D 18, the only extant copy; but in any case its use by a fourteenth-century writer points to its continued popularity among religious. TLG differs from the *Wooing* in two respects: the author of TLG was a monk or a friar who was writing for a specifically masculine audience, and he attempted to transform the *Wooing* into a cadenced prose in which rhyme frequently occurs. The inclusion of TLG in the Vernon manuscript, which includes a number of fourteenth-century religious and contemplative works like the English translation of the *Mirror of St. Edmund*, indicates that it was among the more popular of such treatises. The *Wooing* is thus intimately linked with fourteenth-century devotion through TLG.

Editions: R. Morris, *Old English Homilies and Homiletic Treatises*. EETS o.s. 34 (London 1868).
W. Meredith Thompson, *Þe Wohunge of ure Lauerd*. EETS o.s. 241 (London 1958).

Jesu, swete Jesu, mi druth, mi derling, mi drihtin, mi healend, mi huniter, mi haliwei, swetter is munegunge of the then mildeu o muthe.

2. *swetter is munegunge of the then mildeu o muthe*: cf. *Sed super mel et omnia dulcis eius presentia* from the hymn *Jesu dulcis memoria* (c. 1130–40) attributed to St. Bernard of Clairvaux.

Hwa ne mei luve thi luveli leor? Hwat herte is swa hard that ne mei tomelte i the munegunge of the? Ah hwa ne mei luve the, luveliche Jesu, for inwith the ane arn alle the thinges igedered that eaver muhen maken ani mon luvewurthi to other? Feirnesse and lufsum neb, flesch hwit under schrud makes moni mon beo luved te rather and te mare; summe gold and gersum and ahte of this worlde makes luved and heried; su[m]me fredom and largesce, that lever is menskli to
10 yiven then cwedli to withhalde; summe wit and wisdom and yapschipe of werlde; summe maht and strengthe to beo kid and kene i fiht his riht for to halde; summe noblesce and hehnesse of burthe; summe theaw and hendeleic and lastelese lates; summe menske and milde-schipe and debonairte of herte and dede. And yette over al this kinde makes sibbe-frend euchan to luven other.

Nu, mi derewurthe druth, mi luve, mi lif, mi leof, mi luvelevest, mi heorte-haliwei, mi sawle-swetnesse, thu art lufsum on leor, thu art al schene; al engles lif is ti neb to bihalden. For thi leor is swa uni-mete lufsum and lusti on to loken that yif the forwariede, that wallen
20 in helle, mihten hit echeliche seon, al that pinende pik ne [that wallende] walde ham thunche bote a softe bekinde bath; for yif hit swa mihte beon levere ham were eaver mare in wa for to welle and o that welefule wlite eaver mar to loken then in alle blisse beon and forgan thi sihthe. Thu art swa schene and swa hwit that te sunne were dosk yif hit to thi blisfule bleo mihte beo evenet; tha yif that I wile ani mon for feirnesse luve, luve I wile the, mi leve lif, moder-sune feirest.

A, Jesu, mi swete Jesu, leve that te luve of the beo al mi likinge.

Bote moni wile for ahte lefmon chese, for aihwer with chatel mon mai luve cheape. Ah is ani ricchere then thu, mi leof, that rixles in
30 hevene? Thu art kid keiser that al this werld wrahtes, for as te hali prophete David cwiddes: 'Drihtines is te eorthe and al that hit fulles,

28. moni: nu I

14-15. 'Natural kinship makes close relatives love one another;' cf. l. 104.

20. [that wallende]: in the MS the that has been erased; but TLG reads pich that thei wallen inne (28/7). For the stylistic device of two adjectives surrounding the noun they govern cf. l. 91.

27. This sentence recurs like a refrain and suggests the influence of Latin hymns. TLG has lere (or some modernized form) for leve.

28. moni: cf. l. 58; TLG reads Bote moni for richesse lemmon cheoseth (30/17).

31-2. Ps. 24: 1, 'The earth is the Lord's, and the fulness thereof; the world, and they that dwell therein'. Only the first half of the quotation is strictly biblical, but it was common to offer a free development of a biblical passage.

werld and al that trin wuneth, hevene with the murhthes and ta unimete blisses.' Al is tin, mi sweting, and al thu wilt yive me yif I the riht luvie. Ne mai I na man yive mi luve to swettere biyete. Halde I wile tha to the, mi leof; for the self luve the selven and for thi luve leten alle othre thinges that min herte fram thi luve mihte drahe and turnen.

A, Jesu, swete Jesu, leove that te luve of the beo al mi likinge.

Bote hwat is ahte and weorldes wele wurth withuten fredom? And hwa is frerre then thu? For first thu mades al this werld and dides hit under mine fet and makedes me lavedi over alle thine schaftes that tu 40 schop on eorthe; bote ich hit rewli fordide thurhhut mine sunnes. Ah lest I me al forlesede, thu yef the selven for me to lese me fra pine. Thenne yif I ani wile for largesce luve, luve I wile the, Jesu Crist, largest over othre. For othre large men yiven thise uttre thinges, bute thu, swete Jesu, for me yef the selven that tin ahne heorte-blod ne cuthes tu withhalde. Derre druri ne yef neaver na lefmon to other. And tu that erst [to] me yef al the selven thu hafdes me heht, mi lefmon, to the yive al me selven to rixlen o thi riht hond crunet with the selven. Hwa is ta largere then thu? Hwa for largesce is betere wurth to beo luved then thu, mi luve[s] lif? 50

A, Jesu, swete Jesu, leve that te luve of the beo al mi likinge.

Bote largesce is lutel wurth ther wisdom wontes, and yif that I wile ani mon luve for wisdom nis nan wisere then thu that art wisedom cald of thi fader in hevene. For he thurh the that wisdom art al this world wrahte, and dihteth hit and dealeth as hit best semeth. Inwith the, mi leve lif, is hord of alle wisedom hid as te bok witnesses.

A, Jesu, swete Jesu, leve that te luve of the beo al mi likinge.

Bote moni man thurh his strengthe and hardischipe ek makes him luved and yerned. And is ani swa hardi swa ar tu? Nai! For thu the [self] ane dreddes nawt with thin ahne deore bodi to fihte ayaines alle 60

---

42. me (1) : ne **60.** ahne (*cf.* oune TLG): anre

39ff. The ancress, and by implication each one of us, re-enacts Adam's life. Placed over all created things, we lose that position through our sins. But so that we are not absolutely lost, Christ gave himself to save us from torment. Those of us who give ourselves to him in return can expect to rule with him in heaven.

47. [to]: *cf.* l. 48; TLG has *for* (32/15).

50. It is possible to understand a compound *luve-lif* here; but emendation seems preferable. *Cf.* ll. 130, 153 etc.

56. *bok*: the Bible. The author probably had *Colossians* 2: 3 in mind: 'In whom are hid all the treasures of wisdom'.

60. [*self*]: *cf* l. 169 and TLG 34/11.

the ahefulle develes of helle that hwuch of ham swa is lest latheliche
and grureful mihte he swuch as he is to monkin him scheawe al the
world were offeard him ane to bihalde, for ne mihte na mon him seo
and in his wit wunie bute yif the grace and te strengthe of Crist baldede
his heorte. Thu art yette herwith swa unimete mihti that with thi
deorewurthe hond nailet on rode thu band ta helle-dogges and reftes
ham hare praie that tai hefden grediliche gripen and helden hit faste
for Adames sunne. Thu kene kidde kempe robbedes helle-hus, lesedes
tine prisuns and riddes ham ut of cwalm-hus and leddes ham with the
70   self to thi yimmede bur, bold of eche blisse. Forthi of the, mi lefmon,
was sothliche quiddet: Drihti[n] is mahti, strong and kene i fihte. And
forthi yif me likes stalewurthe lefmon, luve I wile the, Jesu, strongest
over alle, that thi maht felle mine starke sawle-fan, and te strengthe
of the helpe mi muchele wacnesse, and hardischipe of the balde min
herte.

A, Jesu, swete Jesu, leve that te luve of the beo al mi likinge.

Ah noble men and gentile and of heh burthe ofte winnen luve
lihtliche cheape, for ofte moni wummon letes hire mensket thurh
the luve of wepmon that is of heh burthe. Thenne swete Jesu, up o
80   hwat herre mon mai I mi luve sette? Hwer mai I gentiller mon chese
then the that art te kinges sune that tis world wealdes and king and
evene with thi fader, king over kinges, lauerd over lauerdes? And
yette onont ti monhad born thu wes of Marie, meiden mildest o mod,
kine-bearn of burthe, of Davides kin the king, of Abrahames streone.
Hehere burthe then this nis nan under sunne. Luve I wile the tha,
swete Jesu, as te gentileste lif that eaver livede on eorthe. Alswa for in
al thi lif neaver na leaste nes ifunden, mi deore lefmon lasteles; and tat
com the of burthe and of foster alswa, thu that eaver wunedest i the
hurd of heovene. A, mi deorewurthe druth, swa gentile and swa

65ff. Through the crucifixion Christ harrowed hell (66) and thus robbed the devils
of their human captives, who had all been condemned to hell because of Adam's
original sin. The image of Christ being able to rout the devils while nailed (and because of being nailed) to the cross is very striking.

66. helle-dogges: devils are commonly portrayed as dogs or wolves.

70. yimmede bur: the heavenly Jerusalem; cf. Revelations 21: 18ff.

71. Cf. Ps. 24: 8, 'Who is this King of Glory? The Lord strong and mighty, the
Lord mighty in battle.'

87f. TLG is more specific: And that com the nomeliche of kuynde of thi fader, of whom
is al gentilrie and cortesye sprongen (36/7-9).

hende, ne thole me neaver mi luve nohwer to sette o karlische thinges,   90
ne eorthli thing ne fleschli ayaines te yerne ne luve ayain thi wille.

A, Jesu, swete Jesu, leve that te luve of the beo al mi likinge.

Meknesse and mildschipe makes mon eihwer luved; and tu, mi
leve Jesu, for thi mikle meknesse to lamb was evenet. For ayaines al
the woh and te schome that tu tholedest, and ayaines al the wa and te
pinfule wundes neaver ne opnedes ti muth to grucchen ayaines; and
yette the schome and te woh that te sunefule of the world euch dai
don the mildeliche thu tholest hit, ne wrekes tu the nawt sone after
ure gultes, bote longe abides bote thurhut ti milce. Thenne thi deboneirschipe mai make the eihwer luved, and forthi is riht that I luve the   100
and leave alle othre for the for muchel thu haves ti milce toward me
scheawed.

A, Jesu, swete Jesu, leve that te luve of the beo al mi likinge.

Bote forthi that sibbe-frend kindeliche euchan luves other, thu
schruddes te with ure flesch, nam of hire flesch mon born of wummon,
thi flesch nam of hire flesch withuten meane of wepmon, nam with
that ilke flesch fulliche monnes cunde to tholen al that mon mai thole,
don al that mon deth withuten sunne ane—for sunne and unwitschipe
ne hafdes tu nowther. Thenne ayaines kinde gath hwa that swuche
kinesmon ne luveth and leveth. And forthi that trewere luve ah beo   110
imong brethre, thu monnes brother bicom of an fader with alle thoa
that cleneliche singen *Pater noster*—bute thu thurhut kinde, and we

110. kinesmon: kinsemon

---

90. *karlische thinges*: mortal husbands.

94. The symbolism of the lamb is characteristic of the *Book of Revelation*. As a
symbol of meekness it is contrasted with the terrible wolves of hell.

97. Our wicked daily actions are new wounds inflicted on Christ which are equated
with the physical wounds inflicted on him while here on earth.

105. *nam of hire flesch mon born of wummon*: you took from her flesch the quality of
a man born of a woman (i.e. human nature, inherited from a physical mother). This
clause is parallel to and contrasted with the following one. But TLG 28/20–1 reads
Thou clothedest the with oure flesch, mon boren of wommon, and an interpretation along
these lines would be possible for the *Wooing* as well.

111*ff*. 'You became man's brother sprung from one father to all those who sing
"Our Father" in purity (but you are his son through natural relationship and we his
children through grace) and you became man of that same flesch we bear on earth.'
The passage is difficult because several ideas are compressed within it: Christ is brother
to the elect, but also a human being; he is a natural son of his father, but we are sons
by adoption through grace.

C*

thurhut grace—and mon of that ilke flesch that we beren on eorthe. A, hwam mai he luve treweliche hwa ne luves his brother? Thenne hwase the ne luves, he is mon unwreastest. Nu, mi swete Jesu, leaved have I for thi luve flesches sibnesse; and yette borne brethre haven me forwurpen, bote ne recches me na thing hwils that I the halde. For i the ane mai ich alle frend finden. Thu art me mare then fader, mare then moder; brother, suster [other] othre frend narn nawiht ayaines te to
120   tellen.

A, Jesu, swete Jesu, leve that te [luve of the beo al mi likinge].

Thenne thu with thi fairnesse, thu with richesce, thu with largesce, thu with wit and wisdom, thu with maht and strengthe, thu with noblesce and hendeleic, thu with meknesse and mildeschipe and mikel debonairte, thu with sibnesse, thu with alle the thinges that man mai luve with bugge haves mi luve chepet. Ah over alle othre thinges makes te luvewurthi to me tha harde atele hurtes, tha schome-liche wohes that tu tholedes for me, thi bittre pine and passiun; thi derve death o rode telles riht in al mi luve, calenges al mi heorte.

130   Jesu, mi lives luve, min herte-swetnesse, thre fan fihten ayaines me (and yet mai ich sare for hare duntes drede, and bihoves thurh thi grace yapliche to wite me): the werld, mi flesch, the deovel—the world to make me thewe, mi fles to make me hore, the devel thurhut thise twa to drahe me to helle. Arh ich was me self and wak and neh dune-fallen: and mine fan derve, swa bucchede and swa kene that hwen thai sehen me swa wak and swa forhuhande and buhande toward ham thei swithre sohten up o me and wenden of me, wrecche, have maked al hare ahen and hefden for sothe maked, nere helpe ne[v]re the nerre. Thai grennede for gladschipe euchan toward other as wode wulves
140   that fainen of hare praie. Bote therthurh understonde I that tu wult have me to lefmon and to spuse, that tu ne tholedes ham noht fulli fainen of me and allegate have wurpen me in schome and in sinne and terafter into pine. Bote ther the bale was alre meast, swa was te bote nehest. Thu biheld al this and tu allegate seh that I ne mihte stonde

---

134. wak (cf. wok TLG): wah   **137.** up o: up|po

---

119. [other] othre: cf. or eny TLG 30/1.

121. For convenience the refrain is expanded here and at all later occurrences.

137. sohten up o: 'they assailed'.

143–4. A common proverbial expression, cf. B. J. and H. W. Whiting, *Proverbs, Sentences, and Proverbial Phrases* (Cambridge, Mass., and Oxford 1968), B22.

ayain hare wilfulle crokes thurh wit other strengthe that wes in me
selven, bot neh hefde I fulliche buhed til alle mine thre fan. Thu com
me to helpe, feng to fihte for me, and riddes me fram deathes-hus
sorhe and pine of helle. Thu biddes me bihalde hu thu faht for me that I
poverte of worlde ne schome of wicke monnes muth foruten mine
gulte ne secnesse of mi bodi ne flesches pine drede, hwen that I bihalde   150
hu thu was poure for me, hu thu was schent and schomet for me, and
atte laste with pineful death henged o rode.

Jesu, mi lives luve, riche ar tu as lauerd in hevene and in eorthe, and
tah poure thu bicom for me, westi and wrecched: poure thu born was
of the meiden, thi moder, for thenne i thi burth-tid in al the burh of
Belleem ne fant tu hus-lewe ther thine nesche childes limes inne mihte
reste, bot in a waheles hus imiddes the strete; poure thu wunden was i
rattes and i clutes and caldeliche dennet in a beastes cribbe. Bote swa
thu eldere wex, swa thu pourere was. For i thi childhad hafdes tu the
pappe to thi fode and ti moder readi hwen thu pappe yerndes, bote   160
hwen thu eldere was thu, that fuhel o fluht, fisch i flod, folc on eorthe
fedes, tholedes for wone of mete moni hat hungre as clerkes witerliche
in godspel reden. And tu that hevene and eorthe and al this werld
wrahtes navedes in al this werld hwer thu o thin ahen thi heaved
mihtes reste. Bote bathe yung and eldre allegate thu hafdes hwer[with]
thu mihtes wrihe thine banes; ah atte laste of thi lif, hwen thu for me
swa rewliche hengedes on rode, ne hafdes in al this world hwerwith
that blisfule blodi bodi thu mihtes hule and huide. And swa nu, swete
lefmon, poure thu the self was and te poure thu ratheste cheas, poverte
thu luvedes, poverte thu tahtes, and yiven thu haves echeliche thin   170
endelese blisse til alle that clenli for thi luve mesaise and poverte wilfulliche tholien. A, hu schulde I beo riche and tu, mi leof, swa poure?
Forthi, swete Jesu Crist, wile I beo poure for the, as tu was for the
luve of me, for to beo riche with the i thin eche blisse, for with poverte
and with wa schal mon wele buggen.

---

154. poure thu: thoure thi   169. poure: thoure

---

162. There are several biblical references to Christ's hunger, e.g. *Mark* 11: 12.
164-5. *Cf. Matthew* 8: 20.

165*ff.* This sentence develops the idea of Christ's ever-increasing poverty. Both
as boy and man he had clothes to dress in, but at his death he was robbed of all his
clothes for which the soldiers cast lots; *cf. Matthew* 27: 35. For the emendation at
l. 165 *cf.* l. 167 and TLG 42/22.

A, Jesu, swete Jesu, leve that te [luve of the beo al mi likinge].

Bote poverte with menske is eath for to tholien. Ah thu, mi lef, for mi luve with al thi poverte was schomeliche heaned, for hu mon the ofte seide schomeliche wordes and hathfule hokeres long weren
180 hit al to tellen. Bote muche schome thu tholedes hwen thu that neaver sunne dides was taken as untreowe, broht biforen sinfule men, tha heathene hundes, of ham to beo demet that demere art of werlde, ther thu, bote of monkin, schomeliche was demed and te monquellere fra dethes dom was lesed. For as i the godspel is writen, alle thai crieden o wode wulves wise: 'Heng, heng that treitur Jesus on rode, heng him o rode, and lese us Baraban.' Was tat Barabas a theof that with tresun i the burh hafde a mon cwelled. Bote mare schome thu tholedes hwen that te sunefule men i thi neb spitted. A, Jesu, hwa mihte mare tholen cristen other heathen then mon him for schendlac i the beard spitted,
190 and tu i thi welefulle wlite, i that lufsume leor swuche schome tholedes? And al the menske thuhte for the luve of me that tu mihtes with that spatel that swa biclaried ti leor wasche mi sawle and make hit hwit and schene and semlike i thi sihte, and forthi thu biddes me herupon thenche. 'Scito quoniam propter te sustinui op[p]robrium; operuit confusio faciem meam, Understond,' thu seist, 'and herteliche thenke that I for the luve of the tholede schome and bismere and schomeliche spateling of unwurthi ribauz; tha heathene hundes hilede mi neb for the.' As tah he seide: ne dred tu nawt for the luve of me to thole schome of worlde withute thine gulte. Bote schome over schomes tholedes
200 tu hwen thu wes henged bituhhe twa theofes, as hwase seie: he is mare then theof and forthi as hare meister he henges ham bituhhen. A Jesu, mi lives luve, hwat herte ne mai tobreke hwen ha herof thenches hu

198. luve (*sic* TLG): me *erased*, i *above line*   200. is: this is

---

183. *monquellere*: that is, Barabbas.

185f. The quotation is based on *Luke* 23: 18–21. The form *Baraban* is the Latin accusative singular which has been taken over from the Vulgate, where it is usually spelt *Barabbam*.

188–9. Who, whether Christian or heathen, can suffer more than having someone spit in his face?

191. *al the menske thuhte*: it all seemed honour to you.

194–5. *Ps.* 69: 7, 'Because for thy sake I have borne reproach; shame hath covered my face.' The author has offered a free translation to make the psalmist's words harmonize with the story of Christ's trials. *Cf.* l. 292*ff*. This procedure is typical of the *Ancrene Wisse*.

198. *luve of me*: cf. *luve of the* (196)

thu, that menske art of al monkin, of alle bales bote, mon for to menske swuch schome tholedes? Mon spekes ofte of wundres and of selcuthes that misliche and monifald haven bifallen, bote this was te measte wunder that eaver bifel on eorthe, ya wunder over wundres, that tat kidde keiser, cruned in hevene, schuppere of alle schaftes, for to mensken hise fan walde henge bituhhe twa theoves.

A, Jesu, swete Jesu, that tu wes schent for mi luve, leve that te luve of the [beo al mi likinge].   210

Inoh were poverte and schome withuten othre pines, bote ne thuhte the neaver, mi lives luve, that tu mihtes fulliche mi frendschipe buggen hwils the lif the lasted. A, deore cheap hefdes tu on me, ne was neaver unwurthi thing chepet swa deore. Al thi lif on eorthe wes i swink for me saw lengre swa mare. Ah bifore thin ending swa unimeteliche thu swanc and swa sare that reade blod thu swattes for, as Seint Luk seith i the godspel, thu was i swa strong a swing that te swat as blodes dropes eorn dune to the eorthe. Bute hwat tunghe mai hit telle, hwat heorte mai hit thenche for sorhe and for reowthe of alle tha buffetes and ta bale duntes that tu tholedest i thin earst niminge hwen that Judas   220 Scharioth brohte tha helle-bearnes the to taken and bringen biforen hare princes; hu ha the bunden swa heteli faste that te blod wrang ut at tine fingerneiles, as halhes bileven, and bunden ledden rewli and dintede unrideli o rug and o schuldres and bifore the princes buffeted and beten; sithen bifore Pilat hu thu was naket bunden faste to the piler that tu ne mihtes nowhwider wrenche fra tha duntes? Ther thu wes for mi luve with cnotti swepes swungen swa that ti luveliche lich mihte beo totorn and torent, and al thi blisfule bodi streamed on a girre-blod. Sithen o thin heaved wes set te crune of scharpe thornes that with eavriche thorn wrang ut te reade blod of thin heali heaved;   230 sithen yette buffetet and todunet i the heaved with the red-yerde that te was ear in honde yiven the on hokerringe.

213. hwils: hwilf   220. bale: bali

---

216. Of the agony in the garden *Luke* 22: 44 has 'and his sweat was as it were great drops of blood falling down to the ground'. In both medieval art and literature there is considerable emphasis on the blood Christ shed, both to excite pity and to underline the suffering involved in his sacrifice.

219–20. There is no evidence in the gospels that Christ was manhandled when he was captured, though his captors came with 'swords and staves' (*Mark* 14: 48).

229. *girre-blod*: a word confined to the *Ancrene Wisse* and Katherine Group of texts.

231. *red-yerde*: the reed which symbolizes a sceptre which they gave to Jesus to mock

A, hwat schal I nu don? Nu min herte mai tobreke, min ehne flowen
al o water. A, nu is mi lefmon demd for to deien. A, nu mon ledes
him forth to Munte Calvarie to the cwalm-stowe. A lo, he beres his
rode upon his bare schuldres. And, lef, tha duntes drepen me that tai
the dunchen and thrasten the forthward swithe toward ti dom. A,
lefmon, hu mon folhes te, thine frend sariliche with reming and sorhe,
thine fend hokerliche to schome and wundren up o the. A, nu have thai
240 broht him thider. A, nu raise thai up the rode; setis up the warh-treo.
A, nu nacnes mon mi lef. A, nu driven ha him up with swepes and
with schurges. A, hu live I for reowthe that seo nu mi lefmon up o
rode and swa to drahen hise limes that I mai in his bodi euch ban tellen.
A, hu that ha nu driven irnene neiles thurh thine feire hondes into hard
rode, thurh thine freoliche fet. A, nu of tha honden and of tha fet swa
luveli streames te blod swa rewli. A, nu beden ha mi leof, that seith
that him thristes, aisille surest alre drinch menged with galle that is
thing bittrest, twa-bale drinch i blodleting swa sur and swa bittre;
bote ne drinkes he hit noht. A nu, swete Jesu, yet upon al thi wa ha
250 eken schome and bismer: lahhen the to hokere ther thu o rode hengest.
Thu, mi luveliche lef, ther thu with strahte earmes henges o rode, was
reowthe to rihtwise, lahter to the luthere; and tu that al the world
fore mihte drede and divere was unwreste folk of world to hoker-
lahter. A, that luvelike bodi that henges swa rewli, swa blodi, and swa
kalde; a, hu schal I nu live for nu deies mi lef for me up o the deore rode?
Henges dun his heaved and sendes his sawle—bote ne thinche ham
nawt yet that he is ful pinet ne that rewfule deade bodi nulen ha nawt

---

242. nu: mi   **248.** twa: ewa

---

his claims of kingship (*Matthew* 27: 29). This reed has been equated with the one
used to strike him on the head during the scourging (*Mark* 15: 19).

233. Note the sudden shift of the point of view to the first person as though the
ancress was an eyewitness of the events described.

236. *lef*: earlier editors take this as an imperative of *leven*, meaning 'grant, allow'.
But this interpretation lacks immediacy and involvement, so it is better to take it as
a form of address to Jesus, '(my) darling'; TLG 48/31 reads *mi swete lemmon*.

240. *setis*: a plural (Northern) form, 'they set up'.

245. Take *fet* as parallel to *hondes*; they drive nails through his hands and feet.

246. *Cf. Matthew* 27: 34 and *John* 19: 28–30; the author has conflated the two.

248. *twa-bale drinch*: 'a drink of double misery'. Previous editors understand as
'two terrible drinks', but this seems less convincing.

frithie. Bringen forth Longis with that brade scharpe spere: he thurles his side, cleves tat herte; and cumes flowinde ut of that wide wunde the blod that [me] bohte, the water that te world wesch of sake and of sunne. A, swete Jesu, thu oppnes me thin herte for to cnawe witerliche and in to reden trewe luve-lettres, for ther I mai openlich seo hu muchel thu me luvedes. With wrange schuld I the min heorte wearnen sithen that tu bohtes herte for herte. 260

Lavedi moder and meiden, thu stod here ful neh and seh al this sorhe up o thi deorewurthe sune, was withinne martird i thi moder-liche herte that seh to cleve his heorte with the speres ord. Bote, lafdi, for the joie that tu hefdes of his ariste the thridde dai therafter, leve me understonde thi dol and herteli to felen sumhwat of the sorhe that tu tha hefdes and helpe the to wepe that I with him and with the muhe i min ariste o domes dai gladien and with yu beon i blisse that he me swa bitterliche with his blod bohte. 270

Jesu, swete Jesu, thus tu faht for me ayaines mine sawle-fan: thu me derennedes with like and makedes of me wrecche thi leofmon and spuse. Broht tu haves me fra the world to bur of thi burthe, steked me i chaumbre. I mai ther the swa sweteli kissen and cluppen and of thi luve have gastli likinge. A, swete Jesu, mi lives luve, with thi blod thu haves me boht, and fram the world thu haves me broht. Bote nu mai I seggen with the salme-wrihte: 'Quid retribuam, Domino, pro omnibus quae retribuit mihi? Lauerd, hwat mai I yelde the for al that tu haves yiven me?' Hwat mai [I] thole for the for al that tu tholedes for me? Ah me bihoveth that tu beo eath to paie. A wrecche bodi and a wac bere ich over eorthe, and tat swuch as hit is have yiven and yive wile to thi servise, mi bodi henge with thi bodi neiled o rode, sperred 280

260. blod: thlod

---

258. *Longis*: that is, the centurion (*Mark* 15: 39) conflated with the soldier who pierced the side of Jesus (*John* 19: 34) and in later tradition known as St. Longinus. See R. J. Peebles, *The Legend of Longinus in Ecclesiastical Tradition and English Literature* (Bryn Mawr 1911). *Bringen* is pres. pl. with subject 'they' understood, *cf. lahhen* l. 250. Such rapid changes in the syntax help to create the emotional tension of the passage.

262. *in*: here in an adverbial sense, 'within (it)'.

266. *was*: here 2nd sg. of the preterite. 'You who saw his heart pierced by the spear-point were martyred internally in your own heart.' TLG relates these words to *Luke* 2: 35 'yea, a sword shall pierce through thy own soul also', which are Simeon's words to Mary.

275-6. *Cf. Song of Solomon*, 3: 4.   279-81. *Ps.* 116: 12.

284. Thompson understood *henge* as a subjunctive, presumably with the sense 'may

querfaste withinne fowr wahes, and henge I wile with the and neaver
mare of mi rode cume til that I deie. For thenne schal I lepen fra rode into
reste, fra wa to wele and to eche blisse. A, Jesu, swa swet hit is with the
to henge, for hwen that I seo o the that henges me biside the muchele
swetnesse of the, reaves me fele of pine. Bote, swete Jesu, hwat mai mi
290　bodi ayaines tin, for yif ich mihte a thusandfald yive the me selven
nere hit nowt onont te that yef the selven for me. And yet ich have an
heorte unwrest and unwurthi and westi and poure of alle gode theawes,
and tat swuch as hit is tac hit to the nu, leve lif, with treowe luvenesse,
and ne thole me neaver nan other thing ayain thi wille luvie for ne mai
ich nowhwer mi luve bettre sette then o the, Jesu Crist, that bohtes hit
swa dere.

Nis nan swa wurthi to beo luved as tu, swete Jesu, that in the haves
alle thing hwerfore mon ah beo luvewurthi to other. Thu art best
wurth mi luve that for mi luve deidest. Yette yif that I mi luve bede
300　for to selle and sette feor therupon swa hehe swa ich eaver wile, yette
thu wult hit habbe; and teken al that tu haves, yiven wil tu eke mare;
and yif I the riht luvie wilt me crune in hevene with the self to rixlen
werld into werlde.

A, Jesu, swete Jesu, mi luve, mi lef, mi lif, mi luvelevest, that swa
muchel luvedes me that tu deides for luve of me and fra the world
haves broht me and ti spuse haves maked me and al thi blisse haves heht
me, leve that te luve of the beo al mi likinge.

Prei for me, mi leve suster. This have I writen the forthi that wordes
ofte quemen the heorte to thenken on ure Lauerd; and forthi hwen
310　thu art on eise, carpe toward Jesu and seie thise wordes and thenc as
tah he heng biside the blodi up o rode. And he thurh his grace opn[e]
thin heorte to his luve and to reowthe of his pine.

---

my body hang . . .', though this fails to convey the necessary determination of the
ancress. Understand it as an infinitive dependent upon *wile*: 'and I will hang my
body . . .'.

285. The life of the ancress, confined within her cell, is compared with the crucifixion of Christ. Through suffering in this life (here represented by the cell) man
emulates Christ and hopes to share in his reward.

287. This marks the climax of the ecstatic meditation in which the ancress has
virtually merged her own personality in that of Christ.

308. The author of this piece is unknown, though this conclusion may have been
added by a scribe rather than have been composed as part of the original work. *Cf.*
the conclusion to XI.

IV John Gaytryge's Sermon

The pieces known by the titles *John Gaytryge's Sermon* and *The Lay Folks' Catechism* are the same work in slightly modified forms. It is a translation made in 1357 by John Gaytryge, a monk at St. Mary's Abbey, York, of the Latin catechism of Archbishop Thoresby of York. The English version is, however, very much longer than the Latin original. Both the English and the Latin texts were included in the Archbishop's register and both presumably had the status of official versions. Although the register is still extant, I have printed the version in the Thornton manuscript (compiled by Robert Thornton c. 1430–40 and now Lincoln Cathedral Chapter Library MS. A.5.2.) [T] in order to include something from that famous manuscript in this volume. I have compared T with *The Lay Folks' Catechism* i.e. the version found in the register [LFC] and with the version in the fifteenth-century Trinity College Cambridge MS. B.1012 [B]. *John Gaytryge's Sermon* circulated widely, for apart from these three versions, it is found entire or in part in at least eight other manuscripts and it was adapted and expanded by a Wycliffite writer. The Lollard Purvey, in one of his tracts written c. 1403–5, wrote of this piece that Thoresby had sent the catechism 'in smale pagynes to the comyn puple to lerne and to know this, of wiche ben yit manye a componye in Englond'.

Editions: T. F. Simmons and H. E. Nolloth, *The Lay Folks' Catechism.* EETS o.s. 118 (London 1901). [Includes LFC, Thoresby's Latin, Pecham's Latin, and the Wycliffite version.]
G. G. Perry, *Religious Pieces in Prose and Verse.* Rev. edn. EETS o.s. 26 (London 1914). [T]

Here begynnes a sermon that Dan John Gaytryge made, the whilke teches how scrifte es to be made and whareof and in how many thyngez solde be consederide.
Et est Petrus Sentenciarum discrecione prima.

2. *Scrifte* is written in the margin after *in*. Perry included it in the text, but it is better to take it as a marginal note.
4. A corruption of LFC's *Et est secundo Sentenciarum distinctione prima* 'and it is in the first distinction of the *Sentences*'. Peter Lombard's *Sentences*, which is divided into 'distinctions', was written between 1148 and 1151. A systematic treatment of sacred doctrine, it remained a standard textbook in universities till the sixteenth century. The *grete doctour* (5) is Peter.

Als a grete doctour schewes in his buke, of all the creatours that Gode
made in heven and in erthe, in water and in ayere or in oghte elles the
soverayne cause and the skyll whi he mad tham was his awen gud will
and his gudnes. Thurgh the whilke gudnes—alls he es all gude—he
walde that some creatures of thase that he made ware communers of
10   that blyse that evermare lastis. And for that na creatoure myghte
come to that blyse withowtten knaweyng of Godd, als that clerke
teches, he made skillwyse creatours, angelle and man, of witt and
wysdom to knawe God Almyghtyn, and thorowe thaire knawynge
lufe hym and serve hym and so come to that blyse that thay ware made
to. This manere of knawynge had oure formefadyrs in the state of
innocence that thay ware mad in; and so sulde we hafe hade if thay had
noghte synnede—noghte so mekill als hally saules hase now in heven,
bot mekill mare than man hase now in erthe. For oure fourmefadyrs
synned, sayse the prophete, and we bere the wykkydnes of thaire
20   mysdedis. For the knawyng that thay had of Godd Allmyghten thay
had it of Goddes gyfte at thaire begynnynge withowtten travayle or
tray or passinge of tym; and all the knaweyng that we hafe in this
werlde of hym es of heryng and of lerynge and of techyng of other of
the law and the lare that langes till Haly Kyrke, the whilke all creatours
that lufes God Almyghten awe to knawe and to cun and lede thaire
lyfe aftir, and swa come to that blysse that never mare blynnes.

And forthi that mekill folke now in this werlde ne ere noghte wele
ynoghe lerede to knawe God Almyghty ne lufe hym ne serve hym
als thay sulde do, and als thair dedys oftesythes opynly schewes, in
30   gret perell to tham to lyfe and to saule (and perawnter the defaute may
be in thaym that hase thair saules for to kepe and thaym sulde teche,
als prelates and parsouns, vicars and prestes, that ere halden by dett

11. clerke (*sic* LFC): clerkes

---

11. *clerke*: that is, Peter Lombard. The sense of the passage is as follows. Bliss is
acquired through knowledge of God. Our innate knowledge of him was impaired
by the original sin of Adam and Eve, but it was made available again to man by Christ.
But after his time it had to be learned through Holy Church. Hence Christian belief
was essential for salvation, and this sermon expounds its principal tenets.

18. *Lamentations* 5: 7, 'Our fathers have sinned, and are not; and we have borne
their iniquities.'

29. 'as they often publicly reveal through their actions'.

32. The incompetence of priests was a frequent complaint, which was later taken
up by the Lollards. Archbishop Thoresby took steps to improve the quality of the
clergy.

for to lere tham) forthi our fadir the byschope, that God Almyghty
save, that—als Sayn Paule sayse in his pystill—will that all men be
safe and knawe God Almyghten and namely thase undirlowttes that
till hym langes, hase tretide and ordeyned for the comon profett
thorowe the councell of his clergy that ilkane that undir hym hase
cure of saule opynly one Ynglysche apon Sonnondayes preche and
teche thaym that thay hafe cur off the lawe and the lare to knawe God
Almyghty that pryncypally may be schewede in theis sexe thynges: 40
in the fourtene poyntes that falles to the trowthe; in the ten commandementes that Gode hase gyfen us; in the seven sacramentes that er in
Haly Kyrke; in the seven werkes of mercy untill oure even-crystyn;
in the seven vertus that ilke man sall use; and in the seven dedly synnes
that ilke man sall refuse. And he byddes and commandes in all that he
may that all that hase cure or kepynge undir hym enjoyne thair parischennes and thair sugettes that thay here and lere thise ilke sex thynges
and oftesythes reherse tham till that thay cun tham, and sythen teche
tham thair childir, if thay any have, whate tym so thay are of elde
to lere tham; and that parsouns and vycars and all parische prestis 50
enquere delygently of thair sugettes in the Lentyn-tym when thay
come to scryfte whether thay knawe and cun thise sex thynges; and
if it be funden that thay cun tham noghte that thay enjoyne tham
appon his behalfe and of payne of penance for to cun tham. And
forthi that nane sall excuse thaym thurghe unknawlechynge for to
cun tham, our haly fadir the beschope of his gudnes hase ordaynede
and bedyn that thay be schewede opynly one Ynglysche amanges
the folke.

33. John Thoresby, Archbishop of York (1352–73).

34. *1 Timothy* 2: 4, 'Who will have all men to be saved, and to come unto the
knowledge of the truth'. LFC 43 reads *als Saint Paule sais of Jesu Crist*, which reads
better.

35. 'and particularly those subordinates (i.e. priests) entrusted to his care'.

37. *councell of his clergy*: the Convocation of the diocese of York.

41. On this numerical systemization see the Introduction.

45-6. *in all that he may*: 'to the limits of his authority'.

51. All Christians were obliged to go to confession at least once a year. This obligation was frequently performed during Lent so that the congregation could participate
in the Easter communion in a state of purity; *cf.* ll. 229–30.

54. *his*: that is, the Archbishop's. *of payne of penance*: on pain of a penance to be
inflicted upon them.

59ff. The articles of belief varied in number and composition. In *The Book of Vices
and Virtues*, ed. W. Nelson Francis (London 1942), p. 6ff. there are only twelve arti-

Wharefore anence the fyrste of thise sex thynges, that es to knawe the
60 articles that falles to the trouthe, als gret clerkes teches and schewes
in thaire bukes thare falles to the faythe fourtene poyntes, of the whilke
seven falles to Goddes goddhede and other seven falles to Cristes
manehede. The firste poynte that we sall trowe of the godhede es to trow
stedfastely in a trewe Godd and that na nother es for to trowe in.
The tother es that the heghe fadir of heven es stedfaste and sothefaste
Godd Almyghtyn. The thirde es that Jesu Criste, Goddes sone of heven,
es sothefastly Gode even till his fadir. The ferthe es that the Haly
Gaste, that samenly commes of bathe the Fadir and the Sonne, es
sothefaste Godde [and] even to thaym bathe; and the-whethir noghte
70 twa goddes (the Fadir and the Sonne) ne thre goddes (the Fadir and the
Sonne and the Haly Gaste), bot thre sere persouns and noghte bot a
godd. The fyfte artecle es that the Trynyte (the Fadir and the Sonne and
the Haly Gaste—thre persouns and a godd) es makere of heven and
erthe and of all thynges. The sexte artycle es that Haly Kirke, our
modir, es hallyly ane thorowowte the werlde, that es comonynge
and felawrede of all cristen folke that comouns togedir in the sacramentes and in other haly thynges that falles till Haly Kyrke, withowtten the whilke ne es na saule hele. The sevend article that us awe
to trowe es upperysynge of flesche and lyfe withowtten ende. For
80 when the dede hase sundyrde our bodyes and our saules for a certayne
tym, als our kynd askes, unto when that God sall deme the qwykke
and the dede, thane our saules sall turne agayne till oure bodyes and we
thase ilke (and nane other than we are nowe) sothefastely sall ryse up
in body and saule that never mare sall sundir fra that tym furthe; bot
samen, if we wele doo whiles we er here, wende with Godd to that
blysse that evermare lastes; and if we evyll do, till endles payne.

Thir are other seven poyntes of Cristes manhede that are nedfull
to trowe till all that are crystyn. The fyrste es that Jesu Criste, Goddes
sone of heven, was sothefastely conceyvede of the ma[i]den Marie
90 and tuke flesche and blude and become man thurghe the myghte and

---

61. faythe: *wrongly erased in ms*

---

cles, which are linked very closely with the Creed. Of the twelve, one refers to God,
seven to the Son, and four to the Holy Ghost.

69. *the-whethir*: 'nevertheless'; *cf.* OED *Though-whether*.

74-5. For the portrayal of Holy Church as a woman *cf. Piers Plowman*, passus i.

77. After *Kyrke*, LFC 104 adds *In forgyfnes of synnes and hele of thair saules*.

the strenghe of the Haly Gaste, withowtten any merryng of hir modir-hede, withowtten any mynynge of hir maydenhede. The tother artecle es that we sall trowe that he, godd and man bathe in a persoune, was sothefastely [borne] of that blessyde mayden: Godd getyn of his fadire before any tyme, and man borne of his modir and broghte furthe in tyme. The thirde poynte that we sall trowe es Cristes passione that he tholede bodyly for synfull mankynde: how he was betraysede with his disciple and taken with the Jewes, beten with scourges that na skynn helde, naylede one the rude, and corounde with thornes, and many other harde paynes, and dyede at the laste. The ferthe 100 artecle es that whene he was dede and his body tane doun and wonden and dolven, yit the whills his body lay in the grave the gaste with the godhede wente unto helle and heryede it and tuke owte thase that ware tharein, als Adam and Eve and other formefadyrs whilke he in his forluke walde that ware savede. The fyfte poynte es that one the thirde day after that he dyede he rase fra dede to lyfe, sothefaste godd and man in body and in saule; for als he dyede in seknes of our manhede, so he rase thurghe strenghe of his godhede, and swa dystroyed our dede thurgh his diynge and quykkynd us unto lyfe thurghe his rysynge. The sexte artecle es that we sall trowe that one the fourtede day eftyr 110 that he rase thurgh strenghe of hymselfe, he steye intill heven whare our kynde es nowe in his blyssede persoune, noghte anely evynne ne mete till his angells bot hey coround kynge abowve all his angells that before tym was lesse than the kynde of angells. The sevend article es that righte als he dyede and eftirwarde rase and stey intill heven, righte swa sall he come apon the laste day bathe for to deme the qwykke and the dede, whare all the folke that ever was or es or sall be sall sothefastely be schewede and sene before hym and ilke a man answere of his awen dedis, and be saved or dampnede whether-so he serves.

109. rysynge: rysesynge   119. dampnede: daṁpnede

---

99. *na skynn helde*: 'not a piece of skin was left intact'.

102. *the gaste*: Christ's spirit.

103. The Harrowing of Hell figures prominently in medieval treatises, art and drama, *cf*. III, 65*ff*.

112–14. Men when they go to heaven have a rank superior to that of angels, though originally (*before tym*) they were of a lower status. So although the devil seemingly destroyed man through sin, he opened up the possibility of man raising himself to an even higher position.

116. *laste day*: Doomsday or the Day of Judgement.

120 For als his ryghtwysenes nowe es mengede with mercy swa sall it thane be withowtten mercy.

The secund thyng of the sex to knawe God Almyghten es the ten commandementes that he hase gyffen us. Of the whilke ten the thre that ere firste awe us hallyly to halde anence oure Godd, and the seven that ere eftyr anence our even-cristen. The firste comandement charges us and teches us that we leve ne lowte na false goddes; and in this commandement es forboden us alkyn mysbyleves and all mawme-tryes, all false enchauntementes, and all so[r]ceryes, all false charmes, and all wichecraftes, that men of myssebyleve traystes appon or 130 hopes any helpe in withowtten God Almyghten. The tother com-mandement byddes us noghte take in ydillchipe ne in vayne the name of our Lorde Godd so that we trowe noghte in his name bot that es sothefaste, that we swere noghte by his name bot if it be byhovely and that we neven noghte his name bot wirchipfully. The thirde com-mandement es that we halde and halowe our haly day, the Sonondaye, and all other that falles to the yere that er ordeynede to halowe thurgh Haly Kyrke; in the whilke dayes all folke bathe lerede and lawede awe to gyffe tham gudly to Goddes servyce, to here and saye it efter thair state es in wirchipe of Godd Allmyghty and of his gud halowes, 140 noghte than for to tente to tary with the werlde ne lyffe in lykynge ne luste that the flesche yernes, bot gudly to serve Godd in clennes of lyfe. The ferthe commandement byddes us doo wyrchipe to fadir and to modir: noghte anely to fleschely fadyr and modir that getes us and fosters us furthe in the werlde, bot till our gastely fadir that hase hevede of us and teches us to lyffe till hele of our saules; and till our gastely modyr, that es Haly Kyrke, to be bouxome thareto and save the ryghte of it, for it es modir till all that cristenly lyffes; and alswa till ilke man that wyrchipfull es for to do wyrchip eftire that it es. The fyfte comandement byddes us that we sla na man, that es to say 150 bodyly ne gastely nother; for als many we sla in that at we may als we sclaundir or bakbyte or falsely deffames or fandes for to confounde thaym that noghte serves or withdrawes lyfelade fra tham that hase

---

129. *wichecraftes: cf.* II, 484. After *wichecraftes*, LFC has *all fals conjurisons and al wicked craftes*.

136. *and all other:* and all the other days that Holy Church decrees as feast days; the so-called days of obligation.

148. *to do wyrchip eftire that it es:* 'to honour him (each man) in accordance with his position'; some MSS read *he* for *it*.

nede if we be of havynge for to helpe tham. The sexte commandment forbeddes us to syn or for to foly fleschely with any woman, owther sybbe or fremmede, wedde or unwedde, or any fleschely knawynge or dede have with any other than the sacrament of matremoyne excusez and the lawe and the lare of Haly Kyrke teches. The sevend byddis us that we shall noghte stele; in whilke es forboden us robbyng and revyng and all wrangwyse takynge or withhaldyng or hydynge or helyng of other menes gudes agaynes thair witt and thair will that 160 hase ryghte to thaym. The aughten commandement byddes us that we sall bere na false wytnes agaynes our even-cristen; in the whilke es forboden us all manere of lesynges, false conspeꞏacye and false sweryng, wharethurghe our even-cristyn may lese thayr catell, faith, favour, or fame, or anythyng ells, whether it be in gastely or in bodyly gudes. The nyende commandement es that we yerne noghte our neghtbour house; in whilke es forboden all wrangwyse covetyse of land or of lythe or of oghte elles that may noghte be lyftede ne raysede fra the grounde als thynge that es stedfaste and may noghte be styrrede. The tend commandement an[d] the laste es that we yerne noghte the 170 wyefe of oure neghteboure ne of our evyn-cristen ne his mayden ne his knave ne his oxe ne his asse; in the whilke es forboden us to yerne or to take anythynge that may be styrride of other menn's gudes, als robes or reches or other catell, that we hafe na gude titill ne na ryghte to. For what thyng so we take or getes one other wyse than the lawe and the lare of Haly Kyrke teches, we may noghte be assoylede of the trespase bot if we make assethe in that that we may to tham that we harmede withhaldande thair gude. And in case that we hafe thurghe false athes, als in assises or other enquestes, wetandly or willfully gerte our even-cristyn lesse thair patremoyne or thair heritage, or falsely 180 be dyssessede of lande or of lythe, or false devorce be made, or any man dampnede, thofe all we do that we may to the party yit may we noghte be assoylede of the trespas bot of our beschope or of hym that hase his powere, for swylke caas es ryvely reservede till hymselven.

---

160. helyng: helelyng   182. dampnede: daṁpnede

---

163. *false sweryng*: LFC and B read *forswerynge*.

173. *may be styrride*: 'may be moved'—as opposed to the items included in the preceding commandment.

182. *thofe*: 'though'; *cf.* *thof* in MS Harley 1022, but LFC has *of* and B *if*.

Thise ten commandementez that I hafe now rekkenede er umbylowkede in twa of the gospelle: the tane es that we luffe Godd over all
thynges; the tother es that we lufe our even-cristen hallely in our
herte als we do ourselven. For Godd awe us to lufe hally with herte,
with all our myghte, with all our thoghte, with worde and with dede.
190 Our evyn-crysten alsswa awe us to lufe unto that ilke gude that we
lufe ourselfe, that es that thay wele fare in body and in saule and come
to that ilke blysse that we thynke to. And whatesoever that he bee that
thise twa wele yemes, all the ten commandementes for sothe he fulfilles.

The thirde thynge of the sex that I firste touchide es the seven
sacramentes that Haly Kirke gyffes thurghe prelates and other prestes
that hase the powere. Of whilke seven the firste fyve ilke cristen man
awe lawefully to take efter his elde es; and twa lyes in thaire will that
ressayves thaym. The firste sacrament of seven es our baptym that we
take the firste tym that we becom cristyn; in whilke bathe the firste
200 synn that we ere borne with and alkyn other synnes ere waschen
awaye that we ere fylede with are we take it; and the trouthe of Haly
Kyrke es taken tharein withowtten whilke na synfull man's saule may
be savede. And till this sacrament falles foure thynges if it sall ryghtely
be tane als Haly Kirke teches. Ane es ryghte sayeyng and carpyng
of the wordes that hym awe for to say that gyffes this sacrament,
that ere thise: 'I baptise the in the name of the Fadir and the Sonne
and the Haly Gaste.' Ane other es that it be done anely in watir for na
nother licour es lefulle tharefore. The thirde es that he that gyffes this
sacrament be in witt and in will for to gyffe it. And the ferthe es that
210 he that takes it be nother of lerede nor of lewde baptisede before;
for if the preste be in were of hym that sall take it whethir he be baptisede or he be noghte than sall he say the wordes one this wyese: 'If
thou be noghte baptisede, I baptise the in the name of the Fadir and the
Sone and the Haly Gaste.' The secunde sacrament es confermynge,
that the byschope gyffes to tham that ere baptisede, that gyffes thorowe
his powere to tham that takes it the grace and the gyfte of the Haly

185. Notice the change to the first person here.

186. *Luke* 10: 27.

188. *awe us*: *awe* is sometimes used impersonally as here; translate 'we ought'.

196. *that hase the powere*: that is, who are empowered through the Church to
administer the sacraments.

199*ff.* The essential nature of baptism to purify man of his original sin was a cardinal
point of the Church's teaching; thus babies had to be baptized at the earliest possible
opportunity in case they died. For with original sin one could not know God.

Gaste to make thaym mare stallworthe than thay ware before to stande agaynes the fende and dedly syn. That nane hase powere to do bot the byschope allane that hase the state and the stede of Cristes appostilles. The thirde sacrament es callede penance, that es sothefaste 220 forthynkynge that we hafe of our syn withowtten will or thoghte to turne agayne to it. And this sacrament bus have thre thynges: ane es sorowe in our herte that we hafe synnede; another es opyn scrifte of mouthe how we hafe synnede; the [thirde es ryghtwys amendes-making for that we hafe synnede]. Thise thre, with gud will to forsake our syn, clensez us and wasches us of alkyn syn. The ferthe es the sacrament of the autyr, Cristes awen body in lyknes of brede als hale als he tuke it of the blysside mayden, the whilke ilke man and woman that of elde es awe for to rescheyve anes in the yere, that es at say at the Pasch als Haly Kirke uses when thay ere clensede of syn thurghe 230 penance, o payne of doynge owte of Haly Kirke bot if thay forbere it by skyllwyse cause that awe to be knawen to tham that sall gyffe it. For he that tase it worthily tase his salvacyone, and whasa takes it unworthily tase his dampnacione. The fyfte sacrament es the laste enoyntynge with oyle that es hallowede and handelyde of prestes; the whilke sacrament awe anely to be gyffen to tham that he wate ere of skillwyse elde and that he sese sekyrly in perelle of dede, in lyghtenes and alegeance of thair sekenes if Godde will that thay turne agayne to the hele, and als in forgyffnes of venial synnes and in lessynge of payne if thay passe hethen. The sexte sacrament of Haly Kyrke es 240 ordir that gyffes powere to tham that ryghtwysly tase it for to serve in Haly Kyrke efter thair state es, and to tham that takes the ordyre of preste for to synge messe and for to mynystre the sacramentes of Haly

218. It was, and is, a common image to think of Christians as soldiers in a fight against sin and the devil.

224-5. A line has been omitted in T at the bottom of the page; the inclusion is based on LFC; a similar line is found in B.

230. Cf. l. 51.

238. Final absolution was usually given to those on the point of death. But as those who received it did so reluctantly very often because they felt death was now certain, the Church allowed it to be taken by those who were sick but might recover in token that the recovery was a sign of God's grace.

241. That is, Holy Orders through which those who take them are empowered to administer the sacraments, etc.

242. *efter thair state es*: in accordance with which order of priesthood they have proceeded to.

Kyrke that to tham fallys eftyr the state that thay hafe and thair degre askes. The sevend sacrament es matrymoyne, that es lawefull festynn-ynge betwyx man and woman at thair bathere assente for to lyffe samen withowtten any lowssynge whills thair lyfe lastes in remedy of syn and getynge of grace, if it be tane in gude entente and clennes of lyfe.

250 The ferthe thynge of the sex to knawe Godd Almyghty, that us byhoves fullfill in all that we maye, ere the seven dedis of mercy untill our even-cristen that Godd sall reherse us apon the dredfull day of dome and wiet howe we have done tham here in this lyfe, als Sayne Mathewe makes mynde in his gospelle. Of whilke the firste es to fede thaym that er hunngry. The tother es to gyffe thaym drynke that er thristy. The thyrde es for to clethe tham that er clatheles or nakede. The ferthe es for to herber tham that er houseles. The fyfte es for to vesete tham that lyes in sekenes. The sexte es for to helpe tham that lyes or er in presoun. The sevend es to bery dede men that hase 260 myster. Thise ere the seven bodyly dedis of mercy that ilke man awe to doo that es myghtty. Thar are of mercy alswa seven gastely dedis that us awe to doo till tham that hase nede till us. Ane es to consaile and wysse tham that are wyll. Another es to chasty tham that wyrkkys ill. The third es to solauce thaym that er sorowefull and comforthe thaym. The ferthe es to pray for thaym that ere synfull. The fyfte es to be tholemode when men mysdose us. The sexte es gladly to forgyffe when men haves grevede us: the sevend, when men askes us for to here thaym, if we cun mare than thay for to lere thaym. Thise untill our neghtebours ere full nedfull and to tham that duse thaym 270 wondir medefull; for he sall [find] mercy that mercyfull es, and man withowtten mercy of mercy sall mysse.

The fyfte thynge of the sex to knawe God Almyghten are the seven vertus that Haly Writte teches; of whilke seven the thre firste that are hede-thewes teches us how to hafe us unto God Almyghtty, and

---

254. *Matthew* 25: 31*ff.* This passage in which six works of mercy are mentioned gave rise to the concept of the works of mercy; they form the basis of IX.

263*ff.* Notice the use of the rhetorical *similiter cadens* in these lines: *wyll: ill*; *sorowe-full: synfull*; *us: us*; *thaym: thaym*; *nedfull: medefull*; *es: mysse*.

268. *here*: also the reading in LFC. Perry, however, emended to *lere*; but *cf.* l. 23.

273. This follows the normal division of the virtues into the three theological (or divine) virtues: faith, hope and charity, and the four cardinal virtues: justice, prudence, fortitude and temperance. For a more extended treatment see *The Book of Vices and Virtues*, ed. W. Nelson Francis (London 1942), p. 121*ff.*

the foure teches us swa for to lyffe that it be bathe lykande to Godd and
to man. The firste vertu es trouthe wharethurghe we trow anely in
Godd that made all thynges, with all the other artycles I touchede
before. And this es nedfull till all that cristenly lyffes, for trouthe es
begynnynge of all gude dedis; for nother es trouthe worthe withowtten
gud werk, ne na werke withowtten trouthe may pay Godd Almyghtty. 280
The tother gude thewe or vertue es hope, that es a sekyr habydynge
of gastely gude thurghe Goddes gudnes and our gude dedis for to
com to that blysse that never mare blynnes, noghte anely in trayste
of Goddes gudnes ne allanly in trayste of our gude dedis, bot in trayste
of thaym bathe when thay are bathe sammen. For nother sall we fall
sa ferr intill whanhope that we ne sall traiste to hafe that blysse if we
wele do; ne we sall noghte com so ferr into overhope for to trayste so
mekill in Goddes gudnes that we sall hope to have that blysse withowtten gude dedys. The thirde vertue or thewe es charyte, the whylke
es a dere lufe that us awe [to hafe untill God Almyghty and till our 290
even-cristen]: untill Godd Almyghty als for hymselfe and till our
even-cristen for God Almyghttyn, for the tane may noghte be lufede
withowtten the tother; als Sayn John the gospellere sayse in his pystill:
'That commandement,' he saise, 'hafe we of Godd that whasaever
lufes Gode lufes his even-cristyn; for he that lufes noghte his brother
wham he may see, how sulde he lufe God wham he sese noghte?'
The ferthe vertue or thewe es ryghtwysenes, that es to yelde to all
men that we awe tham, for to do to ilke a man that us awe to doo,
for to wirchipe tham that ere worthy, for to helpe the pure that er
nedy, to do no gyle ne wrange unto na man, bot for to do that skill 300
es untill ilke mane. The fyfte vertue or thewe es sleghte or sleghenes

277. artycles: vertus   301. es (2): or

---

275. After lyffe, LFC 385 reads Bathe onentes ourself and our even-cristen.
276. trouthe: see the discussion of this word in J. A. Burrow, A Reading of Sir Gawain
and the Green Knight (London 1965), p. 42ff.
277. artycles: the reading in most MSS; it makes more sense than vertus.
290–91. The inclusion is based on LFC and B.
294ff. 1 John 4: 20–21, 'If a man say, I love God, and hateth his brother, he is a liar:
for he that loveth not his brother whom he hath seen, how can he love God whom
he hath not seen? And this commandement have we from him, That he who loveth
God love his brother also.'
299. pure: 'poor'.
301. Both sleghte and sleghenes (see OED Sleight and Slyness) usually in ME have a

that wysses us to be warre with wathes of the werlde, for it kennes us
to knawe the gud and the ill and alswa to sundire the tane fra the tother,
and for to leve that es evyll and take to the gude, and of twa gud
thynges for to chese the better. The sexte vertue es strenghe or stalworthnes noghte anely of body bot of herte and will, evynly to suffire
the wele and the waa, welthe or wandreth, whethire-so betyde, and
that our herte be noghte to hye for na welefare ne overmekill undir
for nane evyllfare, bot styffely for to stande agaynes our faas whethir
310 thay be bodyly or thay be gastely swa that na fulle fandynge make us
to falle ne be false in oure faythe agaynes God Almyghtty. The sevend
vertue and the laste es methe or methefulnes that kepes us fra owterage
and haldes us in evenhede, lettes fulle lykynge and luste of the flesche
and yemes us fra yernynges of werldly gudes and kepes in clennes of
body and of saule. For methe es mesure and mett of all that we do if
we lyffe skillwysly als the lawe teches.

The sexte thynge and the laste of thase I firste towchede es the seven
hevede or dedly synnes that ilke a man and woman awe for to knawe
to flee and forhewe, for folkes may noghte flee tham bot thay knawe
320 thaym: pride and envye, wreth and glotonye, covetyse and slouthe,
and lecherye. And forthi er thay callede seven hevede synnes for that
all other commes of thaym: and forthi ere thay callede dedely synnes
for thay gastely slaa ilke manes and womann's saule that es haunkede
in alle or in any of thaym. Wharefore the wyese man byddes in his
buke: 'Als fra the face of the neddyre fande to flee syn'; for als the
venym of the neddir slaas manes body swa the venym of syn slaas
manes saule.

The firste of thise seven synnes es callede pryde, that es a lykande
heghenes of a manes herte of offyce or of heghe state or other noblaye
330 that he outher haves of kynde or of grace or he hopes that he haves

318. synnes: synn̄s

---

more derogatory sense such as 'deceit, clever trickery'. But here they are used in the
better sense of Latin *prudentia*.

318. See M. W. Bloomfield, *The Seven Deadly Sins* (Michigan 1952).

325. *Ecclesiasticus* 21: 2. *Ecclesiasticus* or *The Book of Sirach*, the authorship of which
was attributed to Solomon in the Middle Ages, is not usually considered to form a
part of the Anglican Bible. It is an apocryphal book similar in tone and content to
Proverbs and it was frequently quoted in ME texts.

328f. 'which is a self-satisfied elevation of a man's heart as a result of his position,
high rank or other nobility'.

mare than anothir. And of this wikkede synn commes some sere
spyces: boste and avauntynge and unbouxsomnes, despite and ypocrisy
and unschamfulnes, and other that ofte ere sene amanges prowde men.
The secunde dedely synn es hatten envy, that es a sorowe and a syte
of the welefare and a joy of the evyllfare of our even-cristen. Of
whilke synn many spyces sprenges and spredes: ane es hateredyn to
speke or here oghte be spoken that may sown unto gude to thaym
that thay hate; ane other false juggynge or dome of thair dedis, and ay
turne unto evyll that es done to gude; the thirde es bakbyttynge, to
saye behynde tham that we will noghte avowe ne saye before tham—   340
whare noghte anely he that spekes the evyll bot that he that heres it
be spoken es for to blame, for ware thare na herere thare ware na
bakbyttere. The thirde dedly synn or hevede syn es wrethe, that es a
wykkede stirrynge or bollenynge of herte wharefore a man wilnes
for to wreke hym or wykkydly to venge hym appon his evyn-cristyn.
And of this wykkede syn commes stryvynge and flytynge with many
false athes and many foule wordes, sclaunder for to fordo a man's gude
fame, feghtynge and felony and ofte manes-slaughter, and many ma
than nowe es nede for to be nevenede. The ferthe dedely synn men
calles glotonye, that es ane unskilwyse lykynge or lufe in taste or in   350
takynge of mete or of drynke. And thise trespas men duse apponne
sere wyse: ane es outher overarely or overlate or overoftesythe for
to ete or drynke bot if nede gere it; ane other es for to lyffe overdelycately; the thirde es for to ete or drynke overmekyll; the ferthe es
overhastely to ete or to drynke; the fifte es to compas and caste appon
whate wyese we may gette dylicious metis or drynkes to fulfill the
lykynges and the lustes of the flesch other than we may gudly lede our
lyffe with. *Unde versus: prepropere, laute, nimis, ardenter, studiose.* The

---

332. and (1): and | and   333. unschamfulnes (*sic* LFC, B): unhamlynes
349. than (*sic* LFC): that
358. *Unde* (*sic* LFC): Sonde; *prepropere*: preproper'

331ff. Although the sins which formed the seven deadly sins had become regula-
rized by now, their branches are very varied in the extant writings. For a different
selection of branches *cf. The Book of Vices and Virtues*, ed W. Nelson Francis (London
1942), p. 10ff. Cf. also their portrayal in medieval art in A. E. M. Katzenellenbogen,
Allegories of the Virtues and Vices (London 1939), p. 63ff.
358. LFC contains several Latin quotations introduced by *Unde versus*, but in the
Sermon they have usually been put in with the chapter implicits and explicits and so
are omitted in this edition. This particular quotation is an exception. It means 'Whence

fyfte dedly syn es callede covetyse, that es a wrangwyse wylnynge or
360 yernynge to have any maner of gude that us awe noghte. And this es
donne pryncypally appon twyn wyese: ane es wrangwysely to get
anythynge that our lykynge or our lufe lyghtes apon als be sacrelege or
by symony, falsehede or okyr or other gelery whilke thise worldely
men er wounte for to use that castes thaire conaundenes swa unto
covetyse that thay ne rekke whether it be with ryghte or with wrange
bot that thay may gette that at thair herte yernes. Another es wrang-
wisely to halde that at es getyn, that es when we will noghte do to
Godd Almyghten ne till Haly Kyrke ne till our even-crystyn that us
awe for to do by dett and by lawe, bot anely haldes that we hafe for
370 ese of ourselfen, whare noghte anely he that wrangwysely getes bot
he that wrangwysly haldes falles in the synn. The sexte dedly synn es
slewthe or slawenes, that es a hertly angere or anoye till us of any
gastely gud that we sall do. And of this wikkede synn comes sere
spyces: ane es latesomnes or lyte, to drawe apon lenghte or to lache
any gude dedis that we sall do that may turne us till helpe or hele of
oure saules; another es a dullnes or hevenes of herte that lettes us for
to lufe oure Lorde Gode Almyghten or any lykynge to hafe in his
servyse; the thirde es ydillchip that overmekyll es hauntede, that makes
[men] lathe to begynn any gude dedis and lyghtly dose us to leve when
380 oghte es begun, and thare whare we ere kyndely borne for to swynke
als the feule es kyndely brede for to flie, it haldes us evermare in ese
agayne our kynde: for idillnes es enemy to cristen-man saule, stepmodire and stamerynge agaynes gude thewes, and witter wyssynge and
waye till alkyn vices. The sevend dedely syn es hatten lychery, that es a
foule lykynge or luste of the flesche. And of this foule syn comes many

the verse: precipitately, sumptuously, too much, eagerly, zealously.' Each of these
five adverbs formed the basis of the five points mentioned immediately above. The
verse is found in Thoresby's Latin text and in Pecham's original instructions.

380. *Cf. Job* 5: 7, 'Yet man is born unto trouble, as the sparks fly upward'. But the
equivalent Vulgate verse reads *Homo nascitur ad laborem, et avis ad volatum*, 'A man is
born to toil, and a bird to flight'.

381. Because man is born to toil, idleness perverts his true nature by encouraging
him not to work.

382. *stepmodire*: the derogatory sense of this word is common in the later Middle
Ages. It is a translation of the Latin *noverca* which was used frequently in a metapho-
rical sense by Matthew of Vendôme; see E. P. Hammond, *English Verse between
Chaucer and Surrey* (Durham, N.C. 1927), p. 448. The sense of 'hesitation' for *stamerynge*
developed from the meaning 'faltering', but it is not common.

sere spyces; ane es fornycacyon, a fleschly synn betwyxe ane anlypy
man and ane anlypy woman—and forthi that it [es] agaynes the lawe
and the leve and the lare that Haly Kirke haldes, it es dedly syn to
thaym that it duse; another es avowtry, and that es spousebreke whether
it be bodyly or it be gastely, that grevosere and gretter es than the 390
tother; the thirde es incest, that es when a man synnes fleschely with
any of his sybb-frendes or any other that es of his affynyte gastely or
bodyly whether-so it be. Other spyces many sprynges of this syn that
overmekill es knawen and kende in this werlde with thaym that ledes
thair lyfe als thair flesche yernes.

Thise are the sex thynges that I hafe spoken off that the lawe of Haly
Kirke lyes maste in, the whilke we er halden to knawe and to cun if
we sall knawe God Almyghty and come till his blysse. And for to
gyffe yow better wyll for to cun thaym oure fadir the beschope graun-
tes of his grace fourty dayes of pardoun till all that cunnes thaym and 400
ratyfyes alswa that other men gyffes, swa mekill coveites he the hele
of your saules. For yife ye conandely knawe thise sex thynges thurgh
thaym sall ye cun knawe Godd Almyghty whaym, als Sayne John
sayse in his gospelle, cunnandely for to knawe swylke als he es it es
endles lyfe and lastande blysse. To the whilke blysse he brynge us,
our Lorde Gode Almyghty. Amen, amen, amen.

*Per Dominum nostrum, Jesum Christum, qui cum Deo patre et Spiritu
Sancto vivit et regnat omnipotens deus in secula seculorum. Amen, amen,
amen.*

407. *patre*: patri   408. *regnat*: rignat

---

400. Thoresby granted an indulgence of forty days to all who knew his catechism.
Indulgences and pardons were of course to become a subject of bitter debate at a later
date.

400. After *thaym*, LFC 568 includes *Or dos thair gode diligence for to kun tham.*

403. *John* 17: 3, 'And this is life eternal, that they might know thee the only true
God, and Jesus Christ, whom thou hast sent.'

407ff. 'Through our Lord, Jesus Christ, who with God the father and the Holy
Ghost lives and reigns as almighty god world without end.' The Latin is not found
in LFC.

V   The Abbey of the Holy Ghost

This piece is extant in many manuscripts, of which the most important are: Bodley MS. Laud 210 (c. 1370) [L]; the Vernon manuscript (*cf.* VI) [B]; the Thornton manuscript (*cf.* IV) [T]; Columbia University Library MS. Plimpton 263 (c. 1440); and Lambeth Palace Library MS. 432 (fifteenth century). A modified version was printed by de Worde c. 1496. Although in the Lambeth MS. it is attributed to Rolle, it is now accepted that this text is at best a translation from French by one of his followers. Indeed the translation was probably made in the South rather than the North, for it appears in a northern dialect only in T. Its date of composition can be placed between 1350 and 1370. In some manuscripts it is found with a piece called *The Charter of the Abbey of the Holy Ghost*, though this is almost certainly the work of a different author; the two pieces are amalgamated in some manuscripts and in de Worde's print. The French text from which the *Abbey* is derived exists in at least three versions: (i) British Museum MS. Add 39843 [A] and other MSS.; (ii) British Museum MS. Royal 16 E xii [R] and other MSS.; and (iii) Bodley MS. Douce 365 [D], copied by David Aubert 1475 probably for Margaret of Burgundy. The English text is closest to R, though it also has points of similarity with D.

The traditional psychomachia in which vices and virtues were personified and engaged in combat found its expression in England in the thirteenth century in such works as *Sawles Warde* and Robert Grosseteste's *Château d'Amour*. At least four translations and adaptations into English of Grosseteste's work were executed. The *Abbey* continues this tradition forward into the fourteenth century. However, as a manual of piety for those who were unable to enter a monastery or nunnery, it may be compared with the English translation of the *Speculum Vitae* and Walter Hilton's *Epistle on the Mixed Life*. The moral exhortation is only of the most general kind and does not amount to a practical guide to the conduct of life.

The present text is based on L.

Editions: C. Horstmann, *Yorkshire Writers*. Vol. 1 (London 1895). [T]
G. G. Perry, *Religious Pieces in Prose and Verse*. Rev. edn. EETS o.s. 26 (London 1914). [T]

This is the Abbey of the Holy Gost that is founden in a place that is clepud concience.

My dere brother and sister, I se weel that many wolde ben in
religioun but they mowe nowt for poverte or for awe or for drede of
her kyn or for bond of maryage. Therfore I make here a book of
relygyoun of the herte, that is of the Abbey of the Holy Goost, that
all tho that mow nout been in bodylyche relygyon mow been in
gostly.

A Jesu, mercy! Where may thys abbey and this relygyoun best
been ifounden? Sertus, never so weel no so semely as in a place that is   10
clepud concyence. Now behoveth it thanne at the begynny[n]ge that the
place of the concyence be clensed thorow wyse clensynge. The Holy
Goost schal senden ii maydens wel connende: that on is clepud Ryght-
wysnesse; that other is cleped Love-of-clennesse. These two schul
casten out fro the concyence and fro the herte all maner filthes of foule
thoutes and foule yernyggys. Whanne the place of concyence is wel
iclensed, than schal the foundement be made large and dep. And this
schal twey maydens maken: that on is cleped Meknesse that schal
maken the foundement dep thorow lownesse of herself; that other is
cleped Poverte that maketh it large and wyde aboven that casteth   20
out of the herte al that is of erthelyche thynges and wordly thoutes
that thow they have erthely goodes with love they no fast nought
her hertes on hem. And thyse been icleped pouere in spirit; of wyche
God speketh in the gospel and seyth that her is the kyngdoom of
hevene; 'Beati,' inquit, 'pauperes spiritu.' Blessed is thanne the relygyon
that is yfounded in poverte and mekenesse. That is ayeyn many relygyouce that been coveytouse and proude. This abbey schal also be set
on a good ryver: it is the more at ese and more delysyous. On swyche
a ryver was the Maudeleyn yset and ifonded. The[r]fore grace and

10. no (ne B): nō   18. maydens: mayndens
25. inquit: inquid

---

3. The French texts are addressed to a 'sister' only; and the work may originally
have been written for a woman since the abbey is staffed by nuns.

16. yernyggys: There are several words in this MS in which ME ng is represented
by gg.

21. wordly: that is, 'worldly'; cf. l. 284.

24-5. Matthew 5: 3, 'Blessed are the poor in spirit: for theirs is the kingdom of
heaven.' The inquit is found only in L.

28. ryver: B reads here ryveer of teeres, for everi citee and abbey that ben set on goode
rivieres ben the more at ese . . . , which represents the French more closely. The river is
the river of tears or repentance.

29. In French tradition the Mary Magdalen with Lazarus, Martha and others brought

D

30 rychesse of werkus com fully to here wylle. Therfor seyth Seynt
David: '*Fluminis impetus letificat civitatem Dei;*' that is to seyn, 'The
goode ryver that maketh the syte lykende of God,' for it is clene and
syker and ryche of alle goodes and marchaundyses. Ryght so the ryver
of teres clenseth Godys cyte, that is mannes sowle that is Goddes
ce[t]e, as the holy men seyn that the fylthe of synne departeth ryches
of vertues and of alle goode thewes.

Whan this foundement is made than schal come Damisele Buxomnesse on that on half and Damyselle Mysericord on that other half for
to resen the walles on heygh and maken hem stalworthe wit a fre
40 herte largelyche yyvy[n]g to the pouere and to the meseyse. For whan
we doon any good dede of charite thorow grace of good entent, as
many goode stones we leighen on oure housyng in the blysse of
hevene ifastened togederes wit the love of God and of oure evene-
cristene. We reden that Salomon made hys housyng of grete precyouse
stones. Theyse precyouse stones ben almesdedes [and] holy werkes that
schullen been bounden togederes wit quiclym of love and stedfast
byleve. Therfore seyth David: '*Omnia opera eius in fide;*' that is to seyn,
'Al hys werkes ben don in stedfast beleve.' And as a wal may nowt
lasten wytouten syment or morter, ryght so no werk[es] that we doon
50 aryn nought worth to God ne notful for oure sowles bot they been
done in the love of God and in trewe beleve. Therfor all that we
synful doon ys lorn tyl we amenden us.

Christianity to Provence. There she dwelt in a cave, La Sainte Baume, high in the
Maritime Alps; it is still a place of pilgrimage. Because the 'sinner' of *Luke* 7: 37 was
identified as the Magdalen, she became for later Christians the prototype of all peni-
tents. The river is to be understood allegorically as the Magdalen's tears.

30. *Seynt*: this form probably arose from a misreading of *seyt(h)*.

30–2. *Ps.* 46: 4, 'There is a river, the streams whereof shall make glad the city of
God'.

35. *departeth*: 'extracts'; sins lead to penance and hence bring the best out of virtuous
people.

42. *oure housyng*: our spiritual home in heaven. By our good deeds on earth we
build our home in heaven; *cf.* the OE *Phoenix* ll. 451–69.

43. *ifastened*: the bricks of our good deeds which build our heavenly home are
'fastened' with the mortar of love; *cf.* ll. 45–51. This same interaction between good
deeds and love plays a prominent part in *Piers Plowman*.

44. *2 Chronicles* 3.

47. *Ps.* 33: 4, 'and all his works are done in truth'. For the need of love and charity
to accompany one's good deeds *cf.* IV, 279ff.

Sithen Damysel Suffrounce and Damisele the Fort shullen reysen up the pelers and undersetten hem so stedfastly and so stalworthly that no wynd of wordus no of angres ne of gostlyche fondynggus ne of fleshelyche lust, the inner no the uttere, may hym doun casten. After this byhoveth the cloyster be made of foure corners, for-why it is cleped 'cloyster' for it closeth and steketh and warly schal been loken. My dere brother and syster, yyf thow wylt holde the in gostly rely-gyoun and be in rest of soule and in swetnesse of herte, hold the witinne and steke thy yates and so warly kepe the wardes of thi cloyster that non uttere fondyngus no innere mowe have any entre to make thi cylence to breke or stere the to synne. Steke thyn eyghen fro fowle syghtes, thyn eren fro fowle herynges, thy mouth fro foule speches and fro unclene lauters, and thyn herte fro foule thoutus. 60

Shrifte schal make the chapetere-hous, Predicacioun the freytour, Orisoun the chapel, Contemplacioun the dortour, that schal be reysed an hey wit hye yernynggus and wit love-quikyngus to God. Con-templacioun is a devoute rysyng up of the herte: wit brennende love to God to dwelle, and of his dylycys fretheren his soule and sumdel tasten of the swettenesse that Godys chosen schullen have in hevene. 70 Reufulnesse schal be the fermorye, Devocioun the seler; Meditacioun schal maken the gerner. And wan the houses of offyse been made, than behoveth it that the Holy Gost sette the covente of grace and of vertues. Than schal the Holy Gost [come], that is of this relygyoun wardeyn and vysitour, wiche God the Fader foundede thorow his

---

64. fowle (1): fowlo   **67.** Contemplacioun: Comtemplacioun
70. his soule (*sic* T): his halle L, his halewes B

---

53. *the Fort*: 'the strong'. Other English MSS read simply *Fort*, and A, R and D have *Force*. Possibly *Damoiselle Force* was read as *Damoisel le Force*.

55. *wynd of wordus*: that is, force of quarrels or angry words; *cf.* R *vent de tribulacion ou de temptacion*.

58. *cloyster*: ultimately derived from Lat. *claustrum* 'a bar, lock', *cloister* means 'an enclosed place', and hence 'a monastery'. The parallel between ll. 58 and 61 is much closer in D which reads: *doibt estre cloz* (58) . . . *tiens toy close* (61).

61. *yates*: the fives senses, the gates to the body; *cf.* VII, 175.

70. All the scribes had difficulty with this passage and it is impossible to decide what the original reading might have been since the French MSS are no help here. Translate 'and to comfort his soul with the joys of God'.

72. *be*: this is a change in the allegory; one would expect *make*, as in T.

73. *houses of offyse*: those parts of a nunnery set aside for domestic functions; allegorically the human body.

myght. As Davit seyth: '*Fundavit eam altissimus;*' that is, 'The heye
God hath made hit.' The Sone rewleth it, the Holy Gost keput it and
visiteth it; and that synge we in Holy Churche: '*Veni, creator spiritus,*
80 *mentes tuorum;*' that is, 'Com thow God, Holy Gost, the hertes of thyne
thow visite and felle hem with thi grace.'

The goode Lefdy Charite, as sche is most worthy byforn all othere,
schal been abbesse of this holy abbey. And as they that been in relygyoun nothyng schal doon no seggen no goon into no stede no take
no yyve witouten leve of the abbesse, ryght so gostlyche schal non of
swyche thyngus be doon witouten leve of Charite. For thus comaun-
deth Seynt Poule: '*Omnia vestra in carit[at]e fiant;*' that is, 'Watso ye
do or seye or thenk wit herte, al ye mote doon in love.' A dere brother
and soster, wat here is hard comaundement: but yt is notful for oure
90 soules that oure thoughtus and oure wordes and oure werkes be only
doon for love and in the love of God. Weylawey, yyf I dar saye, for
many been in religioun and to fewe relygyous, that don nought after
the comaundement of Seynt Poule no after the counsel of the gode
Lefdy Charite that is abbesse of this sely relygyoun. And therefore
they leson mechel tyme of her mede and eken gretlyche here peyne
bot they amenden hem.

Therfore, leve brother and syster, beth everemore waker and war
and in youre werkes all thenketh bysylyche whatso ye doon that it be
doon in the love of God and for his love. The Levedy Wysdom schal
100 been pryouresse for sche is worthy—*nam prior omni[um] creata est
sapiencia;* that is, 'Alther ferst was wisdom ymaked.' And thorow the
lore and the counsel of this pryouresse we scholden doon al that we

---

84. schal: schol   **86.** swyche: schyche

---

77. *Ps.* 87: 5, 'and the highest himself shall establish her' (i.e. Zion). The translation
given in L is not exact since L may have omitted a few lines here; the other MSS include
a quotation from *Romans* 13: 1 at this point.

79–80. One of the great hymns of the Church, used at Whitsun; its authorship is
uncertain. B provides the full text of the first stanza: *Veni, creator spiritus, mentes tuorum
visita, imple superna gracia que tu creasti pectora,* which is the basis of L's translation.
Cf. l. 336, and see J. Julian, *A Dictionary of Hymnology,* 2nd edn. (London 1907), p.
1206ff. See also A. Wilmart, *Auteurs spirituels et textes dévots* (Paris 1932), pp. 37–45.

87. *1 Corinthians* 16: 14, 'Let all your things be done with charity.'

95. The *mede* is heavenly bliss, the *peyne* the torment of hell.

98. *all:* 'entirely'.

100. *Ecclesiasticus* 1: 4, 'Before them all was wisdom created'.

don. And thus seyt Davyd: '*Omnia in sapiencia tu fecisti;*' that is,
'All that thou hast made thow hast it made avisylyche.' The good
Lefdy Mekenesse, that ever maketh herself ilyche lowe and under all
othere, schal ben suppriouresse; hyr schalt thow onouren and worchepe
wit buxomnesse.

A Jesu, blessed is that abbey and sely ys that relygyoun that hath
so holy an abbesse as Charite, pryouresse as Wysdom, suppryouresse as
Mekenesse. A dere brother and syster, blessed and sely been tho, that 110
is to seyen the sowles been sely, that holden the comaundement of the
abbesse, Levedy Charyte, the techyng of the pryouresse, Lefdy
Wysdom, the counsel of the suppryouresse, Lefdy Mekenesse. For who
ys buxom to the thre lefdyghs and hys lyf reulyth after her techyngus,
the Fader, the Sone, the Holy Gost hem schal counforten wyt many
gostlyche joyes, and hem helpen and socouren in all here fondyngus
and angeres that they been nought overcomen; ne thar hem nought
dreden non wrenches no non wyles of the fende for God ys wyt hem
and stondeth by as a trewe kempe and strong. And thus seyth Davyd:
'*Dominus protector vite mee, a quo trepidabo?*'; as yyf he seyde: 'God, 120
my champyoun stalworth and trewe, that for me, that am so feble
and so unmyghtful, ayeynus myn ennemys hath undertaken for to
fyten, whom schulde I thanne dreden? Treuly noon.' We reden in
a bok of *Daniel* that a myghtful kyng was that men clepede Nabugodo-
nozor that sette in hys rewme thre men that schulden doon and ordeynen and stablen as baylyes of the reume so that the kyng herde no
noyse no pleynt, bot that he myght be in pees and in reste in hys
[reaume]. Also the reaume that these iii bayles been inne and relygyoun
that these thre preletes been inne, that is Charyte, Wysdom and Mekenesse, ther is pees, reste and lykyng in sowle and counfort in lyf. 130

Damysele Descrecioun that is wytty and byfore-war schal be tresou-
resse. She schal have in kepyng al and bysylyche loken that al goo wel.

Orisoun schal be chaunteresse that wit hertly preyers schal travaylen

---

103. *Omnia* (*sic* T, B): Omnis   **133.** travaylen: trawaylen

---

103. *Ps.* 104: 24, 'O Lord, how manifold are thy works! in wisdom hast thou made
them all.'

110. *tho*: *cf. nonnains* (D and R).

114. *lefdyghs*: 'ladies'; L contains some words spelt with a *gh* (MS 3) usually after
a long *i*; *cf.* also *wyghn* 'wine' and *lyghf* 'life'.

119–20. *Ps.* 27: 1, 'The Lord is the strength of my life; of whom shall I be afraid?'

124. *Daniel* 2: 49.

day and nyght. What Orisoun is the holy man seyth: '*Oracio est Deo sacrificium, angelis solacium, diabolo tormentum;*' that is to seyn: 'Orisoun is an holy preyer to God, solas and lykyng to aungels, and torment to the feendes.' It wyttenesseth in the *Lyghf of Seynt Bartolmew* that it is torment to the fend whan the feend cryede and seyde to hym: '*Bartillomew, incendunt me oraciones tue;*' that ys to seyn, 'Bartolmew, thy pre-
140 yers brennen me.' That it is lykyng to aungels Seynt Austeyn bereth wytnesse and seyght: 'Whan whe preyen wit devocioun of herte to God, the aungelys stonden aforn us daunsynge and pleyynge and beryng up our preyers and maken hem present to the Fader of hevene. The wyche preyers our Lord comendeth to be wryten in book of lyghf.' That it is sacrifice to God—ye, and on of thoo that hym most pleseth—therfor he axeth it us and seyt: '*Sacrificium laudis honorificabit me;*' that is, 'Thow schalt worschepe me wit sacrifice of lovynge.' Jubilacion, here felawe, schal helpen. What jubilacioun ys Seynt Gregore telleth and seyght that jubilacioun is a gret joye that is consey-
150 ved in teres thorow brennende love of spyryght that may nought be alle owt schewed noyther al hyd. As it falleth somtyme of tho that God hertly loveth: ye, after that they han been in orisoun, they been so lykyng in God that whereso they been her hertes synggen mornyng-songes of love-longynge to here lef, that they yernen wyt armes of love semly to klyppe and wyt gostly menyngus of hys gladnesse swetly to kysse—and somtyme so deeply that wordes hem wanteth;

136. *preyer*: B and T read *sacrifice* to bring the translation into line with the Latin; *cf*. l. 145.

137. *Cf*. XI, 188*ff*. Little is known of St. Bartholomew except that he was called to be one of the twelve apostles. He is traditionally described as the prophet to Armenia and India. His day is August 24 and one version of his life is printed in *Acta Sanctorum*, August, vol. 5.

140. St. Augustine (354–430), Bishop of Hippo in North Africa and one of the foremost doctors of the Church, is frequently cited as an authority by medieval writers.

143. *maken hem present*: 'make a present of them'.

146-7. *Ps*. 50: 23, 'Whoso offereth praise glorifieth me.' The *honorificabit* is the Vulgate reading, but B and T have *honorificabis*, which is the basis of the translation in L.

148. *Jubilacion, here felawe, schal helpen*: In A and R this line follows l. 134 and the sense is: Jubilation, the companion of Orison, shall help (her to sing praises to God).

149. Gregory the Great, pope from 590 to 604, is another frequently quoted father of the early Church; *cf*. *Moralia* 28: 15.

155. *menyngus*: a rare form meaning 'mournings', see OED *Meaning*, vbl. sb.[2] V reads *moones of his goodnesse*, and T *mourny[n]ge of his gudnes*.

for love-longynge so ferforth ravyscheth here hertes that somtyme they ne wyte what they doon.

Devocioun ys seleresse that kepeth the wynes, bothe whyte and rede, wyt depe thowtes of the goodnesse of God and of the peynes 160 and of the angusches that he soffred and of the joye and the delycys of Paradys that he hath greythed to hys chesoun.

Penaunce schal be cosyner wit gret bysynesse and travayle and peynus bothe day and nyght for to paye for all, and ofte swetyn wyth bytter terres for anger of her synnes. Yhe maketh gode metes, that is many byttere sorowes, al for here gylt; and these metes feden the sowle. But sche spareth herself thorow abstinence and eteth but lytul. For do sche nevere so mykel no so manyfold of goode werkes alwey she holdeth herself unworthy and synful.

And Temperaunce [serveth] in the freytour so that echon loketh 170 that mesure be overalle, that non overmechel no overlytel ete no drynke. Sobornesse redeth at the bord the lyghf of holy fadres and redeth hem what lyghf they ledden here on erthe, for to taken good ensaunple to do as they deden and therethorow swyche mede to wynne as they have.

Pytee is pytauncer that doth of gode al that sche may; and Mercy, her sister, is aumener that yiveth al and can nowt holden to herself.

The Levedy Drede is porter that kepeth bysyly the yate and the cloyster of the herte and of the concyence, that chaseth out all unthewes and cleput in alle goode vertuus and so spereth the yates of the cloyster 180 and the wyndowes that noon evel have entre into the herte thorow the yates of the mought, non thorow the wyndows of the eyen no of the eres.

Honeste ys mayster of the nonnes that techeth hem al corteseye: how they scholen speke or goo, sitte or stonde, how they schollen beren hem witouten, how in, [how] to God and how to man so that al, that hem seen, of hem may taken ensaunple of alle goodnesse.

---

174. do: god

---

164. *swetyn*: understand 'she shall' from the previous clause.

172*ff.* Most monastic rules enjoined that a passage from scriptures or from some moral work should be read during meals; this is why *Predication* made the dining-hall, l. 66.

176. A pittancer was the officer in charge of distributing the pittances; *cf.* l. 254.

182–3. *Cf.* l. 61 and VII, 175.

184. *nonnes*: R, D, T and V read 'novices' here.

Damysel Corteyseye schal been osteler that yhe comynge or goynge schal reseyven heendly so that echon mow speke good of her. And for
190 os meche as non schal been by herselvyn alone among the gestis, for it myght falle that Damysele Cortesye schold ben overbold and over-hardy, therfore sche schal have to felaw Damysel Symplesse. For these to alyed togederes thorow felawchype been syker and semande, for that on witouten that other somtyme is lytel worth, for overgret simplesse may maken overmikel symplete or overlytel, and overgret curteseye may maken overfayr semblant or overglad or overbold for to pay gestes. But fayr and wel and witouten doute of blame mow thei do her offyce bothe togeder.

Damisel Resoun schal be purveyresse that schal ordeyne witouten
200 and witinne so skilfully that ther be no defaute.

Damysel Leaunce schal be fermoresse that schal travaylen abowte and besely serve the syke. And for in the fermorie of this relygyoun be mo syke than hole, mo feble than stalworthe, and over here myghte hem alone for to serven, therfore schal sche have to felawe Damysele Largesse that schal doon the fulle to everycheon after that hem nedeth.

Damycele connyng and wys that is cleped Meditacioun is gerneter. Sche schal gedren and assemblen good wete and other goode cornns togeder, and that fully and that plente, thorow whyche alle the leve-dyghs of the hous mown have here sustynaunce. Meditacioun is good
210 thowtes of God and of hys werkes, of hys wordes and of [hys] crea-toures, of hys peynes that he suffrede, and of his herte-love that he hadde and hath to us for whom he tholed deth. Thys gerner hadde the goode kyng Davyd for he was alwey ryche and in plente. Therfore he seyth in the Sauter: 'In omnibus [operibus] tuis meditabor;' that ys as yyf he seyde: I have alwey [my thowt] deply in thy werkes. And in

---

203. feble: fleble   **207.** gedren (sic V, T): gendren

---

188. yhe: here best understood as 'you'. Translate 'who shall graciously receive you when you come and go.' Cf. A et recevra les alanz et les venanz lieement.

201. Leaunce: Loyalty; cf. V Leaute, D Loialte. The fermoresse was the nun in charge of the infirmary.

203-4. 'It is beyond her strength to nurse them by herself.'

205. the fulle: 'as much as possible'.

206. gerneter: officer in charge of the nuns' granary.

213. ryche: that is in spiritual things, with general reference to the meditations found in the psalms.

214. Ps. 77: 12.

other stede he seyght: '*In lege Domini meditabor die ac nocte*;' that is, 'Lord, in thi lawe I thenke nyght and day.' This ys the begynnyng of all perfeccioun that man se[t] stably hys herte to thenke deeply in God and in hys werkes, for ofte it is beter a good thought in holy medytacion than many wordes seyde in preyer. Ofte it falleth that the 220 herte ys so overcomen and so ravysched in holy medytacion that wot not what he doth, hereth or seth; so deply is hys herte set and fastned in God and in hys werkes that wordes hem wanteth. And the styller that he is in swyche meditacions the ludder he cryeth in Godus erus. Thus seyth David: '*Quoniam tacui dum clamarem tota die*;' as yif he seyde: Lord, therwyl-as myn herte was in dep thowtes of the and of thy werkes and cryede on the in holy meditacions, I was stylle os a dombe thyng. And ther seyth the glose: the grete cryes that we cryen to God been oure grete desyres and our grete yernyggus. And thus seyth Seynt Denys that wanne the herte is lyft op and ravysched to the love 230 of God wyt jelouse yernyng, he no may noght comen wit word that the herte thenketh. This holy meditacion that is a gerner that kepeth the whete, that is red witouten and whyt wytinne and hath the syde cloven, of wyche men maken good bred, that is Jesu Crist that was wytouten reed of hys oune blood and was whyght wytinne thorow mekenesse and tholmodnesse and al maner clennesse of lyghf and hadde hys syde cloven wyt speres dynt. Thys is the bred that we reseiven and seen in the sacrement of the auter.

217. begynnyng (*sic* T, V): regynnyg

---

216. *Ps.* 1: 2, 'But his delight is in the law of the Lord; and in his law doth he meditate day and night.'

220*ff.* The ecstatic state achieved through contemplation, though seemingly without any experience or preparation, may be the sort of danger that the author of VII warned against. Meditation and contemplation (*cf.* ll. 68–72) appear to be the same.

221. *wot*: understand 'he', the person to whom the heart (222) belongs.

225. *Ps.* 32: 3, 'When I kept silence, my bones waxed old through my roaring all the day long.' For the translation *cf.* l. 215.

228. *glose*: probably a mystical commentary on the Psalms; it is referred to simply as a *glose* in the French texts as well. For the place of commentaries in the reading of the Bible see the Introduction.

229–30. The reference is to the Pseudo-Dionysius, a fifth-century Syrian who was mistaken for St. Paul's disciple and martyr, Dionysius of Paris. From A and R it is clear that the reference is to his *De mystica theologia* ch. 3. For his influence on English contemplatives see the Introduction.

237*f.* *Cf.* IV, 226*ff.*

D*

And wel we wyten that the gerner schal been aboven th[e] celer
240 and so schal meditacion been aboven devocion, and therefore Meditacion schal been gerneter and Devocion celerer and Pyte schal been
pytauncer. And of these thre speketh the profeet Davyd, and seyth:
'*A fructu frumenty, vini et olei sui multiplicati sunt;*' that is to seyn, '[Of]
the frught of the whete and wyne and oyle thei ben founded.' In many
places of the old lawe God behoteth to hys chosene these thre. 'Serveth
me weel,' he seyght, 'and Y schal yeve yow plente of whete, of wyne
and of oyle.' Plente of whete [is] to thenkyn on the croys and of the
passyoun of Jesu Crist; and this is meditacion. Plente of wyn, that is
welle of teres, that is welle for to wepen; and that is devocion. Plente
250 of oyle, that is for to have delyt and savour [in God; and that is counfort
for the oyle yiveth odour] to metes and to drynkes and lyghteth in Holy
Churche laumpes. Also whan Goddes servauntes han deply thought
wyt herte on God and on hys werkes wyt love-longyng to hym, than
hath God pyte on hem and sendeth hem pytaunce of counfort and of
gostlyche joye. And this thenketh hym ferst meditacion, and this is the
whete that God byhoteth us, and after the devocion men conceyven
in meditacion. Thanne sendeth Goddes sone after the wyghn of
swete teres. Than sent he the oyle of counfort that yevyt savour and
alyteth hys knowlechyng and sheweth hym of hys privites of hevene,
260 that he hydeth and helyth from tho that folwen fleshlyche yernyngus
and yyven hem to the wysdom of this world and of hys fantesyes.
And wyche that been trewe Godys servauntes, he so enflaumeth hem
wit the blase of hys love that they tasten somdel and felyn hou swete,
hou gode, hou lovynge [it is], but nought all fullyche, for I trowe that

---

243. seyn: *erased in L*   245. chosene (*sic* T, V): cosyne
254. of (1): oof   256. men conceyven: conceyven men
262. he: ho

---

243. *Ps.* 4: 7, 'Thou hast put gladness in my heart, more than in the time that their corn and their wine increased.'

250-51. The omission, common to L and V, is supplied from T.

254. A pittance was a gift or bequest to an abbey to provide wine etc. for festivals or for anniversaries; the word came to be applied to the food and drink itself.

255-7. 'At first this resembles meditation, which is the wheat God promises us, and afterwards devotion which men acquire through meditation.' It is devotion which is the wine of sweet tears. The passage is difficult in all MSS, and this seems the best solution.

noon myght fullyche felon it that his herte ne scholde berste for lykyng of joye.

Seynt Austyn telleth of a prest that whan he herde anythyng of lykyng that were of God, he wolde so be ravysched in joye that he wolde fallen adoun and lygge as he wer ded; and so that tyme yif me leyde brennend fer to hys naked lyche he felt it nought na more than   270 a ded cors. Seynt Bernard speketh up these wordes of Joop ther he seyght thus: '*Abscondit lucem in manibus;*' that is that God hath lyght in hys hondis. Ye weteth wel he that a candel lyght bytwene hys hondes, he may hyden it and schewen hyt at hys wylle. So doth oure Lord God to hys chosene: whan he woll he openet hys hondes and lyghtyth to hem that loven hym wit hevenelyche gladyngus; and whan he wol he closyth hys handes and wytdrawet that lykynge and that counfort, for he wol not that he fele hyt here. But here he yyvyt hyt hym as for to tasten and to savouren sumdel how swete he is. As Davyd seyght: '*Gustate et videte quoniam suavis est Dominus;*' as yif God seyde to us: 280 By this confort and thys lykynge that thou, that this schort tyme hast, of me thou myght tasten and felen how gode, how swete I am to my chosene in my blyssede world wytouten ende. And this he doth for to drawen us fro wordly bysynes and lykyng and for to enflaumen our hertes wyt love-yernyggus for to wynne and for to have lykyng of that joye al at fulle in body and in soule wyt hym for to be evere wythouten ende.

An damysele wys and wel-itaut that men klepyn Jelusye, that is evere waker and bysye evere ylyche wele for to done, yhe schal kepe the orlage and schal wakyn thys othere levedys and maken hem erly   290 for to rysen quiclyche to serven God. Ther is orlage in toune that

288. An: And

---

271. St. Bernard of Clairvaux was one of the early members of the Cistercian order and was principally responsible for its rapid growth. The passage commented on is *Job* 36: 32. The *up* means 'upon'. *Cf.* also the associated image in Hilton's *Scale of Perfection* ii. 32 of a man seeing light through his eye-lids.

278. *here*: in this world.

280. *Ps.* 34: 8, 'O taste and see that the Lord is good.'

281. Worldly life is short, but it is sufficient to gain a foretaste of heaven.

289. *yhe*: 'she', a tautologous subject.

291. *orlage*: the bell in the nunnery.

291. *toune*: here 'manor' or 'farm'.

waketh men to rysen to bodyly travayles and that is the cok; and
ther is oralage in cyte that waketh marchaundes to weenden abowten
her marchaundyse and that is the wayte that blouet day; and ther is
orlage in relygyon that waketh the covent to matyns; and ther is
orlage of contemplacion and that is of thys holy relygyoun that is
fonded of the Holy Gost, and this is gelowseye and this savour of
perfeccion. And ofte it falleth in relygyoun that byfornhond er the
orlage rynge Godes gostly servountes been longe wakyng byforn
300 and han wepte tofor God and han waschen hem wyt here teres, and her
spyrytes been styred wyt devout preyers and gostly counfort. And
why rysen they so erlyche? Trewly, for the orlage of love and Jeluseye
hath wakyd hem byforn that the orlage falleth.

A dere brother and syster, blessed ben the soules that the love of
God and the longynge maketh for to waken that they ne slombere
nought no slepyn in sleuthe of flescelyche lust. Therefore he seyth
in the *Cantykly*: '*Ego dormio et cor meum vigilat*;' that is 'Wyl I slepe
bodyly my flessh for to esen and to resten, my soule is evere wakynge in
jelusie and in love-longynge to God.' The soule that thus waketh to
310 God me thynketh wyth hole conscyence that worldly men thenken,
and is this: '*Jeo ay le quer a* [c]*loche*[*tes*] *revelé pur amours*;' that ys, 'Myn
herte ys stert fro me ywaked wyt love.' What is that that maketh
the herte to sterte fro the flesh and foryet it as it fremd were to hym?
Trewly, jelusye wyt love-terus and mornyng wyt love-longynge
conseyved in devout uprysyng of herte.

Whan this abbey was in al thyng wel ordeynt and God wel served in
reste and in lykynge and in pes of soule, than cam a tyraunt of the

294. Most municipalities employed a watchman or watchmen, whose duties included announcing the hours, by blowing on some wind-instrument. So translate
that blouet day 'which signals the dawn by blowing their trumpets'; *cf.* A *qui corne le
jour.*

307. *Song of Solomon* 5: 2, 'I sleep, but my heart waketh.' In the Vulgate this biblical
book is known as *Canticum Canticorum*, hence ME *Cantykly*. The text was used by
Rolle as the theme of his treatise *Ego Dormio*, also found in B.

309–11. The sense of this sentence is difficult in all the English MSS; perhaps translate
'As for that soul which watches for God in this way, it seems to me in entire conscience
what worldly men think, and that is . . .'. The French quotation (probably part of a
lyric; D calls it *une chanson mondaine*) has been corrupted in transmission, *cf.* R *J'ai
un cuer a clochetes resveillie pour bien amer*, in which *clochetes* is the sound of a bell. Instead
of *pur* (for *pour*), B and T have *par*. The use of secular texts for illustrative material
is found more frequently in sermons than in texts of this type.

londe thorow hys power and dede into this holy abbeye foure doutren
that he hadde that weren lothlyche and of evel maners. The fend was
fader of these foure doutern. Than the ferst of thys foule barentem hatte 320
Envye, that other Pride, the thredde is Groching, the ferthe is Fals-
demynge-of-othere. These foure than hath thys tyraund, the fend of
helle, for evel-wylle and malyce doon into this holy abbeye that they
thorow her wykkednesse al the covent greveth and harmeth so that
they no reste no pees myght have, nyght no day, no lykyng in soule.

Whan the good Levedy Wisdom pryourresse and Levedy Mekenesse suppriourresse and other goode levedys of the holy abbey [saw]
that al the abbeye was in poynt to worthe to nought thorow the
wykkednesse of thyse foure doutren, they rongen the chapeter-belle
and asembled hem togyderes and asked counsel wat was best to done. 330
And the Levedy Dyscrecion hem counselde that they scholde all fallen
in preyours to the Holy Gost that of thys abbeye is visytour that he
hye for to comen, as they gret mester hadde, hem for to helpen and
for to visite wyt hys grace. And thei alle at her counsel wyt gret
devocioun of herte songen to the Holy Gost wyt a swete stevene:
'Veni, creator spiritus, mentes tuorum visita, imple.' And also sone the
Holy Gost cam at here yernyggus and hem all counfortede wyt hys
grace and chased out alle the foule wytes, the lothly feendes doutren,
and clensede the abbey of alle her fylthes and ordeynd yt and restored yt
beter than yt was byfore. 340

Now I prey yow all per charite of God that alle tho that of thys
relygyoun reden or heren that they been boxum wyt al her myght and
suffre that these goode levedys byfore nempned don her office eche
day gostlyche wytinne your hertes. And loke ychon bysyly that ye
do no trespas ayeynes the reule no the obedyaunce of thys relygyoun

---

321. Groching: Grochīng

318ff. The four daughters of the devil were created as a counter to the four daughters
of God, Mercy, Truth, Justice and Peace, in much the same way as the seven deadly
sins were opposed to the seven virtues. On the allegory of the four daughters see H.
Traver, The Four Daughters of God (Philadelphia 1907). Note the shift in approach
introduced by this paragraph: present giving way to past, and theoretical allegory to
temporal action. A similar shift is found in Piers Plowman B. xvi.

326. The French texts include Lady Charity here, which is to be expected. No
doubt she was omitted by the original English translator.

336. Cf. ll. 79-81.

and namly of the sovereyns. And yif it thorow any unhap falle that any
of these foure doutern sekyn in any kens wyse to have entre wytinne
youre hertes to duelle, doth after the goode Levedy Discrecion and yif
you to devocion wyt hertly preyers in hope of Godys helpe and of hys
350 socour, and yhe schulle be delyvered thorow the mercy and the grace
of Almyghty God. He it you graunte thorow the besechyng of hys
dere moder, Seynt Marye. Amen.

Here endeth of the Holy Gost.

346. sovereyns (*sic* B): servountes   347. doutern: douterñ

---

346. *sovereyns*: this represents D more closely and refers to the leading nuns such as
Charity, Wisdom and Meekness. The nuns are not to transgress the rule of the order
or to refuse the obedience due to their superiors.

VI   The Life of Adam and Eve

This life is found only in the Vernon manuscript (Bodley MS. Eng. Poet. a 1, c. 1370–80) [B], one of the more famous collections of medieval religious material (cf. III, V). It is possible that it is a prose adaptation made by the scribe of B from the poetic version of the life found in some later versions of the *South English Legendary* (cf. X). It shows greatest similarity with the version found in Trinity College Cambridge MS. 605 [T], though that manuscript is from the fifteenth century. B shows clear signs of a poetic origin, for there are many passages which still contain rhyme words: e.g. 'Wel fayre he departed the derke from the *liht:* liht he cleped the day and the derknesse the *niht.*' At the same time it is equally clear that B is a prose version, for when compared with T there are many instances in which the rhyme could have been kept where it has not been retained. Possibly the prose version existed before the time of B, but since the scribe of B is noted for his editorial changes it is perhaps best to ascribe this piece in its prose form to him.

Christian interest in Adam stems from the comparisons made by Paul between Christ and Adam in *Romans* 5: 12–21 and *1 Corinthians* 15: 20–22, 45–49. These passages encouraged the growth of apocryphal literature about Adam, which was at first written in Greek. Survivals of this origin are occasionally found, as in the four words which explain the meaning of the name Adam in B. In the Middle Ages the Greek versions were translated into Latin, and the *Vita Adae at Evae*, the ancester of the account in B, was one of the most influential of these translations. Some Middle English poems like the *Canticum de Creatione* are also based on it. In apocryphal literature the story of Adam and Eve became closely linked with the cross so that versions of the one often contain an abbreviated account of the other, as is true of *The Finding of the True Cross* (Xa). Although stories about Adam and Eve existed as independent works, they were also incorporated in adaptations of the Bible like *Cursor Mundi* and in compendia such as the Temporales.

Edition: C. Horstmann, *Sammlung Altenglischer Legenden* (Heilbronn 1878).

This tretys is hou the word was wrought and Adam and Eve, and the wo that Adam and Eve in heore lyve hedden.

1. This treatise is probably an adapted version (see the introductory remarks), since the logical sequence of events is not always clear. *Word:* that is 'world'; cf. V, 21.

Alle that bileeven on Jesu Crist lusteneth and ye mowen heere how muche is the miht of ure hevene-kyng. Furst he schop hevene and sithen the eorthe to beren treo and gras: the eorthe was druyghe and withouten moisture. Ther nas nothing that was quik, neither more ne lasse—the Holi Gost was evere withouten bigining and schal be withouten endyng. God, as his wille was, behihte to make liht. And tho he made angelus of a swithe fair bleo: Sachel was the furste angel that
10   Crist made and sithen he hihte Lucifer, that thorw pruide was forloren. God seih that hit was good to alle goode werkes. Wel fayre he departed the derke from the liht: liht he cleped the day and the derknesse the niht. Of even and of morewen he made a day; and sethen othur thing, as I wol yow tellen. On the secunde day he schop the firmament that is aboven us—ur Lord bring us alle thider yif hit beo his swete wille. The watres undur hevene Crist made togeder weende and alle heore stremes in a luytel stounde and sende hem forth for that the druye eorthe schulde bringe forth fruit; and tho he cleped this water gedering. Crist seih that hit was good. Of even and of morwen he made the
20   thridde day. The feorthe day the sonne and the mone he sette in the firmament and sterres ful brihte; the sonne he sette to the day, the mone to the nighte. The fifthe day Crist comaundet fissches in water for to swymme, mony beestes, and foules to be under the firmament [on] flight. And tho he maked the whal, most of alle fissches; and alle maner beestes he made thermyde and biddeth hem that heo schulden waxe and multiplye and yaf hem his blessyng. The sixte day wolde God enden his werkes: hors and retheren he made forte suffren wo and alle maner beestes that gon uppon fote.

7. bigining: bigīng

---

3. *Cf.* l. 384. The invocations to the audience found in romances may have influenced these passages.

9. More usually the devil is called Lucifer at first and then Satan. The name Sachel is rare.

11. *hit*: the light (l. 8); *cf.* Genesis 1: 4, 'And God saw the light, that it was good.' The sense is difficult because the author has interpolated the creation of the angels into the *Genesis* account of the creation of the world.

13. *Cf.* Genesis 1: 5, 'And the evening and the morning were the first day.'

13. *and sethen othur thing*: understand 'he made' from the preceding clause.

16*ff.* An expansion of the *Genesis* account of the division of the earth from the sea.

16. Take *and alle heore stremes* with *The watres undur hevene*.

18. *Cf.* Genesis 1: 10, 'And the gathering together of the waters called he Seas.'

29. The traditional location of Paradise is in the east beyond Asia; see H. R. Patch,

And tho he made Paradys biyonde the mount of Asye in the est
londe. Hit is wel evene and swithe round abouten with a brennyng   30
wal from hevene to the grounde. The murthe that therinne is non
eorthlich may hit telle no seo. Therinne groweth the treo of lyf that
stont ther wel faire; hose eteth of that fruit schal he never dyghen.
Therinne springeth a welle that was mad with Godes hondes. Four
stremes ther rennen out of into diverse londes: Fyson hette that on
strem that cometh from that welle; anothur hette Gyson that is of
more prys: he passeth bi another coost swithe yeorne withalle, that
colde is inne ifounden—and preciouse stones and yeemstones ther ben
swithe noble for to staunche blood; the thridde hette Eufrate: that
watur is swithe swift; the feorthe hette Tygre: that is briht thorw   40
charbuncle-stones that liggen therinne.

Tho after he made mon of erthe in flesch and bon in the Vale of
Ebron. God reste the seventhe day; nothing wolde he worche for
thulke day men schulde herien God of hevene. Theraftur God bad
foure angelus that heo schulden seche thulke monnes nome that he
hedde imaad. Seint Mihel wente into the est. He seih ther a sterre that
was swithe briht: Anatalim was that sterre ihote with the furste lettre
A. And soone he com ayeyn. Gabriel into the west half wente and he
seigh in the firmament a sterre that hihte Dysus. The furste lettre D
therof soone he broughte. Raphael com to the north; he say ther a   50
sterre that is iclepet Arcis. Anon he fleyh ayein with the furste lettre

---

45. schulden: sc|schulden.

The Other World according to Descriptions in Medieval Literature (Cambridge, Mass.
1950); *est londe* is the east, not a specific country.

30. *wel evene and swithe round abouten*: level and with a circular circumference.

34ff. *Cf. Genesis* 2: 10–14 where the rivers have different names; but similar names
are found in *Cursor Mundi* l. 1317.

38. Gems and precious stones were frequently attributed with special powers and
were traditionally associated with Paradise; information about them was collected
into *Lapidaries*.

42. Adam is thought to have been created and buried in the same place. *Cf.* 'And
in [Hebron] was Adam formed and made, after that sum men seyn. For men weren
wont to clepe that place the Feld of Damasce because that it was in the lordschipe
of Damask, and fro thens was he translated into Paradys of delytes, as thei seyn, and
after that he was dryven out of Paradys he was left there.' (*Mandeville's Travels*, ch. 9).

45ff. The angels went to the four corners of the world to symbolize that man should
be lord of the whole universe. The names are of Greek origin and refer to the four
points of the compass.

A that he con with him bringe. Forth him wente Uriel riht into the
south. Messembrion hihte the sterre that he sih there; with the furste
lettre M he wente swithe ayeyn and brouht hit tofore God with the
othur threo. God took theos foure lettres and bad Uriel rede; and he
radde 'Adam'.

Crist maade Adam ilyk to his owne ymage and bleugh on him the
spirit of lyf with his swete mouth and seide: 'Lo, Adam is on of us,
connynge bothe good and uvel; I wol that ye honoure him.'

60   Seynt Mihel was the furste that dude him honour, and also the othur
angelus aftur him. Tho hit com to Sachel that he schulde honoure him,
so muche was his pryde that he might not lowen him, and seide:
'I was er Adam.'

Tho seide Micael to him: 'Thou schalt honoure Adam or God wole
reyne wreche on the.'

'Ye, yif he beo wroth with me I wot where to abyden: I schal sette
my seete in the north syde and I wol be lyk the hexte that is aboven us.
Therfore I nul not honoure Adam for eighe ne for love.' And seide:
'Whuch of yow seih me be maad?'—as theih he seide: I was er eny of
70   you weore, I wol be evene to the hexte.

And a vois seide aboven: 'I was er then thou.' And tho that yaf
kepe to that word bilaften stille and the othure fellen adoun that
co[n]sented to Lucifer, for heo neoren not stable toforen. And thenne
weore thei stabelichet in that ilke while that heo hedden thenne, bothe
the goode and uvel, so that heo ne mihte never out therof. And after
that while heo beon pynet, summe more and summe lasse; and also
to the other in hevene is heore joye. And he and alle his feeren fullen
out of hevene: heo fullen out as thikke as the drift of the snouh; summe
astunte in the eyr and summe in the eorthe. Yif eny mon is elve-inome

---

75. uvel: u|uvel

53. *him*: best understood as a type of reflexive pronoun.

67. *north syde*: the north, as a land of darkness, is traditionally associated with Satan.
In *The Friar's Tale* the devil says he lives *fer in the north contree* (D 1413). This association
of the devil with the north probably springs from *Isaiah* 14: 13–14; *cf.* also Gregory's
Moralia xvii. 24 (P.L. 76: 26).

73. *heo neoren not stable toforen*: that is, up till this time the good were not confirmed
in their goodness nor the wicked in their evil. This point marked the decisive division.
Heo refers to both good and evil.

77. *he*: Sachel or Satan.

79. Neither *elve-inome* nor *elve-iblowe* is recorded in MED, but *cf. elf-taken* 'bewit-
ched by elves', which has the same meaning.

othur elve-iblowe, he hit hath of the angelus that fellen out of hevene.   80

Tho Paradis was imaad, God nom Adam bi the hond and brouht him therinne and brouhte alle beestes and foules toforen him; and he yaf alle nome after heore kuynde. And he seih that uchon hedde his make and he hedde non. God nolde not that Adam schulde libbe ther alone. He caste sleep in him and made Eve of his owne ribbe for that he scholde have al his wille. And to him he yaf alle thing that tho was o lyve: the fissches and the foules he yaf to heore hondes and alle manere of beestes—al but the appeltre that he him forbade. Tho was Adam wel inouh and riht wys of witte.

Now is heere a skile to asken whi that wymmen ben feirore then   90 men bi kuynde. Herto wol I onswere: for wommon was maad in Paradis of Adames ribbe, and mon was maad of eorthe and of foul fen. Therfore is wommonnes fel cleror then monnes.

Al the blisse of Paradys was taken to Adam and to Eve, his make, but the treo of wisdom that was forboden hem bi the heste of God. Adam hedde the north syde and the est of Paradys, and Eve hedde to hire dele the south and the west.

Heo hedden two angelus to kepen hem and to wissen hem that heo ne schulde have no doute for no maner drede. Tithinges coome anon to the angelus that kepten hem that heo schulden come anon to wor-   100 schupe God Almihti and him to honoure. As soone as the angelus weore went forth to seon heore creatour tho was the stude empti ther thei hedden iben. The angelus of helle, that weore maad with Cristes hond, hedden gret envye of Adames joye and of his blisse. The fend com as a neddre forte begylen Eve and seide to hire: 'What hath God forboden ow?' And Eve tolde him a long tale, al what God hedde iseid. And be hire tellyng the schrewe fond wey of hire frelete. 'Ete nou,' he seide, 'of this fruit and thou schalt eevene ben lyk Crist: bothe thou schalt cunne the goode and the uvel. Bote thou ete therof now, I holde the for wood.' And Eve thorw the fendes red eet of this fruit, and   110 Adam for hire love—and that him rewed ful sore. As soone as heo

90. a skile to asken whi that: a skile whi to asken weore whi that

---

83-4. 'And God saw that each animal had its mate and that Adam had no partner.'
90. 'Now here is a problem, to ask why women are by nature more beautiful than men.'
106. The long conversation between Eve and the serpent is not found in other legends about Adam and Eve, though it is recorded in *Ancrene Wisse*.
111. *Adam for hire love*: that is, Adam ate the fruit for love of her.

hedden therof eten thei knewen wel that heo weren naket; and that
hedde Sathanas maad thorw his tresun. With leves of a fyger heo
hudden heore bodies and hedden muche schome, and therof hedde
Sathanas muche gle and game. What God spak to Adam ye schul
wite sone.

Oure Lord seide to Adam: 'Wher art thou nou? Tel me, Adam, whi
eet thou of the tre?'

'The wommon that thou betoke me, Lord, dude me ete therof.'

120   God seide tho to Adam: 'For thou hast don bi Eves lore, thou
schalt hit abugge afturward. Thou schalt fare into thesternesse, and
from bodilich hele into serwe and wo.' And thenne spak God to Eve:
'Whi hast thou thus iwrouht?'

And heo onswerd and seide: 'Lord, the eddre hath bitrayet me.'

Tho he spac to Eve and seide: 'Wommon, for thou art unwrast, in
muchel travayl thou schalt ben and under monnes heste; children
thou schalt bere with muchel pyne and wo and al that of the cometh
and al thin ofspring.' And God asket the eddre whi he dude so.

And he seide: 'For I hedde to hem envye.'

130   And [God seide]: 'Neddre, for thou bitrayedest mon with nuy[th]
and with oonde, thi breste schal ben thi feet and eorthe thou schalt
eten, and men schal wayte the to slee. Uppe thi breste thou schalt
slyden; feet ne tit the never noone. And whon thou schalt don thi
kuynde, thou schalt smiten thin hed into thin makes mouthe and heo
schal byten hit of. With thyne furste kundles thow schalt bersten on
threo.' Tho seide God to Adam: 'Go out of Paradis; and ye schul
come to that stude that ye schulle agrysen of.'

Tho com the angel Cherubin with a swerd brennynge and drof
hem out of Paradys. Tho was Adam and Eve brought into that stude

117. me: me | me

---

130. *nuy[th]*: it would be possible to emend *nuy* to *envy* (*cf.* l. 129), but *nith and onde*
is a traditional collocation. For the spelling of *nuyth*, cf. *kuynde*, etc.

132. *wayte the to slee*: lie in wait to kill you; *wayte* is here intransitive.

133–5. This account of the snake's procreation was probably taken from the
Bestiaries where a similar story is found about the viper.

138. *Genesis* 3:24, 'So he drove out the man; and he placed at the east of the garden
of Eden Cherubims', was often interpreted as though Cherubin was the name of the
angel placed at the gate of Paradise, *cf. Cursor Mundi* l. 1303. Cherubin was often
equated with Uriel.

139. Hebron, *cf.* l. 43.

ther he was imaad. God yaf hem curteles tweyne of beestus felles, 140
that heo hedden uppon, bitokened that heo and heore ofspring schulde
dye in eorthe. Ther heo lyveden heore lyf in the wrecched weopes
dale. Ofte heo weoren acold and sore of hungred; eddren mihte hem
styngen; foulus and beestes hem mihte totere; the watur that bifore
hem bare hem mihte adrenche. Adam maad him an hous for to wonen
inne; swinke he moste and travaylen and Eve moste spynne. Ther heo
woneden eighte dayes in thulke wonynge in serwe and in muche
teone. Theraftur he eode al one fourtene niht bi water and bi londe
withouten eny lyflode. And ther he com to Eve ayeyn and tolde hire
this tythinge that he ne mihte fynde but more and gras, and that 150
schulde the beestes of the lond ete for God hit hath yeven to hem.

'Weilawey,' quath Eve. 'Ichave iwrouht ful evele, for ich have
ibrouht the in muchel serwe and care. Adam, I bidde the,' quath Eve,
'that thou benyme me my lyf for ichave brouht the in muchel serwe
and wo.'

'Beo stille,' quath Adam. 'Hou miht I so do with my flesch and with
my blode? Ac we schul do penaunce and bidde God of merci yif we
mihte enything amende.'

'Such penaunce,' quath Eve, 'wol I have as I mihte studefastlyche
and wel overcome.'   160

'We schul hope,' quath Adam, 'of foryivenesse. Stond thou in this
water of Tygre up to thi chinne therinne xxx dayes. And alle the while
thou art therinne spek thou no word, for ure lippes ben unworthi to
speken enything to God for we eeten of the fruit that he us hedde
forboden. In thulke manere I wol soffre penaunce in the flum Jordan
fourti dayes.'

Eve stod in hire penaunce til eihte dayes weoren ago. Tho com the
fend in the liknesse of an angel to hire. And Eve loked uppon him and
sore heo bigon to syken and wepte wel sore and hire hondes gan to
wringen. And the angel made muche mornynge and seide tho to Eve: 170
'Cum up of the water, for we angelus of hevene han preyed for the so
that Jesu Crist hath underfongen thi penaunce for thou wold so

162ff. The periods of penance differ in various versions. In the *Canticum de Crea-tione* ll. 115–26 Eve is to endure penance for forty days and Adam for forty-seven, the extra seven symbolizing the period of the creation.

165. The Jordan is the river of Christ's baptism (*cf.* l. 329) and thus provides a further link in the equation that Christ is the second Adam. Perhaps we should under-stand Adam's penance in the Jordan as a form of baptism.

bletheliche dwelle therin so longe. I am set to bringe yow ther ye
schul have mete such as ye weore wont to have and eeten in Paradys.'
The corsud angel nom Eve up bi the hond and ladde hire to druye
londe. As soone as Eve was comen up of the water hire bodi was grene
as eni gras.

The angel ladde Eve forth forte heo coomen to flum Jordan ther heo
seighen Adam stonde. Tho that Adam sauh the angel leden Eve he
180 crighed to hire with muche serwe and seide to hire: 'Eve, Eve, wher
is now thi thought? Al is for nought the penaunce that thou hast idon.'
Anon heo wuste tho that heo was bigiled. Heo thoughte that hire
herte wolde toberste so sore heo was agreved. Adoun heo fel in a
swoune and bigon to tere hire her. Tho was al hire serwe idoublet
more then hit was toforen. Adam cursed the fend and seide to him:
'Whi art thou ur adversarie and ure foo? Constou ever siggen that we
ben omen the eny joye other eny blisse or that we duden the eny unriht?'

Tho the fend onswerde with wel sori cheer: 'Adam, al ich wite hit
the and Eve, thi fere; the cumpaignye of angelus and hevene-blisse
190 ichave forloren. Furst tho thou was ischapet and imaad mon, tho was
I comaundet of God that I schulde honoure the. And I seide I nolde not
honoure the for nothing, and therfore was God wroth with me.
For thulke unboxumnesse was I put out of my sege of hevene.'

Tho spak Adam and seide: 'What mihte we don therto? We ne
knewe the nought.' Adam heold up his honden to the hevene and seide:
'Have merci of me, God Omnipotent. In thi swete hondes I betake
my soule. And do this feondes from us that don us al this wo. I beseche
God Almihti to yive me thulke seete that he hath forloren.' And thenne
at thulke wordus the fend wente away; and Adam stod stille and abod
200 his penaunce.

And tho he hedde don his penaunce he com up and a thunderblast
com, and he and Eve, his wyf, wenten togedere and tho was Caym
biyeten. Tho seide Eve to Adam: 'Ich mot fleo for no lengur in this sory

182. thoughte: thhoughte

176–7. *Was grene as eni gras*: this probably arises from a confusion of what was in the
Vita Adae et Evae 10: 1, 'her flesh was [trembling] like grass from the cold of the water.'
186*ff*. In many versions this section is introduced to allow the author to relate the
story of Satan's fall. As our author included that event at the beginning of his work,
this section has become redundant.
203. Eve fled because she had twice wronged Adam: once by eating the apple in
Paradise and the second time by breaking off her penance.

lyf may I heer dwelle. Bilef thou her, lord, al one and ich wol weenden
to the worldes ende into the west.' Eve tho went hire forth toward
the west syde. And ther heo made hire a logge forte wonen inne for
chele of snough and of forst and for alle maner wikked wederes.
Eve was with childe er heo went from Adam. So twelve moneth heo
dwellet there. And whon the tyme was comen that the child schulde
boren be, heo was so sore adred therof that heo forlees nerhonde hire   210
witte. Ofte heo bad merci to God aboven, ac heo nas nothing herd
of hire biddyng. Heo sent hire stevene and hire sonde bi the hevene to
Adam, hire lord, hou heo was bistad. And Adam was strongliche
aferd and gretliche abascht tho he herde hire leste the fend weore
icomen hire to bitrayen. Tho this tithinges weore come to him thorw
the firmament, he wente to hire sone anon. Tho that Eve him seih, for
blisse heo gon to weopen and seide: 'Lord, wel is me that I the seo on
lyve. Sone so I the seghe I ne felede nothing of alle my pyne. Nou
bidde God that he me wol unbynde of my serwe, for nothing that I
bidde I may fynde no grace.'   220

Tho bad Adam to God his help and his grace. Ther coomen twelve
angelus from hevene and nomen Eve and seiden heo weoren icome
for to helpen hire for Adames love. 'Highe the blyve that thi child
weore boren, for thou schalt have help of us.' That child was soone
iborn: Caym was the childes nome. Tho nom Adam Eve, his wif,
and his child, and wenten ayeynward to the est lond.

Tho God yaf Adam diverse seedes and taughte him to tilye and to
sowe so that he mihte herafturward bothe repe and gedere, and that
he schulde nym yeme to the tilynge of the eorthe for hem and for heore
ofspring that aftur hem comen. And bad Adam to yeven him the   230
tithe dole that coome of the eorthe. And then seide Adam: 'Lord, nym
the halven dole.'

---

205. toward: touward

211–12. 'her prayer was not heard'.

212. *bi the hevene*: 'through the air'. God does not hear her request, but her lament
was carried through the air to Adam. *Cf. Canticum de Creatione* l. 405. *The eyr bar it forth
anon.*

226. *wenten*: 'they went'.

231. *tithe dole*: 'tenth part'; this assumed origin of the payment was often used to
justify the payment of tithes to the Church.

'Nay,' seide ur Lord, 'hit schal the tyme come that the tithe dole schal beo binomen me for fals covetyse of the fendes lore.'

Adam biyat another child: Abel was his name. Theose two children wonede togedere and swonken for heore mete thorwh the teching of heore fader. Eve seide to Adam: 'Icham sore agast that Caym wol sle Abel, his brother. Therfore hit bihoveth, yif we wol wel do, to parte hem atwynne.'

240   Tho was Caym maad tilyere and Abel heerde of scheep and of othur beestes. Abel was tither good of alle thinges and thonked God swithe wel. And Caym tithed falslich and brak Godes hestes for he withheold alway the beste dole and yaf God of the worste. Crist underfong wel fayre the tithe of Abel, for the smoke wente evene upward as hit brende. And the smoke of Caym wente dounwart for he tithede falsliche. This was the lawe of the Olde Testament, for to brenne alle maner tithe, for that God schulde ben heried of that smoke that coome upward the hevene. Abel hedde of God love and grace, and therfore Caym was wroth and bigon to teren his visage. Theraftur God asket
250 Caym whi he was so proud and so stout that he totaar his visage, and seide: 'Yif thou wel dost thou schalt wel fynde; and yif thou enything uvel dost thou schalt beo bounden with sunne.'

After this seide Caym to Abel: 'Go we now to the feelde for to witen ur fader bestes.' So heo wenten forth ifeere.

And ther Caym slouh Abel, with the chekebon of an asse he smot him on the hed; and ther he bilafte ded in the Feld of Damasse. God asket of Caym: 'Wher is thi brothur?'

And Caym onswerde and seide: 'I nam not his kepere.'

'What hastou ido?' quath God to Caym. 'And wher hastou ibeon?
260 The vois of Abel's blod crieth to hevene to me.' God yaf Caym ther his curs for he hedde iculd his brother and sched his blod, and seide: 'The eorthe crieth to me on the for the sunne that thou hast don and wol putte the awey from his face; and alle thinges schul ben ayeynes the, beestes and foules schul sle the.'

Then seide Caym: 'Nou I wot that mi sunne is so muche that I may have no foryivenesse. Nou, Lord,' seide Caym, 'schal alle thing that cometh to me sle me?'

233. *hit . . . the tyme*: a tautologous subject.

248. *upward*: here a preposition, 'up to, in the direction of'.

256. *Feld of Damasse*: cf. note to l. 42; *bilafte* is intransitive with Abel as the subject: 'he remained behind dead'.

'Nay,' seide ur Lord, 'I schal sette a token upon the that alle that sle
Caym sevenfold schal his synne be more.' And tho sette Crist a marke
upon him, that he waggede alwey forth with his heved.   270

Tho tok Caym his wyf Calmana, that was his suster, with him and al
that he hedde and anon riht went him awey from the face of God into
the lond of Edom with serwe and with wo.

And whon Adam wuste that Abel was slayn his herte bigon to waxe
cold; nas never mon for his child so wo. Adam seide: 'Though I thole
wo hit is good riht: for that I nolde not holde Godes hestes I have
forlore Paradys, and nou for Abel, my sone, ne worth I never blithe.'

Theraftur an hundred yeer Adam with Eve engendrede no fruit, ac
evere he was in serwe and in wepyng. Tho the hundred yeer weoren
passet him com aleggaunce of his wo. Crist sent his angel and brouhte   280
tithing that heo schulden asemble and engendre fruit. Tho heo geeten
a child, that hihte Seth. Adam hedde xxx sones and moni doughtres
withouten Caym and Abel. The children of Adam multiplighed swithe.
And Adam comaunded to Seth that non of his kuynde schulde felauschupe with Caymes kuynde ne wedde non wyves in Caymes kuynde,
for tho that coomen of Sethes kuynde ben cleped Godes sones and
Caymes kuynde to men sonus. And thenne at the fiftene hondred
winteres ende heo bigunnen to don heore lecherie priveliche and
afturward openliche. And tho afturward heo weddeden the to kuynde
into that othur and geeten geauns. And thenne God tok wreche and   290
adreynte al the world but eihte soules at Noe flood. God was agrevet
therof and seide that him forthoughte that he hedde imaad mon, so
he nom veniaunce of hem for heore foule synne.

292. forthoughte: forthhoughte

---

270. *waggede*: the author may have understood Cain's mark to be an appendage
fixed loosely on the head.

273. *Cf. Genesis* 4: 16, 'and Cain dwelt in the land of Nod, on the east of Eden'.

278. Adam's abstinence was a vicarious penance for Abel's murder.

282. Seth, whose birth was decreed by God, is a symbol of holiness and stands
in direct contrast to Cain. *Cf. Cursor Mundi* ll. 1203–5.

> Wit this was born an hali child,
> Seth that meke was and mild;
> O[f] quil[k] man that Crist him com.

289. *the to kuynde*: Seth's and Cain's. The giants of Cain's kin take their origin
from *Genesis* 6: 4. They were frequently referred to in medieval literature; an allusion
occurs, for example, in *Beowulf*.

291. Noah and his wife with their three sons and their wives (*Genesis* 7: 7).

Adam livede heere in serwe and in wo nyn hundret yer and more.
Whon hit cometh to the day that he schulde dye, he let sende aftur
alle his sones and seide: 'Ich wot wel, whon I am ded to helle mot
ich wende.' And whon heo weoren alle icomen for to seon heore fader,
heo askeden what him eiled. 'Me is uvele,' quath Adam, 'for seknesse
and for wo. I am biset with uvel in herte and syde and in uche a lime
300 that I may not longe live. For tho that I trespaset and agult to God,
vii and thritti uveles he dude in my bodi. I, wrecche, what schal I do?'
Tho Eve him onswerde, wel sore wepynge: 'Lord,' heo seide, 'do
in me Adames wo for hit is not for his gult, ac hit is for myn.'
Adam bad Eve and Seth weenden to Paradis anon the whiles he
weore on lyve, 'and bidde the angel that he sende me helethe. For wel
I wot, whon I am ded to helle me tit to weende.'
And tho Seth seide to his fader: 'I not what I may do for to Paradys
I con no way.'
'Sone,' seide Adam, 'that gras the wol techen: for al the wey as we
310 out eode the gras is ther unlikelich, for yit into this day nolde hit not
arysen for the sinnen that we duden in Paradys. Go anon forth, leve
sone, and do as I the teche.'
Seth bad his fader his blessing and went anon his wey. Wel sore
wepyng heo eoden into Paradis for the wey was long and brod. Ther
com the fend as a neddre and stynged Seth wel uvele. Eve weop sore
and seide to the cursede wiht: 'Whi artou so hardi to fihte with Godes
ymage?' Seth acursed the fend and wariede him. And heo eoden forth
on heore way riht to the yates of Paradis; ac innore heo ne mighte
winne. Ac there heo seghen the blisse of mony maner foules and muche
320 murthe and joye inouh. And that watur schon as brihte as the sonnebeem and the blosmes weoren so fayre on uche maner treo that unnethe
he mighte hem biholde for heor fairnesse; the stones on the grounde

304. Adam wishes Seth to fetch the oil of mercy from Paradise (l. 326). This is not
granted him immediately; he is told that the oil of mercy (i.e. Christ) will be sent in
due course—to save mankind through the crucifixion and Adam through the harrowing of hell. On Seth's quest see E. C. Quinn, *The Quest of Seth for the Oil of Mercy*
(Chicago 1962).

307. In many versions Seth goes to Paradise by himself. His ignorance of the way
there is inappropriate here as Eve goes with him.

314. *heo*: Seth and Eve.

315. The stinging of Seth by the serpent represents the devil's inability to impede
a good man.

weoren as brihte as hit weore brenninde laite. He seigh there angelus
of wondurfol heuh. And al thulke blisse lees Adam thorw the gilerie
of the feend—and that we mowe sore rewe!

The oyle of merci he asked ful sore wepynge, as his fader him hedde
itaught. And tho the angel spac to Seth and bad him weende ayeyn and
sei to Adam: whon that v thousend yeer and an hundret beon ipasset
then wol Godus sone come into flum Jordan for to beo baptised therinne of water and of the Holy Gost for helthe of Adam and of al his   330
osprunch; and er ne tit him none hele. The angel tok an appel and yaf
hit to Seth and bad him beren hit to Adam and sei him that he knoweth
hit wel, for heo weoren alle at his comaundement til that he agulte
God. Threo curnels of an appel the angel tok to Seth and bad him wite
hem wel forte that Adam weore ded and thenne do that on in his mouth
and the othure in his neosethurles. Swete spices he yaf him and seide
to him: 'Weent hom ayeyn anon for Adam, thi fadur, schal hastiliche
dye.'

Seth turnede ayein wel sore wepynge and with mournynge chere
for that he schulde departe from that grete blisse. And whon he com   340
to his fader, he fel uppon his knes and honoured him and seide: 'Leove
fader, hit ne helpeth not to the forte beseche after helthe into that five
thousend yeer and an hundret be gon. Thenne wol Godes sone ben
baptized in the flum Jordan for the helethe of the and of alle thine;
of alle maner uveles thou schalt have boote.' Of that word was Adam
fayn and swithe glad, and yeorne crighede merci to God of hevene for
he nedde nevere in al his lyve so muche joye as he hedde tho. And tho
louh Adam and never arst.

Adam seide: 'Lord, yif hit weore thi wille hit weore tyme now that
myn olde bones mihte ligge stille, for sethe I com from Paradis ichave 350
lived heere in muchel car. And whon ich am ded I wot wel that I
schal weende to helle. I ne recche,' quath Adam, 'thauh I beo pyned
in alle skinnes wo, for ich hope yit to come to the blisse of Paradis.'
Adam eet that appel that Seth hedde ibrouht him and of no maner

334. In order to atone for Adam's sin Christ must die on the same tree by which
Adam sinned. Hence Seth is given seeds from the tree of life which will produce the
wood on which Christ will be crucified (cf. ll. 381-3).

348. Adam laughed now because he had received a clear sign that there was a limit
to man's suffering which he had caused.

355. The period is given as either three days (Canticum de Creatione) or six (Vita
Adae et Evae).

evel thing he nedde no drede. And theraftur some dayes, as the angel
hedde told to Seth, he wente to Adam and fond his limes colde.
Thenne seide Adam to his sones that weoren tho abouten him: 'I am
ixC yer old and xxx^ti. As swithe as ich am ded, burie mi bodi in the
Vale of Ebron.'

360   Tho Adam hedde so iseid he lay stille and yaf up the gost. In the
tyme that he dyede the day turned into derknesse and neither sonne ne
mone ne sterre ne yaf no liht. Seth bicluppet the bodi of his fader in his
armes and leide his hed wel feire in his barme. Alle heo wepten and
maden serwe til that the angel of God come to hem and beed hem
leven and be stille, and seide to Seth: 'Lo what God wol do with
Adam, thi fader.'

Ther comen the angelus of hevene and herieden God with swete song
for Adames soule. And amonges hem Seth feled ure Lordes hond over
Adam ther he lay; and seide tho to Seint Mihel: 'I betake into thin
370   hond Adam and his osprunch in serwe and in wo forte the day of
grace come. Thene I wol turne al his sorwe into joye and blisse, and
evermore schal laste thulke selve joie that Lucifer les thorw his pruide.'

God comaundet tweyn angelus to bringe twey clothes of sendel
and of bijs, that on to do uppon Adam and that other to don uppon
Abel, his sone. Seint Mihel and Seint Uriel, Eve and Seth buried Adam
and Abel in the eorthe that heo comen of in the Vale of Ebron. Seint
Mihel seide to Seth: 'Thus ye schul burie men whon that heo ben
dede.'

Ther was the eorthe ihalewed at the burieng of Adam of God and of
380   his angelus. Seth dude the greynes of the appel under Adam's tonge and
in the neosethurles. Tho longe afturward sprong threo yerdes of this
greynes that weoren holy and gode, on whuch Jesus schedde his blod
uppon for monnes sunne.

355. some: sone

---

358. That is, 930 years old.   361. The parallel with Christ's death is clear.
   365. 'Behold what God will do with your father, Adam.' Although at l. 358 Adam
asks to be buried after his death, he was the first man other than Abel to die and most
versions imply that Seth did not know what to do. Michael reveals to Seth the essen-
tials of a Christian burial. It would appear that Abel remained unburied till Adam's
death.

369. *seide*: the subject is God.

381–2. There are many accounts of how the rods were found and ultimately transformed into the cross for Christ's crucifixion; *cf.* X(a) 11–20.

Now I have told the lyf of Adam. Now herkeneth of his soule whoder hit was lad. In the ovemaste prison of helle his soule was bounden er the bodi were cold, and therinne he was foure thousend yeer viC and foure, for ther nas nevere so holy mon that he ne was brouht thider til Jesu Crist suffrede deth uppon the roode.

Theraftur eihte dayes that Adam was ded Eve feled hire deth ful neih. Heo comaundet that al hire children schulde beo brought toforen 390
hire and tolde hem in what manere heo hedde agult God and how that God wolde take wreche of monkuynde with watur and with fuir for heore sunne. 'Therfore maketh tables of stones and of cley and writeth therinne the lyf of oure fader and of oure moder and of oure bretheren that ye han of us seghen and herd, that hit may beo founden aftur that we ben dede. And yif that fuir cometh the tables of ston schul tobersten for the hete of the fuir, and yif heo ben of clay heo wolen laste longe.' Tho Eve hedde thus itold, heo heef up hire honden and heried God Almihti and yeld up tho the gost.

Hire children wepten for hire al that sevenniht. Tho com Seint 400
Mihel and brouht hem tithing and beede hem sese of heore wepynge and seide: 'Nou is the seventhe day; resteth and singeth of the heriinge of God, for that bitokeneth the reste of the world that is comynge. God himselven sesed of al his werkes on the Sonenday.'

Tho coome Seth and made tables of ston and of cley and wrot the lyf of his fader and of his moder and of his bretheren theruppon, and leyden hem in Adames oratorie. And ther heo weoren ifounden aftur the deluvie. In the tables weoren iwriten al the deedes of Adam and

394. of (3): or.

___

386–7. That is, 4,604.

387. 'There was no man so holy who was not brought to hell until Christ suffered death on the cross.' Since Christ redeemed mankind, all who died before his coming could not be saved from original sin and so had to go to hell. At the harrowing of hell those who were both virtuous and in the faith were released from hell by Christ; but pagans whether good or bad were not redeemed. The problem of the virtuous pagan caused anguish to many, including William Langland as, for example, in *Piers Plowman* C. xv.

396. If God sends fire the stone tablets will burst with the heat, but the clay ones will be baked even harder; but if God sends water, the clay tablets will disintegrate but the stone ones will survive. So one way or the other posterity would learn the story of Adam and Eve.

403. *the reste of the world*: the day that the world rests or stops, i.e. Doomsday; *cf.* I, 92*ff*.

of othere. Ac no mon that heom seighe ne couthe rede hem. And
410 aftur feole yeeres com Salamon the kyng thider forte seon the tables
and bisouhte God Almihti that he moste wite what was therinne.
And thenne com Seint Mihel to Salamon and dude him to undur-
stonden what was writen in the tables and seide: 'Ich heold Sethes
finger[s] the whiles heo weoren awritynge withouten iren or steel
in the harde ston, and so heo duden.' Yit liggen the tables in that ilke
stude in Adames oratorie ther he bad his beodes.

Tho the kyng dude make a temple of gold and of preciouse stones.
In al the world was non such for the stones in the wal schonen nih as
briht as the sonnebeem. And that hous was clepet the temple of Jeru-
420 salem for Adames children. Tho the folk haden rif Adames pynen,
but soone aftur heo hedden sone foryeten hit for muchel misdoyng
of metes and drinkes and heor othure flessches lustes. And so heo
weoren alle ablent, and therfore God Almihti adreynt al the world:
he dreynte al that was quik aboven the eorthe but onliche eihte soules.

Now ichave yow told al of the furste world; and to the world that
ever schal laste God us thider bring.

414. heo: hit

413-5. Even with emendation this sentence is not entirely happy. The *and so heo
duden* must mean 'and so they did', i.e. and thus the fingers wrote.

415. *Yit liggen . . . beodes*: Horstmann makes this part of Michael's speech, but
it is better to understand it as a general statement by the author. The stones are there
till this present day. Such statements are common enough.

420. *Tho*: 'at that time'; either when the temple was built, or more probably after
Adam's death since l. 424 refers to the Flood.

VII   *Epistle of Discretion of Stirrings*

This epistle is extant in four manuscripts: Cambridge University Library MSS. FF vi 31 [C] and KK vi 26, and British Museum MSS. Harleian 674 [H] and 2373; of which H is from the early fifteenth century, C from the middle of that century, and the other two from its second half. C contains many short pieces ascribed to the author of the *Cloud of Unknowing*, whereas the other three contain the *Cloud of Unknowing* itself as well as some of the shorter pieces. Professor Hodgson, who has edited the works of this author, concluded that H and C were the two best manuscripts of the *Epistle*. She printed H; this edition is based on C so that it can be used for comparison.

The author, who is unknown, is usually referred to by his major work, the *Cloud of Unknowing*. Nothing definite is known about him, but he was probably a priest who lived in the East Midlands and who was writing in the third quarter of the fourteenth century. Some of his works are little more than translations of texts by such authors as pseudo-Dionysius and the Victorines, and those which are not translations are strongly influenced by the contemplative tradition represented by those writers. Nevertheless all his works are marked by the writer's own personality.

Edition: P. Hodgson, *Deonise Hid Diuinite and other Treatises on Contemplative Prayer*. EETS o.s. 231 (London 1955). [H]

Gostly frend in God, that same grace and joy that I wil to mysilf wil I to thee at Goddis wille.

Thou askist me counseil of silence and of speking, of comon dieting and of singuler fasting, of duelling in cumpany and of onely-wonyng bi thiself. And thou seist that thou art in gret were what thou schalt do: for, as thou seist, on the to partie thou art gretly taried with speking, with comyn eting as other folk don and, thou seist, with comyn wonyng in cumpany; and on the tother partie thou dreddist to be streitly stille, singuler in fasting and onely in wonyng, for demyng of more holynes then thou art worthi and for many other perils. For oftetymes   10
now thees daies thei be demyd for moost holy and fallen into many

---

4. *onely-wonyng*: 'living like a hermit, by oneself'. *Onely* could be taken as an adjective here, but it is better to understand *onely-wonyng* as a compound.

6–8. *the to . . . the tother*: 'the one . . . the other'.

9. *for demyng of*: 'lest people think you have'.

perils that moost are in silence, in singuler fasting and in onely-duelling.

And soth it is that thei be moost holy yif grace onely be the cause of that silence, of that singuler fasting and of that onely-duelling, the kynde but suffring and onely consenting. And if it be otherwise then is ther nothing but peril on alle sides; for it is ful perilous to streine the kynde to any siche werk of devocion, as is silence or spekyng or comyn dieting or singuler fasting or duelling in cumpany or in one-
20 lynes (I mene passing the comyn custom and the cours of kynde and degree), but it be ledde therto by grace—and namely to siche werkis the whiche in hemself ben indifferent, that is to sey now good and now yvel, now with thee and now ayen thee, now helping and now letting. For it myght befalle, if thou folwedist thi singuler stiring streitly streyning thee to silence, to singuler fasting or to oonly-duelling, that thou schuldist oftetymes be stille when tyme were to speke, ofte-tyme fast when tyme wer to ete, oftetyme be oonly when tyme wer to be in cumpany; or yif thou yive thee to speking alweies when thee list, to comyn eting or to cumpanous wonyng, then peraventur thou
30 schuldist sumtyme speke when tyme were to be stille, somtyme ete when tyme wer to fast, sumtyme be in cumpany when tyme were to be oonly. And thus myght thou lightly falle into errour, in gret con-fusion, not oonly of thin owne soule but also of others.

And therfor in eschewing of siche errour thou askest of me, as I have perceyvid by thi lettre, two thinges: the first is my conseit of thee and thi stiringes, and the tother is my conseil in this cas and in alle siche other when thei come. As to the first I answer and I sey that I drede ful myche in this matere and in siche other to put forth my rude conseit, siche as it is, for two skils: and oon is this, I dar not lene to my
40 conseit affermyng it for fast trewe; the tother is, thin inward disposicion and thin abilnes that thou hast to alle thees thinges that thou spekist of in thi lettre ben not yit so fully knowen unto me as it were spedeful that thei weren yif I schulde yive ful counseill in this cas. For it is seid of the apostle: 'Nemo novit que sunt hominis nisi spiritus hominis qui in

---

27. be: to be   33. others (sic H): othere

---

16. kynde: 'human nature, one's physical side'.

22. That is, such actions as eating and fasting are neutral, but can become good or bad according to the intentions of the person employing them.

44-5. 1 Corinthians 2: 11.

ipso est; No man knowith whiche ben the privey disposicions of man but the spirit of the same man whiche is in himsilf.' And peraventur thou knowest not yit thin owne inward disposicion thisilf so fully as thou schalt do herafter when God wol lete thee fele it by the profe among many fallynges and risinges. For I knew never yit no synner that myght come to the perfit knowing of himsilf and of his inward 50 disposicion but if he were lerned of it before in the scole of God by experience of many temptaciouns.

For right as among the wawes and the flodis and the stormes of the see on the to partie, the pesible wynd and the calmes of softe weders of the aer on that other partie, the sely schip at the last atteyneth to the lond and the haven; right so among the diversite of temptacions and tribulacions that fallen to a soule in this ebbyng and flowyng lif (the whiche ben ensaumplid by the stormes and flodis of the see on the to partie) and among the grace and the goodnes of the Holy Gost, the manyfold visitacion, swetnes and confortes of spirit (the whiche are 60 ensaumplid bi the pesible wynd and the softe weders of the aire on the tother partie), the sely soule at the liknes of a schip atteyneth at the last to the lond of stabilnes and the haven of heelthe, the whiche is the clere and the sothfast knowing of hymself and of alle hise inward disposiciouns. Thorugh the whiche knowing he sittith quietely in himsilf as a kyng crouned in his rewme myghtely, wisly and goodly governyng himsilf and alle hise thoughtis and stirynges bothe in body and in soule. Of sich a man it is that the wise man seith thus: *'Beatus vir qui suffert temptaciones, quoniam cum probatus fuerit accipiet coronam vite, quam repromisit Deus diligentibus se*; He is a blessid man that suff- 70 ringly berith temptacion, for fro he have be preved he schal take the coron of lif, the whiche God hath hight unto alle tho that loven him.'

The coron of lif may be seid on two maners: oon for gostly wisdom, for ful discrecion and for perfeccion of vertu; thees thre knyttid togider may be called a coron of lif, the whiche bi grace may be comyn to men here in this lif. On another maner the coron of lif may be seid that it is the endeles joy that ech trewe soule schal have after this lif in the blis of heven. And sikerly neither of thees corouns may a man take but

---

53ff. *Cf.* the image in *Piers Plowman* C. xi. 33ff. and the note to that passage in E. Salter and D. Pearsall, *Piers Plowman* (London 1967), p. 110.

68–70. *James* 1: 12, 'Blessed is the man that endureth temptation; for when he is tried he shall receive the crown of life, which the Lord hath promised to them that love him.'

E

he before have ben wel preved in suffring of noy and temptacion,
80 as the text seith: '*Quoniam cum probatus fuerit accipiet coronam vite;*'
that is, 'Fro that he have ben preved, then schal he take the coron of
lif'. As who seith acording to myn undurstonding touchid before:
but if a synner may have ben preved before in diverse temptacions
(now risyng, now falling: [falling] bi freeltee, rising by grace), he
schal never ellys take of God in this lif goostly wisdom in cler knowing
of himsilf and of hise inward disposicions, ne ful discrecion in teching
and conceiling of other, ne yit the thridde the whiche is the perfeccion
of vertu in lovyng of his God and his brother.

Alle thees thre, wisdom, discrecion and perfeccion of vertu, ben but
90 oon and thei be clepid the coron of lif. In a coron ben thre thinges:
golde is the first, precious stones is the secound, and the torettes of
the floured-lise reisid up aboven the heved, tho ben the thridde.
By gold, wisdom; by preciouse stones, discrecion; and by the torrettes
of the flourid-lises I undurstond the perfeccion of vertu. Golde envirouneth the heved and by wisdom we governe our gostly werk in
every side. [Precious stones yiven light in beholding of men] and bi
discrecion we teche and counseile oure bretheren. The torrettes of the
flourid-lises yiven two side-braunches spreding: oon to the right side,
another to the lift, and on even aboven the heved; and bi perfeccion
100 of vertu, the whiche is charite, we yive two side-braunches of love
the whiche ben spreding out to the right side to our frendis and on
the lifte to oure enemyes, and oon even up unto God, aboven mannes
undurstonding the whiche is the heved of the soule. This is the coron
of lif the whiche by grace may be geten here. [And therfor bere]
thee lowe in thi bataile and suffre mekely thi temptacions; for if thou
have ben preved then schalt thou take either coron, or ellys the ton
or the tother, or bothe: that oon her, that other there. For whoso
hath this here, he may be ful siker of the tother there. And ful many

104. [And therfor bere] (*sic* H): if thou (*in margin*)

---

82. 'As if to say, according to my interpretation mentioned earlier.'

92. *floured-lise*: the fleur-de-lys. This symbol of the French monarchy was adopted
by English kings after they laid claim to the French throne at the time of the Hundred
Years' War.

96. The emendation is based on H.

97–9. The heraldic fleur-de-lys consists of a central upright and a petal on each
side; it is these which are allegorized here.

106–7. 'one of the crowns, either this one or the other, or both of them'.

ther ben that ben ful graciously preved here and yit comen never
to this that may be had here in lif; the whiche if thei mekely contenue 110
and paciently abide the wille of our Lord schal ful aboundingly
resceyve the tother there in the blisse of heven. The thinkith this
coron faire that may be had her: ye, bere thee as mekely as thou
maist by grace, for in comparison of the tother there it is but as a
noble to a world ful of gold.

Al this I sey to yive thee comfort in evydence of strengthe in thi
gostly batail the whiche thou hast taken on hande in the trist of our
Lord. And al this I say to lete thee se how fer thou art yit fro the trewe
knowing of thi inward disposicion, and therafter to yive thee warnesse
not oversoone to yive stid ne to folwe the senguler stiringes of thi 120
yong hert for drede of disceyt. Al this I sey for to schewe unto thee
[my conseit that I have of thee] and of thi stirynges as thou hast askid
of me.

For I conceyve of thee that thou art ful able and ful gredily disposid to siche sodeyn stirynges of singuler doynges and ful fast to
cleve unto hem when thei be resceyved; and that is ful perilous. I sey
not that this abilnes and this gredy disposicion in thee or in any other
that is so disposid as thou art, though al it be perilous, that it is therfore
yvel in itsilf. Nay! so sey I not; God forbede that thou take it so. But I
sey that it is ful good in itsilf and ful gret abilnes to ful gret perfeccion— 130
yea, and to the grettest perfeccion that may be in this lif. I meene yif
that soule that is so disposid wol besili nyght and day meke it to God
and to good counseil and strongli rise and martir itsilf, with casting
don of the owne wit and the owne wille in alle siche sodeyn stirings
and singuler, and sey scharply that it wol not folwe siche stirings, seme
thei never so liking, so high ne so holy, but if it have therto the wittes
and the consentis of somme gostli techers—I meene siche as have ben
of long tyme expert in singuler livyng. Siche a soule for gostli contynuance thus in this mekenes may disserve thorugh grace and the
experience of this gostly batail thus with itsilf for to take the coron of 140
lif, touchid bifore. And as gret an abilnes to good as it is, this maner

134. in (sic H): to

110. *this*: that is, this crown.
115. *noble*: a gold coin; *to*: 'in comparison with'.
138. *singuler livyng*: probably 'the way of life characterized by the highest degree
of love'.

of disposicion in a soule that is thus mekyd as I sey, as perilous it is in another soule, siche oon that wol sodeynli withouten avisement of conseil folwe the stiringis of the gredy hert bi the owne wit and the owne wille. And therfor for Goddis love bewar with this abilnes and with this maner of disposicion that I speke of, if it be in thee as I sey; and meke thee contynuely to preier and to conseil; breke don thin owne wit and thi wille in alle siche sodeyn and singuler stiringis; and folwe hem not overlightly til thou wite when[s] thei comen 150 and whether thei be acording for thee or not.

And touching thees stiringis of the whiche thou askist my conseit and my counseil, I sey to thee that I conceyve of hem suspeciously, that is that thei schulde be conceyved on an ape maner. Men seyn comynly that an ape doth as he other seeth. Foryive me if I erre in my suspecion, I preie thee. Nevertheles, the love that I have to thi soule stireth me bi evydence that I have of a gostly brother of thin and of myn, that was now late in your cuntree touchid with tho same stiringes of ful streit sylence, of ful singuler fastingis and of ful oonly-duelling on ape maner, as he grantid to me after long comounyng with me and 160 when he had proved himsilf and hise stiringis. For, as he seide, he had seen a man in your cuntre the whiche man, it is wel knowen, is evermore in gret silence, in singuler fasting and in oonli-duelling. And certis, a[s] I suppose fulli, thei ben ful trewe stiringis, tho that that man hath, causid al oonely of grace that he felith by experience withinne and not of any sight or herdsey that he hath of any other man's silence withouten (the whiche cause, if it were, schulde be clepid apely, as I sey in my symple meenyng). And therfor bewar and prove wel thi stiringis and whens thei comen, for howso thou art stirid, whether fro withinne by grace or fro withoute on ape manere, God 170 wot and I not.

Nevertheles, this may I sey in eschewing of perils liche unto this: loke that thou be none ape; that is to sey, loke that thi stiringis to

149. when[s]: cf. l. 168 and H.

152. Cf. the comment by the author of The Cloud of Unknowing about those who are insufficiently scrupulous in analysing their stirrings, for 'the devil hath his contemplatyves' (ch. 45).

154. An ape imitates what he sees others doing.

161. It is not certain to whom this refers, though the author of The Cloud of Unknowing and Walter Hilton both had reservations about the example of Richard Rolle, whose fervour may have inspired many who had no real vocation towards mystical practices. Cuntre here means 'district'.

silence or to speking, to fasting or to eting, to oonlynes or to cumpany whether thei be comen fro withinne of abundance of love and of devocion in spirit and not fro withouten bi wyndowes of thi bodily wittis, thin eeren and thin ighen; for as Jeremy seith pleynli: 'Bi siche wyndowes cometh in deeth; *Mors intrat per fenestras.*'

This sufficith, so litel as it is, for an answer to the first wher thou askest of me what is my conseyt of thee and of thees stiringis that thou spekist of to me in thi lettre. And as touching the secound thing wher 180 thou askist of me my counseil in this cas and siche othere when thei falle, I biseche Almyghti Jesu, as he is clepid the 'Angel of Grete Counseil', that he of his mercy be [thi] counseillour and thi comfortour in all thi noye and thi nede, and wisse me with his wisdom to fulfille in party by my teching, so simple as it is, the trist of thin herte the whiche thou hast to me before any other—a symple, lewid wrecche as I am, unworthi to teche thee or any other for litelnes of grace and for lacking of kunnyng. Nevertheles, though I be never so lewid, yit schal I sumwhat sey answering to thi desir at my simple kunnyng with a trist in God that his grace schal be lerner and leder when kunnyng 190 of kynde and of clergie defailith.

Thou wost wel thisilf that silence in itsilf ne speking, also singuler fasting ne comon dietyng, onelynes ne cumpany, alle thees ne yit any of hem thei ben not the trewe endis of our desir. But to sum men, and not to alle, thei ben meenes helping to the ende if thei ben don lawe-fully and by discrecion; and ellys ben thei more letting then forthering. And therfore pleynely to speke ne pleynly to be stille, pleynly to ete ne pleynly to fast, pleynly to be in cumpany or pleynly to be onely, think I not to counseil thee at this tyme, for-whi perfeccion stondith not in hem. 200

But this counseil may I yive thee generaly to holde thee by in thees stiringis and in alle other like unto thees, evermore wher thou fyndest two contraries as ben thees, silence and spekyng, fasting and eting, onelynes and cumpany, comon clothing of cristen mennes religion and singuler abites of diverse and divisid bretherhedis, with alle siche othere whatso thei be—the whiche in hemsilf ben werkis of kynde and of men. For thou hast it bi kynde and bi statut of thin utter man now

186. a (*sic* H): as

176. *Jeremiah* 9: 21.
182–3. A title found in the Septuagint and Vetus Itala versions of *Isaiah* 9: 6.

for to speke and now for to be stille, now for to ete and now for to
fast, now for to be in cumpany and now to be onely, now to be comon
210 in clothing and now to be in singuler abit, ever when thee list and
when thou seest that any of hem schulde be spedeful and helply to thee
in norisching of the hevenly grace worching withinne in thi soule;
but if it be so, that God forbede, that thou or any other be so lewid
and so blyndid in the sorweful temptaciouns of the mydday devyl that
ye bynde you by any crokid avow to any siche singulertees, as it wer
undur colour of holynes feyned undur siche an holich thraldome, in
ful and final distroiyng of the fredome of Crist—the whiche is the
gostly abit of the sovereyn holines that may be in this lif or in the
tother, bi the witnes of Poul seiyng thus: '*Ubi spiritus Domini, ibi*
220 *libertas*; There where the spirit of God is, ther is fredom.' And therto
when thou seest that alle siche werkis in their use may be bothe good
and yvel, I preie thee leve hem bothe for that is the moost ese for thee
for to do if thou wolt be meke; and leve the curious biholding and
seking in thi wittes to loke whether is beter. But do thou thus: sette
the tone on the too hande and the tother on the tother, and chese
thee a thing that is hid bitwix hem—the whiche thing when it is had
yyveth thee leeve in freedom of spirit to bigynne and to ceesse in
holding any of the tother at thine ful lyste withouten any blame.

But now thou askist me what is that thing. I schal telle thee what
230 I meene that it is. It is God for whom thou schuldist be stille, if thou
schuldist be stille; and for whom thou schuldist speke, if thou schuldist
speke; and for whom thou schuldist fast, if thou schuldist fast; and for
whom thou schuldist ete, if thou schuldist ete; for whom thou schuldist
be onely, if thou schuldist be onely; and for whom thou schuldist
be in cumpany, if thou schuldist be in cumpany; and so for sothe of
alle the remenaunt whatso thei be. For sylence, it is not God: ne
speking, it is not God; fasting, it is not God: ne eting, it is not God;
onelynes, it is not God: ne cumpany, it is not God; ne yit any of alle
the othere siche two contraries. He is hid bitwix hem and may not be
240 founden bi any werk of thi soule, but al onely bi love of thin herte.

---

214. *mydday devyl*: *cf. Ps.* 91: 6 (Vulgate) *dæmonio meridiano*, where the Authorized
version has 'the destruction that wasteth at noonday'. *Cf.* the use of *the midday feend*
in *An Exposition of Qui Habitat*, ed. B. Wallner (Lund 1954), p. 32.

219-20. *2 Corinthians* 3: 17.

239ff. *Cf.* the images in *The Cloud of Unknowing*, ch. 7, etc.

He may not be knowen by reson; he may not be thought, getyn ne trasid bi undurstonding. But he may be lovid and chosen with the trewe, lovely wille of thin herte.

Chese thee hym: and thou art sylently speking and spekingly silent; fastingly etyng and etingly fasting; and so forth of alle the remenaunt. Siche a lovely chesing of God (thus wisely leesyng and seking him out with the clene wille of a trewe herte bitwix alle siche two, levyng hem bothe when thei come and profren hem to be the poynt and the pricke of oure gostly biholding) is the worthiest trasyng and seking of God that may be getyn or lernyd in this lif—I meene for a soule 250 that wol be contemplatif—yea, though al that a soule, that thus sekith, se nothing that may be conceyved with hir gostly ighe of reson. For yif God be thi love and thi meenyng, the chief and the poynt of thin herte, it sufficith to thee in this lif, though al thou never se more of him with the ighe of thi reson al thi lif-tyme. Siche a blynd schote with the scharp dart of longyng love may never faile of the pricke, the whiche is God; as himsilf seith in the *Book of Love* wher he spekith to a languisching soule and a lovyng, seiyng thus: *'Vulnerasti cor meum, soror mea, amica mea, sponsa mea; vulnerasti cor meum in uno oculorum tuorum*; Thou hast woundid myn herte, my sister, my lemman and my 260 spouse; thou hast woundid myn herte in oon of thin ighen.'

Ighen of the soule there ben two, reson and love. By reson we may trase how myghty, how wise, how good he is in hise creatures, but not in himsilf. But evere when reson defailith, then list love live and lerne for to play. For bi love we may fele him, fynde him and hit him even himsilf. It is a wonderful ighe, love; for [of] a loving soule it is seid of oure Lord: 'Thou hast woundid myn herte in oon of thin ighen;' that is to sey in love, that is blynd to many thinges and seeth but that o thing that it sekith. And therfor it fyndeth and felith, hittith and woundith the poynt and the pricke that it schetith at wel sonner 270

---

244. *Chese thee hym*: the *thee* is a dative of interest, 'choose him for yourself'.

246. *leesyng*: probably the ME present participle of OE *lesan* 'to release'.

255–8. *Cf.* 'for the ighe of thi soule is openid on it and even ficchid therapon, as the ighe of a schoter is apon the prik that he schoteth to,' (*The Cloud of Unknowing*, ch. 5).

258–60. *Song of Solomon* 4: 9. The author borrowed the quotation and its interpretation from Richard of St. Victor's *Explicatio in Cantica Canticorum* ch. 27 (P.L. 196: 484–5).

266. 'Love is a wonderful eye'.

then it schulde if the sight wer sundrid in biholding of many thinges, as it is when the reson ransakith and sekith amongis alle siche sere diverse thinges as ben thees (silence and speking, singuler fasting and comon etyng, onelynes or cumpany, and alle siche othere) to loke whether is beter.

Lat be this maner of doyng, I preie thee, and lete as thou wistist not that there wer any siche meenes (I meene ordeyned for thee to gete God by), for treuly no more ther is if thou wolt be verrey contemplatif and soone spede of thi purpos. And therfor I preie thee and
280 othere liche to thee with the apostle, seiyng thus: '*Videte vocacionem vestram et, in ea vocacione qua vocati estis, state*; Seeth your cleping, and in that cleping that ye ben clepid stondith stifly and abidith in the name of Jesu.' Thi cleping is to be verey contemplatif, ensaumplid by Mary, Martha sister. Do thou as Mary did: sette the poynt of thin herte upon o thing. *Porro unum est necessarium*: 'For o thing is necessarie'—the whiche is God. Hym woldist thou have; him sekist thou; hym list thee love; him list thee fele; and hym list thee holde thee by—and neither by silence ne by spekyng, bi singuler fasting ne bi comoun eting, bi onelynes ne bi cumpanous wonyng. For sumtyme silence is
290 good, but that same tyme speking were beter; and ayenward sumtyme speking is good, but that same tyme silence wer betir; and so forth of alle the remenaunt, as is fasting, eting, onelynes and cumpany, and alle siche othere. For sumtyme the toone is good, but the tother is betir; but neither of hem is anytyme the best. And therfor lat be good al that is good, and betir al that is betir, for bothe thei wol faile and have eende; and chese thee the best with Mary thi myrour that nevere wol defaile. '*Maria*', inquit Optimus, '*optimam partem elegit, que non*

297. *inquit*: inquid

---

271. *sundrid*: 'distracted'.

280-1. Based on several biblical passages; *cf.* 1 *Corinthians* 1: 26, 7: 20 and *Ephesians* 4: 1. *Cf.* the use of part of this quotation in *Piers Plowman* A. x. 109.

283*ff.* From the time of St. Augustine Western Christianity used the figures of Mary and Martha as symbols of the contemplative and active lives. Based on *Luke* 10: 38–42, the distinction is met with frequently in ME writings of a mystical or semi-mystical character. *Cf.* its use in *The Cloud of Unknowing*, ch. 17.

285. *Luke* 10: 42.

293*ff.* The three stages of good, better and best may be compared with Dowel, Dobet and Dobest in *Piers Plowman*.

297-8. *Luke* 10: 42, 'And Mary', (said the Best), 'hath chosen that good part, *auferetur ab ea.*' The Best is almighti Jesu, and he seide that Mary in ensaumple of alle contemplatives had chosen the best, the whiche schulde nevere be taken fro hir. And therfor I preie thee with Mary 300 leve the good and the betir and chese thee the best.

Lete hem be, alle siche thinges as ben thees (silence and speking, fasting and eting, onelynes and cumpany, and alle siche othere) and take no kepe to hem. Thou wost not what thei bemeenen and, I preie thee, covete not to wite. And if thou schalt anytyme thinke on hem or speke, thinke then and sey that thei ben so heigh and so worthi thinges of perfeccion (for to kun speke and for to kun be stille, for to kun fast and for to kun ete, for to kun be onely and for to be in cumpany) that it were but a foly and a foul presumpcion to siche a freel wrecche as thou art for to medyl thee of so gret perfeccion; for-whi 310 for to speke and for to be stille, for to ete and for to fast, and for to be onely and for to be in cumpany, ever when we wol, may we have bi kynde; but for to kun do alle thees we may not but bi grace. And withouten doute siche grace is never geten bi any meene of siche streit silence, of siche singuler fasting or of siche onely-duelling that thou spekist of, the whiche is causid fro withouten by occasion of hering and of seyng of any other man's siche singuler doyngis.

But if evere schal this grace be geten, it bihovith to be lernyd of God fro withinne, unto whom thou hast listily lined many day bifore with al the love of thin herte, utterly voidyng fro thi gostly biholding 320 al maner of sight of anything bynethe him, though al that somme of tho thinges that I bidde thee thus voide schulde seme in the sight of sum man a ful worthi meene to gete God by. Yea, sey what men say wil; but do thou as I sey thee and lat the prove witnesse. For to him that wol be soone sped of his purpos gostly it sufficith to hym for a meene and him nedith no mo but the actuel mynde of good God onely with a reverent stiryng of lasting love; so that meene unto God gete thee noon but God if thou kepe hool thi stiring of love that thou

---

314. streit (*sic* H): foryette

---

which shall not be taken away from her;' in which 'said the Best' is not found in the Authorized Version. The quotation continues that of l. 285.

302ff. *Cf.* the attitude to bodily observances expressed in *The Cloud of Unknowing*, ch. 58.

323-4. 'Let men say what they will'.

E *

maist fele bi grace in thi herte and scaterest not thi gostly biholding
330 therfro.

Then that same that thou felist schal wel kun telle thee when thou
schalt speke and when thou schalt be stille; and it schal governe thee
discretly in al thi livyng withouten any errour, and teche thee m[i]stily
hou thou schalt begynne and ceesse in alle siche doyngis of kynde
with a grete and a soverayn discrecion. For if thou maist by grace
kepe it in custome and in contynuel worching, then if it be nedeful
to thee for to speke, for to comounly ete, or for to byde in cumpany,
or for to do any siche other thing that longeth to the trewe custom
of cristen men and of kynde, it schal first stire thee softely to speke
340 or to do that other comon thing of kynde whatso it be. And then if
thou do it not, it schal smyte as sore as a pricke on thi herte and pyne
thee ful sore and lat thee have no pees but if thou do it. And on the
same maner if thou be in speking or in any siche other werk that is
comon to the cours of kynde, if it be nedeful and spedeful to thee to be
stille and to sette thee to the contrarie (as is fasting to eting, onelynes
to cumpany, and alle siche other the whiche ben werkis of singuler
holynesse), it wil stire thee to hem.

So that thus by experience of siche a blynd stiring of love unto
God a contemplatif soule cometh soner to that grace of discrecion for
350 to kun speke and for to kun be stille, for to kun ete or for to kun fast,
for to kun be in cumpany and for to kun be onely, and alle siche othere,
then bi any siche singulertees as thou spekist of, taken bi the stiringes
of a mannes owne witt and his wille withinne himsilf or yit by the
ensaumple of any other mannes doyng withouten whatso it be. For-
whi siche streynyd doyngis undur the stiringis of kynde withouten
stiringis of grace is a passing pyne withouten any profit but if it be to
hem that ben religious or that han hem bi enjoynyng in penaunce,
wher profit riseth oonly bycause of obedience and not bi siche stretenes
of doyng withouten, the whiche is pyneful to alle that it provith. But
360 lovely and listily to wilne have God is gret and passing eese, trewe
gostly pees and erles of the endeles rest.

361. erles (*sic* H): ernes

---

333. *mistily*: 'mystically'. **352.** *taken bi*: 'inspired, instigated by'.
358. The profit comes from carrying out the penance imposed and not from
the mere severity of the external actions (such as fasting), however much discomfort
they might cause those who attempt them.

And therfor speke when thee list and leve when thee list, ete when thee list and fast when thee list, wone in cumpany when thee list and bi thiself when thee list, so that God and grace be thi leder; lat fast whoso wol and be onely whoso wol, and lat holde silence whoso holde wol; but holde thee by God that no man bigylith. For silence and speking, fasting and eting, onelynes and cumpany, alle may begyle. And if thou here of any man that spekith or of any that is still or of any that etith or of any that fastith or of any that is in cumpany or ellys bi hemsilf, thenk thou and sey if thou schalt that thei can do as thei 370 schulde do but if the cuntrarie schewe in apert. But loke thou do not as thei do (I meene for thei do so on an ape maner), for neither thou canst ne peraventure thou art not disposid as thei ben.

And therfor leve to worche after othere mennes disposicions and worche after thin owne if thou maist knowe what it is. And unto the tyme be that thou maist knowe what it is, worche after tho men's counseil that knowen her owne disposicion, but not after their disposicion; for siche men schulden yive counseil in siche casis and ellys noon.

And this sufficith for answere for al thi lettre. The grace of God be 380 evermore with the. In the name of Jesu. Amen.

VIII   The Art of Dieing

This treatise is part of a longer work known as *The Book of Vices and Virtues* which is extant in three manuscripts: Huntington Library MS. HM 147 [H], and British Museum MSS. Add. 17013 [A] and Add. 22283 (the Simeon manuscript) [S]. A is a copy of H, and H and S both derive ultimately from a common source; H has been used for this edition. The name of the English translator is unknown, but he came from the Midlands and was translating about 1375. *The Book of Vices and Virtues* is a translation of the *Somme le Roi* by Lorens d'Orléans, a thirteenth-century Dominican who was confessor to King Philip the Bold of France (1270–81). It is a composite work consisting of six major sections: the ten commandments, the articles of faith, the seven deadly sins, the seven virtues introduced by an *Ars Moriendi* (or *The Art of Dieing*) which forms an independent section, the *Pater Noster*, and the seven gifts of the Holy Ghost. Most of the six sections, including the sub-section *Ars Moriendi*, are found independently in earlier French manuscripts, though Lorens may have composed the final two sections. Lorens' work was popular and was translated into many other European languages. There were at least eight separate translations into English alone, of which the two best known examples are probably Dan Michel's *Ayenbite of Inwit* (1340) [AI] and Caxton's *Royal Book* (c. 1484) [RB]. It was also used as the basis of the English moralistic work *Disce Mori*.

Edition: W. Nelson Francis, *The Book of Vices and Virtues*. EETS o.s. 217 (London 1942). [H]

The man ne dieth not gladly that hath not lerned hit, and therfore lerne to dye and than schalt thou kunne lyve, for ther schal no man kunne lyve wel but he have lerned to dye. And he may be wel right-fully cleped a wrecche that can nought lyve ne dar not dye. Yif thou wolte lyve frely, lerne to dye gladly. And yif thou askest how schal a man lerne, we schulle teche the al swythe.

The bihoveth to wite that this lif nys but deeth. For deth is a passage, that wot every man, and therfore men seith whan a man is ded he is

4. that (*sic* A): than H

8. *that wot every man*: 'as every man knows', *cf.* l. 38.

passed. This lif is but a passynge tyme—ye, and that a litle; for al the
lif of a man, though he myght lyve a thousand yer, nys but a turnyng 10
of a mannes hond as to that other lif, that ever lasteth withouten ende
or in joye withouten ende or in sorwe and peyne.

And that witnesseth wel the kynges, the erles, the prynces and the
emperoures, that hadde sum tyme the joye of the world, and now thei
lyen in helle and crien and wailen and waryen and seyn: 'Alas, what
helpeth now us oure londes, oure grete power in erthe, honoures,
nobeleye, joye and bost? Al is passed—ye, sonner than a schadewe or
foul fleynge or a quarel of an arblawst; and thus passeth oure lif: now
be we bore and thus sone dede. And al oure lif ne durede nought a
turnyng of an hond, and now be we in endeles peyne. Oure joye is 20
turned to sorwe, oure laughtres into wepynges; corones of perles and
garlandes, riche robes, pleyinges, grete festes and alle othere goodes
beth aweye fro us and faileth.'

Thes beth the songes of helle, as Holy Writ seith; and al is to schewe
us that this lif nys not but a passage, and the deth nys but a passage,
and to lyve here nys but a passage. Than nys lif nought elles but deth,
that is to dye, and this is as soth as the *Pater Noster*, for whan thou
bygynnyst to lyve, thou bigynnist to dye. And al thi tyme and al thin
elde that is passed deeth hath taken and holdeth faste to hym. For thou
seist thou hast fifty or sixty wynter; that is not soth: deth hath hem for 30
nevere wole he yelde the ayen. And therfore the wit of the world is
folye for he that weneth clerly to see is stark blynd. The day and the

9. 'This life is but a transitory time; indeed, it is of the smallest duration'.

10–11. *turnyng of a mannes hond*: cf. ll. 19–20 and II, 352; *as to*: 'in comparison with'.

13*ff.* It was a commonplace to use the dead or old to comment on the passing of
earthly goods. This theme was frequently expressed within the so-called *Ubi sunt*
formula, as in the OE poem *The Wanderer*.

18*f.* The quickness of the passage of man's life is another common homiletic theme,
which owed much to *Ps.* 90: 4, 'A thousand years in thy sight are but as yesterday
when it is past;' *cf.* l. 10.

26. Since our life passes so quickly, life is no more than a preparation for death.

29–30. 'You say that you are fifty or sixty years old'. The *thou hast* is a literal translation from French.

31. *yelde the*: 'give (them) back to you'.

32*f.* The sense is: Day and night lead to one thing (i.e. death) and the more they do
so the less men know, for they must die and do not know how to. The sense is a little
harsh, but a similar translation is found in all the English versions; *cf.* RB *Day and night
they done one thynge, and the more they do the lasse they knowe—alwaye they deyen and
can not deye.*

nyght maketh o thing, and the more thei maken the lesse thei knowen, for they schul ever dye and kunne not dye; and therfore yit, I seye, nyght and day thou diest.

And yit in another wise wole we teche the this craft so that thou lerne to lyve wel and dye wel. Now herkene and understonde. Deeth is but a partynge bitwen the body and the soule, and that wot every man wel. Wise Catoun seith: 'Lerne wee to dye; forbere we ofte the 40 gost of the body.' And so dide thes wise philosophres ofte, that were wise and hatede this world and this lif, and so moche blamede it and so moche desirede endeles lif, that is lif without deeth that clerkes clepeth immortalite. And that soutilede thei and studiede of here owne wittes and willes, but al was for nought for thei ne hadde nother grace ne bileve of Jesu Crist. Bute holy men, that loven God and douten, [bileven] that of thre dethes beth passed two (for we beth dede in synne and we beth ded in the world), and now they abide the thridde deth, that is departyng of the body and of the soule. Bitwene hem and Paradis nys but a thynne wal that thei passen in a thought and in desir, 50 for though the body be here the herte and the gost is there, for there they haven here repeir and conversacioun, as Seynt Poule seith, here solas, here joye, here confort and here desyr. And therfore thei haten this lif that nys but deeth and thei coveiten bodily deeth, for this Damesele Porte-Joye is the deeth that alle the halewen corouneth and setteth in joye. For deth is to goode men ende of al evel and a bigyn-

---

34. dye (1): lyve H, A; sterveth AI; deyen RB

---

39. The *Distichs* of Cato or Catoun was a popular book in the Middle Ages as Chaucer's line in the *Miller's Tale*, *He knew nat Catoun, for his wit was rude*, reveals. The book's popularity is attributable to its use as a school textbook. Its authorship is uncertain, though Cato's name was associated with it only two or three centuries after it was written. It is a collection of moral precepts and gnomic utterances.

40. *philosophres*: that is, the pagan philosophers.

45f. *loven God and douten*, [*bileven*]: A omits *and* and *bileven*; AI has *lovieth God and yleveth thet*; whereas RB has *whiche love God and drede hym, of thre dethes have they passed*. Translate here: 'Holy men who love and fear God believe . . .'.

46. *we*: the translator misunderstood the French; *they* is required, as in RB.

50. *here*: 'in this world'; *there*: 'in Paradise'. The behaviour of these pagan philosophers is almost identical with that of the medieval mystics.

51. *Philippians* 3: 20, 'For our conversation is in heaven.'

54. *Porte-joye*: that is Death, because she opens the gate of heaven to those who have lived well. For allegorical women of this type *cf.* V.

54f. 'Who crowns and sets all the saints in joy'.

nynge of alle goodnesse. Deeth is the brook that departeth deeth and lif, for deeth is here and lif is there.

But the wyse folk of this world, that on the ton side of the brook lyven that seeth so wel here, on that other half thei seeth nothing, and therfore Holy Writ clepeth hem blynde fooles. For this deeth that 60 thei clepen the lif and the deth of goode men that they clepen endynge, that is to hem bigynnynge of lif; and therfore haten thilke fooles so moche deeth for they witeth nought what it is, for thei conversede, that is lyvede, on that other half the brook—and he that nevere yede fro home can no good. Than yif thou wolte lerne good and yvele go fro home, go out of thiself, that is go out of this world and lerne to dye; departe thi soule fro thi body bi thinkynge; send thin herte into that other world, that is into hevene or into helle or into purgatory, and ther thou schalt see what is good and what is yvele. For in helle schalt thou see more sorwe than any man may devyse, and in purgatory mo 70 turmentes than any man myght suffre, in Paradis more joye than any man koude or myght desyren. Helle schal teche the how God vengeth dedly synne; purgatory schal schewe the how God purgeth venyal synne; in Paradis thou schalt see al openly how vertues and goodnesse is yyolde highly in dede. In thes thre thinges is so moche that ther bihoveth no more to kunne good than wel to lyven and wel to dygh.

Nou loke yit a litle, and be nought anoyed, of thes thre thinges for to lerne to hate synne. Foryet thi body ones a day and go into helle while thou lyvest that thou come not there whan thou art ded. And thus doth ofte the holy wise men. There thou schalt see al that herte 80 hateth and fleeth: defaute of al goodnesse and gret plente of al wikkednesse, brennynge fier, stynkynge brymston, foule stormes and tempestes routynge, ydouse develes, hunger, thryst that may nevere be staunched, many manere of turmentrye, wepynges, sorwes more than any herte may thenke or any tunge may devyse, and everemore with-

58. of (2): on   75. that: that | that

---

58. That is, people who are wise in the ways of this world.

60ff. 'As for this death they call that life, and the death of good men, which is to them (the good men) the beginning of life, they (the wise of this world) call that the end.'

64. lyvede: that is, both spiritually and physically.

64-5. A proverbial expression, cf. B. J. and H. W. Whiting, Proverbs, Sentences and Proverbial Phrases (Cambridge, Mass., and Oxford 1969), H425.

80ff. For another description of hell cf. I, 12ff.

outen ende lastynge. And therfore with good right is that penaunce
cleped deeth withouten ende, for everemore a man or a womman
lyveth there dyenge and dyeth evermore lyvynge. Whan thou seest
that a dedly synne mote so dere be bought, thou woldest rathere suffre
90 to lete men flee thi skyn of thi body al quyk er thou dorstest assente
to do o dedly synne.

After go into purgatorye and there schalt thou see the pyne of soules
that repent hem here in this world. But thei were not al fully purched
and clensed, and therfore they suffre now there pyne for the remenaunt
of here penaunce al for to thei ben clene and bright, right as they were
the same tyme that they were taken out of the fontston whan thei were
cristned. And that penance is wel hidous and wel hard, for al that the
holy martires suffrede evere althermost ne womman that travaileth is
no more to acounte ayens here peyne than to bathe a man in cold
100 water to regard of thilke brennynge ovene, there that the soules
brenneth al for to they ben purged and clensed there; as a body that is
fyned and tried bi fier al for to it be fyn and no more filthe is left, for
that fier is of suche kynde that al manere of filthe that it fyndeth in the
soule of dede, of speche or of thought, that longeth to synne, be it litle
or mochel, al it brenneth and clenseth. And there is punysched and
venged al manere of venyal synne, that is to seye smale synnes that we
doth alday, ofte and many tymes in japes, in trefles and in suche othere
vanytees of this world, so that ther be nothing in the soule of no manere
filthe of synne and that sche be worthy to go into hevene, for there may
110 nothing entre but it be right fyn and bright. This fier douteth they
that with al here power kepeth hem fro dedly synne and that kepeth in
holynesse here bodies, here mowthes, here fyve wittes fro alle synnes
and lyven right as thei scholde come every day to jugement tofore

---

88. there (*sic* A): and evermore

---

92. Following certain ambiguous biblical passages, the early fathers developed the
concept of purgatory, a belief in the purging of sins through suffering. The concept
was first fully discussed by St. Augustine, and its later acceptance by St. Gregory
assured it a place in Catholic doctrine. It is frequently referred to in medieval literature,
as in Dante's *Purgatorio*, and depicted in medieval art.

96. One is at one's purest state at baptism, for then all guilt has been washed away
and one has not had enough time to sin again, *cf.* IV, 198*ff*.

97*ff*. 'For all that the martyrs suffered or that a woman suffers in labour is as little
in comparison with their torment as is the giving of a cold bath to a man in comparison
with that burning oven'.

109. *sche*: the soul.

God, for there is non that may lyve without synne. For Salamon seith that sevene tymes falleth a man in the day, and therfore bi schrifte and wepynge teeres and bedes-biddynge thei don her power to arise out and amende hem, and juge hemself in suche wise that thei abideth hardely the laste jugement. For he that jugeth hymself truly dar have no doute to be juged to dampnacioun at Domesday. And thus schal a man lerne to hate synne and flee schrewdnesse; and thus knoweth a man or a womman the holy drede of God that is bigynnynge of good and holy lif and of al goodnesse.

But it is not ynow to lete evele but a man lerne to do wel and to seche the vertues without whiche no good lyveth ne no right. Now yif thou wolte lerne good and to lyve in vertues lerne first, as I have seid, to dye. Departe thi gost fro thi body bi thenkynge and by desir and go out of this world dyenge; go into the lond of lif there non dyeth ne non eldeth, that is in Paradis. There may a man or a womman lerne to lyve wel. There may men lerne wit and wisdom and curtesye, for there may entre no vilenye. There is the joyeful companye of God, of aungeles and of halewen. There is plente of al goodnesse, fairenesse, richesse, worschipe, joye, vertues, love, wit, and joye and likynge everemore lastynge. There is non ypocrisie, ne gile, ne losengerie, ne non evel-acord, ne non envye, ne hunger, ne thrist, ne to moche hete, ne cold, ne non yvele, ne non akynge of heved, ne drede of enemys, but everemore festes grete and realle weddynges with songes and joye withouten ende. That joye is so gret that whoso hadde assayed o poynt of the leste joye that there is, he scholde be so drunke of the love of God that al the joye of this world scholde be to hym stynkynge and tur-ment; richesse, dung; honour, vice and blame; and that wonyng, gret desyr. For whoso wolde gladly and lovede to be there, it scholde make hym the hardere hate synne bi an hundred thousand part and love vertue than al the drede of helle that we have tolde of tofore, for love is wel strengere than drede. And than is a mannes lif fair and honeste

114. *Proverbs* 24: 16, 'For a just man falleth seven times'. The authorship of *Proverbs* is traditionally associated with Solomon, though it is not accepted by modern scholar-ship.

116. *thei don her power*: to the utmost of their ability.

121. An echo of *Ps.* 111: 10, 'The fear of the Lord is the beginning of wisdom.'

127ff. Descriptions of Paradise owed much to the *topos* of the *locus amoenus*, though Paradise is more frequently characterized by what it did not, rather than by what it did, contain. On paradise see N. F. Blake, *The Phoenix* (Manchester 1964), pp. 13–16, and H. R. Patch, *The Other World* (Cambridge, Mass. 1950), ch. 5.

whan men fleeth yvel and doth wel—nought for drede to be dampned,
but for desir to have hevene and for love of God and for the grete
clennesse that vertue hath and good lif.

For he that hath love to his ledere renneth fastere and with lesse
travaile than he that serveth God for drede. The hare renneth and the
150 greyhound renneth: that oon for drede, that other for gret desyr.
That on fleeth, that other chaseth. The holy men renneth as grey-
houndes for thei have evere here eighen to hevene, for there thei seen
the praie that thei honten and chaseth after; and therfore thei foryeten
alle here goodes worldely, right as doth the wrecchede hound whan he
seeth his praie and his chas tofore his eighen. This is the lif of the right
fyn lovers with gentel herte and trewe, that loven so moche vertues
that thei hateth synne. For though thei were siker that no man scholde
wite it ne God scholde nevere venge it, yit wolde they nought do a
synne. But al here thenkynge, al here travail is to kepe here hertes
160 clene and make redy that thei mowe be worthy to have the joye of
Paradis, where no vileyns herte schal entre, ne foles, ne false, ne proude,
for al the felaschipe were the wors.

156. The reference to the *fyn lovers with gentel herte* may imply in this author an
attempt to equate the service of a courtly lover to his mistress with the love of the
devout man for God; such an attempt can be found in many medieval works. *Cf.*
ll. 129–30 and 161.

IX   The Perversion of the Works of Mercy

This text is found complete only in Corpus Christi College Cambridge MS. 296 of the late fourteenth or early fifteenth century [C], but the latter part of it is also found in Trinity College Dublin MS. C III 12 of the fifteenth century [D]. Both manuscripts contain collections of Wycliffite material. While it used to be thought that the majority of them had been written by Wyclif himself, it is now accepted that many are the work of his followers. Most of these tracts were apparently prepared for the benefit of the poor priests who were sent out by the Lollards to preach to the people, and they were evidently written by people with knowledge of the Church's own educational attempts. The emphasis of the teaching by the poor preachers was on the Lord's Prayer, the ten commandments and the seven deadly sins, and they made use of Thoresby's catechism which was available in a Wycliffite version. Orthodox teaching on the works of mercy is exemplified in IV, 250ff. *The Perversion of the Works of Mercy* combines the two elements which run through Wycliffite tracts: the desire to teach the poor and the attack on the hypocrisy and worldliness of the clerics.

Edition: F. D. Matthew, *The English Works of Wyclif hitherto unprinted.* EETS o.s. 74 (London 1880). [C]

Hou Sathanas and his children turnen werkis of mercy upsodoun and disceyven men therinne and in here fyve wittis.

First Crist comaundith men of power to fede hungry pore men. The fend and his techen to make costy festis and waste many goodis on lordis and riche men and to suffre pore men sterve and perische for hunger and othere myschevys. Ye, men that feynen hem ful of charite and religion gadren propre goodis to hemselven and festen delicatly lordis and ladies and riche men and suffre here pore brethren begge for meschef and fare ful harde.

Crist comaundith to yeve drynk to thrusty [men] and wymmen.   10
The fend and his techen to purveye heigh wyn and spised ale and strong

1. upsodoun: upsodom

---

7. *propre*: 'one's own'. The writer was doubtless hinting at the friars who take a vow of poverty and ought not to have any property of their own; *cf.* ll. 25–7.
11. *heigh*: 'luxurious, rich'; a word used in Wycliffite writings to imply excess.

for riche men and lordis to make hem dronken and chide and fightte
and foryete God and his lawe, and to suffre pore, that han nought of
here owene and may not labore for febilnesse or sikenesse and blynde-
nesse, drynke water and falle in feveris or ellis perische.

Crist comaundith to clothe nakyd men and wymmen whanne thei
han noght of here owene. Therto the fend and his techen to yeve costly
clothis and manye to riche men and mynstralis or shavaldours for
worldly name and suffre pore men have nakid sidis and schakynge
20 lippis and hondis for cold that woo is hem with the lif. Ye, prelatis
and men of singuler religion, that taken the charge to ben procuratouris and dispenderis of pore mennus liflode, clothen fatte horsis with
gaie sadlis and bridlis and mytris and croceris with gold and silver
and precious stonys, and suffren pore men and children perische for
cold. And yit thes prelatis and newe religious comen in staat of Cristis
povert and his apostlis, and techen and crien that whatevere thei han
is pore mennus goode. Yit riche men closen dede stockis and stonys
with precious clothis, with gold and silver and perlis and gaynesse to
the world, and suffren pore men goo sore acold and at moche meschefe.
30   Crist techith to herberwe pore men that han non houses ne peny to
peye for here innys. The fend and his techen to herberwe riche men
and lordis with gret cost and deyitte for worldly worschipe and suffre
pore men wander in stormys and slepe with the swyn and many
tymes suffre not hem come withinne here yatis, and to fynde many
excusacions and coloure this doynge. Ye, ypocritis of privat religion

22. with: and   **30.** herberwe: herbwre

---

18. *mynstralis or shavaldours*: minstrels were usually equated with spendthrifts by
religious writers for they were not thought to make any positive contribution to the
community; *cf. Piers Plowman* C. i. 35–6:

    And somme murthes to make as mynstrals conneth,

    That wollen neyther swynke ne swete bote swery grete othes.

Cf. also XI, 249. A *shavaldour* was a robber; the word originated in the North in the
sense 'border-raider', but then became more generalized.

21. *singuler*: *cf. privat* (l. 35); this charge was used in Wycliffite writings of the
friars to imply they were withdrawn from the public body.

25. *newe religious*: the friars; the major orders were founded in the thirteenth century.

27. *closen*: 'wrap, enclose', so that the wood is hidden beneath the finery; but
emendation to *clothen* (*cf.* l. 22) is possible.

28–9. They make them attractive to human sight, but God sees through the finery.

35. *coloure this doynge*: 'provide specious reasons for this action'.

35ff. The friars were often accused of using the confessional to grant absolution

maken grete houses and costy and gaely peyntid more than kyngis and
lordis bi sotil beggynge and confessions and trentalis and meyntenynge
of synne, and herberewe lordis and riche men, and namely ladies, and
suffre pore men lie withouten or geten houslewth at pore men or
ellis perische for wedris and cold. 40

Crist techith to visite sike men and counforte hem and helpe hem of
sustenaunce. The fend and his techen to visiten riche men, lordis and
ladies in here prosperite and lykynge to be holden kynde and curteis,
and to counforte eche other in synne and to have lustis of glotonye,
lecherie and othere schrewidnessis; but of pore men that ben beddrede
and couchen in muk or dust is litel thought on or noght. Yit ypocritis
of feyned religion visiten not fadirles children and modirles and widewis in here tribulacion, and kepe not hemself unbleckid fro this world
as Seynt Jame techith; but visete oft riche men and wymmen and
namely riche widewis for to gete worldly muk bi false disceitis and 50
carien it home to Caymes castelis and Anticristis covent and Sathanas
children and marteris of glotonye.

Crist techith to visite men in prison and helpe to delyvere hem in
good manere and counforte hem bi almes-yevynge. The fend and his
presonen pore men for dette whanne thei ben not at power to paie and
traveile nyght and day and lyven ful harde and toylen with trewthe
and susteynen wif and children; and on hem is no mercy. Yit feyned

---

45. othere: othē
56. toylen: tolyne
49. visite: viseto
57. susteynen: susteynem

---

to the rich in return for money or a contribution towards their building expenses,
cf. Piers Plowman C. iv. 45–67. In that passage a friar approaches a rich lady, a class
specially mentioned here as particularly vulnerable to the friar's flattery. During the
fourteenth and fifteenth century most English kings had friars as their confessors, so
they wielded considerable influence. A trental is a payment made for a set of thirty
requiem masses.

43. *lykynge*: usually used in religious prose in an unfavourable sense implying an
unnatural desire, *cf.* l. 197; *kynde*: 'high born'. The friars can flatter the powerful
because they know the social graces and use them for their own ends.

49. *James* 1: 27, 'Pure religion and undefiled before God and the Father is this,
To visit the fatherless and widows in their affliction, and to keep himself unspotted
from the world.'

51. Caim was used punningly to imply the four orders of friars: C (Carmelites),
A (Augustines), I (Jacobins, i.e. Dominicans), M (Minorites, i.e. Franciscans), giving
CAIM, i.e. Cain. Caim's castle was a typical Wycliffite expression suggesting the com-
fortable living accommodation of the friars who had set themselves up like landed

religious men pursuen pore prestis to prison and to brennynge bi
many cursed lesyngis and sclaundrynge prive and apert for as mochel
60 as thei prechen trewly and frely Cristis gospel and Goddis hestis and
reproven here ypocrisye, symonye, coveitise and othere disceitis.
And yit thes ypocritis blenden lordis and prelatis to enprisone siche pore
prestis techynge the treuthe bi comaundement and ensaumple of Crist
and his apostlis, notwithstondynge that lordis and prelatis ben charged
up peyne of dampnacion to helpe hem and meyntene this treuthe and
prechouris of it.

It is holden a werk of mercy to birie dede men after the techynge
of Goddis lawe. The fend techith worldly riche men, clerkis and
religious to make solempnyte whanne riche men ben dede with dirige
70 and messis and wax and rengynge and grete festis; but whanne pore
men ben dede unnethe wole ony man berie hem or seie derige or masse.
Yit feyned religious wolen come to riche mennus dirige in gret multitude and stire hem to be biried in here chirche, and stryven and fightten
for the dede careyne for love of offrynge and worldly honour; but
pore men schullen not lie among hem though thei axen it nevere so
faste for charite.

And thus in stede of werkis of bodely mercy and charite is comen
in ypocrisie of worldly name and coveitise and norischynge of synne
and sotil excusynge therof; and evyl is clepid good and good evyl.
80 Werkis of mercy ben worse turned upsodoun. Crist seith it is a
sovereyn werk of mercy and charite to teche unlernyd men the rightte

---

gentry. The name Antichrist is derived from the *Epistles of St. John*; in the medieval
period he became an embodiment of all that is evil, *cf. Piers Plowman* C. xxiii. Antichrist has his own convents and martyrs, but they are the perversion of those belonging
to Holy Church.

58. *pore prestis*: the Lollard priests. The statute *De heretico comburendo* allowed for
the burning of heretics, and William Sawtry was the first to suffer this fate in 1401.

64. *Cf. Piers Plowman* C. ix. 23 ff.

69. *dirige*: the first word of the antiphon in the Office of the Dead (*Ps.* 5: 8), and
hence used to mean the Office itself.

70. *wax and rengynge*: candles and the tolling of the church bells.

73. *hem*: the rich men, 'and urge them (the rich men) to be buried in their (the
friars') church'. The passage implies that the friars arrived only when the rich were
dead, but the author no doubt meant that the friars squabbled with the dying men as
to where they should be buried and so destroyed the seemliness of the occasion.

74. Many rich tombs and chapels survive from the fifteenth century for it was a
period in which special attention was paid to death; the prestige attaching to the
churches where such tombs were located was considerable.

weie to hevene, that is the gospel and Goddis comaundementis. The
fend and his seyn it is grete charite to teche yonge men and othere sotil
craftis and nedeles and queynte sleightis to disceyve schepische men
of worldly goodis and make hemself riche and bostful and proude.
And the fend bi sotil menys of ypocrisie and symonye stireth lordis
and myghtty men to make an ydiot and fool curatour of cristene
soulis, that neither may ne kan ne wole for his opyn synne and worldly
lif and ignoraunce of Holy Writt and necligence and worldly vanyte
and drede of worldly shame and loos teche hem Goddis lawe, ne suffre   90
othere to teche hem frely and trewely withouten flaterynge for drede
last his owene falsnesse be knowen; and yit thes cursed avaunsynge
is clepid charite to helpe thus a pore man. But an ydiot and a leccherous
wrecche schal be sett to kepe the soulis for litel pris, and the more
lorel goo on haukynge and huntynge, and serve in lordis courtis in
worldly offices. And the devyl drawith with his helpis alle that he
may to helle—and this is clepid mercy and charite. But this develis
charite puttith oute charite and love of God and bryngith in love of
money and synne and hate of vertues and cristene soulis.

Crist seith it is [a] werk of mercy to conseile at perti hou a man   100
schal best lyve in this or this special poynt. The fend and his seyn it is
mercy and charite to conseile men to holde forth craftis that thei usen
ayenst here conscience and excusen hem bi almes, as masse-syngynge
and makynge of nedles houses and costy. And whanne clerkis schullen
conseile lordis and othere men hou thei may best serve God and save

---

82. The Lollards placed a special emphasis on the availability of the Bible in translation so that all could know the gospel and the commandments.

86ff. It was common complaint that parishes were neglected. Rectors of benefices
often employed someone else to execute their parish duties for a much smaller sum
than the value of the benefice (94); these vicars were often incompetent and ignorant.
The money which should have been used in the parish was employed by the absentee
rector for worldly ends (94–6), for he was often employed in some form of civil or
ecclesiastical administration. There was an enormous gap between the attainments of
the educated clergy and the parish priests, who were often as ignorant as their parishioners; hence Pecham and Thoresby had made attempts to improve their education,
cf. IV. Cf. the portrayal of the parson who does not leave his flock in the *General
Prologue* of the *Canterbury Tales* (A 507–14) and of the bad priests who neglect their
parishes in *Piers Plowman* C. i. 81ff.

96. *his*: this refers to *the more lorel*, who though a priest gives example only of
worldly living and ambition.

100ff. Rich men's sins could be absolved by paying friars to sing masses or by con-
buting to their buildings, cf. ll. 35–7.

here soulis in here astaat, this conseil is turned into worldly wisdom
as bildynge of castellis and arraiynge of housholde in lond of pees and
of werre. And whanne it [is] reserved to the Holy Gost to yeve utterly
conseil in special poyntis that ben not expresly comaundid ne forboden
110 in Holy Writt, worldly clerkis ful of pride, symonye, coveitise and
othere synnys yeven fulbut conseil ayenst the Holy Gost and ayenst
the helthe of the soule for here owene pride and coveitise; and thus
conseil of the Holy Gost and profit of soulis is putt bihynde and conseil of the world and the fleisch and of Sathanas is putt forth.

God biddith that lordis and sovereyns schulden in resonable manere
chastise here sugetis, servauntis and children whanne thei trespassen
opynly in word or dede ayenst Goddis comaundementis. The fend
and his techen that suggettis and servauntis ben cruely beten, pyned,
prisoned, and sumtyme hangid and drawen for worldly trespas and
120 defaute of here servyce-doynge and unreverence ayenst worldly sovereyns but of trespas and dispit of God and his lawe no charge but
myrthe and liynge and japynge. Worldly prelatis of Anticrist seyn
that lordis schullen chastise here sogetis of worldly causes, but not of
lecherie ne pride ne forswerynge, be it nevere so opyn, for that longeth
to jurdiccion of prelatis. Netheles yif thei han money of thes lecherous
theves, thei schullen lie in here cursed synne fro yeer to yeer—ye be
al here lif yif thei paien moche and redily. Clerkis seyn that lordis ben
cursed yif thei chastisen hem, though thei ben nevere so foule lecche-

122. myrthe (sic D): myghthe

106. *this conseil is turned into*: 'the advice they offer consists of'. Because clerks
were used in the civil administration they often advised on matters like castle-building
instead of directing their attention to saving souls.

111. *fulbut*: the word is not recorded in OED or MED; Matthew glosses as 'head-
strong', but perhaps the meaning 'complete, total' is more suitable.

120. *servyce-doynge*: either the execution of official duties or the completion of
feudal service.

121. *no charge*: a shortened form of *it is no charge* 'no importance is attached (to
something)'.

122ff. Clerks were responsible to their ecclesiastical superiors for any breaches of
canon law, which was outside the jurisdiction of the civil authorities.

125-6. The first *thei* refers to the prelates, the second to the 'lecherous thieves', in
this case the lesser clergy. As long as the higher ecclesiastical functionaries (such as bishop
and archdeacon) were bribed, clerks could transgress canon law with impunity.
Cf. the portrayal of the archdeacon and the summoner in Chaucer's *Friar's Tale*.

128. *cursed*: 'excommunicated'; attempts by the civil authorities to discipline the
clergy were frequently countered with excommunication.

rous and nevere so cursed heretikis, for symonye and coveitise and
meyntenynge of synne and robbynge pore tenauntis bi extorcions for   130
Anticristis correccions and veyn halwynge of chirchis and auteris and
othere japis. Lord, soone and esely schulde synne be hurlid oute of
lond yif lordis wolden in al here wille, al here witt and power dispise
synne and synful wrecchis and preise and meyntene vertue and vertuous
men; and certis thei ben holden herto up peyne of dampnacion for
ellis thei failen in mercy and charite.

God techith that it is mercy to counforten men fallen in myschif
and disese. [The] fend and his techen that it is almes to pursuen [men]
to prisonynge and exilynge whanne thei ben brought doun bi sodeyne
loos, as brennynge and robbynge, for riche men beren hem on honde   140
that it is for here synne and mysreulynge of hemself, and ellis othere
brothelis wolden renne awey with riche mennus good; and therfore
thei schulden be seet in strong prison til thei perische for hungur and
myschef and dispeiren and grucchen ayenst God. And thus for love
of rotyn dritt thei don that is in hem to dampne many soulis. Yit
worldly clerkis cursen for dymes and offryngis, though men ben ful
pore and thei don nothing here offis. And veyn religious cessen not to
begge and crave of pore men, though here rente be bihynde and here
werk-bestis in distresse and wif and childe hungry and nakyd. And so
thei bryngen hem into more myschif and counforten hem not but bi   150
lesyngis and fals grauntynge of gostly helpe, that is not in here power
but only in Goddis delynge.

God techith that it is mercy to foryeve trespasis and wrongis don
ayenst men hemself and algatis rancor and evil-wille of herte. The
fend and his seyn that it is manlynesse and rightwisnesse and almes to
betyn gadlyngis and be vengid on hem that don hem wrong, for ellis

---

149. werk- (*sic* D): wrek   **151.** and (*sic* D): of
152. Goddis (*sic* D): goode   **154.** evil: ewil

---

131. *Anticristis correccions*: priests who serve Antichrist rather than Christ enforce
a perverted chastisement upon their parishioners; such an extortion was the one
demanded by the archdeacon and his summoner in *The Friar's Tale*.

140. That is, the possessions of the poor are either burned or stolen. *beren hem on
honde*: 'abuse them by convincing them.'

145-7. As, for example, Chaucer's Pardoner did. A *dyme* is a tenth part or tithe paid
to the Church; the *thei* refers to the clerks. Poor men are forced to pay their dues even
though the priests fail to perform their duties.

154. *ayenst men hemself*: 'against oneself'.

theves and lorellis wolden overrenne hem and here sugetis wolden
not drede hem; but comynly this chastysynge is don bi pride, coveitise
and out of charite. And though lordis and grete men wynnen herby
160 worldly name and temporal goodis, thei lesen charite and here soule
that ben worthi a thousandfold betre than alle erthely tresour.

God seyth it is mercy and charite to suffre men mekely and wisly
whanne thei ben out of reson as wroth and malencolious. The fend and
his seyn that this [is] couwardise and leesynge of worldly name and
boldynge of evyl-doeris; and therfore for o schrewed word a man mot
quyte another or moo. And so of evyl dedis cometh hate and strif,
and fighttynge and pledynge be reised, and witt and reson and charite
exilid, and many men perischid in bodi and soule.

God comaundith us to love oure enemys of oure herte and doo
170 good to men that hatith us and preie for men that pursuen us wrongfully and falsly. The devyl and his seyn that [it] is rightful to hate oure
enemys, and don hevyl and harm to hem that haten us and falsly
pursuen us, and axe vengaunce of oure enemys and false pursueris for
ellis we schullen norische oure enemys in here synne, and overrenne
us and distroie us, oure wifis and children and goodis, and therfore
we willen defende us the while that we may. Trewe men seyn to the
fend and his disciplis that yif we kepen Goddis hestis oure God wole
fighten for us and maken oure enemys afferd, and bi oure goode
pacience and charite and herty preiynge for oure enemys thei schulden
180 bi Goddis grace cesse of here wrong and turne to pees and charite;
and this is lighttere and betere than to conquere al the erthe bi dynt
of swerid. And yif oure enemys ben endurid in synne, as was Pharaoo,
oure Godde wolde ordeyne the beste for us bothe for body and soule
yif we kepen mekenesse, pacience and charite. And sith werris comen

159. *out of*: 'without'.

163. *malencolious*: 'excessively gloomy, morbid'.

165–6. As what a man says in the heat of a moment is not forgiven his words
provoke a lengthy quarrel, and thus he has to pay for his hasty word many times.

172. *hevyl*: 'evil'; because of the instable nature of initial *h*, it was often added to
words to which it did not properly belong.

174. There is a change of subject here; it is our enemies who would overrun us.

176–82. An interesting contrast to the motivation of many ME romances of the
chanson de geste type.

182. Cf. *Exodus* 5–13.

184f. It was a common Christian idea, which stems from the Old Testament, that
God punished the sinful on earth by sending warlike nations against them. Bede had

to men for synnys, let men leve here cursed synne, and God of mercy
and pees wole yeve us reste and pees of alle erthely enemyes.

Bi thes cautelis and many moo the fend and his disciplis distroien
werkis of mercy and fallen into loos of thingis that thei coveiten mochel
and into endelis myschefes that thei wolen to askape, for thei wolen
not be reulid bi Goddis lawe and reson but bi here wille, and therfore   190
alle thingis schal turne ayenst hem at the laste.

Yit the fend disceyveth men bi here fyve wittis and maketh hem
menys to synne where thei schulden be menys to vertue in good
governale of men. First he stirith men to seen vanyte of this world
and setten here herte theronne and foryeten God and his werkis. Also
he stirith men to see faire wymmen and bryngith mynde of hem and
greet likynge of lecherie into mennus hertis til thei consenten to synne
and fulfillen it in dede. Also whanne men seen lordischipis of this world
and precious juelis and gold and silver, faire hors and scheep and othere
goodis, the fend stireth hem to desire hem unskilfully and sette more   200
here herte on hem than on vertues and blisse of hevene; and thanne
thei fallen into pride and coveitise and othere synnys. But men schulden
see Goddis werkis, as hevene and erthe, and Goddis creaturis and herbi
knowen the myght, the wytt and goodnesse of the lord that made alle
thingis of not, and drede hym over alle thingis and love him over alle
creaturis.

Whanne men schulden here Goddis comaundementis and poyntis
of charite and rightwisnesse and treuthe, the fend stirith hem to heren
foul speche of leccherie, of bacbytynge of neigheboris and lesyngis
for to have mynde and likynge of synne and to stire men to hate and   210
envye and pledynge and fighttynge, so that mekenesse and pacience
and charite schullen be lost and cursednesse of synne regneth that

---

190. here: hire   194. he: thei

---

claimed, for example, that the Anglo-Saxon invasion was God's way of punishing
the sinful Britons.

187ff. Because they destroy the works of mercy, the devils will lose what they want
and fall into the mischances they seek to avoid. God is vindicated in the end.

192. hem: that is, our five senses. The five senses are now discussed in turn: sight
(193ff.), hearing (207ff.), smell (215ff.), taste (227ff.), and touch (260ff.). They figure
frequently in religious literature, usually as the means whereby a man sins; for example,
Ancrene Wisse part 2 deals with the custody of the senses.

196. and bryngith mynde of hem: and makes men remember beautiful women and
think about them.

unnethe can ony man kepe his tonge fro fals and veyn swerynge and schrewid spekynge bothe of lecherie and false spekyngis.

Whanne men schullen in spirit smelle the swettenesse and the holynesse of Jesu Crist and his lif, and smelle bi bodily witt the swettenesse and good odour of herbis and spicis and trees and othere creaturis to love God and serve God and herie hym for his goodnesse, the fend stirith men to sette here lust in smellynge of lekerous metis and drynkis

220 to take overemochil of hem til thei lesen here wittis and foryeten God and his servyce and fallen in lecherie and slepen as hooggis, and chiden and fightten as woode houndis, and sweren herte and bonys, and cursen and warien and prechen opynly cursed lesyngis, and yeven ensaumple of synne as cruel fendis of helle. For bi this doynge thei blasphemen God and styren men to synne more spedly than don many thousand fendis bi hemself.

Whanne men schulden taste and take mete and drynk in resonable mesure to sustene here lif and labore and therfore thank God and serve hym mekely and wilfully and love hym hertly, the fend stirith men to

230 sewe here owene lustis of flesch, to walwe in glotonye and drounkenesse as swyn in the feen, that ther is neither witt ne reson in hem ne myght to goo on the erthe sumtyme. And to fulfille this stynkynge glotonye and dronkenes thei seken many stretis and tavernes to seke lekerous morselis and swete drynkis, and borowen other mennus catel and payen not ayen many tymes; for hereby thei wasten here owene goodis and other mennus and comen to povert and ben casten in prison til thei sterven. And bi this glotonye and dronkenesse thei wasten here owen bodi and wittis and fallen into sikenesse on many maneris and

---

230. flesch: flecsch

---

222. *sweren herte and bonys*: they swear by Christ's heart or parts of his body. *Cf. The Pardoner's Tale*:

> Hir othes been so grete and so dampnable
> That it is grisly for to heere hem swere.
> Oure blissed Lordes body they totere. (C 472–4)

223–4. The lives of sinful men encourage others to sin just as the devils entice men to go astray.

231–2. *myght to goo on the erthe*: they are so drunk they cannot walk or stand, as happened with Gluttony in *Piers Plowman* C. vii. 350ff.

233. For a rather different attitude to drunkenness *cf.* 'Monologue of a Drunkard', No. 117 in R. H. Robbins, *Secular Lyrics of the XIVth and XVth Centuries*, 2nd edn. (Oxford 1955).

lesen worldly catel and myghttis of the soule, as understondynge, mynde and reson, and geten peynes of helle in bodi and soule but yif 240 thei amende hem trewely in this world. And the fend techith glotonys and dronkelewe men to excuse this wast on this manere: 'God made alle goode mete and drynke covenable for men schulden spende it and lyve therby.' But thei taken non hede of the mesure ne hou falsly thei lyven ayenst Goddis lawe, and hou Crist and his seyntis taughten and useden abstynence and penaunce, and hou cristene men schulden conquere hevene bi brekynge of fleschly lustis, as Crist techith in the gospel, and hou Crist and Poul and Petir comaunden us that we schullen not fille the desiris of oure flesch, but as gestis or comelyngis and pilgrimes absteynen hem fro fleschly desires that fightten ayenst the 250 soule. And certis the lesse that a man spende bothe of mete and drynk and clothe and alle othere necessaries, so that he be strong to serve God and do his labour aftir the staat that God settith him inne, so moche the betre bothe for body and soule and alle othere men. But houevere we excusen us, we wasten nedeles moche goode both in mete and drynk and clothis werbi pore men schulden be holpen; and we betre serve God and lesse bisi aboute the body and more bisy aboute God and helthe of oure soulis bi lesse cost and spendynge yif we holden goode mesure.

The fend disceyveth men and wymmen bi touchynge of membris 260 ordeyned for genderure of mankynde, and bi kissyng and clippyng is the fier of lecherie kyndlid and norischid in herte til the dede sue, and many tymes long custome in this cursed synne. Therfore seith the wise man: 'He that handlith pich schal be foulid therof.' That is, men handlynge wymmen and kyssynge hem schullen be blickid with lust

250. pilgrimes: ᵢpilgrimes   251. drynk: dry\nk
262. fier: feir   263. in (*sic* D): and

---

244. *Mesure* or moderation is frequently stressed by moral writers as an essential concomitant of man's behaviour; it is sometimes described as the mother of all virtues.

248*ff.* The passage is based on *1 Peter* 2: 11, 'I beseech you as strangers and pilgrims, abstain from fleshly lusts, which war against the soul.' For the concept of pilgrimage *cf.* XI, 143.

257*ff.* We serve God better and are less intent on our physical welfare and more intent on God and the salvation of our souls to the extent that we spend less on ourselves, provided always we observe a due moderation in our spending.

262–3. And frequently this wicked sin is practised for a long time.

263–4. *Ecclesiasticus* 13: 1.

of lecherie other in herte other in body or ellis in bothe. Therfore Jerom and seyntis seyn that fleynge fro suche companye and abstynence and saad traveile is best medecyne ayenst lecherie; but this weiward daliaunce with wymmen is so comyn that unnethe can ony
270 man kepe hym clene, or sengle or weddid or men of ordre of religion.

And thus it is verrifyed that God seith by Jeromye: 'Deth hath entrid bi youre wyndowis,' that ben fyve wittis. Bi thes queyntises and many moo the fend disceyveth men, and of instrumentis or menys and armu[r]e of vertue he makith instrumentis or menys and armour of synne. God graunte us grace to have mynde on the peynes that Crist suffrede in herte, in his hondis and feet, in his heed, in his sightte, and herynge, spekynge, smellynge and tastynge, and in eche place of his bodi fro the heved to the sole of the foot, and to spende alle the myghttis of soule and bodi and oure fyve wittis trewely in his servyce,
280 to seke his worschipe in alle thingis and distroie synne and falsnesse bothe in oureself and othere men, and to holde and meyntene vertuous lif and rightwisnesse and pees and charite. Amen.

267. companye: compayne   **273.** or (*sic* D): of
280. in (*sic* D): and

266ff. The avoidance of women may be considered part of the anti-feminist strain that runs through the works of many Fathers and much ME religious prose; it also emerges as a *topos* in ME verse.

271-2. *Jeremiah* 9: 21, 'For death is come up into our windows.' *Cf.* VII, 176–9.

273-4. As for example the five senses, *cf.* ll. 191–3.

275. Christ suffered in his five senses to give us an example of how we should overcome the sinful inclinations of our senses so that they might be directed to virtue.

X The Golden Legend

The Dominican Jacobus de Voragine, who was Archbishop of Genoa (1291–8) and a famous North Italian preacher and teacher, wrote a book of saints' lives and associated legends in Latin called *Legenda Aurea* (LA). The book, in which the lives were arranged in accordance with the ecclesiastical calendar, was very popular: its stories were used for pictorial narrative by medieval artists and it was translated into most West European languages. There were at least two separate translations into both French and English. The first English translation was made by a friar, who called himself a 'sinful wretch', in 1438. It was translated from the French version associated with Jehan de Vignai and not from the original Latin, and the translator added to his version prose retellings of the poetic lives of some English saints found in the *South English Legendary* (SEL) of the thirteenth century. *The Finding of the True Cross* was translated from French and was part of the original Latin text; *The Life of St. Edmund* was taken from SEL. The second English translation of the *Golden Legend* was made in 1483 by Caxton, who used the earlier English translation as well as the Latin and French texts.

The 1438 translation survives in seven fifteenth-century manuscripts, all of which differ among themselves; their relationship still remains to be investigated fully. I have printed the lives from British Museum MS. Add 35298 [A], but I have compared this text with British Museum MSS. Add. 11565 [B], Harley 630 [H], Harley 4775 [Z], and Caxton's printed text. Of the manuscripts consulted only A contains *The Life of St. Edmund*.

The early translation of the *Golden Legend* has not yet been edited, but Caxton's text is available in F. S. Ellis, *The Golden Legend* (London 1892).

(a) The Finding of the True Cross

The fyndyng of the holy crosse was CC yere and more after the resurreccion of oure Lorde. Men reden in the *Gospelle of Nichodeme* that whan Adam was sike Sethe, his sone, wente to the yeatis of Paradyse terrestre and askid pituously of the oyle of mercy for to

2. The *Gospel of Nicodemus*, an apocryphal work compiled about 425 which deals with the quest of Seth (*cf.* VI) and the harrowing of hell, was very popular, translations into most W. European languages being found. Prose and poetic versions are found in Middle English, see W. H. Hulme, *The Middle English Harrowing of Hell and Gospel of Nicodemus* (London 1907).

have noyntid hys fader to have his hele. To whom Michael the archaun-gelle appierid and saide: 'Ne traveyle thou not ne wepe thou not as thou doyst for to gete the oyle of the tre of mercy, for thoue mayste not have hit in no wyse before vM¹ and vC yere be fulfyllid'—that is to wete from Adam into the passhion of Cryste. Of which vM¹ and vC yere were passid than but iiC and xxxiii^ti yere.

And it is red elswhere that the angelle toke hym a branche and bade hym plante it in the mounte of Lyban. And verily in a story of the Gregis, though it be apocrifie, hit is wretyn that the angelle toke hym of the tre of the which Adam had synned and saide to hym when the tre shalle bere frute his fader shulde be helid. And whan Seth came ayen home he founde his fader ded and than he plantid this braunche on his fader's tombe. And whan it was plantid it grewe and beganne a grete tre and durid unto the tyme of Salaman. But whether these thyngis be true or no, that leve I to the wylle of the reder, for thaye be not wretyn in no cronycle ne in no story autentyke.

Salomon than se this tre so fayre; he commaundid to smyte hym downe and put hym save in the house of Sanxe. And as John Bylet sayeth, that tre wolde never be meten for no maner of werke, for either it was to longe or to shorte; and therefore the werkemen had it in dispite and toke no hede thereof, but laide it over a water as for a bridge for men to passe over. And whan the Queen of Saba came to hire the wysedom of Salomon, as she shulde passe over that water and over the tre she sa in spryte howe that the savyoure of the worlde shulde dye on that tre. And therefore she wolde not passe over, but

---

22. hym: hyn

---

7. The oil of mercy was interpreted as Christ's passion.

10. That is, 5,500 and 233 years respectively; cf. VI, 316.

11. Several versions of the Seth legend mention this, the earliest being apparently John Beleth's *Rationale divinorum officiorum* (c. 1170). *Lyban* is Lebanon.

12. Cf. VI, 319ff.

14. *of the tre*: a branch of the tree (cf. l. 17).

15. The tree which is then the cross bears Christ as fruit at the crucifixion.

17. *beganne*: 'developed into'.

22. *house of Sanxe*: a corruption of LA's *in domo saltus*. Solomon had intended to use the wood in the Temple, but it was always too long or too short for any particular place; God was reserving it for a different task. For *Bylet* see note to l. 11.

26. For the Queen of Sheba's visit see *1 Kings* 10.

wurshippid that tree. And it is red in the *Maister of Storyes* that the 30
Queen of Saba, that segh that tre in the house of Sanxe, and whan she
was gone home to hir owne cuntray, she sente Salamon worde that a
man shulde be hongid on that tre by whos deth the kyngdom of Jeuis
shulde be distroyed. And than Salamon take awaye that tre and hid it
depe in the erthe. And after that the pyssyne of probacion was made
there where men wysshen the sacrifice; and, menn saye, that mevyng
of the water ne the curacion of the people was not only done for that
the angelle came downe but by the vertue of the tre.

And whan the passhion nyghed it is certeyne that the tre floterid
above; and whan the Jewis se it thaye toke it up and made thereof 40
the crosse of oure Lorde. And the crosse was of iiii maner of trees, that
is to saye of palme, of cypres, of sidre and of olyve; whereof a verce
sayeth: 'The trees of the crosse ben palme, olyve, sidre and cypres.'
In the crosse there were iiii difference: that is the tre [uprighte, the tre]
overtharte, the table that was set above, and the morteyse that the
crosse was fastenyd in. In this difference of trees is sayen to touche the
apostle Paule when he sayeth 'that ye mowe comprehende with alle
the seyntis which is the lenght, the brede, the hight, the depnes.' The

---

31. Queen: Queeñ   **48.** is (*sic* H, Z): in A, B

---

30. *Maister of Storyes*: in this instance Peter Comestor's *Historia scolastica*; but in others (l. 93) the *Ecclesiastical History* of Eusebius.

31f. *that segh that*: the first *that* is not found in the corresponding Latin of LA; its inclusion makes the syntax difficult as it leaves *the Queen of Saba* without a predicate. One must take it with *she* (l. 32) as a tautologous subject.

35. *pyssyne of probacion*: the watering place where the beasts for sacrifice in the Temple were washed. It was so holy that an angel used to descend into it and stir the water. The first sick man to enter the water after the angel's visit was cured of his illness. But in this text the stirring of the water and the curing of the sick are said to have been caused as much by the tree as by the angel.

41. *trees*: woods.

42-3. *verce*: This verse, which is taken straight from the source, has not been identified.

44f. The cross was of four parts (the upright, the traverse, the plaque with the inscription, and the block at the foot to support it) and each part was made of a different sort of wood. The omission, common to A, B and H, is supplied from Z.

46f. 'This difference among the four sorts of wood appears to be referred to by Paul when he . . .'; *sayen* means 'seen', cf. LA *videtur*, and *sayyng* (l. 177). The text referred to is *Ephesians* 3: 17–18, 'that ye, being rooted and grounded in love, may be able to comprehend with all saints what is the breadth, and length, and depth, and height'.

F

which wordis Austyn, the holy doctoure, expownyth in this maner:
50 the brede of the crosse of oure Lorde Jesu Cryste is saide in the travers
where oure Lordis hondis were streynid on; the lenght fro the erth to
the brede of the armes where oure Lordis body was streynid on and
turmentid on; the height fro the brede was where the hed enclynyd on;
the depnes was that was hyd in the erth where the crosse was fastenyd
on. In which signes of the crosse alle cristen mennys dedis ben discryvid,
that is to saye to werke welle in Cryste and to cleve in hym perseverantly and to hope in hevynly sacramentis and not mysuse them.

This precyous tre of the crosse was hid within the erthe CC yere
and more, but hit was founde after in this maner by Elyn, the moder
60 of Constantyne the emperoure. In that tyme grete multitude of
barbaryns withoute nombre were assemblid besidis the ryver of
Danibe and wolde have passid over and submyttid alle the region of
the oryent to her lordeship. And whan Constantyne the emperoure
wyste that, he remevid his hooste and came ayenst hem apon the
Danibe. These men of Barbarye encresid alle daye and passid over the
flode, and than Constantyne had grete drede and se that he must
fyght with hem in the morowe. In that same nyght the angelle of
God awoke hym and saide to hym that he shulde loke upwarde. And
than he lokid up to hevynwarde and se the signe of the crosse shynyng
70 right clere with grete light, and ther was wretyn above with letters
of golde 'Thou shalte overcome thyne enemyes by this signe.' And
than he was comfortid by that hevynly vysion and than he lete make a
crosse and ordeynid it to be bore before hym and alle his hoost. And

61. nombre: nōmbre

49ff. Augustine's *Sermo* 165 (P.L. 38: 902–7).

57. *Cf.* LA *sperare coelestia, sacramenta non profanare.*

59. St. Helena (c. 248–328), mother of Constantine, served in an inn in Bithynia
before marrying Constantine's father, also called Constantine, who subsequently
divorced her. Late in life she made a pilgrimage to the Holy Land where she had
churches erected at the sites of the Nativity and the Ascension. She was later credited
with the discovery of the true cross.

60. Constantine the Great (c. 280–337) was the first Roman emperor to become a
Christian, but it is no longer possible to decide how he was converted.

62. The story told here of the Danube is fictional. The battle in question was that
of Milvian Bridge (*cf.* l. 94ff.), which spans the Tiber, fought between the two emper-
ors, Constantine and Maxentius, in 312.

62–3. *Cf.* LA *omnes regiones usque ad occidentem;* in B *occident* is crossed out with
oryent in the margin.

than manly he ranne upon his enemyes and put hem to flyght and slewe
of hem right grete multitude. And after that Constantyne lete calle
to hym the bisshop of the ydols and requyrid of hym diligently of what
god that signe was. And thaye tolde hym thaye wyst never. And than
ther came cristen menn that tolde playnly that it was the signe of the
holy crosse. And than the emperoure belevid perfitly in Jesu Cryste
and receyvid baptyme of the pope Eusebie, or after som other bokis   80
of the bisshop Sesarience.

But many thyngis ben put in this story to the which the *Story Partid
in Thre* ayensayeth, and the *Maister of Stories* also and the *Lyfe of Seinte
Sylvester* and the *Gestis of the Bisshoppis of Rome*. And after som other
wryters this was not that Constantyne which was baptized of Seinte
Sylvester, the pope, lyke as other storyes shewe, but it was Constantyne
the fader of this Constantyne. For this Constantyne came otherwyse
to the feyth, so as men rede in the *Story of Seint Sylvester* that tellith
that he was baptized of Seinte Sylvester and not of Eusebee. For whan
Constantyne the fader was ded, Constantyne the sone remembrid   90
hym of the victory that his fader had by the signe of the crosse [and
sent his moder Elyne to Jerusalem for to finde the verri crosse], so as
it is saide hereafter. And the *Maister of Storyes* tellith that this victory
was done in this wyse. He sayeth that whan Maxence assayled the
Emperoure of Rome, Constantyne the emperoure came besidis the
bridge of Albynum for to fyght with Maxence. He was fulle of ang-

---

86. it: is   94. sayeth: se

---

80. St. Eusebius was pope for only four months in either 309 or 310. There are many
different stories about Constantine's baptism, but it is probable that he remained a
catechumen most of his life, being baptized only shortly before his death.

81. Eusebius, Bishop of Caesarea (c. 265–340), whose writings include a *Chronicle*,
the *Ecclesiastical History* and a *Life of Constantine*.

82. *Story Partid in Thre*: the *Historia Tripartita* by Cassiodorus, so called because it
was a Latin version of three Greek histories. See bk. 1, ch. 5.

84. Many legends associate St. Silvester, pope from 314 to 335, with Constantine.
He is said to have baptized Constantine, to have cured him of leprosy and to have
received the Lateran from him. Constantine for his part is said to have given him dominion over the Eastern patriarchates of the Church in the so-called *Donation of Constantine*, though this is a later forgery. There are many versions of the *Life of St. Silvester*.

91–2. The inclusion is based on H and is also found in Z; it is missing in B.

94. *sayeth*: most other MSS have *seith*, from which A's reading *se* may derive.

96. *bridge of Albynum*: a corruption of Milvian bridge. Maxentius, son of Maximian,
was emperor from 305 to 312. His opposition to Constantine led to his being cast as a
villain by Christian writers.

wissh and oftetyme he lefte up his eyen to hevyn to beseke Almyghty
God of helpe. And as he slepte he had a visyon fro hevyn towarde the
oryent for he segh the signe of the crosse in lykenes of fyre and an
100 angelle after that that saide to hym: 'Constantyne, thou shalte overcome thyne enemyes by thys signe.'

And as it is saide in the *Story Partid in Thre* that, as he merveylid
thereof whate that it myght be, the same nyght folowyng Jesu Cryste
appierid to hym with the signe of the crosse that he had sene in hevyn
and commaundid that he shulde make the fygure of that signe and that
shulde helpe hym ayenste his enemyes in bateyle. Than was Constantyne glad and was fulle sure to have the victory and made in his forehed
that signe that he had sene in hevyn and chaungid alle his baners of
werre and made on them the signe of the crosse, [and he bare a crosse]
110 of golde in his honde. And he besought oure Lorde that he wolde not
suffre that right side which he had wurshippid with the signe of hele
and savacion to be bled with the blode of Romayns, but that he wolde
of his mercy graunte hym victory of the tyrauntis withoute shedyng
of blode. And than Maxence commaundid tho that were with hym
in his shippis that thaye shulde go under the bridge and that thaye
shulde cute the brigg for to disceyve there enemyes that shulde passe
over. And whan that Maxence se that Constantyne approchid the flode,
he forgate his worke that he had do make and wente hastely ayenst
Constantyne with fewe menn and commaundid the remnaunde of the
120 people to come after hym anone; and so he wente forth on the bridge
and was disceyvid with the same disceyte that he wolde have disceyvid
Constantyne. And so he was drownyd in the depe flode. And than was
Constantyne receyvid lorde by alle the accorde. And as it is red in the
story autentyke that Constantyne levid not perfitly in that tyme upon
one god ne had not yet receyvid the holy baptyme; but within a while

111. hele (*sic* Z): the hele H, the hole A, B
112. be bled (*sic* Z, H): blynde A, B; blode (*sic* B, Z, H): blynde A
124. tyme (*sic* Z, H): dayes A, B

---

109. The omission is found in Z, in the margin of H, but not in B.
110ff. 'And he prayed to God that he would not allow the right side which he had
honoured with the sign of (spiritual) health and salvation (i.e. the cross) to be bloodied
with Roman blood.
113. *of*: over.
123ff. Probably based on a *Life of St. Silvester*, but it is also found for example in
Berengosus's *De laude et inventione crucis* III. vi.

after he segh a vision of Seinte Peter and Seinte Paule and than he was
baptized of Seynte Sylvester, the pope, and so he was helid of the lepre;
and after that he belevid in God perfitly.

And than he sent his moder Elyn into Jerusalem for to seke the
crosse of oure Lorde notwithstondyng that Ambrose sayeth in his 130
Epistle of Theodosien, and the *Story Partid in Thre* holdith the same, that
Constantyne abode to be baptized unto his laste dayes, and he did that
to that ende that he wolde be baptized in flom Jordan; and this same
sayeth Jerome in his cronycle. But that is certeyne that he was cristen
under Silvester the pope, but it is a doute whether he abode to be
baptyzed or no; and so men doute in the *Legende of Seynte Sylvester*
many thyngis. For this story of the invencion of the crosse which is
founde in the *Story Ecclesiasticus*, to whom the cronycle accordith,
semyth more autentyke than that is recordid in the Churche, for there
be many thyngis within that that accordith not with the trouthe; but 140
if any peraventure wolde saye, so as it is saide ofte above, that that same
was not Constantyne but Constantyne his fader, the which is not right
autentik, though it be so that it be red in the storys beyonde the see.

And as Elyn was come beyonde the se she commaundid that alle the
wyse Jewis of that regioun shulde be brought before hir. And this
Elyn had furste an osteler, but for hir grete bewty she was joyned to
Constantyne after that Ambrose tellyth by these wordis: 'Men saye,'
sayeth Seinte Ambrose, 'that she was an hosteler, but welle I wote that
she was weddid to Constantyne the olde that was emperoure. She was
a gode osteler that so diligently sought the crybbe of oure Lorde. She 150
was a gode osteler that mysknewe not hym that laye in the stabylle;
a gode osteler that accountid alle thyngis at nought save the love of

152. that: that that

---

127. Leprosy was considered a divine affliction, as in Henryson's *Testament of Cresseid*.

131. *De obitu Theodosii* §42.

134. Jerome translated and wrote a continuation to Eusebius' *Chronicle*.

138. *Story Ecclesiasticus*: the *Ecclesiastical History* by Eusebius.

140–1. *but if*: 'unless'.

143. *storys beyonde the see*: LA has *ultramarinis historiis*, which probably refers to Greek or Eastern versions.

146. 'Helena was married first to an ostler'. But LA has *prius stabularia fuerat*, and it is this idea which is developed in the following lines. On Helena's marriage see note to l. 59.

147. *De obitu Theodosii* §42.

Jesu Cryste and for to gete that was alle hir joye and alle hir laboure—
and therefore oure Lorde lyfte hir up fro that foule place to his endeles
blysse;' and thus sayeth Ambrose. But other say that itt is red in a story
autentyk that Elyn was the doughter of Thoelle, the Kyng of Britayne;
and whan Constantyne was in Brytayne he toke hir to his wyfe. And
than the Ile of Brytayne fylle to hym by the deth of Thoel; and this
the Brytayns witnessith.

160   And than the Jewis drad gretely and saide one to another: 'Whye
trowe ye that the Quene makyth us to appiere before hir?'

And one of hem, that hight Judas, saide: 'I knowe welle that she
wolle knowe of us where the tre of the crosse is that Jesu Cryste was
hongid upon. But none of you knowe that to hir for I wote welle
that oure lawe shal be distroyed and the techyng of oure kynred amentised for Zachie, my graunte-syre, tolde my fader, and my fader tolde
me. And whan my fader died he saide: "Sone, I charge the that when
the tyme comyth that men syke the crosse of Cryste that thou shewe
to no man tofore thou have suffrid to moche turment, for after that it
170   shalle be founde the people of Jewis shalle have no kyngdom. But
they shal have hyt that wurship the crucified, for he is Cryste the sone
of God." And than I saide to hym: "Fader, yf your auncien faders
knewe that he was the sone of God, whye hyng thaye hym in the
gybet of the crosse?" Than saide his fader: "I was never of ther coun-
celle but ayenst hem, for he was a rightwysse man and reprovid the
vicis of the Pheresees, which made hym to be crucified. And he arose
fro deth verily the thrid daye and stied into hevyn sayyng his disciplis.
And Stevyn, thy brother, belevid in hym and therefore [the wode
Jewis stonyd hym to deth. And therefore] kepe the, gode sone, that
180   thou blame hym not ne his disciplis".'

---

166. fader (2) (*sic* Z, H): moder A, B

156ff. In medieval chronicles Helena is said to have been the daughter of Coel of
Caercolvin (i.e. Colchester), a legend which was popularized by Geoffrey of Mon-
mouth, to whom l. 159 may refer.

170. *kyngdom*: spiritual dominion or authority, *cf.* l. 33.

171. The *hyt* refers back to *kyngdom*. The Jewish religion will yield to the Christian
one.

174. *his fader*: the translator has forgotten that Judas is still talking.

177. *sayyng*: 'in the sight of'; LA has *discipulis videntibus. Cf.* l. 46. Our sole information about St. Stephen protomartyr comes from the *Acts of the Apostles*; he was
no doubt a Jew, but the relationship suggested here is fictitious.

178–9. The omission is supplied from Z; it is in the margin of H, but missing in B.

But it is not provable that the fader of this Judas myght have ben
in the tyme of the passhyon of Jesu Cryste, for it was iiC lxx yere fro
the passhion of Cryste unto the comyng of Elyne in which tyme the
crosse was founde; but if it were peraventure that menn levid lengur
in tho dayes than thaye do nowe.

And than saide the Jewis to Judas: 'We herde never of this thyng, but
loke if the Queene enquere of this thyng that thou discover it not.'

And than whan thaye were brought before the Queen and she asked
hem where the place was that Jesu Cryste was crucified in, and thaye
wolde not telle hir in no wyse. And than the Queene commaundid   190
that thay shulde alle be brent in a fyre. So thay drad the dethe and
delyverid unto hir Judas, saying: 'Madam, this is the sone of a rightwysse man and a prophete, and knewe the lawe right welle, and he can
shewe you alle that ye can aske of hym.'

And than she lete go alle the other and kepte Judas allone and than
she saide to hym: 'Chese of ii thyngis, whether thou wylte dye or leve.
Shewe me the place that is callid Galgatha where Jesu Cryste was
crucified so that I maye fynde the crosse.'

Judas aunswerid and saide: 'Howe maye I knowe the place sith it is
iiC yere agone and more, and I was not borne in that tyme?'   200

To whom the Queen saide: 'By hym that was crucified, but thou
telle me the trouthe I shalle make the dye for hungir.' And than she
commaundid that he shulde be caste into a depe pytte and there to be
turment with hongir. And whan he had be ther vii dayes he besought
hir to come oute and he wolde shewe the place to hir. And whan he
[was had oute he come to the place, and whan he] had made his prayers,
the place begane to meve sodenly and men felte a mervelous savoure
of swetnes, so that Judas merveilid and rejoysid and joyned his hondis
togeder and saide: 'In trouthe, Jesu Criste, thou arte the savyoure of
the worlde.'   210

And as men rede in the *Maister of Stories* that the temple of Venus

186. the Jewis to Judas: Judas to the Jewis A, B, H, Z

---

186. *Cf.* LA *Dixerunt ergo Judaei ad Judam.*

206. The omission is supplied from H where it is in the margin; a similar sentence
is found in Z. It is not in B.

211ff. The Emperor Hadrian (76–138) had built a temple and terrace to Venus
there. Constantine ordered a church to be built instead, and its construction was
supervised by Helena.

was in that place the which Adrian the emperoure lete make for that cause that, if any cristen mann came to wurship that place, that he shulde be saide to wurship the ydollis of Venus; and therfore that place was not hauntid but alle forgetyn. And then the Quene made the temple to be distroyed and that place to be wurshippid. And than after that Judas beganne to dygge myghtely and diggid xxx^{ti} pacis depe. And there he founde iii crossis hid, the which he brought to the Quene. And than thaye cowde not knowe the crosse of Jesu Cryste fro
220 the thevis' crossis. Thaye laide hem alle there in the myddis of the cyte and abode the grace of God. And aboute the houre of none men bare a yonge man ded by the waye. And than Judas toke the furst crosse and the secounde and leyde hem on the dede body, but he mevid never the more. But as sone as he was touchid with the iii^{de} crosse, he rose anone fro deth to lyfe. Men rede in the *Story of Ecclesiasticus* that as a lady of Jerusalem which was a lady of the cyte laye in hir bed as halfe dede, Makarie that was Bisshop of Jerusalem toke the furst crosse and the secounde and touchid hir; but thaye profitid hir not. And than he toke the iii^{de} crosse and touchid hir therewith and she arose anone
230 alle hole. Ambrose sayeth howe that thaye knewe the crosse of oure Lorde by the title that Pylate had sette thereon, and was founde and red there.

And the feend cryed in the eyre and saide: 'O thou Judas, whye hast thou done thus? Thou hast not folowid myne other Judas, but thou hast do the contrary. For he did the treson that I counceylid hym and thou hast forsake me and hast founde the crosse of Jesu. By my Judas I have wonne many a soule, and by the I shalle lese tho juels that I had gotyn somtyme. I reignyd by hym in the people and by the I shalle be cast oute of the people. And therefore verily if I maye I shalle overcome the,
240 for I shalle meve ayenste the another kyng that shalle leve the lawe of the crucified.' The which thyng the devylle ment by Julyan the Apostita, which torment after the same Judas with many a grete turment, for he was made Bysshop of Jerusalem after and martir of Jesu Cryste.

238. people (*sic* H, Z): temple A, B

---

237. *juels*: some MSS read *Jues*; but that can hardly have been intended by the scribe of A who spells that word *Jewis*.

241. Julian the Apostate, emperor from 361 to 363. Although he renounced Christianity, he preferred a policy of religious toleration; but his actions were naturally condemned by the Christians; *cf.* XI, 185. He died on an expedition to Persia, *cf.* l. 276.

And whan Judas herde the devylle so crye, he dred hym not but cursid hym strongly and saide: 'Jesu Cryste hath dampned the depe in helle in everlastyng fyre.' And after that Judas was cristenyd and callid Queriacus, and he was ordeynid to be Bisshop of Jerusalem.

And when the blessid Elyn se that she had not the nayles of oure Lorde, she prayed Judas Queriacus that he wolde go the same place and seke hem diligently. And whan he came ther and made his prayers, the nayles of oure Lorde beganne to shyne above the erthe as golde. Then he knelid downe and enclyned his hed and wurshipt hem with grete reverence and bare hem to the Quene. And than she toke one partye of the crosse, and that other she made to be put into a shryne of sylver and bare it into Jerusalem. And that other party she bare to hir sone and the nayles that oure Lorde was nayled with. Of the which nayles, as Cesaryence sayeth, Constantyne made set [oon of] hem in a brydylle, the which he usyd when he went to bateyle; and with the other he arayed his helme.

But many afferme, as Gregory of Toures sayeth, that there were iiii nayles fastenyd in the crosse of oure Lorde; of the which Elyn put ii in hir sones brydelle, and the thirde was set in the ymage of Constantyne that is at Rome and appierith above alle the cyte, and the iiii[th] she caste into the see of Adryan, the which into that tyme had be an deluge and distruccioun of hem that came therein. And she commaundid that the Feest of the Invencion of the Crosse were every yere halowid solemply; and Ambrose sayeth the same also. Elyn sought the nayles of oure Lorde and founde hem; [and of that one she made hir sone a bridylle] and of that other [a] corone; and she made the nayles to be sette right in the forehed, and the corone in the backe of the hed, and the reyne in the honde so that the wytte appierid, the feyth shyned, and the myght governyd.

250

260

270

---

270. and (sic Z): of A, B; H omits   **270.** backe (sic Z, H): balle A, B

---

249. *the same place*: Golgotha, where he had found the cross.

257. *oon of*: found only in H in the margin.

260. *De gloria martyrum* I. vi. The dispute arose because some thought that both feet were fastened with only one nail, while others believed that each foot had been fastened by a separate nail.

262–3. Constantine had a statue of himself holding a cross erected in Rome as a memorial of his victory at the Battle of Milvian Bridge.

264. The Adriatic.

266. The Feast of the Invention is commemorated on 3 May.

268f. The omission is supplied from Z; it is not in H or B.

And after that alle these thyngis were done, Julyan the Apostita slewe Seynte Queryacus, the bisshop, for that he founde the holy crosse, and he enforcid hym alle that he coude for to distroye the holy crosse. For whan Julyan wente ayenst men of Perce, he toke Queriacus and wolde have made hym to do sacrifice to the ydollis. And whan he had denyed hit, he made cut of his right honde and saide: 'He hath wryte to manye letters with this honde, by the which he hath with-
280 drawe moche people fro the sacrifice of oure goddis.'

And Queriacus saide to hym: 'Thoue wode hounde, thoue hast done to me a grete profite, for or I was cristen I wrote ofte in to the synagoge of Jewis that non shulde leve in God—and nowe thoue hast cast awaye alle that sclaundre of my body.'

And than anone Julyan lete molte ledde and powre hit in hys mouthe. And after he made a grede-yron of yron and made hym to be layde thereon and grete coolys of fyre to be put under. And thaye made his woundis to be frotid with salte and grece; and Queriacus hilde hym stylle withoute meovyng. And than Julyan saide to hym: 'If thou
290 wylte not do sacrifice to oure goddis, renye that thou arte a cristen man.'

And whan he had do to refuse that in scornyng, Julyan commaundid to make a grete pytte in the erthe and put therein Queri[a]cus, and cast upon hym venomys serpentis. But these serpentis were ded anone. And than Julyan commaundid Queriacus to be put in a cawdryn boylyng fulle of oyle alle hote. And he blessid hym and entrid in with gode wylle and prayed oure Lorde that he wolde baptize hym ayen in the lavatory of martirdome. And than was Julyan wroth and commaundid that he were smyte thurgh the body with a spere; and so
300 he deservyd to fulfylle his martirdome.

Howe moche the vertue of the crosse is hit appierith in the true notary, that an enchauntoure wolde have [deceived and] brought [hym] into a place where he callid the feendis and behight hym that

276. Perce (sic Z, H): Proce A, Prece B   **283.** non (sic Z, H): men A, B
287. thereon: thereoñ

---

276. *Perce*: Persia.
301ff. 'The story of the faithful notary reveals how powerful the cross is. A magician intended to deceive him and brought him to a place where he summoned up devils, and he promised the notary that he should wallow in riches.' The omissions are supplied from H.

he shulde habounde in alle maner of riches. And than he segh a grete
Ethiope sit on hye upon a sege and had aboute hym many a Ethiope
that hilden swerdis and stavis in her hondis. And than he askid of the
enchauntoure whate mann that was. And than he saide: 'Lorde, it is
youre servaunt.'

And than the Ethiope saide: 'Wolle ye wurship me and be myne
and renye thy Cryste, and I shalle make the sytte on my right side.' 310

And than anone this notary made on hym the signe of the crosse
and saide that he was the servaunt of Jesu Cryste, and anone that
multitude of feendis vanysshid awaye. And after that as this notary
in a tyme went with his maister and entrid into a churche of Seinte
Sophie and stode bothe before an ymage of Seinte Savyoure, his maister
segh howe that the ymage behelde the notary veryly and had his eyen
sette on hym ententifely. And whan he segh this he had grete mervayle
and made hym turne into the right side of the ymage and yet he segh
the ymage alwayes have his eyen upon hym. And than he turnyd hym
to the furst side and the ymage turnyd his eyen upon hym and behelde 320
hym. And than his maister conjurid hym and prayed hym to telle hym
whate he had deservid towardis God that the ymage behilde hym so.
He saide that he coude not remembre hym of no gode dede that he
had done but that he wolde not renye hym afore the feend and the
enchauntoure.

(b) *The Life of St. Edmund*

Seynt Edmounde the confessoure, that lyethe at Pounteney in
Fraunce, was bore in Ynglond in the towne of Abyngdon. Mabely the
ryche was his moder's name; she was right holy, bothe wyfe and
wydowe. And upon Seynt Edmoundis daye the kyng the sayde Seynt

319. than: thañ

305. The devil was often thought of as an Ethiopian because of the latter's black skin; *cf.* the devil in *St. Marharete.*

307. *he*: that is, the Ethiopian or devil.

309. Condition through inversion: 'If you will . . .'.

314–15. St. Sophia is the mother of the legendary St. Faith and her sisters.

1. St. Edmund (c. 1170–1240) was the son of Reynold (or Richard) and Mabel Rich of Abingdon.

4. St. Edmund, king and martyr, was killed in 870 at Hoxne in East Anglia; his day is November 20.

Edmond was bore. And in his byrthe noo clothe was fowlyd by hym. And he was bore in the furst spryngyng of the daye, and al that daye tyl it was evyn he laye as he had ben dede. And than the mydwyff wolde have had hym buryed, but his moder sayde naye. And anone thurgh the myght of God he revyvved and than he was bore to the churche to be cristenyd. And bycause he was bore on Seynt Edmondis daye the kyng he was namyd Edmond. And as this chelde grewe in aige he encresyd gretely in vertu. And than the moder sent the sayde Edmounde with his brother Robert to scole. And she had ii doughters, Dame Mary and Dame Alys; bothe theye were made nonnys at Catesby in Northaumptonshire by the laboure of Seynt Edmond. And there moder gave theym yeftes to fast the Fryday, and so she drewe theym to good levyng by yeftes and fayre beheestes; and when thaye came to more aige it grevyd theym not. The moder hirself weryd the hard heyre for oure Lordis love and lad hir lyff in grete penaunce.

But in a tyme as Mabely his moder put oute wolle to spynne, she toke hir spynners so moche for the libra that thaye myght not leve thereon, but complaynded to Seynt Edmond hir sonne. And he toke the yerne and rekyd it in the colys, and the libra was savyd that she payd for and the overplewse was brente. Wherefore she dyd never so after to hir lyves ende.

And than she sent hir ii sonnys, Edmond and Robert, to Paryce too scole. And she toke theym mony for theyre costes wyth theym, and she delyveryd to theym ii harde hayres, made lyke shurtes, and she prayd theym for here love to were theym onys or tweys in the weke, and they shulde lake nothyng that nedid to theym. And then thay fulfylled theire moder's desire, and in shorte tyme after thaye werid the heyre every daye and every nyght. This was a blessyd moder that soo vertuosly brought fourth hir chyldren. And then Seynt Edmond encresyd so gretely in vertu that every creature joyed thereof and preysed God in his holy servaunt Edmond.

5. That he was born in such a pure state without the normal defiling that accompanies a human birth is indicative of his own purity.

15. A house of Cistercian nuns formed by Edmund (cf. l. 83).

16. the Fryday: 'every Friday'.

21. libra: 'a pound', in money. Because Mabel gave the spinners more wool to spin than she ought to for a pound in payment, they complained to Edmund. So he put all the wool in the fire, and only that amount of wool which was justly spun for a pound was untouched; the rest was burned.

And in a daye as his felowys and he wente to playe he left his felow-
ship and went allone into a medowe under an hedge saying his devo-
cions. And sodenly there appierid before hym a fayre chelde in whyte
clothyng and sayd: 'Hayle, felowe that goyst allone.' And than
Edmounde merveylid from whens the chylde come; and the chelde   40
sayde: 'Edmond, knowyst not me?'

He sayde: 'Naye!'

And he sayde: 'I am thye felowe in scole, and in eche other place
where that thu goyst I am alweye on thy ryght syde; and yet thu
knowyst me not. But loke thu in my forehed and there thu shalte
fynde my name wryte.' (And than Edmond lokyd in his forehed and
se wryte therein *Jesus nazarenus, rex Judeorum, fili Dei, miserere mei.*)
And then the chelde saide: 'Drede the not, Edmond, for I am thy lorde,
Jesu Cryste, and shall be thye defendoure whyle thue levest.'

And than Edmond fylle downe mekely and thankyd our Lorde of   50
his grete mercy and godenes. And oure Lorde bade hym when he
shall go to his bed and when he shall aryse to blesse hym with the
syngne of the crosse and saye the prayer affore-wryten in mynde of
hys passhyon, 'and the devyll shall have no power over the'. And anone
the chylde vanysshyd awaye, and Seynt Edmond usyd ever after that
prayer and blessyng to his lyvys ende, and suffryd ever grete penaunce
for Goddis sake in weryng of the heyre.

And when he had contynued many yeris at Paryce at the scole,
than he came to Oxford. And he dyd never lechery nor consentyd
therto, and that was a special grace of oure Lorde. And on a daye he   60
came to an ymage of oure Lady and put a ryng upon hir fyngur and
he promysed hyr verely never to have other wyff but hir whyles he
levyd. And he greete oure Lady withe these iiii wordis: '*Ave, Maria,
gracia plena*', which was wryte in the ryng. Hys oste had a doughter
that labouryd gretely Seynt Edmond to synne by hir and she desyred
long tyme to come to his chambir. And at the last this holye man
grauntyd hir. And she was ryght gladde and spyed hir tyme and came

---

40. merveylid: merveyvid

47. 'Jesus of Nazarus, king of the Jews, son of God, have pity on me.' In the early
Latin lives and Caxton, only the first four Latin words are found; they are from
John 19: 19. The rest of the Latin, which is probably modelled on the psalms, is given
later where the prayer (l. 52) is mentioned.

63–4. 'Hail, Mary, full of grace'.

to his chambir and made hir redy to go to bed and stode nakyd before
Seynt Edmond. And he toke a sherp rodde and layde upon the mayde
70 tyll the rede blode ranne downe fro hir body in every syde. And than
he sayde to hyr: 'Thus thu shalt lerne to caste awaye thye sowle for
the fowle lustis of thye bodye.' And ar he lefte of she had no lust to syn
with hym for all hir fowle desyres were clene gonne. And after that
she levyd a clene virgyn to hir lyves ende.

Than sone after Mabely his swete moder nyghed hir ende and sente
for Seynt Edmond hir sonne and yeaff hym hir blessyng and all hir
chyldren. And than she prayed hym for Goddes love and oure Ladys
also that he wolde se that hys susters were well guyded in the nonry
of Catysby affore-sayde. And so she passid to our Lorde full of vertues,
80 and is buryed in the churche of Seynt Nycholas at Abyngdon in a
tombe of marbyll before the rode. And this scripture is wryte on hir
tombe: 'Hir lyeth Maboly, flowre of wedows.' And than Seynt
Edmonde made a chapell at Catysby, and after bothe his susters were
buryed therein, for the one of theym was pryoras of the same nonry
and dyd there many myraclys. And theye ben buryed before the high
auter in the same nonry.

And than this holy man Seynt Edmond dwellyd at Oxford and
contynued there in ful holy levyng for he weryd the hard heyre knett
with knottes lyke a nett. And the knottis stekyd faste to his flessh that
90 oftyntymes it causid his body to blede and to be full sore. And in this
maner was bothe hys shurte and hys breche imade, and he bounde it
faste with a corde to hys body that the heyre myght cleve fast to his
body in every place. Hyt sate so strayte upon hym that unnethe he
myght bowe his body, the which was a ful grete penaunce to hym.
And in a tyme whan his shurte of heyre was fowle and tobroke, he
toke it his man too brenne in a grete fyre. But he cowde not brenne
hem in no wyse, but ever thaye laye hole and unbrent in the fyre.
Than his mann toke an hevy stone and bownde the shurte thereto
and caste it in the water where was a depe ponde; and there he left
100 theym. But he tolde hys maister that thaye were brente.

71. SEL 116–17 reads:
> 'Maide, thu schalt lurny thus awei forto caste
> Thi fole wil of thi flesch with suche discipline.'

84. Margaret was prioress of Catesby and died in 1257.

97. *hem . . . thaye*: the writer was probably thinking of both shirt and trousers here; *cf.* l. 91.

Seynt Edmond and his felowys on a daye came fro Lewkenowre to Abyngdon and as thaye came into a grete valey thaye se many black fowlys lyke crowys, among which there sate one that was all totoryn with the other black crowys; and thaye cast hym from one to another that it was grete pety to beholde it. Therefore his felowys were nye madde for fere of that syght. And then Seynt Edmond comfortyd hem and tolde theym whate it was. He saide that thaye beth feendis of helle that berith a mannys sowle that dyed at the towne of Chalfegrove right nowe, and that sowle shall never come in the blysse of hevyn for his cursyd levyng. And than Seynt Edmond and his felowis wente to the towne of Chalfegrove and fownde al thyng lyke as Seynt Edmond tolde theym.

And fro thens thaye wente too Abyngdon and theire Seynt Edmond wente into the churche and sayde his prayers lyke as he was wonte to doo, the which prayer was *O intemerata*, the which he sayde every daye in the wurship of Jesu Criste, oure blessyd Lady, and of Seynt John the Evaungelyst. And this prayer he usyd to saye dayly or he dyd ony wordely workys. But in a tyme he forgate to saye this holy oryson and than Seynt John the Evaungelyst came to Seynt Edmond in a ful gastfull maner and blamyd gretely Seynt Edmond. But after that to his lyfys ende he never forgate to saye that holy prayer.

And after this holy man encresyd so gretely in Oxforde in all the vii sciences that all men had grete joye of hym. And in a nyght as he sate in his studye, hys owne moder Maboly appierid unto hym in a vysyon. And she sayde to hir sonne: 'Loke fro hense forewarde that thue laboure in devynyte and in no nother science, for that is the wylle of God lyke as he hathe sente the worde by me.' This saide she vanyshed awaye fro hym. And after that this holy mann labourid

101. Lewknor (Oxon.).

103. *one*: in SEL 189 it is a 'lute blac sac'. Black is of course the colour of wicked men and devils. Examples of the witnessing of the progress of a soul to heaven or hell are common in medieval literature.

111. Chalgrove (Oxon.).

115. 'O, chaste one', a prayer to the Virgin and St. John, see A. Wilmart, *Auteurs spirituels et textes dévots* (Paris 1932), pp. 474–504.

120. *gastfull*: in SEL 211ff. St. John appears with a cane, with which he offers to beat Edmund as though he were a lazy pupil.

123. The basis of medieval education was the trivium (grammar, rhetoric and logic) and the quadrivium (arithmetic, geometry, astronomy and music). These seven subjects led on to theology.

alweye in devynyte to fulfylle the wylle of oure Lorde Jesu Cryst.
130 And he encresyd so mervelously in that scyence that al Oxford had
grete wondyr of hym for his grete connyng, for there was none lyke
hym in all Oxford. For he had that grace when he radde in the scole
of devynyte, he profyted more to the herers in one weke than other
mennys techyng dyd in a moneth, for many one of his scolers thurgh
his gracious techyng forsoke the worlde and became relygious men.

And in a daye as the holy man sate in the scole for to dispute of the
holy trynyte, he came long ar his scolers came, and he felle in a sclombryng as he sate on his chayre. And ther came a white dove and brought
hym the body of oure Lorde and he put hyt into his mouthe. And
140 than the dove flye upwarde from hym and hevyn openyd ayenst hym
as Seynt Edmonde behelde hit. And ever after he thought that the
savoure of oure Lordis flessh was ever in hys mowthe. And thereby
he knewe full moche privyte of the pure state of Jesu Cryste and of
hys magestye in hevyn, for he had mervelouse connyng above al other
doctors that were in Oxforde for he expownyd so hye maters to
theym that they thought he was more lyke an angel than a man.

And in every lesson that this holy man taught he thought in oure
Lordis passhyon. And in a nyght he studyed so long on his bokys that
sodenly he fylle aslepe and forgate to blesse hym and thynke on the
150 passhyon of oure Lorde. And than the feende that had gret envy to
hym laye so hevye on Seynt Edmond that he had no power to blesse
hym with the ryght honde ner with the lyft honde. And than Seynt
Edmond wyst not whate to doo, but at last thurgh the grace of oure
Lorde he remembryd his blessyd passhyon; and then the feend had no
power on Seynt Edmond, but fylle downe anone fro hym. And than
Seynt Edmond commaundid hym by the vertue of oure Lordis passhion that he shulde telle hym howe he shulde best defende hym that he
shulde have no power over hym. And the feende aunsweryd to Seynt
Edmond: 'That that thue haste sayde and thought on the passhyon of
160 oure Lorde Jesu Cryst; for whate mann or womann that hath hys mende
on oure Lordis passhyon, I have no power over theym at no tyme.'
And ever after Seynt Edmond the holy mann had ful grete devocyoun
in the passhyon of our Lorde and in holy orysons for therein was all
hys delyte bothe nyght and daye. But when he ete, slepte and rode, all
that tyme he thought was but in ydelnes and hevy onto hym. But all

138. The dove is a symbol of the Holy Ghost.

that he labourid in holy studye or bedis-byddyng or almesdede-doyng, all suche thynges was moost plesaunce to hym, and he was never wery of suche werkys for he was all hole yevyn to Goddys servyce and to hys plesyng. And also he was a notable prechoure and gretely his techyng edefyed in the people that all people had grete devosyon to hyre his prechyng. 170

In that tyme the pope sente his crosser to the bysshoppis of Ynglonde that thaye shulde chese a wyse clerke that shulde proclayme the popys entent thurgh this realme of Ynglond for to have helpe and socoure ayenste the Turke, Goddes enmy. And so by one assent theye chose Seynt Edmond to proclayme the popys wylle. And soo he dyd that charge full welle and dyligently thurgh this londe, and moche people he causyd to take the crosse and for to go into the Holy Londe. And as a yong mann came with other to resseyve the crosse, a woman that lovyd hym lette hym of hys purpose and she drewe hym fast 180 awaye fro thens with hir hondys. And anone bothe hir hondis were styffe and harde as a borde and also hir hondis wax all crokyd. And than she made grete sorowe and cryed God mercye; and she prayed Seynt Edmond to praye for hir to oure Lorde.

And he sayde to hir: 'Woman, wylt thue take the crosse?'

And she sayde: 'Yee, sir, full fayne.'

And than she resseyvid it and was made hole. And than she thankyd oure Lorde, Jesu Cryste, and his holy servaunt, Seynt Edmond. And thurgh this grete myracle moche more people toke the crosse.

In a tyme as this holy man prechyd at Oxforde in the churcheyerthe 190 of Alhalwyn and moche people was there to hyre his holy prechyng. Sodenly there waxed so derke weder that alle the people were sore agast; and moche people beganne to go awaye, the wynde and the weder was so horryble. And than this holy man sayde to the people: 'Abyde ye stylle here for the power of God is strenger than the feendis power, for thus he doyth for envye to distrouble Goddes worde.' And than Seynte Edmond lyfte uppe his mynde to oure Lorde and besought of mercy and grace. And when he had endid his oryson, the weder beganne to withdrawe bye the other syde of the churche. And all the people that abode there stylle to hyre the prechyng had not one drope 200

172. Gregory IX (1227-41). He was responsible for launching the so-called sixth crusade of 1228-9.

190. In the medieval period it was almost as common to preach outside as inside a church.

of rayne. But thaye that wente awaye fro the sermon were thurghwette with the rayne, and there fylle so moche rayne in the hye strete that men myght neither go ner ride therein. And than alle the people preysid God in his servaunt for this grete myracle. And at Wynchester another tyme, when he prechyd, was shewid there a lyke myracle for there he chasyd awaye suche a derke wether by hys holy prayer.

Than for his holy levyng he was chose hye chanon at Salysbury and there he was made rewler and tresourer. And there he levyd a full gode lyve, for all the mony that he myght gete he yeaff hyt in almes
210 to pore folkys for the love of God that he had nothyng to leve by hymself. And than he wente to th'abbey of Stanley and sojournyd there tylle hys rentys came in, for Maister Stephyn Lexston that there was abbott was somtyme his scoler in Oxford. He was so lytle an etyr that menn woundryd howe he levyd. And yett he wolde ete no coste-lewe mete for full selde he ete any flessh. And fro Shroftyde tyll Ester he wolde ete no mete that suffryd the dethe, nor in Advent he ete never but Lente-mete.

And when the Archiebisshopp of Canterbury was dede, he was chose by all the covent to be there bysshopp. And anone thaye sent
220 there messyngers to hym to Salysbury, but he was then at Calne which was then one of hys prebendis. There he was prevyly in hys chambir allone in his prayers; and one of his chapeleyns came into his chambyr and tolde hym that he was chose Archiebysshopp of Canter-bury and that messyngers were come to hym for the same cause. But Seynt Edmond was nothyng gladde of the tydynges. And then the messyngers spake with Seynt Edmond and delyverid to hym the letters for to rede theym. And he sayde: 'I thanke you of youre laboure and gode wylle, but I am nothyng gladde of these tydynges. But I wolle go to Salysbury and take councell of my felowys in this mater.'
230 But when he came theder he was chose there in the chapyterhowse

---

211. Stanley was a Cistercian abbey southeast of Chippenham.

212-13. Stephen de Lexington was one of the pupils who had been turned away from the world by Edmund while a pupil at Oxford; he was later abbot of Clairvaux. Edmund had gone to Stanley because he had given so much of his own income away that he had not enough left to feed himself. He used to go to Stanley to live until he received the next instalment of his salary.

217. *Lente-mete*: 'food appropriate for Lent, for a fast'.

219. Edmund was elected Archbishop upon the insistence of the pope.

220. Calne is a few miles from Stanley. A prebend is that portion of the revenues of a cathedral or collegiate church granted to a canon as his income.

by all the feloushypp, but he denyed hytt in alle wyse to hys power.
But the Bysshop of Salysbury with his brethern chargyd hym by the
vertue of obedyence that he shulde take it upon hym. And then he
mekely toke it upon hym fulle sore wepyng. And so thaye had hym
to the hye auter and there thaye beganne to syng ful devoutly *Te
Deum laudamus* ful merely. But ever this holy man wepte with full
bytter tyres and sayde: 'Lorde, I beseche the to have mercy on me,
thyne unworthy servaunt, and yeffe me grace ever to guyde me to thy
plesyng and wourshypp; and blessyd Lady, helpe me ever at my nede;
and the holy virgyn, Seynt John the Evaungelyst, be my socoure and 240
helpe at my moost nede.'

And than he was brought fro Salysbury to Canterbury, and there
he was stallyd Archiebysshopp. And than he rewlyd Holy Church full
wysely and godely that every man spake gode of hym, for he ledde
his lyff in grete penaunce and almysdede. And ever he holpe the poor
in theyre grete nede. In a tyme a pore tenaunt of hys dyed and then his
bayly fette the best beest that he had for his lordis heryott. And than
the poor wydowe that had lost hyr hosbande and hir best beste came
to this holy bysshopp and complaynd to hym of hir grete povertye.
And she prayd hym for the love of God that he wolde yeff hir ayen 250
hyr beest. Than seyde this gode bysshopp to the poor woman: 'Ye
knowe welle that the cheff lorde must have the best beest.' And sayde:
'Woman, yf Y leve the my beest, wylte thue kepe hym welle to my
behofe tylle Y aske it ayen of the another tyme?'

And she sayde to the bysshopp: 'Yee, sir, at all tymes to youre
pleasyng or else God defende, for I am fulle moche bownde unto
yowe that ye wolle to me, a poor wrecche, shewe thys youre gode
grace.'

And so he lete sende hir hyr best ayen; and she kept hytt stylle to hir
lyfys ende. And thys holy bysshopp was ever fulle mercyfulle to the 260
poor.

232. brethern: bretherñ

---

240. The word *virgin* may be applied to those of either sex who have remained in
a state of chastity.

247. The heriot was originally the return of those weapons, etc., which a lord had
bestowed on a retainer, upon that retainer's death. But it became transmuted into a
feudal due payable to the lord upon a tenant's death; it was usually the best animal
on the tenant's farm.

And trewly he rewlyd and maynteyned the right of Holy Churche.
And therefore the devyll of helle had grete envy unto hym for his holy
guydyng and sette debate betwene the kyng and hym, the which kyng
was Kyng Harry, that was Kyng John's sonne. And this kyng dyd to
Seynt Edmond leke as hys unkylle Herry dyd to Seynt Thomas, for
alwey he was sturdy ayenst Holy Churche. And yett Seynt Edmond
prayed hym oftymes to be mercyfulle to the Churche of God, and
strenght hym in ther right for the love of God and of his blessid
270 modyr, Mary. But for alle his godely entretyng the kyng toke aweye
the lybertyes and the fraunchyes thereof; and he thretenyd gretely
Seynt Edmonde. And whan he se it wolde no better be, than he spake
sherpely to the kyng and sayde: 'Though ye put me oute of youre
londe, yette I maye go to Paryce and dwelle there, as I have do here-
before, tylle ye be better dysposyd to Holy Churche.'

The kyng hyryng this was ever moor and more ayenst hym and
Holy Churche. Than Seynt Edmond cursyd all tho that troublyd Holy
Churche by unright and shame. And when the [kyng] herde of this
cursyng, he was gretely meovyd ayenst Seynt Edmond. But alweye
280 the holy man kepte the right of the Churche to hys power and myght.
And then Seynt Thomas appierid to hym and bade hym holde uppe
the right of Holy Churche with alle hys myght and rather for to suffre
dethe than lese the fredome of the Churche, and to take that in sample
of hym. Than Seynt Edmond fylle on hys kne and wolde have kyssed
the fete of Seynt Thomas with weepyng teerys, but he denyed hytt.
And then he kyssed the mouth of Seynt Thomas, and he vanyshyd
awaye. And then Seynt Edmond was more stedefast to Holy Churche
than ever he was before and wolde rather dye than lese the right
thereof.

290 And he toke ensample by Seynt Thomas howe he wente over the
se into Fraunce. And then Seynt Edmond went prevely over the see
intoo Fraunce trustyng in God that the kyng wolde amende his levyng
and withdrawe his malyce fro Holy Churche. Than Seynt Edmond

265. John's: Jhons

265. Henry III (1216–72), the son of John (1199–1216). The dispute had been caused
more by Henry's administration of England and his unworthy ministers than by his
clerical policy.

266. Henry II (1154–89) who was responsible for Thomas à Beckett's death in 1170.
For *unkylle*, SEL 496 reads *grandsire*, the correct relationship.

283–4. *in sample of hym*: 'following his example'.

came to Pounteney and there he bode in fulle holy levyng, and ever he prayde for the gode state of the churche of Ynglond.

And vi yere he dwellid stille at Pownteney in fulle grete holynesse. And than this holy mann waxyd seke and feble and was counselyd to remove thens to a towne xx myle thens that is callyd Solye. And than the monkys of the abbey of Pounteney made grete sorowe for his departyng thense, but he comfortyd theym in the beste wyse that he cowde and promysed theym to be there ayen upon Seynt Edmondis daye the kyng. And as sone as he came to the towne of Soly he waxe right sore seke and he knewe welle he sholde not long abyde in this worlde. And he desired to resseyve the sacramentes of the churche; and so he did with fulle grete reverence, and passyd to oure Lorde full of vertues in the yere of oure Lorde M^l iiC xlii. And fro the towne of Solye he was brought to Pounteney upon Seynt Edmondis daye the kyng. He myght not kepe his promyse to the monkis of Pounteney on lyve, and therefore he kepte hys promys dede, for he was brought thedir and resseyvid ryght devoutly and buryed with grete solempnyte and put into a fulle worshipfulle shryne in the abbey of Pounteney before the high auter, where oure Lorde shewith many a grete myracle for his holy servaunt Seynt Edmond.

300

310

294. Pontigny, the refuge earlier of both Thomas à Beckett and Stephen Langton.
298. Soisy.
306. That is, 1242. The date of his death was actually November 16, 1240.

XI   Remedies against the Seven Deadly Sins

This is one of ten religious tracts found in a volume usually known by the name of the longest one, *The Treatise of Love*. The volume was translated from French in 1493. Although there is no printer's name or date, the book was almost certainly printed by de Worde in 1493 or 1494. Most extant copies of the *Treatise* are bound with *The Chastising of God's Children*, printed by de Worde in 1491, with which it shares two characteristics: a Burgundian connection and the use of the *Ancren Riwle* as a source. Of the ten tracts in the *Treatise* volume, the first three (the *Treatise* itself, *Remedies* and *The Hours of the Cross*) were probably written by the same author and may have been intended as three parts of one work, though *Remedies* has an opening which suggests an independent work. The conclusion at the end of *Remedies*, the last of the three pieces, may have been designed to conclude all three pieces. These three were written for a rich, noble lady whose identity is not disclosed. It may have been Margaret of Burgundy or someone close to her; manuscripts of the French texts with Burgundian connections are extant.

Edition: J. H. Fisher, *The Tretyse of Loue.* EETS o.s. 223 (London 1951).

Here begynneth a treatyse moche prouffitable for reformacion of soules defoyled wyth ony of the vii dedely synnes.

To his riht dere suster salute and helthe of soule and of body in him that is true Savyour, in whom is alwaye charyte, pacyence, and chastyte, whyche in trouth defendeth us fro evyl-dooyng and mevyth us to the Holy Trynite. This he graunt us by his holy pyte, the swete Jesus Cryste, of whom as moche more as man understondeth and sayth of his merveylous godenes soo moche more loveth he and hath joye in him; for spyrituell joye comyth of the love of our Lorde, the
10   right swete Jesus, and the very signe of love is to thynke often on hym. Wherfore remembre you oft of the humilite of his incarnacion, of the goodnes of his conversacion, and of the charytee of his passion;

3. The lady for whom this treatise was written has not been identified; *cf.* Introduction.

7–9. The more a man understands and speaks of Christ's goodness, the more he (the man) will love and have joy in him (Christ).

and who well remembre thyse may fynde sure medycyne ayenst every dedely synne and temptacion.

Fyrst, who that entendeth to be proude, bethynke hym of the grete humylite of our Lorde Jesu Cryst whiche is soo grete that heven and erthe maye not comprehende hym and by his mekenes list to close him wythin the wombe of a mayde. 'Thus was the Sone of God ensample of humylite and medycyne of pryde,' as Saynt Austyn sayth; for he hath shewed to us mekenes in alle his werkes, for he wolde have an humble moder, the blessyd Vyrgyne Marye, and an humble howse where he was borne, whiche was callyd a dyversorye, and soo humble a bedde as the manger for bestes. And whan he came to the age of xii yere, by his mekenes he was obedyent to Joseph and to his blessyd moder, as it is shewed in the gospell. And whan he came to more age, he choos meke persones as Saynt Peter and Saynt Andrew, poor meke fisshars, wyth other suche to be in his company, in token that what man or woman that wold be with him in his perdurable joye, it behoveth hem to be humble and meke. As Saynt Austin sayth: 'By the humylite of Jesu Criste ye may come to the joye perdurable, for in as moche as Jesu Criste is kyng of that countree whether we entende to goo and for as moche as he is man, he is sure waye wherby we shall goo, for he is our example.' Soo as he saith in the gospel: 'I have given you ensample of humylite.' Now may the proude folke understonde that they may goo by none other way but by Jesu Cryste, this is by the waye of mekenesse. For as Saynt James sayth: 'For God resisteth to the hie and proude folkes, and to the humble he gyveth his grace.' They ben humble that can marke ther owne proper defawtes and holde theymself for foles and wretches, for the more they disprayse theymselfe the more largely shalle they have the grace of our Lord. Wherefor it is sayd in scrypture: 'The gretter that ye be in auctoryte, the more

---

18-19. St. Augustine's *Sermo* 123 (P.L. 38: 684).

23-25. Possibly a reference to *Luke* 2: 41ff.; passages based upon and quotations from the Bible have been freely adapted in this text, for the treatise has a long textual history.

25-27. *Cf. Matthew* 4: 18.

29. *hem*: today we would use a singular form here; though the plural may have been employed to avoid a specific gender. *Cf.* l. 308.

29. *Sermo* 123 (P.L. 38: 685). **33.** Possibly based on *James* 5: 10.

36. *James* 4: 6.

41ff. There is no exact parallel from the Bible, though there are many similar passages.

humble shold ye be in your herte, in worde and in werke: and thenne shal ye finde grace at our Lord, and after the joye without ende;' whiche us graunte the swete Jesu Cryst that so moche lovyth humylite.

Who sholde rejoyce the hurte of other or be sory of the wele of other, as envyous folke done, yf they beholde bi the eye of ferme fayth how grete charyte the swete Jesu, very god and man, shewed us not for his wele but for the wele of other, whan he soo dere boughte us from th'infernal pryson, whiche was wyth noo lityll raunson, whan he gaaf hymself for our salvacyon—and all this made charyte? For he rejoyseth the wele of other: and the sorow of other was more paynful to hym than his owne, whiche shewed well by his moost pyteous and paynfull deth that ever man suffred in erth for the releef and comforte of other. This charyte was the gyfte that he lefte wyth his discyples at his departyng, as he saith in the gospel: 'By this shal all folkes knowe yf ye ben truely my dyscyples, for thenne shall ye have truly charite and love among you.'

Now, dere suster, remember well what marke he setteth upon al his. Wherfore yf ye wyl be one of his ye must be of that marke, as wolde our Lorde I were one of the leest of theim. For God is ordener of love, and in love restyth hymselfe; soo as Saynt John sayth: '*Deus caritas est*, etc.' Now take gode hede by thyse ensamples, that be soo open, how good a thyng is humylite of herte wyth true love of Jesu Cryst, for there is noothyng under heven that he loveth so moche. And yf ye have that, ye shall have alle weles and God hymself; and yf ye fayle that, ye shall fayle all that may torne to your wele. And as Saynt Poul sayth: 'Know ye not wel that where many folkes fyghte togyder in grete oostes that thoos that holde theym ferme togyder may not lightly be dyscomfyted in noo wise?' And soo is it of the spyrituell batayll agaynst the fende, for he doeth all his force to dysceve and departe our hertes and to take fro us true love and charyte. And as sone as the hertes ben therfro departed, the fende entreth and sleeth

45. *sholde*: perhaps translate 'would'; *Ancrene Wisse* has *is*. *Other*: 'other people'; here and in many other instances *other* is plural.

55. *John* 13: 35.

61–2. 'God is love,' *1 John* 4: 8.

67ff. There is no parallel from the Bible. The passage, however, closely resembles a sentence in *Ancrene Wisse* which has probably been incorrectly attributed to St. Paul.

71ff. As soon as our hearts are parted from love, the devil interposes himself between us and love and destroys us.

on every parte. For where a man gooth alone in a cumbrous waye and stumblith, comunely he falleth; but and there were many togyder, everyone myghte helpe other: for yf one stumble another is redy to holde hym uppe or he falle, and yf one of theym wexe wery his felawe wyll helpe to lede hym. This temptacion is stumbling, that makyth many to falle in the myre of synne yf he be not susteined by other with tru charyte; and soo sayth Saynt Gregorye. By thyse ensamples appe-reth it thenne that who that is bounden wyth other in true charyte 80 and love hath a mighty helpe ayenst temptacion and who that is un-bounde by hatrede sone synkith and overthroweth. Beholde wel thenne how moche is worth the alyaunce of true charyte and love that al good and godenes holdeth togyder soo that none may perysshe that hath that. Moche loveth us our swete Lord Jesus and claymeth of us none other rewarde but to love him agayn; and this sholde noo man denye, for alway he maye fynde mater ynough in his herte yf he ensērche well. In good hour are they born that can love him aryght, whyche Almighty God graunt us soo to doo by his holy pyte.

Who shold be inpacient with onythyng or kepe wrathe in his herte 90 that beholdeth the pacyence that our swete Lorde Jesu Cryst had in al his lyf? Thre degrees ben there in pacyence. The fyrst is hye, that is whan ye suffre humbly for your owne gylte. The seconde more hye, yf ye suffre humbly wythout your desert. The thyrde is best and moost high, yf ye suffre payne humbly for your good dede. For though we suffre harme for our deserte, we maye not wyth right complayne us. Now full unhappi and unwyse were he that wolde rather chose to be felowe of Judas than the felowe of Jesu Cryst; and yet bothe two were hanged on the tree: Judas for his deserte, and Jesu wythout deserte for his grete bounte was cruelly hanged on the crosse. By this may ye take 100 ensample that what man that wrongeth you or hurteth you in worde or dede is your lighte; it giveth you clernes and takith fro you the

---

82. synkith: stynkith   **90.** inpacient: inpaceint   **93.** gylte: gylti

---

79. The author has omitted the passage from St. Gregory included in *Ancrene Wisse*, which is translated: 'When we unite together in prayer, we are like persons walking on slippery ground, who hold each other by the hand for mutual support.' *Cf.* also *Troilus and Criseyde* I, 694–5.

100. In his remorse for the death of Jesus Judas hanged himself (*Matthew* 27: 5), though Christian authors interpreted his end as a just punishment for his crime. Jesus and Judas form an obvious contrast between loyalty and treachery.

102. *lighte*: in *Ancrene Wisse* the image is a file which sharpens man to good. It is

clowde of synne. But is not this evyll that man torneth to derknesse this that shold be his lyght so that it makyth hym moche more derke— as whan a man hathe trybulacyon or adversite and takyth it impacyently, he dooth ayenst nature and as evyl metall, for that thyng derkyth him that of his nature sholde gyve hym lighte and cleernes?

Wherfore, my dere suster, thynke on the pacyence of Jesu and of the remedyes ayenst wrath. That one remedye is to answer debonayrly to the angry, for Salamon sayth: 'Fayre answere refreyneth ire.' The seconde is scylence: whan mouth is stylle, the fyre quencheth and the hete aswageth, thenne ben they stylle fro chydynge; and therfore saith Saint Poul to the irous folke: 'Holde your peas and speke not to the wrathful.' The thirde is to beholde to our owne proper defautes, for a man in that is more apte to perceive the fawtes of other than of himselfe; and Salamon sayth: 'The poure man that hath defawt of godes, he is mesurable to other.' This is to saye, a man that perceyveth hymself disposed to wrath and felith in him many defawtes of impacyence, he forbereth and suffreth moche more other wyth gretter pacyence; but he that can perceyve noo defawte in hymselfe lightly is wroth wyth other. The fourth is to behold in what condycion the wrathfull is, for the wyse man callith wrath a lityl woodnes; and thenne a man that is wrothe semyth as oute of his witte—and to a madde man is foly to answere. For the irous man that is redy to saye evyll and curse may unneth suffre ony man or woman to be in the hous in rest wyth hym, he makyth soo moche chidyng. Wherof the gospell sayth: 'viM fendes, viC, lx and vi were entred by that synne into one man and never one of theim departed from other;' for this the wrathfull hath the cursinge of our Lorde, and the peasible and pacyente of meke hert hath his

104. lyght: ly|ight

---

possible that the word was misunderstood or misread at some stage. Cf. l. 106.

103. We should use the wrongs that others do to us for our spiritual improvement; but if instead we get angry with them, we make our spiritual condition worse, not better.

110. *Proverbs* 15: 1.

113. Possibly based on *Colossians* 3: 8.

116–17. Possibly based on *Proverbs* 18: 23, 'The poor useth intreaties; but the rich answereth roughly.'

126*ff.* Possibly based on *Mark* 5: 9, 'And he (the devil) answered, saying, My name is Legion, for we are many' (*cf. Luke* 8: 30); the figure six was often used to suggest a large size: here the number is 6,666.

blessynge. Wherof he sayth in the gospel: 'Ble[s]syd be the peasible   130
for they shall be callid the chyldern of God;' and to the contrary,
unhappy be the wrathfull for they shall be callyd the chyldern of the
fende.

Wherfore, good suster, remembre often the pacyence of Jesu Cryst
and of all his blessyd apostles, marters, confessours, and virgyns, how
grete anguysshe and payne they suffryd wyth pacience for to have the
joye perdurable. Wherof sayth Saynt Poul: 'By mani trybulacions
behoveth us to entre into the reygne of God.' Now take good hede
how those that ben pacyent, peasible, and debonayr ben well byloved
wyth the swete Jesu. Now ye know well whan dere frendes departe   140
asondre, the last wordes that they speke at theyr departyng is beste
remembryd; and amonge the last wordes that our Lorde sayd whan
he ascended to heven and lefte his dere frendes in a strange countree
were of swetnes and of peas, for thus sayd he to theim: 'Peas be amonge
you; my peas gyve I to you.' This peas graunt us Jesu Cryste by pacyence in herte, in mekenesse by worde, and in dede by debonayrtee.

Who is it that by slouthe sholde leve to lerne or to labour to doo
wel that beholde by true fayth how Jesu Cryst was in erthe in gooyng,
in prechynge, and in all well-dooyng? After all this beholde how in
the ende of his lyfe he was traveyled whanne he prayed, soo that wyth   150
his swette ranne from hym droppes of blood rennyng down on his
blessid body to th'erthe. And after beholde whan he was at the pyler
how sorowfully he was scorged of the felon Jewes, not oonly on his
legges but over all his fayr body. And at the last beholde how he upon
the harde crosse was sore traveylled the daye of his letyng blood, where
other folkes take rest and eschewe the light and kepe theym cloos in
theyr chambers whan thei ben lete blod of ony veyne. But our blessyd
Lorde Jesu Criste went upon the Mount of Calvarie and yet more on

---

| 132. the wrathfull: they wrathfull | 145-6. pacyence: paeyence |
| 150. traveyled: travelyd | 158. went: vent |

---

130. *Matthew* 5: 9.

137. *Cf. 2 Thessalonians* 1: 5, 'That ye may be counted worthy of the kingdom of God, for which ye also suffer.'

143. *strange*: 'foreign, not one's own'. The real home of good men is paradise from which they were exiled through Adam's sin, so this world is 'foreign' to them. This idea is a commonplace in medieval religious literature. *Cf.* IX, 249.

144-5. *John* 14: 27.

158. Instead of hiding away in a room he was fully exposed on the top of Mount Calvary.

the crosse, and was lete blood in v places wyth woundes large and depe
160 and in the veynes capytall, for he was lete blood in his hede and in
many places. Than who by the eye of true fayth beholde wel this traveyle of Jesu Cryst wolde joyefully traveyle for his love and never
wolde be ydle; soo as sayth Saynt Jerom: 'For bi slouth comyth many
evylles.' And therfore sayth an holy fader: 'Doo alwaye well that ye
be not founde idle of the fende, wherby he may tempte you.'

Another medycyne ayenst spyrytuell slouth is in the hope and comforte of everlastyng joye, and this may a man have by holy medytacion of the passion of the swete Jesu Cryst and of his joye of heven.
And thise medytacions comen ofte by good lessons herde of other folke
170 or by redyng theymself, that makyth man and woman fermly to trust
in God and for noo synne to be in dyspaire of his mercy. For thus sayth
Saynt Bernarde: 'I have synned gretly, wherwyth my conscyence is
trowblid; but for this I dyspayre not, for I shall thynke of the woundes
of our Lorde that he suffryd for synnars, and thenne cann I not be
afrayed for noo synne that I have done in tyme paste, but that I shall
be savid yf I have grace to come wyth repentaunce to the mercy of
our Lorde.'

Another remedie there is ayenst slouth and ayenst every evyll,
and a mene to purchace every wele. This is oryson. And therfore
180 the fende dredeth moche the charytable prayer, for this cause that
prayer entreth so moche in the court of Jesu Cryst ayenst the fende
that it doth two thingis: it byndeth hym and brenneth hym. We rede
that a holy man was in his prayers and the fende came fleyng over hym
in the eyre and sholde passe towarde the occydent by the commaundement of Julian, the Emperour of Rome; and there became he soo faste

166-7. comforte: comforto

---

159. The five places are both hands and both feet and the side. The veneration of
the wounds of Christ grew in importance during the fourteenth and fifteenth centuries; the wounds are frequently depicted in art and literature.

163. The necessity for keeping busy was stressed by Jerome and many other Fathers,
and their words were frequently repeated in prologues and epilogues to medieval
books as a justification for their being written.

170. *theymself*: a somewhat rare emphatic object meaning 'them, i.e. the lessons'.

172. *Sermones in Cantica* 61 (P.L. 183: 1072).

180-2. Prayer ascends immediately to Christ in heaven, who quickly aids the person
praying to the detriment of the devil.

185. For Julian *cf.* X(a), 241.

bounde by the prayers of the holy man, that to hym ascended as wynges mountynge towarde heven, that in noo wise he myght remeve bi the space of x dayes enteerly. And of another fende rede we in the *Lyf of Saynt Bertylmew* that, as he was in his prayers, the fende sayd to him: 'Grete pane have I wyth you for your praiers brenne me sore.' And for thys I pray you, good suster, that ye oft remembre thise thynges, and thenne shall ye have the joy of heven that shal be gyven to theym that traveylle for our Lord Jesu Cryst. Soo as he hymselfe sayth in the gospell: 'Calle,' sayth he, 'the labourers and gyve them theyr hire;' that is, the joye of heven.

Who shold be coveytous or scarse, as ben thei that will for the purchasyng and receyvyng of erthly weles trespace ayenste God, yf they beholde by true fayth the grete povertee that was in the swete Jesu that conteyned fro the begynnyng of his lyf more and more unto th'ende? For at the fyrst tyme whan the kyng was borne that made bothe heven and erth, he had not soo moche place on all the erth upon whiche his lityl body myght reste, and therfore his piteous moder wrapped him in pour clothes and layed him in a manger betwyx an oxe and an asse, as it is sayd in the gospell. Yet after this was he more pour, so as he hymself sayd, that he had not soo moche place wheron he might rest his hede, so pour was he of erthly loggyng. But yet foloweth a greter poverte, for the Kinge of Glorye was dyspoyled and alle nakyd put upon the crosse; and yet what is more merveile, that of all the large erthe and brode might he not have space to laye his body to deye upon, for the crosse was not of brede past a fote or lityll more. This was a thyng of grete merveyle that he, that was almyghty in heven and in erthe, wolde wylfully be so pour as I have here befor touchid. Thenne unhappy ben they that overmoche desyren erthly goodes and love and honour of this world; wherof Saynt Poul

190

200

210

---

192. thenne: thennel

189*ff*. For St. Bartholomew *cf.* V, 137*ff*.   **194.** *Matthew* 20: 8.

200*ff*. *Cf*. III, 153*ff*. Probably through the influence of the thirteenth-century *Meditationes vitæ Christi*, increasing emphasis was placed on the pathos of Christ's birth and life in the later medieval period. Similarly in the art of this period Christ's suffering is more frequently portrayed than his glory. *The Book of Margery Kempe* contains many examples of this affective devotion to the humanity of Christ.

204. *Cf. Luke* 2: 7. The ox and the ass are not biblical, though they became associated with the birth of Christ at an early date.

spekyth sore ayenste and saith in this wyse: 'It is not evyl to have them, but rather it is evyll to love theym.' For the rychesse of this worlde is but thyng that gooth and comyth, and therfore who that hath rychesse and loveth it becometh pour, and they that have riches and loveth poverte is ryche. For thyse riche folkes that overmoche 220 loven this worlde have the curse of God, soo as he sayth in the gospell: 'Cursed be ye ryche folkes that have your comfort in your ryches.' But to theim that lityll love it hath he gyven his blessyng and the joye perdurable; and thus sayth he in the gospell: 'Blessyd be the poore, for theyrs shall be the reame of heven;' thys graunt us the swete Jesus that soo moche lovyd povertee.

Who sholde ete overmoche by wyll or custome, or drynke wherby that the naturel forces of the soule or body sholde be destourbed soo that they maye not doo th'office that they are ordeyned to? Suche that ben thus accustomed ben the glotons that are ofte grutchyng for 230 mete and drynke. But who that by true fayth beholde well the poure petaunce that our Lorde Jesu Cryst had the day that he was lete blood on the crosse, they sholde have lityll appetyte to that glotenie. There ben two maner of folkes that have grete nede of good and comfortable metes: this is to knowe, they that traveyle and they that blede; and the day of his passion our Lorde was both in harde traveyle and bledyng, and his pour petaunce was thenne but a draught of eysell and galle, as the gospel sheweth. Who thenne sholde grutche for defawte, though he have somtyme not plente at his wyll of mete or drynke, for the servaunt ought not to be better servid than his lord? 240 Wherof oure Lorde spekith by Jeramye: 'Remembre you,' sayd he, 'that have soo moche trespased of my grete poverte, and of the bytternesse of the eysell and galle that was gyven to me to drynke, and yet had I noothynge trespased.' Alas, wretches that we ben, for truely if we thought of this grete defawte, we sholde be content wyth lityll, and furnyssh penaunce wyth abstinence, and helpe those membres of our Lorde that have grete defawte, whiche ben the pour nedy. But it is grete merveyle that thise ryche men have not grete remorse

215–16. Probably based on *1 Timothy* 6: 10.

221. *Cf. Luke* 12: 21.   **223–4.** *Matthew* 5: 3.

231. *petaunce*: *cf.* V, 254.

234. *this is to know*: namely, that is to say; *blede*: let blood.

236–7. *Matthew* 27: 34.   **239.** *Cf. Matthew* 10: 24.

240. There is no exact parallel from *Jeremiah*.

of conscyence to thynke how they wythdrawe from the mouth of God in the pour and gyve it to the chyldern of the fende, as to thise mynst- relles and triflers, glotons and unthryftes, and doon ayenst the comma- undement of oure Lorde Jesu Cryste and to the peryll of her soules. For the book sayth: 'For the commaundement of God receyve the pour,' whiche is to meane to helpe them after your power. And yf ye may not, yet have compascion on theym and be of good wyll to helpe theim, and God wyll rewarde you. And Saynt Austin sayth: 'The ryche be made to helpe the pour and the pour to pray for the riche, and God wyll gyve to eche of theim richesse and joye wythout ende;' the whiche joye us graunt the swete Jesus that fastyd xl dayes in erthe.

Ayenst lecherye is to be noted the clennesse of the pure Vyrgyn Mary, for he sholde be overvyle of his body that by tru fayth beholde the clene byrth of Jesu Cryst and of his riht clene and pure moder, the blessyd vyrgyn Saynt Mary, and the clennesse of the lif that thei ledde in erthe and all theyrs and, on that other partye, how shamfully evyll and unclene is that vyle sinne. They sholde hate it wyth all theyr hertes and flee it as the deth, yf they were not out of theyr wyttes or of suche frowardnesse that they raughte not of theyr dampnacion. For we rede in *Genesis* that God for that vyle shamfull synne dystroyed al the worlde by the Floode, for it rayned xl dayes and xl nyghtes and this water was soo hye that it was above the hyest mountayn in erthe xv cubytes, whiche drowned al folkes and bestes and fowles in the world savyng Noe and his wyfe, his thre sones and their iii wyves, and those bestes and fowles that were saved in the same arke. The whiche water roos soo hye over al erth to wasshe away the filth and foilyng of that vyle synne of lecherye; and as hye shall ryse the fyre before the Daye of Jugement to purge the erthe of synne. As a wise fader sayth: 'A, how unclene a thyng and vyle is that fowle synne of lecherye whiche foyleth not oonly th'erthe but the ayre; the whiche fylthe to wasshe awaye suffyseth not all the water that was in erth, but that God sente fro heven rayne xl dayes and xl nyghtes.' And for simple fornycacion that the folke of Israhel dyde wyth the women of

250
260
270
280

---

250. *Cf.* IX, 18.

252. *Cf. Ps.* 41: 1, 'Blessed is he that considereth the poor.'

255. *Sermo* 80 (P.L. 38: 496).   **267.** *Genesis* 7: 12ff.

274-5. A common idea in sermons, *cf.* Chaucer's *The Parson's Tale* (*Canterbury Tales* X (I) 838).

279ff. For the Israelites' fornication with the Midianites, see *Numbers* 25.

Madyan, rede we that there were slay[n] of theim in one daye by the commaundement of Moyses xxiii thousande men; and Saynt Poul wytnesseth. And for the avoutrye that the folke of Gaba dyde one nyghte in the ravysshyng the wyf of a man were slayne lx and vM men. And for that vyle and shamfull synne ayenste nature, God dystroyed v cytees, for it regned upon Sodome and Gomore stynkyng sulphur and brennynge fyre, and overthrewe the cytees and all the reame aboute, and all tho that enhabyted in the cytees, and all the thynges growenge in that londe. And this was done in signe that God took noo vengaunce
290 upon the sinners oonly, but on the place where they enhabyted and of al the place aboute theim that eyther usid it or knewe it and myghte amende theym and wolde not.

And knowe well that in all maners that ony man or woman procureth or assenteth therto oute of maryage, it is dedely synne and one of the gretest synnes that is; for Saynt Austin sayth in the decre: 'Avoutry is gretter synne than fornycacyon; and woors and more vyle is a man to sinne wyth his own moder then with another woman; but overevyl and abhomynable is it of the synne ayenst nature, and the leest of all, oute of mariage, is dampnable.' Wherfore ye wretches that folow soo
300 the vile desires of your flessh, bethinke ye and repent you and remembre how grevous is this vyle synne of lecherye. And therof sayth Saynt John in th'*Apocalipsis*: 'The vicyous wretches and avouterers that will not leve their synne shall be payned perdurably in a lake of stynkyng sulphur and brennyng fire for this that they ben now soo brennyng in the fowle desire of theyr wretchid flessh before God and his angelles and all good folkes.'

But yet the mercy of our Lord is soo grete that whan the wretchid

---

285. ayenste: a ayenste

282–3. *Ancrene Wisse* quotes *Hebrews* 12: 3 and 5: 4 in the corresponding passage, and the author of *Remedies* may have had one of these texts in mind.

283–4. For the rape of the woman by the men of Gibeah, see *Judges* 20.

284. That is, 65,000 men.

285–9. The destruction of Sodom and Gomorrah is related in *Genesis* 19.

295ff. *De bono conjugali* 11 (P.L. 40: 382). The sense of 297–9 is: Unnatural sexual relations are all evil, and even the least sin of this type, which is that committed outside marriage, leads to damnation. According to Augustine unnatural sexual practices were more reprehensible inside than outside marriage: *iste qui est contra naturam exsecrabiliter fit in meretrice, sed exsecrabilius in uxore.*

302. Based on *Revelations* 9: 17–21.

man or woman repenteth hem of hir synnes, have they ever so moche offended in ony synne what soo ever it be, so that they kepe hem clene forthe in body and herte shall goo to the joye perdurable where they shall see Jesu Cryst, the Fader, and the Holy Goost; soo as sayth the gospell: 'Blessyd be the clene of herte for they shal see God,' and swete Jesu, the sone of Marye, and all the holy company of heven. My dere suster, there I trust we shall be togyder bothe body and sowle at the grete Daye of Jugement; and this graunt us Almighti God of his infinite mercy. Amen.

And all ye that rede or here this, pray ye for hym that made it and for theym that wrote it and for hir that was the cause that it was made and of your charite for theym that translated it and wrote it out of Frenssh into Englissh one *Pater Noster* and one *Avee*, that God have mercy on us and that we may come to hym after this mortall lyfe into the everlastyng lyf wythout departynge. Amen.

312. *Matthew* 5: 8.

317*ff.* This conclusion probably served for the first three tracts of the *Treatise of Love*; see the introductory remarks.

G

Select Glossary

The glossary is designed as a guide to reading the texts only, and an elementary knowledge of Middle English is assumed on the part of the reader. Words glossed in the notes are not recorded here unless they occur in another context. Since the texts cover such a wide range of dates and of ME dialects some words appear in a variety of different forms; but in order to prevent the glossary from becoming too bulky, full cross-references and textual references are not provided. The arrangement is strictly alphabetical.

a *prep.* to, into, II 289

a, aa, ay *adv.* ever, always, II 209, 308, IV 338

abascht *pp.* upset, frightened, VI 214

abeh *pt.3 s.* bowed in homage, I 70

abeoren *v.* to endure, II 240

abilnes *n.* fitness, VII 41; proneness, VII 127

abit *n.* habit, dress, VII 210

ablent *pp.* blinded, led astray, VI 423

aboundingly *adv.* abundantly, VII 111

abowve *prep.* above, IV 113

abuggen *v.* to pay for, II 420; *pp.* **aboht** II 385

abuten *adv.* about, around, I 45

abyde *v.* to remain, X(b) 303; to expect, II 239; **abod** *pt.3 s.* completed, VI 199, waited (for), X(a) 135, 221

accorde *n.:* **alle the a.** unanimously, X(a) 123

accordith *pr.3 s.* agrees, X(a) 138

acold *a.* freezing, VI 143

acording *a.* suitable, VII 150

acoverunge *n.* recovery, II 390

acovrin *v.* to regain, recover, II 138; *pp.* **acoveret** II 131

acwiketh *pr.3 s.* be reborn, II 228

adamantines *a.* (*quasi-n., gen.*) of adamant, adamantine, II 554

adred *a.* afraid, VI 210

adrenche *v.* to drown, destroy by water, VI 145; *pt.3 s.* **adreynte** VI 291

adun *adv.* down, II 37

afferd *pp.a.* afraid, terrified, IX 178

aforn *prep.* before, V 142

agast *a.* frightened, VI 237

agayne(s) *see* **ayein(es)**

ageasteth *pr.3 s.* frightens, II 457

ago *pp.* past, VI 167

agrisen *v.* to shake with fear, II 458; **agrysen of** to abhor, loathe, VI 137

agulte *pt.3 s.* sinned against, VI 333; *pt.pl.* **agulten** II 695

ah *conj.* but, I 54, II 177

ah, awe *pr.3 s.* ought, II 8, IV 369; *pr.2 s.* **ahest** II 140; *pr.pl.* **awe(n)** I 96, IV 25; *pt.2 s.* **ahtest** II 510

ahefulle *a.* terrible, III 61

ahne, awen(e) *a.* own, I 23, III 45

ahonge *pp.* hanging, I 14

ahte *n.* cattle, livestock, II 435; possessions, III 8

aihwer, eihwer *adv.* everywhere, III 28, 100

aisille, eysell *n.* vinegar, III 247, XI 236

akeasteth *pr.3 s.* casts down, II 124; *pp.* **akeast** II 39

akennesse *n.* incarnation, birth, II 669

ald *a.* old, I 45; *comp.* **eldere** III 159

alegeance, aleggaunce *n.* relief, mitigation, IV 238, VI 280

aleid *pp.* destroyed, corrupted, II 352

alesen *v.* to redeem, II 191

alesendnesse *n.* redemption, salvation, II 139

al for to *conj.* until, VIII 95

algatis *adv.* always, IX 154

alkyn, alle skinnes *a., quasi-a.* of all kinds, IV 127, VI 353

al(l) *adv.* entirely, I 29, V 88

allane *adv.* only, IV 219

allanly, alonly *adv.* only, merely, IV 284

allegate *adv.* altogether, III 142; always, III 144, 165

alles, allunge *adv.* entirely, completely, II 265, 696

alls, alswa *conj.* as, I 9, IV 12

almes *n.pl.* work(s) of charity, IX 155

almesdedes, almesdede-doyng, almesyevynge *n.* alms-giving, performance of charitable deeds, V 45, IX 54, X(b) 166

alre, alther *a.* (*gen.pl.*) of all, II 496, V 101

alswa *prep.* like, I 92

Alwealdent *n.* Almighty, II 516

alyaunce *n.* association, XI 83

alyteth *pr.3 s.* illuminates, V 259

amanges *prep.* among, IV 57

amansed *pp.* cursed, I 91

amead *a.* mad, II 554

amende *v.* to reform, X(b) 292

amendes-making *n.* restitution, reparation, IV 224-5

amentised *pp.* destroyed, X(a) 165-6

and *conj.* if, XI 74

ane *a., pron.* one, IV 386; **anes** *gen.* own, II 261; *adv.* alone, only, II 45; *art.* a, I 20

anely, onely *adv.* only, IV 143; alone, VII 9

anence *prep.* with respect to, IV 59

anes, eanes *adv.* once, II 133, IV 229

angere *n.* anguish, distress, IV 372

angoise *n.* anguish, II 533; **angusches** *pl.* torments, V 161

anlypy *a.* single, IV 386

anon *adv.* immediately, VI 313; **anan riht** II 217

anoye *n.* affliction, IV 372

anoyed *pp.* vexed, VIII 77

anuppon *prep.* upon, I 48

apely *adv.* in the manner of an ape, imitatively, VII 167

apert *a.* open, public, IX 59; **in apert** openly, VII 371

apocrifie *n.* fiction, X(a) 13

appon(ne) *prep.* upon, IV 351

ar, are, or *conj., adv.* before, previously, IV 201, X(b) 137

arayed *pt.3 s.* adorned, decorated, X(a) 259

arblawst *n.* cross-bow, VIII 18

areare *pr.subj.s.* raise, II 297

arh *a.* cowardly, frightened, III 134

ariste *n.* resurrection, I 93

arraiynge *n.* fitting out, IX 107

arst *see* **erest**

aryght *adv.* properly, fittingly, XI 88

as *conj.* where, II 426

asemble *v.* to copulate, VI 281

askes *see* **axe**

asondre *adv.* apart, XI 141

assayed *pt.3 s.* made trial of, VIII 137

assethe *n.* recompense, reparation, IV 177

assoylede *pp.* absolved, IV 176

astaat *n.* rank, position, IX 106; state, condition, II 159

astunte *pt.pl.* came to a halt, VI 79

aswageth *pr.3 s.* dies down, XI 112

at *pron.* that, IV 366; *adv.prep.* to, IV 150, 229

atele *a.* dreadful, horrible, III 127

athes *n.pl.* oaths, IV 179

a thet, a tha *conj.* until, I 76, 78-9

at perti *adv.phr.* privately, IX 100

atteyneth to *pr.3 s.* reaches, VII 55

attri *a.* poisonous, II 194

aturn *n.* appearance, dress, II 318

atwynne *adv.* in two, apart, VI 239

auctoryte *n.* authority, XI 41

aughten *num.a.* eighth, IV 161

aumener *n.* almoner, V 177

auncien *a.* old, X(a) 172

auriole *n.* crown or halo of a saint, II 322

autentyke *a.* reliable, authoritative, Xa 20

autyr *n.* altar, IV 227

avaunsynge *n.* promotion, preferment, IX 92

avauntynge *n.* vice of boastfulness, IV 332

aveallet *pp.* fallen into sin, II 230

avisement *n.* thought, consideration, VII 143

avisylyche *adv.* prudently, V 104

avouterers *n.pl.* adulterers, XI 302

avow *n.* promise, vow, VII 215

avowe *v.* to say, admit, IV 340

avowtry *n.* adultery, IV 389

awakenin *v.* to spring, arise, II 19; to quicken, receive life, II 519

awarpen *pp.* cast away, II 712

awe *n.* fear, V 4

awe *see* **ah**

aweariede *pp.a.* cursed, II 640

awundret of *pp.* amazed at, II 594

axe *v.* to ask, IX 173; **askes** *pr.3 s.* requires, IV 81; *pt.3 s.* **escade** I 45

ayein(es), ayeynus, againe(s) *prep.* in comparison with, II 61, III 119; in return for, II 83; in anticipation of, II 455; against, IV 387, V 122; *adv.* back, II 207

ayeinwart *adv.* back, II 638; on the other hand, VII 290

ayensayeth *pr.3 s.* contradicts, X(a) 83

ayere, aer, eyre *n.* air, IV 6, VII 55, X(a) 233

ba *pron.* both, II 54

bacbytynge *n.* slander, defamation, IX 209

bakbyte *pr.pl.* slander, IV 151

bakbyttere *n.* slanderer, IV 343

baldede *pt.3 s.* strengthened, III 64

bale *n.* torment, misery, II 20; poison, evil, II 483; disaster, danger, III 143; *a.* baleful, deadly, III 220

band *pt.2 s.* bound, III 66; *pt.pl.* **bunden** III 222; *pp.a.* in chains, III 223

banes *n.pl.* bones, body, III 166

baptym *n.* baptism, IV 198

barbaryns *n.pl.* barbarians, X(a) 61

bare *pt.3 s.* flowed, VI 145

barme *n.* breast, VI 363

basme *n.* balm, embalming ointment, II 167

bathe *pron.* both, IV 69; **bathere** *gen.* of them both, IV 246; *adv.* as well, II 28

baylyes, bayles *n.pl.* stewards, V 126

be *prep.* by, VI 107

bearn *n.* child, II 542

bearnen *v.* to burn, II 566; *prp.* **bearninde, beorninde, berninde** I 13, 16, II 109

bearnteam, barentem *n.* brood, progeny, II 450, V 320

beddin *v.* to lodge, dwell harmoniously, II 635

beddrede *a.* bed-ridden, IX 45

bede *pr.subj.s.* offer, III 299; **beot** *pr.3 s.* orders, I 105; *pt.3 s.* **beed** VI 364; **beode** *inf.* to pray, I 87

bedes-biddynge *n.* prayer, VIII 116

befalle *v.* to happen, VII 24

beheestes *n.pl.* commands, instructions, X(b) 17

behilde *pt.3 s.* beheld, X(a) 322

behofe *n.* benefit, use, X(b) 254

behoteth *see* **bihate**

bei *imper.* bend, II 4; *pr.subj.s.* **beie** II 205

bekinde *a.* warm, fomenting, III 21

bemeenen *pr.pl.* signify, symbolize, VII 304

benyme *pr.subj.s.* deprive, take away, VI 154; *pt.pl.* **benomen** VI 187

beodes *n.pl.* prayers, VI 416

beo(n) *v.* to be, II 41, 56; *pr.1 s.* **icham** VI 237; *pr.3 s.* **bith** I 55, **es** IV 74; *pr.pl.* **beoth** I 35, **ere** IV 27, **aryn** V 50; *pr.subj.s.* **beo** I 86; *pr.subj.pl.* **beon** II 72; *pt.3 s.* **wes** I 7; *pt.pl.* **weren** I 18, **weore** VI 70; *pt.subj.* **ware** IV 9; *pp.* **iben** VI 103

beore *pr.subj.s.* incline, II 203

be(o)rninde *see* **bearnen**

bere *n.* outcry, shouting, II 458

bersten *v.* to burst, shatter, VI 135

beseke *v.* to beseech, X(a) 97

bestelich *a.* loathsome, foul, II 110

betake *pr.1 s.* entrust, commit, VI 196; *pt.2 s.* **betoke** VI 119

beten *v.* to atone for, II 303

bethynke *pr.subj.s.* consider, reflect, XI 15

betraysede *pp.* betrayed, deceived, IV 97

betyde *pr.3 s.* befalls, IV 307

bi- *see also* **be-**

biburien *v.* to bury, be buried, II 104

bichearret *pp.* deluded, deceived, II 90

biclaried *pp.* besmirched, III 192

bicleopest *pr.2 s.* speak to, II 477

bicluppeth *pr.pl.* encompass, enclose, II 250; **bicluppet** *pt.3 s.* embraced, VI 362

bicumeth *pr.3 s.* is fitting, I 81; **bikimeth** becomes, II 54

bidde *pr.1 s.* ask, I 64; *pp.* **ibeden** I 78; **bad** *pt.3 s.* prayed, VI 211; **bit** *pr.3 s.* commands, II 105; **bedyn** *pp.* ordered, IV 57

biddyng *n.* prayer, VI 212

bifunden *pp.* encompassed, II 468

bigan *v.* to omit, II 560

bihalde *v.* to look (at), III 148; *pr.3 s.* **bihalt** II 31; *pt.2 s.* **biheld** III 144

bihate *pr.1 s.* promise, II 246; *pr.3 s.* **behoteth** V 245; *pt.pl.* **biheten** II 89; *pp.* **bihaten** II 252; **behihte** *pt.3 s.* commanded, VI 8

bihe(a)ste *n.* promise, II 252, 573

biheve *n.* profit, advantage, II 376

biholding *n.* observation, inspection, VII 223

bihoveth *pr.3 s.* is fitting, necessary, II 47; **byhoves** IV 251

bihynde *adv.* in arrears, IX 148

bijs *n.* a dark fur, VI 374

bikimeth *see* **bicumeth**

bileave, byleve *n.* faith, II 48, 276

bilef *imper.* remain, VI 204; *pt.pl.* **bilaften** VI 72

biluketh *pr.3 s.* incorporates, expresses, II 550

bimong *prep.* among, II 146

bireavin *v.* to deprive of, II 425

biremen *v.* to bewail, deplore, II 700

bireowe *v.* to repent of, II 86

bireowseth *pr.3 s.* repents of, II 658

bireowsunge *n.* repentance, contrition, II 180

birie *v.* to bury, IX 67

biseon (on) *v.* to look (at), II 260; *imper.* **bisih** II 475; *pt.3 s.* **biseh** II 673

biset on *pp.* encumbered with, II 99, VI 299

bismere *n.* scorn, mockery, II 224; **tuketh the to b.** treats you shamefully, II 459

bistad *pp.* placed, VI 213

bisuncken *pp.* sunk, II 473

bitacneth *pr.3 s.* represents, symbolizes, II 26; **bitokened** *pp.* signified, VI 141

bithencheth *pr.pl.* reflect, II 94

bitterlukest *adv.superl.* with most pain, II 505

bittre, bittri *a.* grievous, dire, II 20, 96; *quasi-n.* torment, II 403

bituh(h)e(n), bitweonen *prep.* between, II 689, III 208

biwepe *pr.1 s.* shed tears for, I 60

biwinneth *pr.pl.* acquire, win, II 431; *pt.3 s.* **biwon** I 6

biwitene *v.* to guard, II 283; *pt.pl.* **biwisten** I 21

biyeotene *v.* to acquire, obtain, II 87; *pt.3 s.* **biyat** VI 235; **biyeten** *pp.* begotten, VI 203

biyete *n.* possessions, profit, II 388; gain, II 578

blase *n.* fire, V 263

blede *v.* to let blood, XI 234

blenden *pr.pl.* blind, mislead, IX 62

bleo *n.* complexion, face, III 25

blescede *pp.a.* blessed, II 720

blesse *v.* to make the sign of the cross, X(b) 52

bletheliche, blitheliche *adv.* joyfully, II 240, VI 173; *comp.* **blitheluker** II 8

bleugh *pt.3 s.* blew, filled, VI 57

blickid *pp.* stained, besmirched, IX 265

blisfule *a.* blessed, III 168

blissith *pr.pl.* rejoice, live in bliss, II 689

blithe *a.* glad, VI 277

blodleting *n.* letting or shedding of blood, III 248

blostme *n.* blossom, II 133

blynnes *pr.3 s.* ceases, IV 26

blyve *adv.* quickly, promptly, VI 223

bodily *a.* mortal, human, IX 216; material, IV 165; physical, V 7

bold *n.* home, abode, III 70

boldynge *n.* encouragement, IX 165

bollenynge *n.* swelling (of heart with rage), IV 344

bord *n.* table, V 172

boste *n.* arrogance, presumption, IV 332

bostful *a.* arrogant, IX 85

bote *conj.* unless, VI 109

bote, boote *n.* remedy, deliverance, III 99, 143

bounte *n.* goodness, XI 100

bouxome, buhsum *a.* obedient, II 11, IV 146

brade *a.* broad, III 258

bread *n.* food, II 449

breche *n.* trousers, X(b) 91

brede *v.* to beget, rear, II 450; **bredest** *pr.2 s.* cause, breed, II 92

brede *n.* width, X(a) 52; breadth, Xa 53

brekene *v.* to torment, tear apart, I 31; **breoke** *pr.3 s.* break, II 205

brekynge *n.* conquest, IX 247

brenne *v.* to burn, X(b) 96; *prp.* **brennende** V 69

brethe *n.* smell, I 44

bretherhedis *n.pl.* religious orders, VII 205

brethre(n) *n.pl.* brothers, kinsmen, I 80, III 111; monks, members of a religious community, X(b) 232

broke-rugget *a.* hunch-backed, II 370

brothelis *n.pl.* rogues, IX 142

brought fourth *pt.3 s.* educated, X(b) 33

bruche *n.* sin, loss of virginity, II 147; transgression, II 284

bruchele *a.* brittle, II 154

brude *n.* bride, II 41

brudgume *n.* bridegroom, II 160

brudlac *n.* marriage, II 16

bruken *v.* to enjoy, II 486

brune *n.* burning, II 109

bucchede *pp.a.* cursed, vile, III 135

buffetet *pp.* beaten, III 231

buggen *v.* to buy, II 101; *pt.3 s.* **bohte** III 272

buheth *pr.pl.* obey, bow to, II 42; **buhed** *pp.* submitted, III 146; **buhande** *prp.a.* weak, flexible, III 136; **bowe** *inf.* to bend, X(b) 94

buhsumnesse, buxomnesse *n.* obedience, II 606, V 107

bunden *see* **band**

bur *n.* dwelling, III 70; room, chamber, III 275

burde *n.* natural state, II 162

burh *n.* town, III 155

burtherne *n.* pregnancy, II 495

burth-tid *n.* time of birth, nativity, III 155

bus *pr.3 s.* ought, IV 222

busteth *pr.3 s.* beats, thrashes, II 460

bute(n) *prep.* without, I 29; except, II 97

bute yef *conj.* unless, II 91

but onliche *prep.* except, VI 424

byde *v.* to stay, VII 337; **bode** *pt.3 s.* remained, X(b) 294

byfore-war *a.* cautious, V 131

byforn *prep.* before, above, V 82; *adv.* earlier, V 299

byfornhond *adv.* previously, V 298

byhovely *adv.* fittingly, appropriately, IV 133

bysyly(che), besely *adv.* diligently, carefully, V 98, 178, 202

bysynes *n.* activity, occupation, V 284

cader-clutes *n.pl.* baby clothes, II 560

caldeliche *a.* coldly, III 158

calenges *pr.3 s.* claims, III 129

capytall *a.* principal, XI 160

care *n.* anxiety, VI 153

careyne *n.* corpse, IX 74

carie(n) *v.* to look after carefully, II 46; to grieve, be sad, II 397

carpe *imper.* talk, converse, III 310

carpyng *n.* utterance, IV 204

caste appon *v.phr.* to plot the means, IV 355; **castes unto** *pr.pl.* employ, IV 364

catell, chatel *n.* possessions, wealth, III 28, IV 164

cause *n.* reason, X(a) 213

cautelis *n.pl.* tricks, stratagems, IX 187

cawdryn *n.* cauldron, X(a) 295

chanon *n.* canon, X(b) 207

chapeter-belle *n.* bell in the chapter house, V 329

charbucle, charbuncle-stone *n.* carbuncle, precious stone, II 651, VI 41

charge *n.* duty, IX 21

charges *pr.3 s.* instructs, IV 126

charite *n.* love, IX 184

charytable *a.* loving, XI 180

chas *n.* quarry, game, VIII 155

chasty *v.* to correct, IV 263; **chastieth** *pr.3 s.* disciplines, II 202

chastysynge *n.* punishment, IX 158

chatel *see* **catell**

chaunteresse *n.* precentor, nun who leads the singing, V 133

ch(e)affere *n.* transaction, bargain, II 103, 378

cheap *n.* purchase, bargain, III 213; **lihtliche c.** at little cost, III 78

cheape *v.* to buy, III 29; *pp.* **chepet** III 214

cheff lorde *n.* tenant-in-chief, overlord, X(b) 252

chelde *n.* child, X(b) 38; *pl.* **childir** IV 49

chele *n.* coldness, VI 207

cheorl *n.* bondsman, servant, II 567

cheoweth *pr.3 s.* nags, vexes, II 458

chere *n.* expression, II 477, VI 339

cherre *n.* time, II 335; **sum c.** sometimes, II 134

chese *v.* to choose, III 28; *pt.3 s.* **cheas** II 697; **chose** *pp.* elected, X(b) 207

chesing *n.* choice, VII 246

chesoun *n.pl.* chosen ones, V 162

chide *v.* to quarrel, IX 12; **chit** *pr.3 s.* rails, scolds, II 458

chief *a.* as *n.* principal object, VII 253

childir *see* **chelde**

chirche-bisocnie *n.* attendance at church, I 86

churcheyerthe *n.* hallowed ground around church, churchyard, X(b) 190

clatheles *n.* naked, IV 256

cleane *a.* pure, unsoiled, II 145; *adv.* neatly, chastely, II 147

cleannesse *n.* purity, II 145, IV 141

cleanschipe *n.* purity, II 302

cleneliche *adv.* purely, III 112

cleopien *v.* to call, II 673; *pr.3 s.* **cleopeth** II 6, **cleput** V 180, **clepeth** VIII 60; *pp.* **icleped, icleopet, icleoped, clepud** II 25, V 2

cleping *n.* vocation, VII 281

clere *a.* plain, VII 64; *comp.* more beautiful, VI 93; *adv.* brightly, X(a) 70

clergie *n.* learning, scholarship, VII 191

clerke *n.* doctor of the church, learned man, IV 11

clernes *n.* light, brightness, XI 102

clethe *v.* to clothe, IV 256

cleve *v.* to cling, X(a) 56; to smite in two, III 259; *pp.* **cloven** V 234

cloos *a.* private, XI 156

close *v.* to enclose, be enclosed, XI 17

cluppen, klyppe *v.* to embrace, III 276, V 155

cluppunge, clippyng *n.* embrace, intercourse, II 16, IX 261

clutes *n.pl.* rags, III 158

cnawe, knowe *v.* to know, recognize, III 261; to reveal, tell, X(a) 164; **that es to k.** namely, IV 59

cnotti *a.* knotted, III 227

cokkunge *n.* struggling, striving, II 711

comelyngis *n.pl.* guests, strangers, IX 249

comfortable *a.* comforting, sustaining, XI 233–4

communers *n.pl.* partakers, sharers, IV 9

comonynge, comounyng *n.* congregation, IV 75; conversing, VII 159

comounly *adv.* in company, VII 337

comouns *pr.pl.* commune, participate, IV 76

compas *v.* to plan, devise, IV 355

conandely, cunnandely *adv.* expertly, IV 402

conaundenes *n.* knowledge, skill, IV 364

conceyve *pr.1 s.* understand, think, VII 152

confermynge *n.* confirmation, IV 214

confort *n.* security, pleasure, II 73

conjurid *pt.3 s.* urged solemnly, X(a) 321

connende, connyng *prp.a.* wise, competent, V 13, 206; knowing, VI 59

connyng *n.* knowledge, X(b) 131

conseit *n.* opinion, judgement, VII 39

consented to *pt.pl.* followed, VI 73

constou *pr.2 s.* can you?, VI 186

contemplatif *a.* devoted to the contemplation of God, VII 251

contynuance *n.* perseverance, VII 138-9

conversacioun *n.* living place, VIII 51; manner of life, XI 12

conversede *pt.pl.* lived, VIII 63

coolys *n.pl.* coals, fire, X(a) 287

coroun, cruni *v.* to crown, II 714, III 302; *pp.* **corounde** IV 99, **crunet** III 48

cors *n.* corpse, V 271

corsud *see* **cursid**

cos *n.* kiss, II 222

cost *n.* choice entertainment, IX 32; *pl.* expenses, X(b) 27

costly, costelewe *a.* expensive, sumptuous, IX 17, X(b) 214-5

costy *a.* extravagant, IX 4

cosyner *n.* cook, V 163

couchen *pr.pl.* lie, sleep, IX 46

counforte *v.* to encourage, strengthen, IX 44; to comfort, IX 54

cours *n.* ordinary procedure, VII 20

coveiten *pr.pl.* desire, are eager for, VIII 53

covenable *a.* appropriate, fitting, IX 243

covent *n.* monastery, members of a monastery, X(b) 219

coverunge *n.* recovery, II 142; deliverance, redemption, II 626

covetyse *n.* covetousness, IV 167

coveytous *a.* greedy, gluttonous, XI 196

creft, craft *n.* skill, handicraft, II 536; *pl.* trickery, stratagems, IX 102

crighed *pt.3 s.* called out, VI 180

cristenly *a.* in a Christian manner, IV 147

croceris *n.pl.* crosiers, IX 23

crohe *n.* pot, jug, II 567

crokes *n.pl.* wiles, deceptions, III 145

crokid *a.* defective, misguided, VII 215

crosser *n.* one who carries the crosier, X(b) 172

croys *n.* cross, V 247

crune, coron *n.* crown, II 280, VII 76

crupel *n.* cripple, II 476

cubyt *n.* a measure of length (usually about eighteen inches), XI 270

cumbrous *a.* difficult, uneven, XI 73

cumeth *pr.3 s.* comes, I 96, **kimeth** II 242; *pt.3 s.* **com** I 58; *pt.pl.* **coomen** VI 178; *pt.subj.s.* **cume** I 66; *pp.* **icomen** VI 215; **cum up of** come out of, VI 171

cumpanous *a.* in company, VII 29

cun *n.* family, II 501

cun, kun *v.* to know, be familiar with, IV 25; *pr.pl.* **cunnen** II 536; **kunne** *pr.2 s.* know how to, VIII 2; **cuthes** *pt.2 s.* were able, III 46

cunde *see* **kind**

cunqueari *pr.subj.s.* vanquish, acquire, II 487

cuntasses *n.pl.* countesses, II 93

curacion *n.* healing, cure, X(a) 37

curatour *n.* guardian, IX 87

cure *n.* responsibility, IV 38

curious *a.* careful, meticulous, VII 223

curnels *n.pl.* pips, VI 334

cursednesse *n.* wickedness, IX 212

cursid *pt.3 s.* reviled, invoked evil upon, X(a) 245; excommunicated, X(b) 277; *pp.a.* wicked, IX 223

cursyng *n.* excommunication, X(b) 279

curteis *a.* noble, refined, IX 43

curteles *n.pl.* dresses, garments, VI 140

curtesye *n.* refinement of manners, VIII 129

custome *n.:* **in c.** in use, VII 336

cwalm *n.* murrain, plague, II 435

cwalm-hus *n.* prison, house of torment, III 69

cwalm-stowe *n.* place of execution, III 235

cwedli *adv.* meanly, niggardly, III 10

cwelled, iculd *pp.* killed, III 187, VI 261

cweme *a.* pleasing, agreeable, II 140

cwemen, quemen *v.* to please, gratify, II 46, III 309

cwiddes *pr.3 s.* says, III 31; *pp.* **quiddet** III 71

cwike, qwykke *a.* living, II 168, IV 81

cwikede *pt.3 s.* was born, II 641

dale, dele, dole *n.* portion, part, II 95, VI 97

daliaunce *n.* coquetry, IX 269

dampne *v.* to condemn, IX 145

dart *n.* arrow, VII 256

dawes *n.pl.* days, I 105

deadbote *n.* penance, II 181

deadliche *a.* mortal, II 158

dealeth *pr.3 s.* disposes, bestows, III 55

deathes-hus *n.* abode of death, hell, III 147

debate *n.* strife, X(b) 264

debonairte, deboneirschipe *n.* gentleness, mildness, III 14, 100

debonayr *a.* mild, humble, XI 139

debonayrly *adv.* courteously, humbly, XI 109

decre *n.* ruling, judgement, XI 295

dede *n.* death, IV 109

defailith *pr.3 s.* fails, is lacking, VII 191

defaute *n.* fault, IV 30; lack, want, V 200; absence, VIII 81; omission, IX 120

defende *pr.3 s.* forbid, X(b) 256

deffames *pr.pl.* slander, IV 151

defoyled *pp.a.* stained, polluted, XI 2

degre *n.* rank, position, II 184, IV 244; stage, level, II 328, XI 92

dehtren, doutren *n.pl.* daughters, II 247, V 318

deie, dyghen *v.* to die, II 602, VI 33; *pt.2 s.* **deidest** III 299

delicatly *adv.* luxuriously, IX 7

delit *n.* pleasure, II 17

deluge *n.* great danger, X(a) 265

deluvie *n.* flood, VI 408

delycys *n.pl.* joys, delights, V 161

delynge *n.* disposition, IX 152

delysyous *a.* delightful, V 28

deme *v.* to judge, IV 81; *pp.* **demet, demd** III 182, 234

demere *n.* judge, III 182

demyng *n.* estimation, opinion, VII 9

dennet *pp.* lodged, sheltered, III 158

denye *v.* to refuse, X(b) 231

deopliche *adv.* earnestly, seriously, II 12

deor *n.pl.* animals, wild animals, I 28

de(o)re *a.* dear, II 9; precious, IV 290; *comp.* **deorre, derre** II 283, III 46

deore *adv.* expensively, III 214; *comp.* **derure** II 283

deoreliche *adv.* zealously, carefully, II 141

deorewurthe *a.* precious, II 22, III 16

deovel *n.* devil, II 184; *pl.* **deoflen** I 45

departe *v.* to separate, XI 71

departyng *n.* separation, VIII 48; departure, XI 55

depness *n.* depth, X(a) 48

der *pr.3 s.* dares, II 642

derennedes *pt.2 s.* vindicated by fighting, III 274

derf *n.* affliction, hardship, II 240

derf *a.* cruel, dreadful, II 688; **derve** *pl.* severe, difficult, II 275

derkyth *pr.3 s.* obscures, sullies, XI 107

derling *n.* sweetheart, lover, III 1

derure *see* **deore** *adv.*

derveth *pr.3 s.* injures, torments, II 74; *pp.* **idervet** II 82

deserte *n.*: **wythout d.** undeservedly, XI 99; **for our d.** deservedly, XI 96

deservid *pt.3 s.* earned, X(a) 322

despite *n.* haughtiness, defiance, IV 332; disobedience, IX 121

destourbed *pp.* stopped, hindered, XI 227

dett *n.* duty, obligation, IV 369

devynyte *n.* theology, X(b) 126

devyse *v.* to describe, VIII 70

deyitte *n.* provision of food, IX 32

dihten *v.* to prepare, order, II 57

dintede *pt.pl.* hit, struck, III 224

disceyt *n.* deception, VII 121

discover *pr.2 s.* reveal, X(a) 187

discrecion *n.* understanding, discrimination, VII 93

discryvid *pp.* described, illustrated, X(a) 55

dispenderis *n.pl.* stewards, IX 22

disposicion *n.* temperament, VII 40; *pl.* inclinations, VII 45

disprayse *pr.pl.* disparage, underestimate, XI 39

disserve *v.* to earn, merit, VII 139

distrouble *v.* to hinder, impede, X(b) 196

divere *v.* to make tremble, III 253

divisid *pp.a.* divided, separated, VII 205

do, don *v.* to do, perform, cause to do, II 55; *pt.2 s.* **dides** III 39; *pt.3 s.* **dude** II 189; *pp.* **idon** II 570; **doon** *inf.* to arrange, V 125; **deth** *pr.3 s.* sends, submits, II 57; **dede** *pt.3 s.* placed, V 318

doctor *n.* teacher, lecturer, X(b) 145

dol *n.* grief, III 269

dolven *pp.* buried, IV 102

dome *n.* judgement, IV 338

don *adv.* down, VII 134

dorstest *pt.2 s.* dared, VIII 90

dortour *n.* monastic dormitory, V 67

dosk *a.* dark, dim, III 24

doskin *v.* to become dim, II 523

doute *n.* fear, V 197

douteth *pr.pl.* fear, VIII 110

doynge *n.* action, IX 224; **doynge owte** excommunication, IV 231

drahen *v.* to drag, II 37; *pp.* **idrahe(n)** II 39; **dreaieth** *pr.pl.* lead, entice, II 15; *pp.* fastened, II 323

dream *n.* song, joy, II 254

drechunge *n.* trouble, disturbance, II 57

drede *n.* fear, VIII 135

drede *v.* to cause to fear, III 253; **drad** *pt.pl.* feared, X(a) 191

dredfull *a.* awe-inspiring, IV 252

drehen *v.* to endure, suffer, II 55

dreori *a.* lamentable, unfortunate, II 227

dreynte *pt.3 s.* destroyed by drowning, VI 424; **idrencte** *pp.* dipped, covered, II 194

drihten, drihtin *n.* lord, I 58, III 1

drinch *n.pl.* drinks, III 247

dringan *v.* to oppress, I 49

dritt *n.* dirt, filthy lucre, IX 145

drivel *n.* drudge, menial, II 419

driveth *pr.pl.* fall headlong, II 295; **drof** *pt.3 s.* drove, VI 138

dronkelewe *a.* drunk, IX 242

dronken *pp.* drunk, IX 12

druri *n.* love-token, III 46

druth *n.* darling, III 1

druyghe, druye *a.* dry, VI 5

dunchen *pr.pl.* strike, III 237

dune-fallen *a.* cast down, overcome, III 134-5

dunt, dynt *n.* blow, II 228, V 237; **dynt of swerid** warfare, IX 181-2

durede *pt.3 s.* lasted, endured, VIII 19

dyscomfyted *pp.* destroyed, conquered, XI 69

dyspoyled *pp.* stripped of clothing, XI 207

dyssessede *pp.* deprived, dispossessed, IV 181

dyversorye *n.* lodging place, XI 22

eadi *a.* blessed, II 307; *comp.* **ediure** II 157

eadinesse *n.* blessedness, II 156

ealdren *n.pl.* parents, II 382

eanes *see* **anes**

eani *a., pron.* any, I 18

ear *adv.* earlier, previously, II 34

eardin *v.* to live, II 636

earewen *n.pl.* arrows, II 194

earm *a.* wretched, II 84

earmhwile *n.pl.* wretched moments, II 497

e(a)rming-saulen *n.pl.* souls of wretches, I 5, 22

earmthe *n.* wretchedness, grief, II 400, 638

earnnesse *n.* pledge, token, II 77

earre *a.comp.* previous, former (one), II 53

easki, easkest *see* **axe**

eateliche *a.* terrible, horrible, I 18; *superl.* **eatelukest** II 626

eath *a.* easy, light, III 177

eaveres *n.pl.* boars, II 174

eavriche *a.* every, III 230

eawbruche *n.* adultery, II 631

eawiht, eawt *n.* anything, ought, II 620, 648

ec, ek *adv.* also, I 4, III 58

eche *n.:* **to e.** in addition to, II 343

eche *a.* eternal, II 77

echeliche *adv.* eternally, III 20

ecnesse *n.* eternity, II 407

ed, et *prep.* at, II 335

edefyed in *pt.3 s.* strengthened, instructed, X(b) 170

edhalt *pr.3 s.* preserves, keeps intact, II 162; *pp.* **ethalden** II 597

ediure *see* **eadi**

edstont *pr.3 s.* restrains, II 202; **etstonde** *pr.subj.s.* continue, II 708

edwiteth *pr.pl.* reproach, II 538

efr(e) *adv.* ever, I 27, 79

eft *adv.* afterwards, I 90

efter, after *prep.* in accordance with, II 670; *num.a.* second, IV 125

efter thon, eftyr *adv. (phr.)* afterwards, after, I 24

efterwart *adv.:* **beon e.** desire, long for, II 540

eftire that *conj.* according as, IV 148

egede *a.* foolish, absurd, II 564

eggi *v.* to encourage, prompt, II 568

eggunge *n.* prompting, incitement to evil, II 36

eghen, ehnen, eyghen *n.pl.* eyes, I 29, II 10, V 63; **ighe** VII 252

ei *a., pron.* any, anyone, II 76

eie, eighe *n.* fear, terror, II 456; anger, II 657

eihwer *see* **aihwer**

eil *a.* loathesome, grievous, II 357

eili *v.* to trouble, afflict, II 708

eise, eese *n.* satisfaction, comfort, II 17, VII 360

eisliche *adv.* terribly, horribly, I 12

either *pron.* each of two, both, II 392

eken *pr.pl.* increase, add, III 250

elde *n.* age, IV 49

eldeth *pr.3 s.* grows old, VIII 128

elleshwer *adv.* elsewhere, II 423

elmesyeorn *a.* charitable, I 54

elne *n.* strength, vigour, II 379

en *num.* one, II 335

enclynyd *pp.* rested, X(a) 53

ende *n.:* **ed ten e.** in the end, II 60; **to that e.** for that purpose, X(a) 133

enden, endin *v.* to complete, fulfil, I 32, II 122

endurid *pp.a.* obdurate, hardened, IX 182

enflaumen *v.* to kindle, inspire, V 284

enforcid *pt.3 s.* did one's utmost, X(a) 275

engendre *v.* to conceive, VI 281

engles, englene *n.pl.* angels, I 73, II 32

enhabyted *pt.pl.* lived in, XI 288

enjoynyng *n.* instruction, VII 357

enquere *pr.subj.s.* ask, X(a) 187

ensaumple, ensaunple, *n.* example, illustration, V 174, IX 223

ensaumplid *pp.* represented, signified, VII 58

enserche *pr.subj.s.* seek, XI 88

enteerly *adv.* in entirety, wholly, XI 188

entent *n.* purpose, V 41

ententifely *adv.* intently, with close attention, X(a) 317

entretyng *n.* pleading, negotiation, X(b) 270

envirouneth *pr.3 s.* surrounds, encloses, VII 94–5

eode, eoden *see* **gan**

eolie *n.* oil, II 678

eordlich *a.* earthly, II 146; **eorthlich** (as *n.*) human being, VI 32

eornen *v.* to run, II 567; *pt.3 s.* **eorn** III 218; *pt.pl.* **urnen** I 20

eorthe-threlles *n.pl.* men bound to earthly pursuits, I 99

eoten *v.* to eat, I 87

eow *see* **yhe**

erest, arst *adv.* first, I 6, VI 348; **alre earst** first of all, II 235

eritage *n.* spiritual inheritance, allotted place in heaven, II 372

erles *n.* foretaste, promise, VII 361

erlyche *adv.* early, V 302

erming-licome *n.pl.* bodies of wretches, I 31

escade *see* **axe**

eschewe *pr.pl.* avoid, XI 156

eschewing *n.* avoidance, VII 34

esen *v.* to rest, relax, V 308

estat *see* **astaat**

este *n.* delight, bliss, II 421

etforen *prep.* in front of, I 13

ethele-theowe *n.* domestic servant, II 460

eth(e)lich *a.* worthless, weak, II 84; **etheluker** *comp.* of low rank, II 102

ethem *n.* breath, I 30

etlunge *n.:* **withuten e.** beyond calculation, II 597

etstonde(n) *see* **edstont**

etstutten *pr.subj.pl.* come to a halt in, II 292

etyr *n.* one who eats, X(b) 213

euch, euchan, echon, uchon *pron.* each, each one, each other, III 104, V 170, VI 83

evel-acord *n.* disagreement, VIII 134

even *a.* equal, like, IV 69

evenald *a.* contemporary, of like age, II 624

even-crystyn *n.* fellow Christian, IV 43

evene *n.* stage, condition, II 323; nature, kind, II 641

evene *adv.* straight, VI 244

evenhede *n.* moderation, temperance, IV 313

evenin *v.* to compare, II 259; *pp.* **evenet** III 25

evening, evenunge *n.* equal, peer, II 153; **withuten e.** beyond comparison, II 63

evil-wille *n.* malevolence, IX 154

evydence *n.* example, VII 116, 156

evyl-doeris *n.pl.* criminals, IX 165

evyl-dooyng *n.* wickedness, XI 5

evyllfare *n.* misfortune, IV 309

evynly *adv.* equally, IV 306

excusacion *n.* excuse, IX 35

excusen *v.* to atone, IX 103; allow, permit, IV 157

excusynge *n.* justification, IX 79

exilynge *n.* exile, IX 139

expownyth *pr.3 s.* explains, X(a) 49

eysell *see* **aisille**

fa *n.* enemy, II 149; *pl.* **fan** II 439

fainen of *pr.pl.* rejoice at, III 140

falewi *pr.subj.s.* wither, fade, II 134

falle *v.* to happen, befall V 191; **falles** *pr.pl.* belong, IV 60; **falleth** *pr.3 s.* sounds, V 303; **fylle** *pt.3 s.*, **fullen, fellen** *pt.pl.* tell, VI 72, 78, X(b) 149

falsehede, falsschipe *n.* falseness, II 384, IV 363

fame *n.* reputation, IV 165

famon *n.* enemy, II 620

famplin *v.* to stuff, II 560

fandes, fandynge *see* **fondi, fondunge**

fant *pt.2 s.* found, III 156; *pp.* **funden** IV 53

fantesyes *n.pl.* illusions, V 261

fare *n.* appearance, bearing, II 262

fare *v.* to proceed, go, VI 121; *pr.3 s.* **feareth** II 64; *pt.3 s.* **ferde** I 10; to suffer, IX 9; **feare with** to treat, II 386

fast *adv.* undeniably, VII 40; firmly, VII 125

fast *pr.pl.* fasten, attach, V 22

favour *n.* esteem, IV 164

fawtes *n.pl.* faults, moral defects, XI 115

fayle *v.* to be lacking in, XI 66; *pr.pl.* **faileth** VIII 23

fayn *a.* glad, VI 346

fayne *adv.* gladly, X(b) 186

fayre *adv.* exactly, precisely, VI 11; beautifully, VI 33; **feire** courteously, II 478

feader *n.* father, II 7

feahi *imper.* make beautiful, adorn, II 680

feahunge *n.* adornment, II 643

feareth *see* fare

fearlac *n.* fear, anxiety, II 431

fe(e)n *n.* mud, dirt, VI 93

feghtynge, feht *n.* fighting, II 209, IV 348

fehten *v.* to fight, II 236; *pt.3 s.* **faht**, **feht** III 148

feier *a.* fair, beautiful, II 262; *superl.* **feherest** II 598; **fayre** gentle, peaceful, XI 110

feierlec, feirnesse *n.* beauty, II 596, III 6

fel *n.* skin, VI 93

felauschupe *v.* to associate with, marry, VI 284-5

felaw *n.* companion, V 192; *pl.* **feolahes** II 253

felawrede, felaschipe *n.* company, fellowship, IV 76, VIII 162

felon *a.* wicked, evil, XI 153

felte *pt.pl.* were aware of, smelt, X(a) 207

feng to *pt.2 s.* undertook to, started to, III 147

fenniliche *adv.* vilely, miserably, II 124

feole, fele *a.* many, II 58; much, III 289

feond, feont *n.* devil, II 36; enemy, II 555

feor *n.* value, price, III 300

ferde *see* fare

fere *n.* companion, wife, VI 189; *pl.* **feeren** VI 77

ferforth *adv.*: **so f.** to such a degree, V 157

ferliche *adv.* suddenly, quickly, II 295

ferme *a.* constant, steadfast, XI 46; *adv.* steadfastly, XI 68

fermorie *n.* monastic infirmary, V 202

ferr *adv.* far, IV 286

festen *pr.pl.* entertain with food and drink, IX 7

festni *pr.subj.s.* become fixed, II 201

festynnynge *n.* union, IV 245

fether-fotetd *a.* four-footed, I 29

fette *pt.3 s.* fetched, X(b) 247

feyned *pp.a.* false, IX 57

fille *v.* to fulfil, satisfy, IX 249; **felle** *imper.* fill, V 81

fla *n.* arrow, II 200

flee *v.* to flay, VIII 90

fleo *v.* to flee, VI 203; *imper.* **flih** II 233

fleoth *pr.pl.* fly, II 207; *pt.3 s.* **fleyh, flye** VI 51 X(b) 140; *prp.* **fleynge** VIII 18

fleschely *adv.* carnally, IV 154

fleschliche *a.* physical, temporal, II 14

fliche *n.* flitch of bacon, II 566

flod(e) *n.* sea, river, III 161, X(a) 66; *pl.* currents, VII 58

floterid *pt.3 s.* floated, X(a) 39

flowinde *prp.* flowing, III 259; **flowyng** rising, VII 57

fluht *n.* flight, II 238

flum, flom *n.* river, VI 329, X(a) 133

flurs *n.pl.* flowers, II 322

fluttunge *n.* maintenance, provisioning with necessities of life, II 380

flytynge *n.* quarrel, dispute, IV 346

foilyng *n.* stain, sin, XI 274

foles *a.* foolish, VIII 161

folhin *v.* to follow, II 256; *pt.2 s.* **folwedist** VII 24

folliche *adv.* foolishly, II 219

foly *v.* to have illicit sexual relations, IV 154

fondi *v.* to make trial of, experience, II 414; *pp.* **ifondet** II 302; **fandes** *pr.pl.* attempt, strive, IV 151

fondunge, fandynge, fondyng *n.* temptation, II 707, IV 310

fontston *n.* font, VIII 96

for *prep.* against, VI 206; instead of, II 704

forbeddes *pr.3 s.* forbids, IV 154; *pt.3 s.* **forbeode** II 195; *pp.* **forboden** IV 127

forberest *pr.2 s.* refrain from, II 241; **forbere** *pr.subj.pl.* part, separate from, VIII 39; **forbereth** *pr.3 s.* puts up with, XI 119

forbisne *n.* example, model, II 667

forbuh *imper.* avoid, refrain from, II 234

forcarien *v.* to worry about, provide for, II 544

force *n.*: **all his f.** his utmost, XI 70

forcorven *pp.* cut down, cut off, II 134, 244

forcuthest *a.superl.* most vile, II 471

fordemde *pt.3 s.* condemned, II 629

fordo *v.* to bring to naught, destroy, IV 347

fore *adv.* before, III 253

forewart *n.* word, II 246

forgan *v.* to forgo, II 702

forgulten *v.* to sin against, II 702; **forgult** *pp.* guilty, sinful, I 22

forheccheth *pr.3 s.* repudiates, rejects, II 618

forhohien, forhewe *v.* to despise, avoid, II 373, IV 319; **forhuhande** *prp.* self-despising, III 136

forhorest *pr.2 s.* are unfaithful to God, fornicate, II 615

for-hwen *conj.* because, for, II 357; **for-hwon thet** when, II 189

for-hwi, for-whi *adv.* wherefore, for which reason, II 312; *conj.* because, VII 199

forleoseth *pr.pl.* lose, forfeit, II 431; *pt.1 s.* **forlesede** III 42; *pt.3 s.* **forleas, forlees** II 187, VI 210; *pp.* **forloren** VI 10

forlith *pr.3 s.* seduces, II 617

forluke *n.* provision for the future, IV 105

forme *num.a.* first, I 25

formefadyrs *n.pl.* forefathers, IV 15

forneh *adv.* almost, II 624

forrotieth *pr.pl.* decay, rot, II 176

forschuppet *pp.* misshapen, monstrous, II 506

forst *n.* frost, VI 207

forswerynge *n.* perjury, IX 124

forte, for to *conj.* to, in order to, II 24

forte that *conj.* until, VI 335

for that, forthi that *conj.* in order that, IV 55, VI 17

forthering, *a.* helpful, VII 196

forthi, forthi the *conj.* because, I 5; *adv.* therefore, I 92

for(th)lich *a.* thriving, vigorous, II 502, 507

forthon *conj.* because, I 40

forthoughte *pt.3 s.* regretted, VI 292

forthre *adv.* later, II 96

forthward *adv.* forward, III 237

forthynkynge *n.* repentance, contrition, IV 221

foruten *prep.* without, III 149

forwariede *pp.a.* cursed, III 19

for-whi *see* **for-hwi**

forwurpen *pp.* cast out, rejected, III 117

forwurthen *v.* to perish, II 436

foryelt *pr.3 s.* gives in return, repays, II 60; *pp.* **foryolden** II 158

foryet *imper.* forget, leave, II 4, VIII 78; *pt.3 s.* **forgate** X(b) 149

foryeve *v.* to forgive, IX 153

foryevenesse *n.* forgiveness, II 659

foster *n.* foster child, II 208; upbringing, III 88

fosters furthe *pr.pl.* bring up, educate, IV 144

fostrunge *n.* nursing, II 497; feeding, II 559

foule *adv.* wickedly, IX 128; *a.* dirty, X(b) 95

foundement *n.* foundation, V 17

founden *pp.* established, V 1

fourtede *num.a.* fortieth, IV 110

foyleth *pr.3 s.* defiles, XI 277

fra, fro *prep.* from, III 184; *conj.* from the time that, VII 71

frakele *a.* wretched, worthless, II 82

fraunchyes *n.pl.* rights, privileges, X(b) 271

freameth *pr.3 s.* helps, benefits, II 444

freel *a.* weak, simple, VII 309

freinin *v.* to ask, enquire, II 470

frelete *n.* frailty, VI 107

fremmede, fremd *a.* strange, foreign, IV 155, V 313

freo *a.* liberated, free, II 34; **frerre** *comp.* more liberal, III 39

fre(o)dom *n.* nobility, II 49; generosity, III 9

freolec *n.* freedom, II 61

freoliche *a.* noble, gracious, III 245

fret *pr.3 s.* eats, destroys, II 435

freytour *n.* monastic refectory, V 66

frithie *v.* to leave in peace, spare, III 258

fro that *conj.* since, from when, VII 81

frommart *adv.* away, II 568

frotid *pp.* rubbed, chafed, X(a) 288

frowardnesse *n.* obstinacy, disobedience, XI 266

frumthe *n.* beginning, II 580

frut *n.* profit, reward, II 329

fuhel, feule, foul *n.* bird, fowl, III 161, IV 381

ful *n.* abundance, II 111

ful *adv.* very, entirely, VII 130

fule *a.* evil, foul, II 177; **fulle** IV 310

fuleth *pr.3 s.* stains, II 150; *pp.* **foulid** IX 264

fulfill *v.* to satisfy, IV 356; **fulfyllid** *pp.* past, accomplished, X(a) 8

fulieth *pr.pl.* follow, II 656

fulitohschipes *n.pl.* ill-mannered behaviour, II 467

fulle *a.* complete, absolute, II 440; satiated, II 595; **at fulle** completely, V 286

fullen *v.* to perform, carry out, II 275; to fill, III 31; *pp.* **ifullet**, II 188

fulliche, fully *adv.* entirely, completely, II 133, III 146

fully *a.* complete, entire, V 208

fulst *n.* help, ally, II 216

fulthe *n.* vice, sin, II 111

fure, fuir, fer *n.* fire, I 16, II 567, V 270

furthe, forth *adv.* forward, in future, I 79, IV 84

fyger *n.* fig tree, VI 113

fygure *n.* representation, emblem, X(a) 105

fyn *a.* pure, VIII 102

fyned *pp.* refined, VIII 102

gadlyngis *n.pl.* fellows, persons of low birth, IX 156

game *n.* pleasure, happiness, VI 115; **gomenes** *n.pl.* love-making, II 468

gan, goon *v.* to walk, go, I 45, V 84; *pr.3 s.* **gath** III 109; *pr.3 pl.* **gath** II 319; *pt.3 s.* **eode, yede** I 10; *pt.pl* **eoden** I 9; *pp.* **igan** II 136; **wenten togedere** had intercourse, VI 202; **in iyongen** embarked upon, II 724

gaste, gost *n.* spirit, soul, IV 102, VIII 50

gasteli(ch), gostly *a.* spiritual, II 421, III 277, V 8

gastfull *a.* terrifying X(b) 120

gealde *a.* sterile, barren, II 490

gedering *n.* gathering, VI 18

gederunge *see* **yederunge**

gedren *v.* to gather, collect, V 207; *pr.pl.* **gadren** IX 7; *pp.* **igedered** III 5; **gedere** *inf.* to harvest, VI 228; **iyederet** *pp.* united, II 392

gelery, gilerie *n.* guile, deceit, IV 363, VI 324

gelowseye *n.* carefulness, watchfulness, V 297

genderure *n.* reproduction, procreation, IX 261

gentile *a.* noble, refined, II 100

gere *v.* to do, cause, make, IV 353

gerlondesche *n.* chaplet, coronet, II 321

gerner *n.* granary, storeroom, V 73

gerneter *n.* nun in charge of granary, V 206

gersum *n.* costly gift, riches, III 8

getes *pr.pl.* beget, conceive, IV 143; *pt. pl.* **geeten** VI 281; *pp.* **getyn** IV 94; comprehended, VII 241

girre-blod *n.* bloody stream, III 229

gladien *v.* to rejoice, III 271

gladyng *n.* delight, pleasure, V 276

gle *n.* joy, pleasure, VI 115

gleden *n.pl.* live coals, sparks, I 35

gledscipe, gleadschipe *n.* gladness, bliss, I 87, II 607

glidende *prp.* falling, running, I 36

glotonys *n.pl.* wastrels, IX 241

gnegheth *pr.3 s.* gnaws, chews, I 34

goddede *n.* benefit, favour, II 264

godely, gudly *adv.* piously, beneficently, X(b) 244

godhede *n.* divinity, IV 103

godles *a.* poor, poverty stricken, II 449

godspel *n.* gospel, III 163

gon, gat *pt. 3 s.* began (*used as a weak auxiliary*), I 71, VI 169

gospellere *n.* evangelist, IV 293

gostlyche *adv.* spiritually, V 344

governale *n.* rule, self-control, IX 194

granin *v.* to groan, lament, II 705; *prp.* **graninde** I 34

graunte-syre *n.* grandfather, X(a) 166

grauntyd *pt.3 s.* gave permission to, X(b) 67

greden *v.* to weep, bewail, II 705

gredily, grediliche *adv.* eagerly, III 67, VII 124

gredy *a.* eager, VII 127

greitheth *pr.3 s.* prepares, makes ready, II 217; *pp.* **greythed** V 162

gremien *v.* to disturb, trouble, II 396

grenin *v.* to bloom, become green, II 135; to turn green, lose colour, II 522

grennede *pt.pl.* grinned, III 139

gretely *adv.* to a great extent, vigorously, X(b) 65, 169

grette, greete *pt.3 s.* greeted, II 668, X(b) 63

grevede *pp.* injured, IV 267

grevosere *a.comp.* more grave, serious, IV 390

greynes *n.pl.* pips, seeds, VI 380

gripen *pp.* grasped, III 67

grithe *n.* peace, harmony, I 87

grome *n.* anger, hatred, II 193; grief, sorrow II 58, 462

grucchen, grutche *v.* to complain, grumble, III 96, XI 237

grure *n.* torment, suffering, II 705

grureful *a.* terrible, fearful, III 62

gulte *n.* sin, guilt, III 99

gulteth *pr.3 s.* sins, II 515

gume *n.* man, husband, II 160

guydyng *n.* government, rule, X(b) 264

gybet *n.* gallows, X(a) 174

gyffe *see* **yiven**

habbe *v.* to have, II 69; *pr.1 s.* **ichave** VI 154; *pr.2 s.* **havest** I 78; *pr.3 s.* **hafth, haveth** I 97, II 3; *pr.pl.* **habbeth, hase, han** I 5, V 252; *pt.3 s.* **hefde, hedde** II 53; *pt.pl.* **hefden, hedden** II 302, VI 2; **hastou** have you?, VI 259

habydynge *n.* expectation, IV 281

halden *v.* to observe, keep, I 48; *imper.* **halt** II 128; *pr.3 s.* **halt** II 165; *pt.3 s.* **heolt** II 302; **heold, hilde** *pt.3 s.* held, VI 195, X(a) 288; *pt.pl.* **hilden** X(a) 306; **holden** *pp.* considered, IX 67; obliged, IV 397; **halt on** continues, II 708; **holde forth** use, IX 102; **holdith the same** agrees, X(a) 131

hal(e), hole *a.* whole, in good condition, II 166, IV 227; healthy, V 203

haleghen, halhen, halhes *n.pl.* saints, I 74, II 44, III 223

H

half *n.* side, hand, II 80

halie, heali, holich *a.* holy, blessed, I 38, III 230, VII 216

halighen, halowe *v.* to honour, keep holy, I 82, IV 135; **ihalewed** *pp.* consecrated, VI 379

halinesse *n.* holiness, II 166

haliwei *n.* balm, potion, III 2

hally(ly) *adv.* entirely, completely, IV 75, 188

halschipe *n.* chastity, purity, II 43; wholeness, II 510

halwynge *n.* consecration, IX 131

handelyde *pp.* administered, IV 235

hantith *pr.pl.* use, practise, II 354; *pp.* **hauntede** IV 378; frequented X(a) 215

hard *a.* harsh, coarse, X(b) 19

hardely *adv.* confidently, VIII 118

hardi *a.* brave, III 59; presumptuous, VI 316

hardischipe *n.* bravery, III 58

hastiliche *adv.* soon, VI 337

hat *a.* sharp, severe, III 162

hat *n.* condition, rank, II 327

hateredyn *n.* hatred, IV 336

hathfule *a.* mocking, scornful, III 179

hatte, hihte *pt.3 s.* was called, V 320, VI 10; *pp.* **ihaten, hatten, ihote** I 3, IV 334, VI 47; **het, hat** *pt.3 s.* commanded, I 10, II 271; *pp.* **ihaten** II 283; **heht** *pp.* promised, III 247

haunkede *pp.* attached, bound, IV 323

havynge *n.* possessions, wealth, IV 153

he *pron.* he, I 12; **heo, ha, yhe** she, I 52, II 7, V 165, **hine** him, I 71; **heo** her, I 51; **hys** its, V 261; **ha, heo** they, I 9; **hare, heore, her** their(s), I 32, 36, V 23; **ham, tham, heom** them, I 5, 6, 9

healden *pt.subj.pl.* cure, heal, II 291; **helid** *pp.* cured, saved, X(a) 15

heale, hele *n.* health, II 511, X (a) 5

healend *n.* saviour, III 1

healewi *n.* poisonous unguent, drug, II 194

heame *n.* stranger, II 149

heaneth *pr.3 s.* injures, oppresses, II 150; *pp.* humiliated, III 178

hearde *adv.* severely, II 74, IX 9; *comp.* more firmly, VIII 142

hearmi *v.* to harm, II 66

heasci *pr.subj.s.* be angry, II 454

heateth *pr.3 s.* hates, II 555

heaved, heavet, heved *n.* head, II 9, VII 99; **hase h.** is in charge of, IV 145

hede-thewes *n.pl.* theological virtues, IV 274

heerde *n.* shepherd, VI 240

he(g)he, hey(gh), hie *a.* high, I 12, IV 113; elevated, IV 308; *quasi-n.* height, II 268; *comp.* **herre** II 183; *superl.* **heste, hexte** II 44, VI 67

hehin *v.* to raise, ascend, II 725; *pp.* **ihehet** II 333

hehnesse *n.* elevated position, II 27; excellence, nobility, III 12

hehschipe *n.* glory, honour, II 249

hele *a.* safe, saved, IV 78

helest *pr.2 s.* hide, conceal, II 20; *prp.* **helyng** IV 160

helethe *n.* health, VI 344

helle-bearnes *n.pl.* children of hell, devils, III 221

helle-dogges *n.pl.* devils, III 66

helle-grunde *n.* bottom of hell, II 626

helle-hus *n.* hell, III 68

hellene *a.* infernal, devilish, II 629

helle-yete *n.pl.* gates of hell, I 13

helply *a.* helpful, useful, VII 211

hende *a.* gracious, merciful, II 71

hendeleic *n.* nobility, courtliness, III 13

henge *v.* to hang, III 288; *pt.pl.* **hyng** X(a) 173; *pp.* **henged** III 152

heofene *n.* heaven, I 5

heorte *n.* heart, I 16

heorte-haliwei *n.* heart's balm, III 17

heoven *v.* to raise, II 372; *pt.3 s.* **heef** VI 398

heovenlich *a.* heavenly, II 32

heowe, heuh *n.* colour, I 17, VI 324

herber, herberwe *v.* to shelter, IV 257, IX 30

herdsey *n.* report, hearsay, VII 165

here *n.* army, host, II 23

here *v.* to teach, IV 47

herere *n.* listener, IV 342

herien *v.* to praise, II 146

heriinge *n.* praise, VI 402

herkene *imper.* listen, VIII 37

herte-love *n.* heartfelt love, V 211

herte-swetnesse *n.* heart's delight. III 130

hertly *a.* deadly, dire, IV 372; sincere, passionate, V 133

hertly *adv.* passionately, V 152; sincerely, IX 229

her towart *adv.(phr.)* in comparison with this, II 391

herty *a.* heartfelt, IX 179

heryede *pt.3 s.* ravaged, IV 103

heryng *n.* instruction, IV 23; *pl.* what one hears, V 64

heste *n.* commandment, VI 95

heteli *adv.* cruelly, fiercely, III 222

hethen *adv.* hence, away, IV 240

hevede *a.* capital, IV 318

hevel-bedd *n.* bed with canopy, II 294

hevene-kyng *n.* king of heaven, VI 4

heveneriche *n.* kingdom of heaven, I 58

heyre *n.* hairshirt, X(b) 19

hidous *a.* intense, severe, VIII 97

hilde(n) *see* **halden**

hilede *see* **hule**

hine *n.* member of a household, II 149; servant, II 419

hirdmen *n.pl.* retainers, II 453

hofles *a.(quasi-n.)* something unreasonable, II 648

hoker *n.* scorn, II 648; contemptible word or act, III 179

hoker-lahter *n.* derision, III 253–4

hokerliche *adv.* distastefully, with nausea, II 529; scornfully, III 239

hokerluker *a.comp.* more contemptible, II 197

hokerringe *n.* mockery, III 232

hole *adv.* entirely, X(b) 168

holpen *pp.* helped, IX 256

honde, hande *n.:* **take on h.** to undertake, VII 117; **bere on h.** to persuade, IX 140

hondhwile, honthwile *n.* short time, moment, II 130, 663

hondlith *pr.pl.* handle, II 225

honte *n.* to hunt, VIII 153

hopes *pr.pl.* expect, put faith in, IV 130

hoppin *v.* to jump with joy, II 230

horedom *n.* fornication, II 628

horlinges *n.pl.* fornicators, II 354

hose *see* **hwase**

hosteler *n.* stable-girl, X(a) 148

houseles *a.* homeless, IV 257

houslewth *n.* lodging, IX 39

hu *conj.* how, I 10

hude *n.* animal skin, II 566

huide *v.* to hide, III 168; *pt.pl.* **hudden** VI 114

hul *n.* elevated state, II 286

hule *v.* to cover, III 168; *pt.pl.* **hilede** III 197

huler *n.* lecher, II 459

huniter *n.* honey-drop, III 2

hurd *n.* court, company, III 89

hure *adv.* especially, II 620

hure *n.* payment, II 59

hurte *n.* misfortune, XI 45; *pl.* affliction, suffering, III 127

hus-lewe *n.* lodging, III 156

hwa *pron.* anyone, I 6; who, I 104; **hwas** whose, II 253; **whaym** whom, IV 403

hwase, whasa, hose *pron.* whoso, whosoever, II 552, IV 233, VI 33

hweol *n.* wheel, II 433

hwervore *adv.* why, for what reason, II 207

hwerwith *pron.* something with which, III 167

hwetse *pron.* whatsoever, II 621

hwiderse *conj.* wheresoever, II 256

hwile, while *n.* time, VI 74; **ane h.** for a short time, II 241

hwilinde *a.* transitory, II 355

hwit *a.* white, III 192

hwuch *a.,pron.* what, what sort of, II 17; whichever, III 61

hwuchse *pron.* whosoever, II 278

hye *v.* to hasten, V 333; *imper.* **highe** VI 223

i *prep.* in, II 2

iblissieth *pr.pl.* rejoice, I 5

ibohte *pp.a.* bought, II 460

iboren *pp.* born, II 502

iborenesse *n.* birth, giving birth, II 496

ibureghe *pr.3 s.* saves, redeems, I 37; *pp.* **iborhen** II 139

ic(h) *pron.* I, I 7, II 34

icnawen *v.* to understand, comprehend, II 328

icnawlecheth *pr.pl.* confess, II 94

icnut *see* **knet**

icorene *pp.a.* (as *n.*) the chosen, I 74, II 72

icrunet *see* **coroune**

iculd *pp.* killed, VI 261

icweme *a.* pleasing, acceptable, II 593

idoublet *pp.* redoubled, VI 184

idrechet *pp.* tormented, II 418

ifeere *adv.* together, VI 254

ifinden *v.* to find, II 69; *pp.* **ifunden** II 87; *pt.3 s.* **ifont** II 675

ifounden, yfounded *pp.* established, V 10, 26

ighe *see* **eghen**

ihal *a.* intact, II 204

ihente *v.* to catch, II 285

iheortet *pp.* hearted, II 553

iheren *v.* to hear, I 72

ihuret *pp.a.* hired, wage-earning, II 419

ihwer *adv.* everywhere, II 578

ikepte *pt.3 s.* restrained, held, II 266

ikepunge *n.* prevention, II 338

ilahet *pp.* made legal, allowed, II 285; abased, lowered, II 290

ilatet *pp.a.* mannered, II 479

ilich *prep.* like, II 42

iliche *adv.* alike, II 273

ilicnesse *n.* semblance, similarity, II 345, 371

ilimpeth *pr.3 s.* happens, occurs, II 499

ilkane *pron.* everybody, IV 37

ilke, ilca *a.* same, very, I 28; each, IV 45

iloken *v.* to observe, keep, I 91

ilome *adv.* frequently, I 36

iloten *pp.* allotted, II 127

imeane *a.* common, II 274; *adv.* together, II 557

imiddes *prep.* in the middle of, III 157

imong *prep.* between, among, III 111

inc *pron.* you two, II 128

inker *a.,pron.* your, II 18; **i. either** both of you, the two of you, II 454

innan *prep.* within, I 24

inner *a.* internal, V 56

innore *adv.* inside, VI 318

innys *n.pl.* lodgings, IX 31

inoh *adv.* enough, II 61

inoh-reathe *adv.* quickly enough, II 482

intill *prep.* in, into, IV 111

into that *conj.* until, VI 342

invencion *n.* finding, X(a) 137

inwardluker *adv.comp.* more inwardly, II 658

inwith *prep.* within, II 14

iopenet *pp.* revealed, II 583

ipaiet *pp.* pleased, II 392

irest *n.* rest, I 4

irikenet *pp.* enumerated, II 488

irnene *a.(pl.)* iron, III 244

irous *a.* angry, XI 113

is *n.* ice, I 25

iscrippet ut *pp.* scratched out, II 339

iseo *pr.1 s.* see, I 61; *pt.3 s.* **iseh** I 50; *pp.* **isahe** II 568

ismethet *pp.* fashioned, II 384

ismiret *pp.* embalmed, II 168

istihe *see* **steye**

iteiet *pp.* knit, bound, II 403

itholien *v.* to endure, I 41

itimeth *pr.3 s.* happens, II 504

iunnen *pp.* granted, II 172

iweddede *pp.a.* (as *n.*) the married, II 264

iwiss *adv.* indeed, surely, II 472

iwrat, iwrouht *pp.* done, performed, I 86

iwurthen *v.* to become, II 378
iyederet *see* **gedren**
iyettet *pp.* granted, II 137
iyotten *pp.* fused, II 663

jacinct *n.* jacinth, II 651
japes *n.pl.* frauds, trifles, VIII 107
japynge *n.* joking, mockery, IX 122
jelouse *a.* ardent, V 231
joyed *pt.3 s.* rejoiced, X(b) 34
joyned *pp.* married, X(a) 146
juggynge *n.* judgement, IV 338
jurdiccion *n.* jurisdiction, IX 125

kalde *a.* cold, III 255
keasten *v.* to throw, cast, II 37
keiser *n.* emperor, III 30
kelf *n.* calf, II 567
kempe *n.* warrior, III 68; *gen.pl.*
  kempene II 320; conqueror, II 643
kenchinde *prp.* laughing, II 230
kene *a.* brave, III 11
kennes *pr.3 s.* makes known, teaches, IV
  302; *pp.* **kende** IV 394
kens *quasi-a.* kind of, V 347
kepe *n.* heed, VI 72
kepe *imper.* guard, V 61; *pr.3 s.* **keput**
  V 78; take care, X(a) 179
kepynge *n.* charge, care, IV 46
kid(de) *pp.a.* renowned, III 11
kimeth *see* **kumeth**
kind, kuynde *n.* nature, II 115, 364;
  flesh, II 522; race, IV 112; natural
  constitution, VII 17
kindeliche, kyndely *adv.* naturally, by
  natural inclination, III 104, IV 381
kine-bearn *n.* royal-child, III 84
kinedome *n.* spiritual sovereignty of
  God, I 72; kingdom, II 589
kineriche *n.* kingdom, II 246
knave *n.* lad, servant, IV 172
knawyng *n.* knowledge, IV 20; intercourse, IV 155
knett, icnut *pp.* tied, knotted, II 475,
  X(b) 88

knowlechyng *n.* understanding, V 259
kumelich *a.* becoming, appropriate, II
  362
kundles *n.* litter, brood, VI 135
kunnyng *n.* knowledge, VII 189
kynde *a.* courteous, noble, IX 43
kynred *n.* race, X(a) 165

labouryd *pt.3 s.* endeavoured, X(b) 65
lache *v.* to neglect, IV 374
lacking *n.* lack, deficiency, VII 188
lad(de) *see* **leaden**
ladli(che), latheliche, lothlyche *a.*
  loathsome, hateful, II 353, III 61;
  comp. **ladluker** II 358; *superl.* **lad-**
  lukeste II 599
lah, lowe *a.* lowly, in a low condition,
  II 30, V 105
lahe *n.* law, II 266; *pl.* **lawen** I 47
laheliche *adv.* lawfully, II 176
lahhen *pr.pl.* laugh, III 250; *pt.3 s.*
  louh VI 348
lahter *n.* laughter, scorn, III 252;
  lauters *pl.* ribaldry, V 65
la hwure, lanhwure *adv.(phr.)* at any
  rate, at least, I 65, II 265
lake *v.* to lack, X(b) 30
lam *n.* earth, clay, II 51
lami *a.* formed of earth, II 721
langes *see* **longeth**
lare, lore *n.* teaching, II 11, IV 24
large *a.* liberal, generous, III 44
largeliche *adv.* copiously, II 411
largesce *n.* generosity, III 9
lasse *a.comp.* small, VI 7
last *conj.* lest, IX 92
laste *n.:* **atte l.** at the end, III 166
lasteles *a.* blameless, flawless, III 13
lastis *pr.3 s.* endures, IV 10
lates *n.pl.* habits, manners, III 13
latesomnes *n.* sluggishness, IV 374
lath *a.* hateful, loathsome, II 398; loath,
  IV 379
lathe *n.* hatred, loathing, II 487
lathi *v.* hate, loathe, II 85
lauerd, louerd *n.* lord, I 40, 64

lauerdom *n.* lordship, dominion, II 116

lavatory *n.* washing, cleansing water, X(a) 298

lawede, lewid *a.* lay, IV 137; simple, ignorant, VII 186; stupid, ignorant, VII 213

layde upon *pt.3 s.* beat, X(b) 69

leaden *v.* to lead, II 24; *pr.3 s.* **lead, leat** II 32, 307; *pt.pl.* **ledden** I 45; *pp.* **lad** VI 385

l(e)afdi, lavedi, lefdigh *n.* lady, II 42

leafdischipe *n.* rank as a lady, II 52

leafeth *see* **leve**

leanin *v.* to grow lean, II 522

leareth *pr.3 s.* teaches, II 7; *pr.2 s.* **learst** II 12

leasse *adv.comp.* less, II 52

leaste *n.* flaw, III 87

leatere *a.* second, II 52

leathieth *pr.pl.* invite, prompt, II 15, 106

ledene *n.* language, II 26

leesynge *n.* loss, IX 164

lefte *pt.3 s.* lifted, X(a) 97

lefulle *a.* legal, permissible, IV 208

leies *n.pl.* flames, I 17

leifen *n.* sea, bog, II 473

leighen *pr.pl.* lay, V 42

leirwite *n.* punishment, fine for adultery, II 704

leit, laite *n.* lightning, I 30, VI 323

lekerous *a.* luxurious, dainty, IX 219

lene to *v.(phr.)* to rely upon, VII 39

lenghte *n.:* **drawe apon l.** to procrastinate, delay, IV 374

lengur *adv.comp.* longer, X(a) 184

leoden *n.pl.* peoples, II 674

leof, leve *a.* dear (one), beloved, I 80, II 143; *superl.* **leoveste** II 274

leoflukest, luvelevest *a.superl.* most lovely, II 144; dearest, III 304

le(o)fmon, lemman *n.* lover, II 41, III 28, VII 260; **leofemen** *pl.* beloved (brethren), I 1

leor *n.* face, countenance, III 3

leosen, lese, lesse *v.* to lose, II 406, IV 180; *pt.3 s.* **les, lees** VI 324, 372; *pp.* **lorn** V 52; to redeem, III 42; to release, III 184

leote(th) *see* **lete(n)**

leoth *n.* song, II 297

lere *v.* to teach, IV 33; to learn, IV 47; **lerede** *pp.a.* educated, IV 28

lerned *pp.* taught, VII 51

lerner *n.* teacher, VII 190

lerynge *n.* instruction, IV 23

lese *see* **leosen**

lessynge *n.* diminution, IV 239

lest forth *pr.3 s.* continues, II 353

lesynges *n.pl.* lies, IV 163

let *a.* late, II 546

lete(n), leoten *v.* to allow, II 239; to leave, abandon, III 35, VIII 123; **leoteth** *pr.pl.* esteem, II 656; **lette** *pt.3 s.* considered, II 675; caused, VI 295; **l. to** to value, II 481

lettes *pr.3 s.* hinders, IV 313; *prp.* **letting** VII 23

leve *n.* permission, IV 388

leve *pr.pl.* believe (in), IV 126; *pt.3 s.* **levid** X(a) 124

leve *v.* to stop, leave off, IV 379; *imper.* VII 362; **leafeth** *pr.3 s.* remains, II 353; **le(a)ve** *pr.subj.s.* grant, II 720, leave, remain, II 201; **leaved** *pp.* abandoned, III 115

lever *adv.comp.* rather, III 9

levyng *n.* life, manner of life, X(b) 110

libben, lyffe *v.* to live, II 342, IV 145; *prp.* **liviende** I 44

lich, like *n.* body, III 227, 274

liche *n.* likeness, I 59

liche *a.* like, VII 171

licome *n.* body, I 53

licomliche *a.* bodily, carnal, II 16; *adv.* physically, II 33

licour *n.* liquid, IV 208

licunge, likinge *n.* delight, enjoyment, II 70, III 277; desire, IV 140

licwurthe *a.* agreeable, II 142

liflade, lyflode *n.* way of life, II 32; sustenance, IV 152, VI 149

lif-sithen *n.pl.* lifetime, II 664

lighere *a.* lying, deceitful, I 55

liheth *pr.pl.* deceive, II 581

lihte *a.* easy, II 275; **lighttere** *comp.* easier to accomplish, IX 181

lihte *v.* to descend, II 50; *pp.* **iliht** II 345; to be born, II 498

lihting *n.* dawn, I 79

lihtlice, lightly *adv.* readily, easily, II 239, VII 32

liknes *n.:* **at the l. of** in accordance with the metaphor of, VII 62

limen *n.pl.* limbs, II 169; offspring II 723

limpeth *pr.pl.* belong, I 2; *pr.3 s.* ought, is fitting, II 549

lined unto *pp.* desired after, VII 319

lire *n.* flesh, muscle, II 296

lisse *n.* delight, I 4

list *pr.3 s.* pleases, VII 29; *pt.3 s.* chose, XI 16

list, lith *see* **lygge**

listily *adv.* with pleasure, VII 319

litelnes *n.* smallness, paucity, VII 187

lith *n.* limb, II 295

liveneth *n.* food, means of sustenance, II 409

logge *n.* small dwelling, VI 206

loggyng *n.* accommodation, XI 206

lokien, locan, loken *v.* to observe, have regard to, I 48, III 19

longeth, langes *pr.3 s.* appertains to, IV 24, VII 338

loos *n.* reputation, IX 90; loss, IX 188

lordeship *n.* dominion, X(a) 63; *pl.* seignories, domains, IX 198

lorel *n.* worthless person, IX 95

lorn *see* **leosen**

losengerie *n.* flattery, deceit, VIII 133

lothlyche, latheliche *a.* repulsive, horrible, III 61, V 319

love-longynge *n.* longing experienced by love-sick souls, V 154

lovely *a.* loving VII 246; *adv.* lovingly, VII 360

love-quikyngus *n.pl.* stirrings prompted by love, V 68

love-terus *n.pl.* tears of love, V 314

love-yernyggus *n.pl.* yearnings prompted by love, V 285

lovynge *n.* praise, V 147

lowe *adv.* humbly, VII 105

lowen *v.* to humble, VI 62

lownesse *n.* humility, meekness, V 19

lowssynge *n.* divorce, IV 247

lowte *pr.pl.* worship, IV 126

lude *adv.* loud, I 33; *comp.* **ludder** V 224

lufsum *a.* beautiful, III 6

lupe *n.* spring, leap, II 335

lure *n.* loss, II 21

lusten, lustin *v.* to listen, I 1, II 8; *pr.pl.* **lusteneth** VI 3

lusteth *pr.3 s.* desires, II 361

lusti *a.* beautiful, III 19

lut, lyte *a., quasi-n.* few, little, II 275

luteth *pr.3 s.* lurks, II 646

luthere *a.* cruel, relentless, II 657; (as *n.*) the wicked, III 252

lutlin *v.* to diminish, II 52

luveli(che), luvelike *a.* beautiful, III 227, 254; **luvelevest** *superl.* (as *n.*) dearest one, beloved, III 16

luveliche *adv.* lovingly, II 7

luvenesse *n.* love, III 293

luvewurthi *a.* worthy to be loved, III 6

luvie *a.* loving, in love, II 398

lyfe *n.* body, IV 30

lygge *v.* to lie, V 269; **list** *pr.2 s.* are subject to, II 85; **lyethe** *pr.3 s.* is buried, X(b) 1

lyghtenes *n.* alleviation, IV 237

lykyng, liking, lykande, lykende *a.* pleasant, agreeable, V 32; enthralled, V 153

lyste *n.* desire, pleasure, VII 228

lyte *n.* delay, tardiness, IV 374; *see also* **lut**

lythe *n.* subjects, IV 168

ma, mo *a., adv.* more, IV 348

mahe *n.* stomach, II 529

maht *pr.2 s.* may, might, can, II 328;
pr.3 s. **mei, mahe** II 67, 234; *pr.pl.*
mawen, mahe(n), muhen, mowe
I 40, V 4; *pt.3 s.* **mahte, mihte** I 43,
II 18; *pt.pl.* **mihte** VI 143; *pr.subj.s.*
muhe III 270

maht *see* **mihte**

mahti, mihti *a.* strong, III 71

make *n.* mate, partner, II 365

makunge *n.* cause, II 644

malencolious *a.* inclined constitution-
ally to melancholy, IX 163

maner *n.* kind (of), X(a) 23

manly *adv.* bravely, X(a) 74

manlynesse *n.* kindness, human kindness, IX 155

mare, more *a.* larger, IV 18; big, VI 6;
adv. more, III 118

marhen, morwen *n.* morning, II 465,
VI 19

marheyeve *n.* gift made by husband to
wife, II 589

marke *v.* to recognise, give heed to,
XI 38

mawmetryes *n.pl.* idolatry, IV 127

me *adv., conj.* but, now, lo, II 463

me, mon *indec.pron.* one, I 37, 105, V
269

meadschipe *n.* madness, II 554

mealten *n.* to melt, disintegrate, II 171;
pp. **imelt** II 663

meane *n.* intercourse, III 106

meast *adv.superl.* most, II 100

meastling *n.* brass, II 89

meche, myche *adv.* much, VII 38

mede *n.* reward, II 73

medefull *a.* meritorious, IV 270

medycyne *n.* remedy, XI 166

meene *n.* manner, means, VII 323

meene *pr.1 s.* think, VII 230

meenyng *n.* opinion, VII 167; intention,
VII 253

meidenhad *n.* virginity, II 168

meister *n.* leader, III 201; *pl.* **meistres**
I 23

meister-deoflen *n.pl.* principal devils,
I 21

meistrie *n.* rule, II 116

meith-had *n.* virginity, II 27

meith-theawes *n.pl.* behaviour suitable
for virgins, II 3

meke *v.* to humble, VII 132

mekill *adv.* much, IV 18; *see also*
muchele

membris *n.pl.* genitals, IX 260

mene *n.* method, course of action, XI
179

menged *pp.* mixed, III 247

menske *n.* honour, courtesy, II 193

menske *v.* to honour, dignify, II 220

mensket *n.* honour, virginity, III 78

menskli *adv.* courteously, III 9

meoke *a.* meek, II 654

meokelec, meokeschipe *n.* meekness,
II 633, 666

merely *adv.* joyfully, X(b) 236

merren *v.* to mar, II 171

merryng *n.* impairment, IV 91

mesaise, meseyse *n.* trouble, misery,
III 171; the afflicted, V 40

meschefe *n.* poverty, distress, IX 29;
pl. misfortunes, IX 6

messe *n.* mass, IV 243

mesurable *a.* modest, XI 117

mesure *n.* moderation, II 605

met *n.* measure, II 277

mete, met(t) *n.* moderation, II 605,
IV 315

mete *n.* food, VI 174

mete *a.* equal, like, IV 113

metelec *n.* gentleness, mildness, II 609

meten *pp.* measured, X(a) 23

methe, methefulnes *n.* moderation,
temperance, IV 312

meve *v.* to tremble, X(a) 207; to stir,
propel, XI 5; **meovyd** *pp.* enraged,
X(b) 279

mevyng *n.* stirring, X(a) 36

meyntene *v.* to support, IX 134

meyntenynge *n.* maintenance, IX 37

mid *prep.* with, I 48

middewarde *a.* the middle of, I 42

mihte, maht *n.* quality, virtue, I 99; physical strength, III 11

milce *n.* mercy, II 292

milcien *v.* to have mercy on, I 68

mildeu *n.* honey, III 2

miltschipe, mildeschipe *n.* mildness, II 609, III 13–14

mis *adv.: on mis* wrongfully, sinfully, II 235

misboren *pp.a.* misshapen at birth, II 499

misfeare *pr.subj.s.* come to grief, II 500

misliche *a.(pl.)* various, II 135

moche *adv.* very, XI 1; liberally, IX 127

mod *n.* temper, disposition, III 83

moderliche *a.* maternal, III 266–7

moder-sune *n.* man, III 26

modi(e) *a.* proud, I 54

modirhede *n.* condition of being a mother, IV 91–2

monhad, manehede *n.* humanity, incarnation, III 83, IV 63

monifolde, monifald *a.(pl.)* manifold, I 60, III 205

monkin, moncun *n.* mankind, man, II 187, III 62

monquellere *n.* murderer, III 183

more *n.* moorland, VI 150

mornyng *n.* passionate grief, V 314

mornyng-songes *n.pl.* passionate songs, V 153–4

most *a.superl.* largest, VI 24; great, X(b) 241

most *pr.2 s.* must, are allowed to, II 237; *pr.3 s.* **mot** II 209; *pr.pl.* **mote(n)** II 308, V 88

motien *v.* to dispute at law, I 49

mought *n.* mouth, V 182

mountynge *prp.* rising, XI 187

muche *a.* great, big, II 335; **muchel m.** very much, II 429

muchele, mikle, mekill *a.* great, big, II 21, III 94; many, IV 27; **mucheles** *gen.adv.* by much, I 82; **muchele** *adv.* much, I 18

H*

muchli *v.* to increase, II 709

munegheing, munegunge *n.* memorial, memory, I 93, III 2

munnen *v.* to tell, relate, II 344

murhthe *n.* happiness, II 70

murie *a.* pleasant, sweet, II 255; happily, II 342

myche *adv.* greatly, VII 38

myghtely *adv.* vigorously, X(a) 217

myghtful *a.* mighty, powerful, V 124

myghtty *n.:* **es m.** has the ability to, IV 261

mynde, mende *n.* memory, mind, X(b) 53, 160; spirit, X(b) 197; **makes m.** mentions, IV 254

mynynge *n.* diminution, IV 92

mysbyleve, myssebyleve *n.* error, heresy, IV 127

mysdose *pr.pl.* commit wrong against, IV 266

mysknewe *pt.3 s.* failed to recognize, X(a) 151

mysreulynge *n.* sinful conduct, IX 141

mysse *v.* to do without, go without, IV 271

myster, mester *n.* need, necessity, IV 260, V 333

mytris *n.pl.* mitres, IX 23

na *a.* no, IV 162

nabbe *pr.2 s.* have not, II 448; *pr.3 s.* **naveth** II 50; *pr.pl.* **nabbeth** II 100; *pt.2 s.* **navedes** III 164; *pt.pl.* **nefden** II 361

nacnes *pr.3 s.* strips of clothing, III 241

nam *pr.1 s.* am not, VI 258; *pr.3 s.* **nis** II 39; *pr.pl.* **narn** III 119; *pt.3 s.* **nere, nes** I 54; *pt.pl.* **neren** II 289

name *n.* reputation, position, IX 78

nan *a., pron.* no, no one, I 44

nat *pr.3 s.* knows not, II 97; *pt.3 s.* **nuste** II 637; *pr.pl.* **nuten** II 472

nathing *n., pron.* nothing, I 86

nawhit, nawt *n.* nothing, nought, II 45; *adv.* not, in no way, II 72

ne *adv.* not, I 43; **ne . . . ne** neither . . . nor, I 31

neaver the leatere *adv.(phr.)* nevertheless, II 135

neb(be) *n.* face, I 36, II 522; *pl.* animals, II 363

nebscheft *n.* countenance, II 595

neddir, eddre *n.* snake, IV 326; *pl.* **neddren, eddren** I 26

nede *adv.* of necessity, II 272; *n.* necessity, VII 184

nedeles *a.* unnecessary, IX 84

nedfull, notful *a.* necessary, IV 87, V 50

nedid *pt.3 s.* was necessary, X(b) 30

nefre *adv.* never, I 31

neghtbour *n.* neighbour, IV 166

ne(i)h, nye *adv.* near, II 97; near, at hand, VI 390; almost X(b) 105; *comp.* **nerre** III 138; *superl.* **nest, nehest** II 319, III 144

nempnede *pt.1 s.* named, II 35; *pp.* **nempned** V 343

neomen *v.* to take, II 365; *pr.3 s.* **nimeth** II 160; *pt.3 s.* **nom** VI 81; **nam** III 105; to take in marriage, II 688; **nim to** *imper.* entrust, II 80; **nimest** *pr.2 s.* regard, II 12

neosethurles *n.pl.* nostrils, VI 336

neother *adv.* down, II 334

nerhonde *adv.* almost, VI 210

nesche *a.* tender, III 156

netheles *adv.* nevertheless, IX 125

neven *pr.pl.* name, IV 134; *pp.* **nevenede** IV 349

never the more *adv.* not at all, X(a) 223–4

nim, nimest *see* **neomen**

niminge *n.* capture, III 220

no *conj.* nor, and not, V 93

noblesce *n.* nobility, noble birth, III 12

nobeleye *n.* nobility, VIII 17

nohtunge *n.* scorn, II 85

nomeliche *adv.* particularly, II 198

non(e) *n.* noon, I 78, X(a) 221

nonry *n.* nunnery, X(b) 78

norische *v.* to support, cause to grow, IX 174

norischynge *n.* support, IX 78

not *n.* nothing, IX 205

nother *pron.* no other, IV 64; *adv.* neither, IV 285; **noyther** V 151

nothing *adv.* in no way, not at all, IX 147

nower *adv.* in no way, II 97

nowhwider *adv.* not at all, III 226

nowther *adv.* not at all, III 109

noy *n.* distress, trouble, VII 79

noyntid *pp.* anointed, X(a) 5

nul(l)e *pr.3 s.* will not, II 72; *pt.2 s.* **naldest** II 70; *pt.3 s.* **nalde** I 47; *pt.pl.* **nalden** I 32

nurrice *n.* nurse, II 548

nurth *n.* noise, confused sound, II 458

nuthe *adv.* now, II 157

nuyth *n.* envy, VI 130

nyende *num.a.* ninth, IV 166

nyghed *pt.3 s.* approached, X(a) 39

o *num.* one, IX 165

o, one *prep.* on, II 215; **on** beside, on the banks of, V 28

occasion *n.* reason, VII 316

of *prep.* by, IV 23; from, out of, IV 330

ofdret *pp.* afraid, terrified, II 656

ofearnest *pr.2 s.* earn, II 152

offearet, offeard *pp.* frightened, II 183

offyce *n.* duty, task, V 198

ofhungred *pp.a.* starving, VI 143

ofter *adv.comp.* more often, I 48

oftesythes *adv.* often, IV 29

ofthunchunge *n.* vexation, disgust, II 353

okyr *n.* usury, IV 363

on *art.* an, I 45

ondswerie *pr.1 s.* answer, II 114; *pt.3 s.* **onswerede** I 77

onely *adv.* alone, solitary, VII 9

onely-duelling, onely-wonyng *n.* living as a solitary, VII 4, 15

onelynes *n.* solitariness, VII 19–20

onhalsien *v.* to implore, entreat, I 71

onont *prep.* equal to, II 101; in respect of, III 83

onouren *v.* to honour, V 106

ontful *a.* envious, I 55

o(o)nde *n.* evil, envy, II 608, VI 131

oostes *n.pl.* armies, XI 68

open, opyn *a.* public, IV 223; manifest, XI 63

openlich, opynly *adv.* clearly, plainly, III 262, IV 38

or . . . or *conj.* either . . . or, VIII 12

ord *n.* point, III 267

ordener *n.* ordainer, ruler, XI 60

ordeynen *v.* to arrange, order, V 125; **ordeynid** *pp.* consecrated, X(a) 247

orisoun *n.* prayer, V 152

orlage *n.* clock, V 290

os *adv.* as, V 190

osprunch *n.* offspring, VI 331

oste *n.* host, landlord, X(b) 64

osteler *n.* nun in charge of guests, V 188

other *adv.* or, II 394

other *num.a.* second, I 25; **other . . . other** *pron.* the one . . . the other, II 271–2

otherhwiles *adv.* sometimes, II 644

ovemaste *a.superl.* highest, uppermost, VI 385

overalle *adv.* entirely, II 34

overarely *adv.* too early, IV 352

overbold *a.* too forward, V 191

overcome *v.* to perform, VI 160

overdelycately *adv.* too fastidiously, IV 353–4

overeorninde *prp.* overflowing, II 277

overfayr *a.* too agreeable, V 196

overfullet *a.* abundant, II 277

overgeath *pr.3 s.* surpasses, II 330

overhardy *a.* too forward, V 192

overherren *n.pl.* superiors, II 434

overhohe, overhope *n.* pride, II 634, IV 287

overkim *imper.* overcome, II 123

overlate *adv.* too late, IV 352

overlightly *adv.* too readily, VII 149

overmekyll *adv.* too much, IV 354

overoftesythe *adv.* too frequently, IV 352

overplewse *n.* surplus, X(b) 24

overrenne *v.* to overwhelm, IX 157

oversoone *adv.* too quickly, VII 120

overstihen *v.* to get the better of, II 199

overtharte *a.* traverse, X(a) 45

overthroweth *pr.3 s.* stumbles, falls, XI 82; **overthrewe** *pt.3 s.* destroyed, XI 287

overvyle *adv.* too polluted, XI 260

overwarpen *pp.* cast down, II 528

owterage *n.* excess, IV 312

owther *pron.* one of two, either, II 503

pappe *n.* breast, III 160

paraise *n.* paradise, II 694

parischennes *n.pl.* parishioners, IV 46–7

partie *n.* part, hand, VII 6

Pasch *n.* Easter, IV 230

passeth *pr.3 s.* surpasses, II 578

passing *a.* surpassing, pre-eminent, VII 360; *prep.* beyond, more than, VII 20

patremoyne *n.* inheritance, IV 180

pay *v.* to please, gratify, V 197

payned *pp.* tormented, punished, XI 303

pelers *n.pl.* pillars, V 54

per *prep.* through, V 341

perawnter, peraventur *adv.* perhaps, IV 30, VII 29

perdurable *a.* everlasting, XI 28

perdurably *adv.* for ever, XI 303

perfitly *adv.* absolutely, X(a) 79, 124

perischid *pp.* destroyed, IX 168

perseverantly *adv.* persistently, X(a) 56–7

perti *see* at **perti**

pesible *a.* peaceful, gentle, VII 61

pich, pik *n.* pitch, III 20

pine *n.* torment, I 6

pinen *v.* to torment, I 22; *prp.* **pinende** III 20

pinfule *a.* painful, III 96

pituously *adv.* pitiably, so as to inspire pity, X(a) 4

pledynge *n.* litigation, IX 167

pleien *v.* to rejoice, be merry, II 603

plente *a.* abundant, V 208

plesaunce *n.* pleasure, desire, X(b) 167

plesyng *n.* satisfaction, X(b) 169

pleyinges *n.pl.* sports, VIII 22

pleynly *adv.* fully, VII 197

pleynt *n.* complaint, V 127

povert *n.* poverty, IX 26

powere *n.* authority, IV 216; **ben at p.** have the ability, IX 55; **don p.** do all one can, VIII 116

poynt *n.* object, VII 248; little bit, VIII 137; **was in p.** was about to, V 328

preoveth *pr.3 s.* proves, II 333; *pp.* **preved** VII 79

presonen *pr.pl.* imprison, IX 55

prevyly, priveliche *adv.* by himself, X(b) 221; secretly, VI 288, X(b) 291

pricke *n.* object, VII 249; target, VII 256

prisonynge *n.* imprisonment, IX 139

prisuns *n.pl.* prisoners, III 69

privat *a.* separated from the public body, IX 35

prive(y) *a.* private, VII 45; surreptitious, IX 59

privites *n.pl.* mysteries, V 259

procunges *n.pl.* incitements, II 15

procuratouris *n.pl.* agents, stewards, IX 21

profitid *pt.pl.* were of service, helped, X(a) 228

prokie *v.* to incite, prompt, II 708

proper *a.* own, XI 114

prove *n.* result, VII 324

prud *a.* proud, I 54

prude *n.* pride, II 614

prys *n.* estimation, worth, VI 37; payment, reward, IX 94

psalm-wruhte, salme-wrihte *n.* psalmist, II 2, III 279

purched *pp.* cleansed, VIII 93

pursueris *n.pl.* persecutors, IX 173

purveye *v.* to provide, supply, IX 11

purveyresse *n.* nun in charge of provisions, V 199

puttith oute *pr.3 s.* expels, IX 98; **putt bihynde** *pp.* retarded, IX 113; **putt forth** *pp.* expedited, IX 114

pystill *n.* epistle, IV 293

pytauncer *n.* nun in charge of pittances, V 242

pyteous *a.* pitiful, affecting, XI 53; merciful, full of pity, XI 202

qu- *see also* **cw-**

quarel *n.* arrow, bolt, VIII 18

quencheth *pr.3 s.* goes out, XI 111

querfaste *adv.* transversely, III 285

queynte *a.* crafty, cunning, IX 84

queyntises *n.pl.* tricks, stratagems, IX 272

quiclyche *adv.* promptly, V 291

quiclym *n.* mortar, V 46

quykkynd *pt.3 s.* gave new life, IV 109

quyte *v.* to repay, IX 166

radde *pt.3 s.* gave a lecture to, X(b) 132

rancor *n.* hatred, IX 154

rase *see* **riseth**

ratheste *adv.superl.* most readily, III 169

rattes *n.pl.* rags, III 158

re(a)d *n.* advice, II 19, VI 110

reade *pr.1 s.* advise, counsel, II 271; *pr.3 s.* **read, reat** II 107, 272; *pt.3 s.* **readde** II 580

realle *a.* royal, VIII 136

reavers *n.pl.* robbers, II 434

reaveth *pr.3 s.* robs, II 445; *pt.2 s.* **reftes** III 66

recches *pr.3 s.* cares for, III 117; *pt.pl.* **raughte** XI 266

reches *n.pl.* riches, IV 174

redliche *adv.* promptly, I 70

reformacion *n.* curing, XI 1

refreyneth *pr.3 s.* puts a restraint on, XI 110

refuse *v.* to avoid, shun, IV 45

reherse *v.* to repeat, IV 48

rejoyce *v.* to feel joy on account of (something), XI 45

rekke *pr.pl.* consider, IV 365

rekkenede *pp.* enumerated, IV 185

rekyd *pt.3 s.* swept, X(b) 23

religioun *n.* monastic life, V 4; monastery, nunnery, V 108

relygyouce *n.* religious, member of religious order, V 27

remeth *pr.3 s.* cries, screams with pain, I 33

remeve *v.* to stir, depart, XI 188; **remevid** *pt.3 s.* conveyed, moved, X(a) 64

reming *n.* lamentation, III 238

remnaunde *n.* remnant, X(a) 119

reng *n.* rank, II 299

renne *v.* to run, IX 142

renye *v.* to renounce, abjure, X(a) 310

reowfulnesse, reufulnesse *n.* pity, compassion, II 607

reowliche, rewli *adv.* pitifully, wretchedly, I 34, III 41; with no pity, III 223

reowthe *n.* pity, II 228

repeir *n.* resort, dwelling, VIII 51

requyrid *pt.3 s.* asked, X(a) 76

resceyve, rescheyve *v.* to receive, VII 112; *pr.pl.* **ressayves** IV 198

resen, reysen *v.* to raise, V 39, 53; **reised** *pp.* brought about, IX 167

resisteth *pr.3 s.* rejects, XI 36

rest *n.* peace, quiet, XI 125

retheren *n.pl.* oxen, VI 27

reulyth *pr.3 s.* controls, orders, V 114

revyng *n.* robbery, IV 159

rewe *v.* to regret, VI 325

rewfule *a.* pitiful, sorrowful, III 257

rewler *n.* manager, steward, X(b) 208

rewli *see* **reowliche**

rewme, reaume, reygne *n.* kingdom, V 125, XI 138

ribauz *n.pl.* knaves, III 197

riche *n.* kingdom, II 445

richedom *n.* royal power, kingdom, II 18

riddes *pt.2 s.* saved, III 147

rightful *a.* just, IX 171

rightfully *adv.* justly, properly, VIII 4

riht *n.* rights, III 12, IV 147; justice, VI 276

riht *adv.* properly, III 33; very, X(a) 75

rihtwise *a.* (as *n.*) the righteous, III 252

rihtwissnesse *n.* righteousness, II 604; justice, IV 120

ring *n.* circle, II 300

riseth *pr.3 s.* arises, comes, VII 358; **rase** *pt.3 s.* rose, IV 106

rit *pr.3 s.* rides, mounts, II 178

rive, rif *a.* prevalent, widespread, II 88; plentiful, II 424; commonly in mind, VI 420

rixlen *v.* to rule, III 48

rode, rude *n.* cross, III 129, IV 99

rongen *pt.pl.* rang, V 329

rotunge *n.* decay, II 168

routynge *n.* raging, roaring, VIII 83

rude *a.* ignorant, VII 38

rudie *a.* ruddy II 522

rug *n.* back, III 224

rychesse *n.* riches, excess, V 30

ryghte *a.* correct, just, IV 204

ryghtely *adv.* correctly, IV 203

rysynge *n.* resurrection, IV 109; **r. up** elevation, V 69

ryvely *adv.* currently, prevalently, IV 184

saad *a.* steady, serious, IX 268

sabaz *n.pl.* sabbaths, II 245

sake *n.* strife, III 260

salme-wrihte *see* **psalm-wruhte**

salute *n.* greetings, XI 3

samen(ly) *adv.* together, IV 68, 85

sar *a.* grievous, vexatious, II 456

sar *n.* sorrow, II 395

sare, sariliche, sore *adv.* sorrowfully, grievously, I 33, II 48, VI 143; *comp.* **sarre** II 183

sari *a.* sorrowful, II 177; *comp.* **sarre** II 401

Sauter, Sawter *n.* Psalter, II 2, V 214

save *v.* to guard, protect, IV 146

savour *n.* taste, V 297; smell, X(a) 207

savurure *a.comp.* more tasty, II 406

savyng *prep.* except, XI 271

sawl, saul *n.* soul, I 7, IV 17; *pl.* **saulen** I 14

sawle-fan *n.pl.* enemies of the soul, devils, III 73

sawle-swetnesse *n.* soul's sweetness, III 17

sayeyng *n.* utterance, IV 204

scarse *a.* niggardly, XI 196

scawede *see* **schawin**

scean *pt.3 s.* shone, I 30

schad *n.* distinction, II 361

schaftes *n.pl.* created things, creatures, III 40

scharp *a.* piercing, VII 256

scharply, sherpely *adv.* sternly, VII 135; peremptorily, X(b) 273

schawin, scheawe *v.* to show, II 383; *pt.3 s.* **scawede, sceawede** I 11, 12; **schewed** *pp.* revealed, V 151

schendlac *n.* disgrace, infamy, II 223

schene *a.* beautiful, shining, II 259

schent *pr.3 s.* humiliates, II 459; *pp.* humiliated, III 151

scheome *imper.* shame, II 220; **schomet** *pp.* humiliated, III 151

scheome, schome *n.* disgrace, ignominy, II 707, III 95

scheomelese *a.* shameless, II 111

scheomeliche *adv.* shamefully, II 459

sch(e)op *pt.3 s.* created, II 113; *pp.* **ischapet** VI 190

schepische *a.* simple, silly, IX 84

schetith *pr.3 s.* shoots, VII 270

schilde *pr.subj.s.* protect, II 470

schimminde *prp.a.* shining, II 307

schomeliche *a.* shameful, III 127-8

schreamen *v.* to scream, II 565

schrewdnesse *n.* wickedness, VIII 120

schrewe *n.* wicked being, devil, VI 107

schrewed *a.* malicious, IX 165

schrud *n.* dress, clothing, III 7

schruddes *pt.2 s.* clothed, III 105

schucke *n.* devil, II 629

schuldi *a.* guilty, II 515

schunien *v.* to avoid, II 511

schuppere *n.* creator, III 207

schurges *n.pl.* whips, III 242

sciences *n.pl.* branches of knowledge, X(b) 123

sclaundrynge *n.* false accusation, IX 59

sclombryng *n.* sleep, doze, X(b) 137-8

scole *n.* university, X(b) 58

scrift(e) *n.* confession, penance, I 32, IV 2

scripture *n.* inscription, X(b) 81; the Bible, XI 41

se, swa *adv.* so, much, II 59, III 61

seche *v.* to seek, VI 45; **seken** *pr.pl.* visit, IX 233

secnesse *n.* sickness, III 150

sege *n.* place, seat, VI 193

seggen, siggen *v.* to say, I 2, VI 186; *pr.3 s.* **seyght, seyt, seith** I 83, V 141, 146; *pt.1 s.* **seide** II 48; *pt.3 s.* **seit** I 90; *pp.* **iseid, iseit, seyen** I 88; to mean, signify, II 6

seil *n.* seal, II 128

seileth *pr.3 s.* seals, unites, II 128

seke *a.* sick, II 285

sekyrly, sikerliche *adv.* assuredly, with certainty, IV 237; indeed, II 64

sel *n.* happiness, II 726

selcuthes *n.pl.* marvels, miracles, III 204

selde *adv.* seldom, X(b) 215

seler *n.* cellar, V 72

seleresse, celerer *n.* nun in charge of provisions, V 159, 241

selhthe *n.* happiness, bliss, II 575

seli, sely *a.* blissful, II 49; helpless, VII 55

seltscene *a.* rarely seen, II 393

semande *a.* suitable, fitting, V 193

semblant *n.* intimation, II 464; appearance, II 606; expression, V 196

semely *adv.* fittingly, V 10; chastely, V 155

semeth *pr.3 s.* is fitting, III 55

semlike *a.* pleasant, handsome, III 193

sendel *n.* rich silk, VI 373

seofe *num.* seven, I 17

seofethe *num.a.* seventh, I 27

seolcuthre *a.comp.* rare, strange, I 17

seolf *a., pron.* himself, I 83

seon *v.* to see, III 20; *pr.3 s.* **sith** II 191; *pr.pl.* **seoth** II 229; *pt.3 s.* **seigh, sih, sauh** VI 179; *pr.pl.* **seighen** VI 179; *pp.* **seghen** VI 395

seorhfuliche *adv.* sorrowfully, II 230

seothan, sethe(n), sithen *adv.* afterwards, I 16, III 229; **sithen that** *conj.* since, III 263-4

sere *a.* separate, distinct, IV 71

serpentis *n.pl.* snakes, X(a) 294

sertus, certis *adv.* indeed, assuredly, V 10, VII 163

serve *v.* to deserve, IV 119

servin *v.* to enslave, II 81

serwe, sorhe *n.* sorrow, II 395, VI 122

sette *pr.subj.s.* establish, V 74; **yset** *pp.* placed, V 29; **set** *pp.* appointed, VI 173; **seet** *pp.* set, IX 143

sevenniht *n.* week, VI 400

sewe, sue *v.* to follow, IX 230, 262

shamfully *adv.* disgustingly, XI 263

sherp *a.* sharp, painful, X(b) 69

Shroftyde *n.* Shrovetide, Quinquagesima Sunday and following two days, X(b) 215

sibbe-frend *n.* relative, III 104

sibnesse *n.* relationship, kinship, III 116

sidre *n.* cedar, X(a) 43

siheth *pr.3 s.* descends, II 727

sihthe *n.* sight, view, II 26

siken *v.* to sigh, II 397

sikere, sekyr *a.* secure, firm, II 660, IV 281

sikernesse *n.* security, II 56

simplesse *n.* innocence, guilelessness, V 195

simplete *n.* simplicity, II 606

singuler *a.* special, extraordinary, VII 4; solitary, VII 138

singulertees *n.pl.* differences from others to attract attention, VII 215

siste *num.a.* sixth, I 26

sith *n.* time, II 86

sith *conj.* since, IX 184

skillwyse *a.* rational, IV 12

skillwysly *adv.* sensibly, reasonably, IV 316

skinnes *see* **alkyn**

skyll *n.* reason, IV 7

slawenes *n.* sloth, IV 372

sle *v.* to kill, VI 238; *pr.3 s.* **sleath, slaas** II 435, IV 326; *pr.pl.* **sla** IV 150; *pt.3 s.* **slouh** VI 255

sleightis *n.pl.* tricks, stratagems, IX 84

slewthe *n.* sloth, IV 372

smechunge *n.* taste, II 170

smeorteth *pr.pl.* cause pain, II 461

smirles *n.* ointment, II 166

smyte *v.* to cut, X(a) 21; to thrust, VI 134

snaw, snouh *n.* snow, I 25, VI 78

socoure *n.* help, support, X(b) 240

softe *a.* gentle, mild, VII 54

softely *adv.* gently, VII 339

sojournyd *pt.3 s.* stayed, X(b) 211

solas *n.* delight, pleasure, V 136, VIII 52

solauce *v.* to comfort, IV 264

solempnyte *n.* ceremony, IX 69

somet *adv.* together, II 636

sompnunge, somnunge *n.* union, copulation, II 111, 443

sonde *n.* message, VI 212

songen *pt.pl.* sang, V 335

soone *adv.* immediately, VI 48; **sone so** *conj.* as soon as, VI 218; **sonner** *comp.* more quickly, VIII 17

sorceryes *n.pl.* magic, witchcraft, IV 128

sorhfule *a.* sorrowful, II 533

sorhin *v.* to sorrow, II 397; to cause sorrow, II 505

soth *a.* true, II 298

soth *n.* truth, II 94; **sothes** *gen.* in truth, II 238; **to sothe** truly, I 7; **for sothe** indeed, truly, VII 235

sothefaste *a.* true, IV 65

sothefastly, sothlice *adv.* truly, III 71, IV 67

sotil *a.* clever, false, IX 37

soutilede *pt.pl.* argued cleverly about, VIII 43

soverayne *a.* principal, IV 7

sovereyns *n.pl.* officers, V 346

sown *v.* to redound, IV 337

space *n.* period, time, XI 188

spareth herself *pr.3 s.* lives frugally, V 167

spatel *n.* spittle, III 192

spateling *n.* spitting, III 196

speatewile *a.* disgusting, II 350

spede *v.* to succeed, fare, VII 279

spedeful *a.* profitable, advantageous, VII 42

spedly *adv.* quickly, IX 225

spekynge *n.* utterance, statement, IX 214

speoken *v.* to speak, II 350; *pt.1 s.* **spec** II 89; *pt.3 s.* **spak** VI 115

spere *v.* to shut, lock up, V 180; *pp.* **sperred** III 284

spousebreke *n.* adultery, IV 389

spreding *prp.* growing, flowering, VII 101

sprenges *pr.pl.* arise, IV 336

spruteth *pr.3 s.* blooms, II 134

spryngyng *n.* rising, dawn, X(b) 6

spuse *n.* wife, spouse, II 3

spyces *n.pl.* species, IV 332

spyed *pt.3 s.* watched stealthily, X(b) 67

spyryght *n.* spirit, V 150; **in spryte** in the mind, imagination, X(a) 28

staat, state *n.* rank, condition, IV 139, IX 253; guise, status, IX 25

stabelichet *pp.* established permanently, VI 74

stabilnes *n.* stability, VII 63

stable *a.* fixed, firm, VI 73

stablen *v.* to ordain, order, V 126

stably *adv.* firmly, V 218

stal *n.* seat, throne, II 40

stalewurthe, stallworthe *a.* brave, courageous, III 72, IV 217; strong, V 203

stallyd, istald *pp.* instituted, installed, II 267, X(b) 243

stalworthly *adv.* securely, V 54

stalworthnes *n.* bravery, IV 305–6

stani *a.* insensible, II 231

stark blynd *a.(phr.)* completely blind, VIII 32

starke *a.* strong, fierce, III 73

staunched *pp.* satisfied, VIII 84

stedfaste *a.* unchanging, IV 65, V 46

stedfastly *adv.* firmly, V 54

steketh *pr.3 s.* shuts, encloses, V 58; **stekyd** *pp.* stuck, X(b) 89

steorre *n.* star, II 136

sterte *v.* to spring, V 313

sterve *v.* to die, IX 5

stevene *n.* voice, V 335

steye, stied *pt.3 s.* ascended, arose, IV 111, X(a) 177; *pp.* **istihe** II 184

stiche *n.* sharp pain, II 496

sticheth *pr.3 s.* afflicts with sudden pain, II 98

stikelunge *adv.* intently, II 216

stikinde *prp.a.* painful, throbbing, II 533

stille *adv.* quietly, X(b) 296

stilthe *n.* peacefulness, II 606

stinkinde *prp.a.* loathsome, disgusting, II 111

stire, stere *v.* to prompt, VII 347; to encourage, IX 73; **stirrynge** *prp.* boiling, IV 344; **styrrede** *pp.* moved, IV 169

stiring *n.* prompting, VII 24

stockis *n.pl.* blocks of wood, IX 27

stont *pr.3 s.* stands, II 29; **stonde in** to be an attribute of, VII 199–200

stounde *n.* time, VI 17

stout *a.* arrogant, VI 250

strahte *pp.a.* extended, III 251

strayte *adv.* tightly, X(b) 93

streine *v.* to force, constrain, VII 17

streitly *adv.* strictly, VII 8

strengeluker *adv.comp.* more firmly, II 196

strengest *a.superl.* most painful, II 496

strenghe *n.* power, might, IV 91

strenght *pt.3 s.* fortified, strengthened, X(b) 269

strengre *adv.comp.* more terrible, I 18; more powerful, VIII 144

streon *n.* offspring, progeny, II 381

streoneth *pr.3 s.* conceives, II 586

streonunge *n.* conception, procreation, II 494

stretenes *n.* rigour, severity, VII 358

streynid *pp.* stretched, X(a) 52

stronge *a.* severe, II 533; well-guarded, IX 143

strongly, strongliche *adv.* vigorously, X(a) 245; severely, grievously, VI 213

stryvynge *n.* contention, IV 346

stude, stede, stid *n.* place, I 42, IV 219; **to yive s.** to yield, VII 120

studefastlyche *adv.* with constancy, VI 159

stunch *n.* stink, I 27

sturdy *a.* harsh, intractable, X(b) 267

styffely, stifly *adv.* unflinchingly, IV 309, VII 282

stylle *a.* quiet, V 227; silent, VII 9; **ben stylle fro** cease, stop, XI 112

styngen *v.* to bite (of a snake), VI 144

submyttid *pp.* conquered, X(a) 62

suffringly *adv.* with patient endurance, VII 71

suget *n.* tenant, subordinate, IX 116; *pl.* parishioners, IV 47

suken *v.* to suck, II 567

suleth *pr.3 s.* defiles, II 203

sullen *v.* shall, II 389; *pr.2 s.* **schalt** II 65; *pr.3 s.* **schal, sall** II 49; *pr.pl.* **schule(n)** II 64; *pt.3 s.* **schulde, solde, sulde** II 366, IV 3; *pt.pl.* **scholden** V 102; **schulden** *pt.pl.* ought, IX 207

sulli *a.* marvellous, II 251

sum *adv.* in some way, II 500

sumdel *adv.* to some extent, V 279

sumhwile *adv.* once, II 25

sunderliche *adv.* individually, II 5

sundrith *pr.3 s.* separates, II 325; *pp.* **sundyrde** IV 80

sunegilt *n.* sinner, II 657

sunfulle, sinefule *a., quasi-n.* sinful (people), I 11

sunne *n.* sin, wickedness, III 261

suppriouresse *n.* subprioress, V 106

sur *a.* sour, bitter, III 248

sure *a.* confident, X(a) 107; certain, unfailing, XI 32

susteynen *pr.pl.* support, IX 57

suteliche *adv.* clearly, I 2

suti *a. (as n.)* foulness, II 558

swa *conj.* as, I 30; *prep.* like, I 33

swat *n.* sweat, III 217

swattes *pt.2 s.* sweated, III 216

sweameth *pr.3 s.* causes grief, afflicts, II 505; *pp.a.* grieved, II 229

sweoke *n.* traitor, II 692

swepes *n.pl.* whips, III 227

sweting *n.* darling, III 33

swikel *a.* treacherous, I 55

swikelliche *adv.* deceitfully, II 582

swiken *v.* to cease, I 31

swilc, swylke, swuc(c)h *a., pron.* such, like, II 40; *conj.* as if, I 21

swilc swa *prep.* like, I 29

swing *n.* hardship, affliction, III 217

swink *n.* toil, labour, III 214

swinke *v.* to toil, labour, VI 146; *pr.3 s.* **swinketh** II 587; *pt.2 s.* **swanc** III 216; *pt.pl.* **swonken** VI 236

swithe, swythe *adv.* very, I 19; greatly, VI 283; **al swythe** quickly, VIII 6; **as swithe as** as soon as, VI 358; **swithre** *comp.* rather, III 137

swithelice *adv.* especially, I 97

swote *a.* fragrant, II 166; agreeable, II 421; *quasi-n.* pleasure, II 403

swoteliche *adv.* joyfully, II 599

swotnesse *n.* sweetness, II 609

swoune *n.* swoon, VI 184

swungen *pp.* beaten, III 227

sy *n.* happiness, victory, II 575

sybbe *n.* kin, family, IV 155

syngne *n.* sign, X(b) 53

synkith *pr.3 s.* falls, XI 82

syte, cete *n.* city, V 32

syte *n.* sorrow, IV 334

tables *n.pl.* tablets, VI 393

tah, that, thow, theih *adv.* though, however, II 62, 315; *conj.* although, I 23

tahtes *pt.2 s.* taught, III 170
takynge *n.* consumption, IV 351
tane *pron.* the one, IV 292
taried *pp.* hindered, VII 6
tase *pr.3 s.* takes, IV 233; *pp.* **tane** IV 101;
  tac to *imper.* entrust, commit, II 65;
  pp. **itake, tane** II 47; **toke** *pt.3 s.* gave,
  X(a) 11; **taken bi** *pp.* directed by, VII
  352
taste *n.* tasting, enjoyment, IV 350
tasten *v.* to experience, V 282
te *prep.* to, for, II 285
teames *n.pl.* offspring, II 492
teke(n) (thet) *conj.* considering that, II
  444; *prep.* in addition to, II 450
telest *pr.2 s.* count, consider, II 646;
  telles *pr.3 s.* claims, III 129
tellyng *n.* account, narration, VI 107
temen *v.* to conceive, procreate, II 489
tendreth *pr.3 s.* becomes tender, II 462
tente *v.* to give heed to, IV 140
teone *n.* vexation, annoyance, II 196,
  VI 148
teonith *pr.pl.* enrage, irritate, II 466
teren *v.* to tear, scratch, VI 249
terrestre *a.* terrestrial, X(a) 4
tha, tho *adv.* then, I 11, III 25
than, thon *a.,art.* the, that, those, I 2, 4;
  dat. **tham, ther** I 37, II 295
thar, the(a)rf *pr.3 s.* is necessary, II 409,
  V 117
thar neh *adv.(phr.)* near there, I 43
the *pron.* who, which, I 22
the hwile, tha hwile *conj.* while, I 63;
  the whills IV 102
theaveth *pr.3 s.* permits, II 709
theaw *n.* habit, virtue, III 12
theawfule *a.* virtuous, moral, II 666
then, thenne *conj.* than, I 27, II 646
thenchen *v.* to think, II 17
thenkynge *n.* thought, VIII 159; **bi**
  thinkynge in your mind, VIII 67
theo, tho(a), tha(se) *a.,pron.* those, II
  244
theonewart, theonne *adv.* thence, II
  636, 637

theostri *a.* dark, II 679
theow, thewe *n.* slave, servant, II 54,
  III 133
theowdom *n.* servitude, slavery, II 24
theraftur that *conj.* after, VI 389
therefter, threfter *adv.* afterwards, I 12,
  II 77
thermyde *adv.* in addition to, besides,
  VI 25
therthurh *adv.* from that, III 140
thervore *adv.* as a result of this, consequently, II 689
therwyl-as *conj.* while, V 226
thesternesse *n.* darkness, VI 121
thilk, thulke *a.,pron.* that, such, VI 45
tho *conj.* when, VI 190
tholemode *a.* patient, IV 266
tholien, tholen *v.* to endure, I 19, III
  190; to allow, III 90
tholomodnesse *n.* patience, II 606
thonkes *n.pl.* thoughts, inclinations, II
  14
though al *conj.* although, VII 254
thought *n.* intention, VI 181; **thoutus**
  pl. thoughts, V 65
thrasten *pt.pl.* press, force, III 237
thre(a)l *n.* thrall, serf, II 55, 83
threat *pr.3 s.* threatens, II 221
threl-weorkes *n.pl.* toil suitable for
  slaves, I 100
threo *num.* three, VI 136
thridde *num.a.* third, III 268
thriftre *n.* physical growth, II 546
thrin *adv.* therein, II 17
thristes *pr.3 s.* thirsts, III 247
thristy, thrusty *a.* thirsty, IV 256
thrittuthe *num.a.* thirtieth, II 334
throf *adv.* from it, II 70
thron *adv.* on it, II 323
thruppe *adv.* above, II 89
thryst *n.* thirst, VIII 83
thuften *n.* handmaiden, II 673
thulli(ch) *a.* such, suchlike, II 106, 710
thuncheth *pr.3 s.* seems, II 20
thunre *n.* thunder, I 30
thurghwette *a.* wet through, X(b) 201

thurhhut *prep.* by means of, III 41

thurles *pr.3 s.* pierces, III 258

thusent *num.* thousand, II 83

till *prep.* to, IV 144

tilye *v.* to plough, VI 227

tilyere *n.* ploughman, VI 240

time *n.:* **et sume t.** on one occasion, I 9; **in a tyme** once, X(a) 314

timeth *pr.3 s.* happens, II 690

tit *pr.3 s.* falls as lot or portion, VI 133; must, VI 306

tithed *pt.3 s.* paid tithes, VI 242

tither *n.* one who pays his tithes, VI 241

tithing *n.* news, message, VI 281

titill *n.* claim, IV 174; tablet, inscription, X(a) 231

to, too, tone *num.* one, VII 6

toberste *v.* to break into pieces, VI 183

tobreke *v.* to burst, crack, III 202; **tobroke** *pp.a.* worn out, X(b) 95

todunet *pp.* beaten, struck, III 231

tofor *prep.* before, V 300

tolimet *pp.* dismembered, II 295

tomelte *v.* to melt, III 4

torent *pp.* torn to pieces, III 228

torettes *n.pl.* turrets, VII 91

toswelleth *pr.3 s.* swells up, II 193

totere *v.* to tear to pieces, VI 144; *pt.3 s.* **totaar** VI 250; *pp.* **totor(y)n** III 228, X(b) 103

tother *num.a.* second, IV 65

totweame *pr.subj.s.* separate, divide, II 156

touchid *pp.* mentioned, VII 141; affected, VII 157

toweddest *pt.2 s.* married, II 616

toyederes *adv.* together, II 54

toyeines *adv.* in reply, I 64

trase *v.* to search out, VII 263

trasyng *n.* searching out, VII 249

travayle *n.* work, labour, IV 21

travaylen *v.* to labour, V 133; to torment, distress, XI 150; *imper.* be grieved, X(a) 6

tray *n.* trouble, vexation, IV 22

trayste *n.* trust, faith, IV 283

trayste *v.* to have confidence in, IV 287

trefles *n.pl.* jests, VIII 107

treon *n.pl.* trees, I 12

treowe *a.* faithful, II 151

trespas *v.* to sin, XI 241

trespase *n.* sin, IV 177

tretide *pp.* arranged, provided, IV 36

trewely, treowliche *adv.* faithfully, II 65, IX 279

trie *v.* to refine, VIII 102

triflers *n.pl.* jesters, XI 250

trist *n.* trust, faith, VII 117

trouthe *n.* faith, IV 276; **in trouth** truly, assuredly, XI 5

trowe *v.* to believe, IV 63

trubuil *n.* affliction, distress, II 421

trukien *v.* to deceive, beguile, II 51; to fail, be wanting, II 210

trume *n.* band, company, II 307

tukest *pr.2 s.* ill-treat, II 517; **ituket** *pp.* afflicted, II 495

tur *n.* tower, castle, II 26

turment *pp.* tormented, X(a) 204

turmentrye *n.* torment, torture, VIII 84

turn *n.* trick, stratagem, II 712

turne agayne *v.(phr.)* to return, IV 82

turnunge *n.* activity, II 523; **turnyng of an hond** a moment, VIII 20

tweamen *v.* to divide, separate, II 398

tweien, twa, twey, twyn *num.* two, I 9, II 83; **tweire** *gen.pl.* of two, II 361

twinnin *v.* to separate, II 398

twinnunge *n.* separation, II 401

tyraund *n.* tyrant, V 322

tyres *n.pl.* tears, X(b) 237

uchan, uche *see* **euch**

umbe *adv.* busied with, seeking after, II 24

umbehwile, umbestunde *adv.* at times, II 59, 396

umbylowkede *pp.* included, comprehended, IV 185

unbisorweliche *adv.* with lack of care, I 51

unbleckid *pp.a.* undefiled, IX 48

unbotelich *a.* irredeemable, II 234

unbounde *pp.a.* unsupported, XI 82

unbouxsomnes *n.* disobedience, IV 332

unbrent *pp.a.* unburned, X(b) 97

unbruche *n.* sinlessness, with virginity intact, II 613

unbynde of *v.(phr.)* to remove, do away, VI 219

unclene *a.* impure, V 65

uncoverlich *a.* irrecoverable, II 387

uncumelecheth *pr.3 s.* dishonours, II 514

uncumelich, unkumelich *a.* improper, unseemly, II 362; hateful, II 537

undeadlich, undeathlic *a.* immortal, II 159, 588-9

underneomen *v.* to understand, II 270

undersetten *v.* to secure, V 54

underveth *pr.3 s.* receives, II 529; *pr.subj.s.* undervo II 695; *pt.3 s.* underfong VI 243; *pt.pl.* underfongen VI 172; undervoth *pr.pl.* understand, II 269

unforgult *a.* without sin, II 660

unhap *n.* misfortune, II 425

unhende *a.* improper, II 109

unlich, unilich *a.* unlike, II 304

unimete *a.* immeasurable, III 32

unimete(liche) *adv.* excessively, III 19, 215

unknawlechynge *n.* ignorance, IV 55

unlahcliche *adv.* unlawfully, II 354

unlicnesse *n.* strangeness, II 162

unlikelich *a.* poor, withered, VI 310

unlust *n.* distaste, II 530

unlusti *a.* listless, II 660

unmyghtful *a.* weak, V 122

unne(a)the *adv.* scarcely, hardly, VI 321

unnet *n.* idleness, II 219

unreverence *n.* lack of respect, IX 120

unrideli *adv.* harshly, violently, III 224

unright *n.* injustice, X(b) 278

unroles *a.* restless, II 533

unschamfulnes *n.* shamelessness, IV 333

unseli *a.* wretched, II 354

unskilfully *adv.* unreasonably, IX 200

unskilwyse *a.* unreasonable, IV 350

unstronge *a.* (as *n.*) the weak, II 267

untheaw *n.* vice, sin, II 108; *pl.* unthewes V 179

unthryftes *n.pl.* wasters, XI 250

untill *prep.* to, unto, IV 43

untohe *a.* wanton, II 111

untreowe *a.* faithless, III 181

untuliche *adv.* wantonly, II 226

unwedde(de) *pp.a.* (as *n.*) the unmarried, IV 155

unwemmet *pp.a.* undefiled, II 43

unwiht *n.* devil, II 615

unwil *n.* dislike, II 467

unwitschipe *n.* folly, ignorance, III 108

unword *n.* slander, II 478

unwrast, unwre(a)st *a.* wicked, evil, III 253, VI 125

unwurth(e), unwurthi, unwurthliche *a.* poor, worthless, II 103, 390; unworthy, false, II 480; wicked, III 197

unwurthgeth *pr.3 s.* treats disparagingly, II 514

unwurthliche *adv.* dishonourably, II 479

unwyse *a.* foolish, XI 97

up *adv.* upright, II 371

up, up o, uppe *prep.* upon, II 595, VI 132, IX 65

upbrud *n.* reproach, II 501

upperysynge, uprysyng *n.* resurrection, IV 79; elevation, V 315

upsodoun *adv.* upsidedown, IX 1

urnen *see* eornen

use *v.* to be accustomed to, X(b) 117

ute *adv.* out, away from home, II 455

utewith *adv.* externally, II 644

uthe *n.pl.* waves, I 25

utlahe *n.* exile, II 163

utnume *a.* abundant, II 572; *adv.* especially, II 255

uttere, uttre *a.* external, physical, III 44, V 56

utterly *adv.* sincerely, IX 108

uvele, yvel *a.* wicked, terrible, I 37; *quasi-n.* evil, II 66; misery, II 533; *adv.* wickedly, severely, VI 315 uwilc *pron.* each, I 89

veat *n.* vessel, II 165

venge *v.* to avenge, IV 345; to punish, VIII 72

veniaunce *n.* vengeance, VI 293

venomys *a.* poisonous, X(a) 294

very, verrey *adv.* truly, VII 278

veryly *adv.* indeed, X(a) 316; truly, X(b) 62

vesete *v.* visit, IV 258

veyn *a.* false, IX 131

vilenye *n.* lack of courtesy, boorishness, VIII 130

vileyns *a.* villainous, wicked, VIII 161

visage *n.* face, VI 249

voide *v.* to avoid, cut off, VII 322

wa *n.* misfortune, II 59; *quasi-a.* unhappy, I 70

wac, wake *a.* insignificant, II 59; weak, II 123

wacliche *adv.* meanly, II 99

wacnesse *n.* weakness, III 74

waheles *a.* without walls, III 157

wahes *n.pl.* walls, II 449

wakenin *v.* to spring, II 442; to be born II 623

waker *a.* vigilant, V 97

walh *a.* insipid, II 528

wallen *pr.pl.* are in boiling liquid, III 19; wallende *prp.* boiling, III 20

walwe *v.* to wallow, IX 230; *pr.pl.* walweth II 177

wandreth *see* wontrethe

wanes *n.pl.* dwellings, II 456

wanteth *pr.pl.* are lacking, V 156

wanunge *n.* lamentation, II 542

warde *n.* protection, II 57

wardes *n.pl.* entrances, V 61

warh-treo *n.* gallows cross, III 240

warly *adv.* prudently, V 58

warnesse *n.* caution, VII 119

warpeth *pr.3 s.* throws, II 36; *pt.3 s.* warp, weorp I 17, II 636; *pp.* wurpen III 142

war(re) *a.* cautious, vigilant, IV 302

warschipe *n.* prudence, II 604

waryen *pr.pl.* curse, VIII 15; *pt.3 s.* wariede VI 317

wasche *v.* to wash, III 192; *pt.3 s.* wesch III 260; *pt.pl.* wysshen X(a) 36

wa-sith *n.* time of distress, II 536

wasten *pr.pl.* destroy, IX 235; wastinde *prp.a.* consuming, II 662

wathes *n.pl.* dangers, perils, IV 302

wawes *n.pl.* waves, VII 53

waxunge *n.* growth, II 546

wealden *v.* to rule, wield, II 584; *pr.2 s.* wealdes III 81; *pr.3 s.* wealt II 68

weane *n.* misery, woe, II 88

wearnen *v.* to refuse, III 263

wecches *n.pl.* stratagems, II 559

weddede *pp.a.* married, II 314; (as *n.*) the married, II 28

weden *n.pl.* clothes, II 259

weder *n.* storm X(b) 192; *pl.* tempests, bad weather, VI 207, IX 40; breezes, VII 54

wedlac *n.* marriage, II 266

weenden *v.* to go, V 293; *pr.3 s.* wendeth, went II 257; weent *imper.* turn, VI 337

wei *n.* way, II 638; alles weis in every respect, II 392; nanes weis in no way, not at all, II 399; other weis differently, II 282; summes weies in some ways, II 112

weila, wala, weilawei *interj.* alas, II 102, 228

weimer *n.* lamentation, II 297

weiward *a.* perverse, IX 269

welefare *n.* prosperity, IV 308

wel-itaut *pp.a.* well-educated, V 288

wel-itohe *pp.a.* genteel, II 358

well-dooyng *n.* performance of good deeds, XI 149

welle *v.* to boil, rage, III 22

wemmunge *n.* imperfection, II 169

wenest *pr.2 s.* think, II 99; *pt.2 s.* wendest II 87

wengen *n.pl.* wings, II 717

we(o)le *n.* joy, prosperity, II 91, 249

we(o)lefule *a.* fortunate, blessed, II 426; beautiful, III 190

weolewunge *n.* nausea, II 528

weopen *v.* to weep, VI 217; *pt.3 s.* **weop** I 58

weord *n.pl.* words, I 71

weorre *n.* war, II 609

weorrin *v.* to fight against, II 217

wepmon *n.* man, III 79

wepynges *n.pl.* tears, VIII 21

werbi *adv.* through which, IX 256

werc, werke *n.* deed, act, II 246, 510; occupation, function, X(a) 23

were *n.* man, husband, II 175

were *n.* doubt, IV 211

werk-bestis *n.pl.* beasts of burden, IX 149

westi *a.* desolate, II 449; destitute, III 154

wetandly *adv.* knowingly, IV 179

wex *pt.3 s.* grew, III 159

whanhope *n.* despair, IV 286

whareof *pron.* of what, IV 2

wharethurghe *adv.* whereby, through which, IV 164

whasaever *pron.* whosoever, IV 294

whether *pron.* which of the two, VII 224

whether-so, whethire-so *pron.* whichever of two, IV 307; *conj.* according as, IV 119

whilke *pron.* which, IV 1

whoder, whether *adv.* whither, VI 385, XI 31

widewe *n.* widow, II 654

widewehad *n.* the state of being a widow, II 327

wifmen *n.pl.* women, I 100

wiht *see* **wytes**

wikked *a.* severe, VI 207

wil *n.* desire, lust, II 206

wilfulle *a.* determined, III 145

wilfulliche, willfully *adv.* willingly, III 171; purposely, IV 179

willeliche *adv.* willingly, I 1

willes ant waldes *adv.(phr.)* of your own accord, II 703; **al willes** willingly, II 517

wilnin, wilne *v.* to will, desire, II 120, VII 360

wilnunge *n.* prompting, II 366

winne *v.* gain entrance, go, VI 319

wirchipe *n.* honour, IV 139

wirchipfully *adv.* with honour, IV 134

wise, wyse *n.* manner, way, IV 352, VIII 36

wisly *adv.* understandingly, IX 162

wissen, wysse *v.* to guard, VI 98; *pt.3 s.* **wiste** I 53; to counsel, guide, IV 263; **wysses** *pr.3 s.* directs, teaches, IV 302

wit *n.* reason, intelligence, II 723; *pl.* approval, VII 136; mind, VII 224

wite *pr.1 s.* blame, VI 188

witeghe *n.* prophet, I 38

witen *v.* to keep, observe, I 62; to protect, II 141; to guard against, II 225

witen, wiet *v.* to know, II 470, IV 253; *pr.1 s.* **wat** I 67; *pr.2 s.* **wast** II 90; *pr.3 s.* **wot** V 221; *pr.pl.* **weteth** V 273; *pt.3 s.* **wuste, wiste** II 267, VI 182; **that is to wete** namely, X(a) 9

witerliche *adv.* truly, clearly, II 39; *comp.* **witerluker** II 341

with *prep.* by, IV 98; against, IV 302

withbreide *pr.subj.s.* withdraw, II 92

withbuhe *v.* to avoid, II 553

withouten *prep.* apart from, VI 283 outside, II 512; *adv.* outside, IX 39

witith *pr.pl.* punish, II 434

witter *a.* certain, IV 383

wleateful, wleatewile *a.* loathsome, II 110, 557

wlecche *a.* tepid, II 660

wlecheunge *n.* lukewarmness, II 664

wlite *n.* beauty, countenance, II 126, III 23

wlonke *a.* magnificent, II 452

wode, wood *a.* mad, III 139

wodeluker *adv.comp.* more ferociously, II 196

woh(e) *n.* wrong, harm, I 48

won *a.* dark, II 652

wonden, wunden *pp.* wrapped, III 157; wrapped (in a shroud), IV 101

wondir *adv.* very, exceedingly, IV 270

wondrinde *prp.a.* amazing, II 534

wone *a.* lacking, II 450

wone *n.* want, lack, II 412

wonnin *v.* to become dark, II 523

wont, wounte *a.* accustomed, IV 364

wonti *v.* to be lacking to, II 68

wontrethe, wandreth *n.* misery, II 88; poverty, IV 307

woodnes *n.* madness, XI 122

wopes, weopes *n.pl.* weeping, II 658

worche, wurchen *v.* to work, VII 374; to act, II 121; *pr.pl.* **wyrkkys** IV 263

worchepe *v.* to honour, V 106

worching *n.* occupation, VII 336

wordely *a.* worldly, X(b) 118

wori *pr.subj.s.* distract, trouble, II 723

worlt *n.* world, II 31; **from worlde into worlde** world without end, II 407

worltlich *a.* earthly, II 455

worthe *v.* to become, V 328; *pr.subj.s.* **wurthe** II 388

worthi *a.* valuable, IX 161

wracfulliche *adv.* in vengeance, II 629

wrahtes *pt.2 s.* created, III 30; *pp.* **wraht, wrought** II 370, VI 1; **iwrat** *pp.* done, I 86

wrang *pt.3 s.* flowed through squeezing, III 222

wrange *n.* evil, IV 300; **with w.** wickedly, III 263

wrangwyse *a.* wicked, IV 159

wrangwysely *adv.* wrongfully, IV 361

wrath *a.* angry, II 453

wrathfull *a.* (as *n.*) the angry, XI 121

wreathe, wrethe *n.* anger, II 608, IV 343

wreathen *v.* to anger, enrage II 396

wreche *n.* vengeance, VI 65

wreke *v.* to avenge, IV 345

wrenche *n.* deceit, guile, V 118

wrenche *v.* to escape, III 226; *pr.subj.s.* pervert, turn, II 724

wrenchfule *a.* deceitful, crafty, II 701

wrethful *a.* angry, irate, I 55

wrihe *v.* to cover, III 166; **wrist** *pr.2 s.* protect yourself, II 717

writ *n.* book, treatise, II 580

wulle, chulle *pr.1 s.* will, I 68; *pr.2 s.* **wult** II 237; *pr.3 s.* **wule** I 6; *pr.pl.* **wulleth** I 2; *pt.3 s.* **walde** I 48; *pt.pl.* **walden** II 265; **wullen ha nullen ha** whether they will or not, II 438

wunderliche *a.* amazing, II 79; *adv.* very much, I 57

wundi *v.* to wound, II 194

wundre *n.:* **tukin to w.** to be amazed, II 220-1

wundren *v.* to gape, gaze, III 239

wunie, wonen *v.* to remain, III 64; to live, VI 145; *pr.pl.* **wunieth** II 29

wunne *n.* joy, delight, II 87

wununge, wonyng *n.* dwelling, dwelling place, II 639, VIII 140; living, VII 7

wurchen *see* **worche**

wurdliche *a.* noble, excellent, I 98

wurmene *n.pl.(gen.)* of worms, II 631

wurth *a.* valuable, excellent, II 53

wurth *n.* value, worth, II 390; *pl.* II 491

wurthe *see* **worthe**

wurthien *v.* to honour, I 82; *pr.3 s.* **wurthgeth** II 490

wurthinge *n.* filth, moral corruption, II 174

wurthschipe *n.* honour, II 40

wyll *n.* straying, IV 263

wylnynge *n.* desire, IV 359

wyrchipe *n.* honour, IV 142

wyrchipfull *a.* honourable, IV 148

wyssynge *n.* enticement, IV 383

wytes *n.pl.* devils, V 338

wytty *a.* wise, V 131

ya *interj.* yea, indeed, III 206

yapliche *adv.* readily, III 132

yapschipe *n.* prudence, III 10

yarketh *pr.3 s.* prepares, II 718

yates, yeatis *n.pl.* gates, entrances, V 61, X(a) 3

ydillchipe *n.* vanity, vain, IV 131; idleness, IV 378

ydouse *a.* terrible, VIII 83

yederunge *n.* assembly, II 14; copulation, II 110

yeemstones *n.pl.* precious stones, VI 38

yef, gif *conj.* if, I 1, 6

yeftes *n.pl.* gifts, X(b) 16

yeigheth *pr.pl.* cry out, I 37

yelde *v.* to give, pay, III 280; to give up, VI 399; **yyolde** *pp.* repaid, VIII 75

yeme *n.:* **nim y.** pay attention, II 5

yemes *pr.3 s.* gives heed to, IV 193

yeohthe *n.* lust, II 109

yeomerunge *n.* lamentation, II 534

yeorne *adv.* eagerly, I 37

yerdes *n.pl.* saplings, VI 381

yerne *n.* yarn, X(b) 23

yerne *v.* to desire, III 91; *pt.2 s.* **yerndes** III 160

yernynge *n.* desire, lust, IV 360; *pl.* **yernyggys** V 16

yettede *pt.3 s.* granted, II 303

yetten *adv.* yet, II 156

yhe *pron.* she, V 165; you, V 350; **yu, eow, ow** you, II 225

yimmes *n.pl.* gems, II 323

yimmede *pp.a.* bejewelled, III 70

yisceunge *n.* covetousness, II 608

yiscith *pr.pl.* covet, II 429

yiven, yeoven, yeve, yyve *v.* to give, II 247, III 10, V 85, IX 10; *pr.3 s.* **yeveth** I 99; *pr.subj.s.* **yefe** I 65; *pt.3 s.* **yef, y(e)af** II 309, X(b) 76; *pp.* **gyffen, yiven** III 232, IV 123; **iyeven** *pp.* given in marriage, II 99

ymage *n.* statue, X(b) 61

yong *n.* journey, II 261

ypocrisie *n.* false religious belief, pretence, VIII 133

ypocritis *n.pl.* those who pretend to have religious feelings, IX 35

Index of Names

The first reference in each passage is given; the inclusion of an ff. after the reference indicates that there is more than one occurrence of the name in that passage. The various names of the deity are disregarded.

Abbey of the Holy Ghost, V 1ff.
Abel, VI 235ff.
Abraham, III 84
Abyngdon, X(b) 2ff.
Adam, II 114, III 68, IV 104, VI 1ff., X(a) 3ff.
Adrian (Emperor Hadrian), X(a) 212
Adryan (Adriatic Sea), X(a) 264
Albynum (Milvian Bridge), X(a) 96
Alhalwyn (All Saints), X(b) 191
Alys (Alice, St. Edmund's sister), X(b) 14
Ambrose, X(a) 130ff.
Anatalim, VI 47
Anticrist, IX 51ff.
Apocalipsis (Book of Revelation), XI 302
Arcis, VI 51
Asye (Asia), VI 29

Babilon, II 23ff.
Barabas, Baraban (Barabbas), III 186ff.
Barbarye, X(a) 65
Bartillomew, Bartolmew, (St. Bartholomew), V 138ff.
Belleem (Bethlehem), III 156
Book of Love (Song of Solomon), VII 257
Britayne, X(a) 156ff.
Brytayns, X(a) 159
Buxomnesse (Obedience), V 37
Bylet, John (John Beleth), X(a) 22

Calmana (Cain's wife), VI 271
Calne, X(b) 220
Calvarie, III 235, XI 158
Canterbury, X(b) 242
Canterbury, Archiebisshopp of, X(b) 218ff.
Cantykly (Song of Solomon), V 307
Catesby, Catysby, X(b) 15ff.
Catoun (Cato), VIII 39

Caym (Cain), VI 202ff., IX 51
Chalfegrove (Chalgrove, Oxon), X(b) 111
Charite (Lady Love), V 82ff.
Cherubin, VI 138
Constantine (the emperor), X(a) 60ff.
Constantine (father of the emperor), X(a) 86ff.
Contemplacioun, V 67
Corteyseye, Cortesye, V 188ff.
Crist, Jesu Crist (used both of Christ and of the deity in general), I 47ff., II 41ff., III 1f., IV 62ff., V 9ff., VI 3ff., VII 182ff., VIII 45, IX 3ff., X(a) 9ff., X(b) 47ff., XI 7ff.

Damasse, Feld of, VI 256
Danibe (River Danube), X(a) 62ff.
Daniel, V 124
David, Davit, I 38, II 2ff., III 31ff., V 31ff.
Descrecioun, Dyscrecion, V 131ff.
Devocioun, V 72ff.
Drede (Fear), V 178
Dysus, VI 49

Ebron (Hebron), VI 43ff.
Edom, VI 273
Elyn (St. Helena), X(a) 59ff.
Envye, V 321
Epistle of Theodosien, X(a) 131
Ethiope, X(a) 305ff.
Eufrate (River Euphrates), VI 39
Eusebie, also Sesarience (Eusebius Bishop of Caesarea), X(a) 81ff.
Eusebie (Pope Eusebius), X(a) 80
Eve, II 114, IV 104, VI 1ff.